British Military Policy between the Two World Wars

by

BRIAN BOND

CLARENDON PRESS · OXFORD
1980

Oxford University Press, Walton Street, Oxford OX2 6DP

OXFORD LONDON GLASGOW

NEW YORK TORONTO MELBOURNE WELLINGTON

KUALA LUMPUR SINGAPORE JAKARTA HONG KONG TOKYO

DELHI BOMBAY CALCUTTA MADRAS KARACHI

NAIROBI DAR ES SALAAM CAPE TOWN

Published in the United States
by Oxford University Press, New York

British Library Cataloguing in Publication Data

Bond, Brian
British military policy between the two World Wars.
1. Great Britain. Army – History – 1918–1939
I. Title
355′.00941 UA649 79–41664
ISBN 0–19–822464–8

Phototypesetting by Parkway Group, London and Abingdon
Printed in Great Britain by Lowe and Brydone, Thetford

For Madeleine

ACKNOWLEDGEMENTS

My thanks are due first and foremost to Lady Liddell Hart for allowing me to quote extensively from the late Sir Basil Liddell Hart's books and papers in which she holds the copyright. Most of the research for this book was completed before the Liddell Hart library and papers were transferred to the Centre for Military Archives at King's College, London, but I am most grateful to the archivists Julia Sheppard and her successor Elizabeth Bennett for their help in checking numerous references and for enabling me to consult other collections in the Archives. I am also appreciative of Willoughby Pownall-Gray's patience in allowing me to retain the Pownall diaries for reference while working on this book. The librarians and archivists of Churchill College, Cambridge, the Imperial War Museum, the Old War Office (now Central and Army) Library, and the Central Library at the Royal Military Academy, Sandhurst, all assisted my researches by their courteous efficiency. The staff of the Public Record Office formerly in Portugal Street and now at Kew have been equally helpful: documents in the PRO are quoted by permission of the Controller of Her Majesty's Stationery Office. The cost of xeroxing documents at the PRO was partly met by a grant from the Central Research Fund, University of London. Davis-Poynter Ltd have generously allowed me to reproduce extracts originally published in my book *France and Belgium, 1939–1940* (1975), and Constable and Company Ltd have permitted me to quote several passages from *The Ironside Diaries, 1937–1940* (1962). My indebtedness to other publications which I have quoted less extensively has been fully acknowledged in the footnotes and in the list of sources.

I am especially indebted to Michael Howard for discussing this subject with me on several occasions and above all for reading my typescript in draft and suggesting several alterations and additions. Dan Davin scrutinized my occasionally tired and repetitive prose with a critical literary eye and his amendments have improved virtually every page. Major-General James Lunt, Derek Waldie, Harold Winton, and John Rawson all kindly gave me their expert assessments of individual chapters. While they have saved me from numerous errors, I of course am entirely responsible for any which have escaped detection.

I am glad of this opportunity to thank my colleagues Michael Dockrill and Bryan Ranft for lightening my teaching load while this book was being written, particularly in the Lent term of 1978; and also to thank our invaluable departmental secretary, Sylvia Smither, whose firmness saved me from many avoidable chores.

My thanks are due to many others who helped by their recollections of the inter-war period and in a variety of other ways, including (with apologies for any inadvertent omissions): General Sir Ronald Adam, Brigadier R. G. S. Bidwell, Major-General H. L. Birks, Viscount Bridgeman, Peter Dennis, Professor Norman Gibbs, John Gooch, Paul Harris, Lesley Jackman, Lieutenant-General Sir Ian Jacob, Mark Jacobsen, Keith Jeffery, Paul Kennedy, Ronald Lewin, Colonel Roderick Macleod, General Sir James Marshall-Cornwall, Williamson Murray, Major-General R. B. Pargiter, George Peden, R. John Pritchard, Major-General E. K. G. Sixsmith, John Terraine, Howard Welch, and Robert J. Young.

It is a great pleasure to acknowledge the encouragement and friendly assistance I have received from Oxford University Press in the persons of Dan Davin, Ivon Asquith, and Oliver Metcalf.

Finally, my indebtedness to my wife is inadequately acknowledged by the dedication of this book. No matter how often the tribute has previously been made by grateful authors, in this case it is certainly true that without her help and understanding this study would not have been completed.

Medmenham, Bucks.
June 1979 Brian Bond

CONTENTS

LIST OF MAPS

ABBREVIATIONS

AA	Anti-Aircraft
AASF	Advanced Air Striking Force
ADGB	Air Defence Great Britain
AFV	Armoured Fighting Vehicle
AG	Adjutant-General (also DAAG Deputy Assistant Adjutant-General)
AOC.-in-C.	Air Officer Commanding-in-Chief
BEF	British Expeditionary Force
Bt.	Brevet (the prefix to a rank)
Cab	Cabinet (also CP, Cabinet Paper and Cab Cons., Cabinet Conclusions)
CAS	Chief of the Air Staff
CGS	Chief of the General Staff
CID	Committee of Imperial Defence
CIGS	Chief of the Imperial General Staff (also DCIGS Deputy Chief, and VCIGS Vice Chief)
CNS	Chief of the Naval Staff
COS	Chiefs of Staff Sub-Committee of the CID (also DCOS, Deputy Chiefs of Staff)
DC(M)	Disarmament Committee (Ministerial)
DMI	Director of Military Intelligence (also DDMI, Deputy Director)
DMO and I	Director of Military Operations and Intelligence (also DDMO, Deputy Director)
DMT	Director of Military Training (also DDMT, Deputy Director)

DP(P)C	Defence Plans (Policy) Committee
DPRC	Defence Policy and Requirements Committee
DRC	Defence Requirements Committee
DRO	Director of Recruiting and Organization
DSD	Director of Staff Duties (also DDSD,—Deputy Director)
FF	Field Force
FSR	Field Service Regulations
GHQ	General Headquarters
GOC	General Officer Commanding
GOC.-in-C.	General Officer Commanding-in-Chief
GSO1	General Staff Officer First Grade
GSO2	General Staff Officer Second Grade
GSO3	General Staff Officer Third Grade
IDC	Imperial Defence College
JIC	Joint Intelligence Committee
JPC	Joint Planning Sub-Committee
MGO	Master-General of the Ordnance
NCO	Non-commissioned Officer
p.s.c.	Passed Staff College (Camberley or Quetta)
PUS	Permanent Under-Secretary
QMG	Quartermaster-General (also DAQMG, Deputy Assistant)
RA	Royal Artillery
RAC	Royal Armoured Corps
RAOC	Royal Army Ordnance Corps
RASC	Royal Army Service Corps
RE	Royal Engineers
RFA	Royal Field Artillery
RFC	Royal Flying Corps (RAF after 1918)
RGA	Royal Garrison Artillery
RHA	Royal Horse Artillery
RTC	Royal Tank Corps

RUSI	Royal United Service Institution (Royal United Services Institute for Defence Studies since 1971)
TA	Territorial Army
WO	War Office

INTRODUCTION

> From the cliffs of Dover on a clear day it is possible to see a grey rim of land shutting in the south-eastern horizon. It is not the coastline of Asia; nor of Japan; nor of Arabia, Africa or Asia Minor, but of Europe. England lies only twenty-two miles from the European shore. Simple, obvious, indeed well-known a fact as this was, the English were prone from time to time to forget all the implications which it bore for English policy and strategy.[1]

The truth of the last admonitory sentence in the epigraph above can never have been more applicable to the mood of British public opinion than in the years succeeding 1918. The continental commitment, so enthusiastically accepted by hundreds of thousands of volunteers in 1914, was now bitterly condemned as an unwise—worse still, an unnecessary—departure from an allegedly traditional maritime strategy in which small military expeditionary forces played a valuable but subsidiary role. The influential military journalist and critic Captain B. H. Liddell Hart, in particular, persuasively presented the seductive alternative concept of a 'British Way in Warfare' in which any future commitment of land forces to the Continent would be strictly limited as, he contended, had always been the case before 1914. Though there were dissentient voices, mostly, one might expect, from former army officers, they did not receive a sympathetic hearing in the 1920s and early 1930s. In perspective it now seems obvious that the continental commitment, though on a much vaster scale in 1914–18 because of changed strategic conditions, nevertheless accorded with the traditional British preoccupation of maintaining a balance of power in Europe and preventing a hostile power from seizing the Low Countries and the Channel ports. In short the continental and maritime modes of operation were complementary not alternative strategies. What served to blur this fairly obvious conclusion was of course the frightful nature and high cost of the war on the Western Front: 'postwar differences of view about how the fighting was actually conducted tended, even if unintentionally, to obscure the basically correct reasons which took Britain into that war in the first place. Her involvement was a continuation of, not a break with, a proper tradition of self-interest.'[2] In other words, Germany was far less vulnerable than previous enemies to attack on her overseas trade and colonies; amphibious operations against her coastline would at best create minor diversions; and, most important, it was extremely doubtful if France could or would withstand an all-out land attack from Germany without substantial British military support.

Quite apart from this failure to understand the restraints on strategic options imposed by geography, commerce, and the military preponderance of Germany before 1914, the British public was masochistically prone to dwell on defeats and casualties rather than to exult in a unique national war effort that had culminated in a series of impressive victories. We have recently been reminded of these achievements by military historians such as the late Hubert Essame and John Terraine, who have stressed the fact that Haig's forces bore the brunt of German attacks on the Western Front in the last two years of the war and played the major role in defeating the enemy's main armies in 1918.[3]

A few pages must suffice to convey an impression of this enormous military expansion which provides such a sharp contrast to the period of contraction, fragmentation, and uncertainty that followed. In August 1914 the Expeditionary Force consisted of a professional army of six infantry and one cavalry divisions, highly trained and efficient no doubt, but with logistical backing—notably in guns and ammunition—for only a short and limited campaign comparable to the last war in South Africa. This *corps d'élite* had largely been sacrificed before the New 'Kitchener' Armies and conscripts, backed with adequate reserves and munitions, became available from 1916. By the end of the war Britain and her Empire had no less than 80 infantry and eight cavalry divisions on active service (i.e. outside the United Kingdom and India), and of these 61 infantry and three cavalry divisions were serving on the Western Front. Of the total 80 infantry divisions 12 were Regular, 30 New

Army, 21 Territorial Force, 10 Dominion, six Indian, and one Royal Naval.[4]
By 1918 the higher formations on the Western Front consisted of five Armies and nineteen Corps (including the Canadian, Australian, and Cavalry Corps). While not all the senior commanders were as good as, say, Haig, Rawlinson, Plumer, Monash, and Jacob, it is only fair to remember that at the beginning of the war no serving British officer had had the experience of commanding so much as a Corps. The problem of finding competent staff officers for the expanding Army was even more intractable because the Staff Colleges at Camberley and Quetta had produced enough p.s.c.s only for the original BEF. The 1914 Army List contains a total of 447 p.s.c.s. Moreover, many of these qualified staff officers were killed or wounded in the opening months of the war. By 1918 at least 3,310 officers were holding staff appointments in France at GHQ and the HQs of armies, corps, divisions, and brigades. The overwhelming majority of these officers were specially selected from the regiments for their outstanding ability and many had been decorated for conspicuous acts of courage. This gives the lie to the understandable but for the most part baseless accusations against 'the Staff' for incompetence, ignorance of front-line conditions, and even cowardice.[5]

The staggering rate of expansion is equally evident in terms of manpower. On the outbreak of war the total strength of the Regular Army, Reserves, and Territorial Forces was 733,514, whereas at the Armistice 1,794,000 soldiers (with over one million combatants) were serving on the Western Front alone. Britain's contribution to France had previously reached a maximum strength of over 2 million troops and the total employed there during the war amounted to nearly 5½ million. Total white enlistments numbered over 7 million for all theatres and the grand total was in excess of 8½ million. Britain's increasing contribution to the Western Front is more graphically suggested by the amount of line held—all of it in the zone of intense fighting. In 1914 the BEF's frontage was only 20–5 miles out of approximately 460 miles between the Channel coast and the Swiss border; by 1916 it had increased to a maximum of 90 miles; rising to 110 in 1917 and a peak of 123 in February and March 1918. Expenditure on the Army alone in the year ending

31 March 1919 totalled £824,259,300; while the average daily expenditure on the war as a whole in the final six months was nearly £7½ million.[6]

In the final phase of the advance on the Western Front between 8 August and 11 November, Haig's armies fought and won nine important battles. These were the battles of Amiens (8–13 August), Bapaume (21 August–1 September), the Scarpe (26 August–3 September), Havrincourt and Epéhy (12–18 September), Cambrai and the Hindenburg Line (27 September–5 October), Flanders (28 September–14 October), Le Cateau (6–12 October), the Selle (17–25 October), and the Sambre (1–11 November). During these battles the five British Armies captured no fewer than 188,700 prisoners and 2,840 guns which almost matched the aggregate captures of their French, American, and Belgian allies together during the same period. In General Rawlinson's opinion the capture of Mount St. Quentin and Péronne by the Australian Corps stood out as 'the finest single feat of the whole war', but it was closely matched by the Canadian Corps's breaking of the Drocourt–Quéant line on 2 September, the forcing of the Canal du Nord two days later by the Fourth Army and the breach of the Hindenburg Line by 46th Division on 29 September. As General Essame wrote of this last action: 'By any standards the achievement of the 46th Division was magnificent . . . The dash, determination and initiative of their junior officers and non-commissioned officers on this day reached a standard not surpassed even by the Australians.' In this same writer's judgement, these battles 'constitute the most impressive chain of victories in the history of the British Army since the Peninsular War'. Strangely, however, they never at the time captured the imagination of the war correspondents or the public; indeed their very titles had to be invented by the official historians after the war.[7]

The expansion of the Army in France from 6 to more than 60 infantry divisions with corresponding increases in the other arms and auxiliary corps inevitably entailed a vast increase in the supply services. At its peak the British and Dominion armies in France approached a grand total of 2,700,000 men. The addition of even one ounce to each man's daily rations involved carrying an extra 75 tons of goods. The maintenance of a single division for one day represented a shipping tonnage of nearly 450 tons. At least 800,000 tons of stores arrived at the base ports every month. GHQ controlled a transport system which used half-a-million horses and mules, 20,000 lorries, and light railways carrying more than half a million tons a month. A division normally consumed a train load of ammunition every day and at least an additional train load of supplies per day, much of this consisting of forage for the animals. Each set-piece battle required hundreds of additional train-loads of shells. For a ten-division attack the rail traffic to and in the sector would be multiplied fifteen times.[8]

No single aspect perhaps conveys a more vivid impression of the magnitude of the great siege war on the Western Front than the enormous expenditure of ammunition. By August 1918 no less than 14,000 British firms were engaged in munitions production and at last the shortage of ammunition which had so handicapped commanders in the early years of the war was virtually ended. Between 8 August and 11 November 621,289 tons of ammunition were pumped into the German defences facing the British sector. To soften up the formidable Hindenburg Line at the end of September in a gigantic effort surpassing any British operation until the final year of the Second World War, a bombardment of 30,000 tons of mustard gas was followed up by forty-eight hours of sustained shelling in which a million and a quarter rounds were expended. In three days British guns fired nearly 65,000 tons of ammunition. At the Armistice Haig's artillery consisted of 6,437 guns and howitzers, not counting anti-aircraft guns and mortars.[9]

So rapid was the acceleration of British war production in 1917–18 not only of ammunition but also of tanks, guns, and all types of equipment that the huge losses suffered in the German March offensive were speedily made good. Indeed, the problem in the final months of the war was not so much one of production as of movement: first to the theatre of war, then to the railheads and, most difficult of all, beyond the railheads once the advance began. Logistic and engineering problems were exacerbated by the Germans' systematic destruction of all communications and installations as they withdrew, thus creating a ravaged desert some 30 miles wide. To overcome these obstacles there grew up an enormous staff under the Quartermaster General, which by 1918 could be aptly likened to a great modern industrial organization such as Shell or ICI. The QMG had two major-generals as deputies and under them were no fewer than five inspector-generals and seventeen directorates. Their responsibilities included all kinds of construction, docks, inland water transport, railways, roads, postal services, engineer stores, hiring and requisitioning, labour, pay, remounts, war graves, and works. The creation of this vast infrastructure from the meagre base existing in 1914 was as impressive an achievement as the raising of the great armies which it was designed to feed and maintain. Certainly its smooth functioning was absolutely essential to the brilliant operations which ended the war.[10]

Field-Marshal Sir Douglas Haig proudly summed up his Army's achievement in his penultimate dispatch as follows:

> The annals of war hold record of no more wonderful recovery than that which, three months after the tremendous blows showered upon them on the Somme and on the Lys, saw the undefeated British Armies advancing from victory to victory, driving their erstwhile triumphant enemy back to and far beyond the line from which he started, and finally forcing him to acknowledge unconditional defeat.

And in praising the work of the troops he concluded: 'By the long road they trod with so much faith and with such devoted and self-sacrificing bravery we have arrived at victory, and today they have their reward.'[11]

Unfortunately this fleeting sense of a great achievement was in effect to be the troops' only reward, for within a few months of the ending of the war this huge Army with its higher formations and headquarters, its vast administrative structure, and its industrial base at home all rapidly disappeared like some insubstantial vision. The British public has traditionally been quick to forget the sacrifices and hardships of its returning soldiers, and in 1919 the pressures to cut back the Army to its pre-1914 scale and imperial role were irresistible. What in retrospect is somewhat surprising, however, is that so little effort was made, even on paper, to garner the lessons of unpreparedness in 1914 and of the unprecedented national war effort that followed; much less to preserve the administrative and industrial basis for a future mobilization on a similar scale. In an atmosphere of war weariness, economic disturbance, and disillusionment with the fruits of victory such forethought was quite simply impossible.

In the 1920s a combination of domestic crises, extended imperial commitments, and growing retrospective revulsion against the experience of the First World War together provided powerful discouragement to military involvement in Europe. Some historians, including Mr A. J. P. Taylor, have suggested that the real error lay in not pushing this tendency towards isolationism to its logical conclusion. According to this view, Britain would have done better to have concentrated on home and imperial defence and kept entirely free from European involvements. Attractive though this altenative policy appears with the wisdom of hindsight after the French collapse and Dunkirk, it was surely never a realistic option in the inter-war period. Britain was unavoidably a party to the Versailles and Locarno treaties; she maintained a military contingent in the Rhineland until 1930; and it was a fundamental political assumption that she would be an ally of France in the event of renewed German aggression in western Europe. Until this danger began to loom ominously in 1933 Britain's military preoccupation with the security of her overseas Empire, particularly India and the Middle East, is understandable. What seems more surprising, and receives careful attention in this study, is the marked unwillingness of the British Government, aided and abetted by many of its Service advisers, to make a definite commitment to the Continent of its small Expeditionary Force until the beginning of 1939.

The question of the Army's role, or more precisely of which role was to be given priority, has interested me for many years. In editing Henry Pownall's diaries covering the years 1933–9 I encountered the forthright views of a soldier who consistently argued that, however undesirable, a continental commitment of the Army was probably unavoidable, and who played an important part in eventually getting it accepted as government policy. Pownall's outlook provided a sharp contrast to that of my mentor in the 1960s, Basil Liddell Hart, who had been a leading advocate of a policy of 'limited liability'. In my recent study of Liddell Hart's intellectual development I attempted to clarify the many elements in his arguments on this topic and also to assess their influence. In the meantime research for my study of British policy and strategy in 1939–40 had further impressed on me the view that the most important cause of the Army's unpreparedness at the start of the Second World War lay in protracted political and military indecision over its role.[12]

This present study emphasizes the appalling way in which the Army was allowed to degenerate in the 1920s to the extent that by 1933 it was incapable of providing in reasonable time an Expeditionary Force equipped to meet even a second-class opponent outside Europe. Special attention has been given to the development of armoured forces in Britain, partly to bring out the effects of financial stringency on the Army's most progressive and potentially important branch, but more specifically to argue the point that it was the lack of a definite European role more than 'military conservatism' which impeded the growth of armoured divisions in the later 1930s. The aim in following in detail the tortuous debates on the Army's priorities in the 1930s has by no means been to 'whitewash' the Army's political and military spokesmen, though it must be said that Hailsham, Duff Cooper, Montgomery-Massingberd, Gort, and others emerge with more credit (and their opponents such as Neville Chamberlain, Simon, Hoare, and the Air Staff representatives with less) than in many accounts of the period which assume or accept that the Army deserved the lowest priority in rearmament. By viewing the Army's position sympathetically, though not uncritically, it is hoped to modify the very unfavourable impression created by Liddell Hart's scintillating *Memoirs* which cannot convey the whole truth since their author was patently concerned to justify and defend his own important part in the events described. Viewed from the Army's standpoint the strategic aspects of the Munich crisis and its aftermath also appear in a light very different from that provided by the many accounts which are concerned solely with politics and diplomacy.

To sum up, two main themes are explored. First, the shaping of military policy is traced using more evidence from General Staff and other influential Army officers than was feasible for other scholars who have surveyed the subject in a wider context of national strategy.[13] Second, an attempt has been made to rescue the Army from the charge of 'Blimpery' by establishing that the most serious obstacle to military preparedness in the period of rearmament was continuing uncertainty over the Service's priorities.

Though this study seeks to fill an important gap in the formulation of military policy where, by contrast, the other two Services have received more scholarly attention,[14] it does not claim to be a comprehensive history of the Army between the wars. I have had the benefit of drawing on a great deal of research which was not available a decade ago, but there is still scope for much more work, particularly on the Army as a social institution. We know, for example, almost nothing about the recruitment of officers and other ranks, the development of military education, or the progress of doctrine and training of arms other than the Royal Tank Corps, which has been something of an obsession with popular and technical authors.

Since the relaxing of the Fifty Year Rule to thirty years and the consequent release of public records for the whole inter-war period, British foreign policy and strategy in the 1930s have been subjected to intense scrutiny. But on closer inspection this attention has been remarkably patchy: scholars have trodden on each other's heels in some areas—such as disarmament, the Far East, and above all Munich—whereas other important topics—such as the Treasury and its influence—have until recently been neglected. Just as in the 1930s, the Army has aroused less interest for its own sake than the other two Services whose policies seem more attractive perhaps, or controversial. This is a pity, because, whether they realise it or not, scholars' judgements are considerably affected by the area they chose to work in and by the documents they principally rely on. The popular image of the British Army in the inter-war period has been profoundly influenced by the wickedly effective cartoons of David Low and by the satiric pens of brilliant mavericks and outsiders such as Fuller and Liddell Hart. For all its faults and shortcomings the 'Cinderella Service' is long overdue for more understanding treatment.

CHAPTER 1

The Aftermath of War and The Return to 'Real Soldiering', 1918–1923

In the aftermath of the First World War the British Empire reached its apogee. Through the allocation of mandates, Britain and her Dominions added to their island possessions in the Pacific, acquired vast areas of Africa, and extended their control of Egypt through Jerusalem to Baghdad and the valley of the Tigris and Euphrates. More of the world's map was coloured red than it was ever the case before or ever would be again.

Yet this enormous increase in territory and political responsibility did not bring with it a corresponding increase in real power. On the contrary, the elements of weakness were becoming ever more apparent; the 'gouty giant' of pre-1914 had become 'a brontosaurus with huge, vulnerable limbs which the central nervous system had little capacity to protect, direct or control'.[1]

The elements of weakness were various and their effects were cumulative. First and most obvious were the war losses and the burdens which these imposed on the survivors. The three quarters of a million dead represented nine per cent of all men under forty-five including many of the finest young men of their generation, and to this outright loss must be added over a further one and a half million badly wounded. It would be difficult to overestimate the psychological effects of these losses in a country unused to casualties on the Continental scale.

Secondly, although the Empire as a whole had made an invaluable contribution to the war effort, and the heads of the Dominion governments had participated directly in policy-making in the Imperial War Cabinet, this closer co-operation did not mean that the long-cherished British concept of Dominion-sharing in the burdens of imperial defence would flourish after the war. On the contrary, the white Dominions emerged with a far stronger sense of their own national identities and, correspondingly, of their own separate security problems which they sensed, correctly, Britain would be unable to meet. Equally they showed no enthusiasm for sharing Britain's military burdens as an imperial and mandatory power. A British request in 1920 for Dominion troops to share the garrison duties in Mesopotamia met with a firm refusal from all but New Zealand who offered one battalion, while the Chanak crisis of 1922 made the Dominions' isolationism from post-war problems in Europe even plainer.[2] 'If Britain were to take an active share in reshaping Europe and in upholding a European settlement, then she would sooner or later be forced to contemplate parting from the Dominions.'[3]

India's role in the new imperial structure was even more problematic, not least because British official thinking at home and on the spot was so divided about the methods and the timing of gradual progress towards self-government. Despite the growth of the nationalist movement chiefly embodied in the Congress Party, the Viceroy and his Government remained firmly in charge of India's external affairs and internal security.[4]

Although anti-imperialism was far from new in 1918 and was composed of many divergent elements, the extension of the Empire as a consequence of the First World War weakened the sense of a moral basis for imperial rule on two counts. On the one hand it was increasingly asked whether Britain had the moral right to remain in India, Egypt, and the mandated territories in the face of growing nationalist opposition unless she could genuinely confer greater benefits on the peoples than would accrue from self-government. On the other hand, where British commercial and strategic issues were really at stake, it seemed that British financial and military weakness would make continued direct rule difficult if not impossible. And would indirect or 'concealed' imperialism, operating behind a facade of local self-government, be much cheaper or more effective in the long run?[5]

When one adds to these real losses and anxieties for the future the genuine if exaggerated belief in the possibility of revolution in Britain, it is easy to understand the sensation of 'pulling up with relief at the winning post' that occurred in 1918. Indeed after the ephemeral junketings at the Armistice the savouring of victory brought little cause for rejoicing. The memories of the terrible campaigns on the Western Front were too recent and searing while the high costs of victory were poignantly brought home to the civil population by the erection of mutely eloquent war memorials in every town and village.

On the less emotional political plane, victory did seem to signify the disappearance or crippling of those Continental giants who had constituted a real or imagined threat to British interests before 1914. Russia, broken by war and now engulfed by revolution and anarchy, was incapable of posing any direct threat to Britain, though the indirect influence of Communist propaganda both at home and in India was widely feared. Germany had been defeated in battle and her western frontier zones occupied by the victorious allies; she had been stripped of all her overseas possessions; her fleet was destroyed and her land and air forces seriously limited by the Treaty of Versailles. True, France was at odds with Britain both as regards her security against a revived Germany and the division of the spoils in the Middle East, but it was difficult to believe that a nation which had suffered much more heavily than Britain would seriously contemplate another major war. Thus in contrast to the pre-1914 era the dangers either of being invaded or of involvement in a great Continental war seemed to have disappeared. Military experts could not afford to take such a sanguine view of course, but the general public's mixture of exhaustion, relief, and disillusionment with the outcome of its great military effort was summed up in the popular slogan of the day: Never Again.[6]

Britain's military policy in the inter-war period was decisively influenced by the additional commitments accepted during and immediately after the First World War. The understandable preoccupation of many historians with the final stages of the war on the Western Front and the prolonged controversy preceding the signing of the Versailles Treaty have tended to obscure the growing imperial concerns and ambitions of an influential group of British policy-makers and strategists. Indeed, as Michael Howard noted, 'The Imperial War Cabinet in 1917 regarded the Western Front as little more than a disagreeable necessity. A policy-making group consisting of Curzon, Milner and Smuts, and serviced by such men as Leo Amery and Mark Sykes, was not likely to give to the European theatre any larger priority than it could help.'[7]

By the end of 1917 Russia was in a state of anarchy while the Ottoman Empire teetered on the brink of total disintegration. In these circumstances it was hardly surprising that statesmen obsessed with the security of India, such as Curzon, should exaggerate the nightmare prospect of a German advance through the Ukraine to the Caucasus with the ultimate aim of controlling Armenia, Mesopotamia, and Persia while preserving the remainder of the Ottoman Empire under German protection. In 1918 the General Staff apparently gave its support to this view, the CIGS, Sir Henry Wilson,* noting with typical hyperbole 'From the left bank of the Don to India is our preserve.'[8] The same apprehensions caused Wilson to argue that there could be no question of Britain giving up the conquered territories of the Ottoman Empire, though he was dubious from the first about the necessity of retaining a garrison in Persia. As in the nineteenth century, these alarmists greatly underestimated the logistical problems—quite apart from the likelihood of local guerrilla operations—which would hamper a European power advancing towards the north-west frontier of India, but one should bear in mind that Ludendorff and his entourage did actually entertain such grandiose ambitions, and the German forces came close to fulfilling them in the Second World War.

Thus it was initially to counter possible German thrusts that British troops marched from Mesopotamia into the Caucasus, from Persia towards the Caspian and from India into Trans-Caspia. Germany's sudden collapse in November 1918 might appear to have rendered these onerous undertakings pointless, particularly as regards the contingents sent into Russia to stiffen resistance, but in fact the German menace was speedily replaced by fears of ubiquitous Bolshevik revolution. In consequence of these fears, and also of more straightforward desires to extend the Indian Empire while restricting France's foothold in the Middle East to a minimum, Britain accepted responsi-

*Indicates biographical note in Appendix I.

bility for Mesopotamia and Palestine as mandates and attained a temporary financial and military hegemony in Persia. There was even some discussion, by ministers ill-acquainted with the facts of geography, about accepting a Protectorate over the Caucasian Republics. In this immediate post-war period of uncertainty with its pervading fear of rampant Bolshevism, a 'high-minded itch for responsibility' briefly held ascendancy over the sober realism of statesmen like Arthur Balfour who pertinently asked whether Britain could find either the troops or the money for these immense commitments.[9]

The armistices that brought the First World War to an end by no means led to a smooth or rapid transition to peace. Russia was plunged into civil war and revolution; the newly emancipated countries of eastern Europe clashed over disputed boundaries; Greeks fought Turks; and Arab leaders contested the succession to the dismembered Ottoman Empire in the Middle East. The end of the war also brought a new surge of nationalism in India, in Egypt, and, most important of all as far as Britain was concerned, in Ireland. In virtually every one of these trouble spots British troops were involved, and even where Britain was not directly committed militarily she could not afford to stand entirely aloof 'since no country had a greater interest in a restoration of general tranquillity and resumption of ordered economic intercourse.'[10]

There could consequently be no calm period of stock-taking concerning the future organization and policy of the British Army in the months after the Armistice. Though the number of men under arms rapidly decreased, Britain's military commitments actually increased with the nominal ending of war. Even by the end of 1918, for example, seven generals with independent commands and 14,000 troops had been dispatched to Russia. Bridgeheads were established at Archangel and Murmansk, in Siberia, the Caucasus and Trans-Caspia. Early in 1919 it was becoming clear that the Supreme Council at the Peace Conference could not provide sufficient troops to make intervention in Russia a success, and that the anti-Bolshevik forces would have to stand on their own feet supported only with arms and money. The Dominions understandably displayed no enthusiasm whatever for involvement in the Russian civil war, and there was very little in Britain either, especially as the conflict in

Ireland became increasingly intense and bitter. Unfortunately, initially modest commitments in Russia designed to keep her at war with Germany, had the almost inevitable effect of drawing in reinforcements of men and supplies—which in turn had to be protected. For example, the northern expedition began with a mere 150 men sent to guard munitions at Murmansk but eventually, in the absence of a definite policy, absorbed nearly 20,000 British troops. Lloyd George insisted on disengagement against Churchill's objections and the last British troops in North Russia embarked at Archangel in September 1919. By that date British participation in Siberia was confined to small military missions. In October a British-backed expedition by General Yudenich to capture Petrograd from the Baltic was defeated, leaving Denikin's southern armies as the last White Russian recipients of British and French support. Lord Curzon strongly advocated a British military presence in South Russia on strategic grounds, but in June 1920 the Cabinet decided on evacuation. Meanwhile Denikin had been defeated early in 1920, leaving Britain's sole anti-Bolshevik commitment as two battalions at Batum. These were withdrawn after the Soviet conquest of Azerbaijan.[11]

The extension of British commitments in the Middle East resulted from a combination of pressure from the Government of India and rivalry with France. The San Remo Conference in April 1920 confirmed the secret wartime arrangements by allocating Mesopotamia and Palestine to Britain and Syria and Lebanon to France as mandates. In the summer of 1920 nationalist revolts broke out in both Syria and Mesopotamia. In the former French forces succeeded in regaining control, but in the latter troop withdrawals made the suppresssion of an insurrection in July more difficult. In August and September Sir Henry Wilson secured reinforcements from India amounting to no less than nineteen infantry battalions but he was warned that no more were available. Eventually it was decided to offer the throne of Iraq (as Mesopotamia was now styled) to Faisal, whom the French had expelled from Syria. This arrangement was confirmed at the Cairo Conference in March 1921, but Britain retained responsibility for preserving internal order. As regards Persia, by contrast, Churchill and Henry Wilson successfully pressed for withdrawal because of the shortage of troops. Much against the wishes of Curzon and Milner withdrawal was completed by June 1921.

Iraq proved to be an impossibly heavy burden for the Army. In addition to internal disturbances, the Turks laid claim to the Mosul vilayet—about a third of the whole country including the most fertile areas—and there was a serious danger of war. At the beginning of 1921 the British garrison amounted to 32 infantry battalions and supporting arms but such a large force could not be maintained indefinitely. In October 1922 military control of Iraq passed from the War Office to the Colonial Office which henceforth relied mainly on the RAF. This change proved an outstanding success in terms of both economy and efficiency. The substitution of eight RAF squadrons assisted by armoured car companies enabled the military garrison to be steadily reduced until in 1929 the last regular British and Indian army units were withdrawn. The cost of the Iraq garrison to the British tax-payer fell from over £20 million in 1921–2 to just over £1¼ million in 1927–8.[12]

Palestine was viewed by the Foreign Office and General Staff alike as a strategically desirable buffer-state for Egypt. The mandate was therefore accepted and military occupation theoretically ended on 1 July 1920. Unfortunately from the start Britain found it impossible to reconcile the pledge to create a Jewish national home with the aspirations of Arab nationalism. The situation, already difficult enough, was further complicated by the entry of Faisal's brother, Abdullah, into Trans-Jordan where he was proclaimed ruler in 1920. By recognizing him as Emir under the same High Commissioner as Palestine's, Britain effectively killed a plan for the possible resettlement of Palestinian Arabs in Trans-Jordan. The first outbreak of Arab violence in May 1921 caused the High Commissioner to promise that Jewish immigration would be controlled, thus placing the British authorities and forces of order in a position where they were bound to arouse the enmity of one community or the other, and often of both. Palestine was destined to become an increasingly serious military liability for Britain in the inter-war period.

After the Treaty of Versailles had been signed, Britain still had to maintain two armies of occupation: one at Constantinople and one in the Rhineland. As for the former, Britain still had 17,000 troops in the Black Sea area in 1919 (including six

Indian battalions) but, when early in 1922 Mustapha Kemal's Turkish nationalist forces threatened to involve Britain in a major war by invading the neutral zone at Chanak *en route* for Thrace, General Sir Charles 'Tim' Harington* had only one battalion at Chanak and three in Constantinople. Reinforcements were rushed out from Britain, Malta, Gibraltar, and Egypt with the result that at the height of the crisis he had six infantry battalions at Chanak, three and a Royal Marine battalion at Constantinople, and two more in the Ismid Peninsula. This theatre remained a major commitment until the British and other allied contingents were withdrawn following the Treaty of Lausanne in 1923.[13]

By contrast the occupation of the Rhineland was maintained until 1930, but units in Germany were counted as being on home service. Initially, Britain and France had to maintain large armies in the occupied zone in case Germany failed to sign the peace terms and needed to be coerced. Thus Foch originally requested ten British divisions on a war footing with at least another twenty in reserve, but Haig was hard pressed to spare even ten divisions. In June 1919 Foch and Sir Henry Wilson seriously discussed a 200 km advance to the line of the river Weser but this fortunately proved unnecessary. As British units, including the Guards Division, were rapidly demobilized or withdrawn for use in Ireland, it was only possible to maintain her contingent by compelling newly joined conscripts to serve for another year and by raising 69 battalions from 'young soldiers' aged 18 who were being trained at home when the war ended. At the end of 1919 the British Army of the Rhine still comprised 45,000 troops, but thereafter the higher formations and headquarters were broken up and the permanent garrison was reduced to a token force of eight infantry battalions and one cavalry regiment. After France's abortive attempt in 1923 to compel Germany to maintain her reparations payments by military force it was clear that the Anglo-French military contingent in the Rhineland was unlikely to be called upon to fight.[14]

The military commitment which above all others overtaxed Britain's resources, prevented an orderly transition to a peace establishment, and created grave misgivings about the efficacy of military force for repressing violent nationalism and preserving internal order was Ireland. Although Ireland's value to Britain was seen from Whitehall primarily as strategic, the bitter controversies aroused by the attempt to crush the rebellion by armed forces raised doubts whether Ireland as a whole was worth keeping in the Empire. On the one hand, as the General Staff pointed out in 1917, Ireland was a net loss from the viewpoint of military manpower since more troops were required to keep order there than had been raised in Ireland for service abroad. On the other hand diehard imperialists like Carson and Sir Henry Wilson believed that the loss of British control would signify the first irrevocable step in the inevitable break-up of the Empire. As Carson put it: 'If you tell your Empire in India, in Egypt and all over the world that you have not got the men, the money, the pluck, the inclination, and the backing to restore order in a country within twenty miles of your own shore, you may as well begin to abandon the attempt to make British rule prevail throughout the Empire at all.'[15]

When due allowance is made for the bias of Sir Henry Wilson's fulminations in his diaries against 'the frocks' for their failure either 'to govern Ireland or get out', it remains true that Lloyd George's Cabinet did not pursue a consistent policy or give the Army a clear mission either before or after the proclamation of a Republic by Dáil Eireann in Dublin in January 1919. The fundamental problem was that the Government never defined the nature of the conflict, or the respective roles of the police and military forces.[16] The British garrison, which totalled 53,000 troops in May 1919 and increased to the colossal total of 80,000 in July 1921, was also handicapped by the Government's failure to introduce martial law except (from December 1920) in eight of the most troublesome counties in the south west, and even in this limited area martial law was not wholeheartedly enforced. The employment of the notorious Black and Tans to assist the Irish constabulary and illegal reprisals for the murder of Royal Irish Constabulary (RIC) policemen and British troops further embittered the conflict.

The British Army's experience in Ireland between 1919 and 1921 had a deleterious effect on its reputation and morale. Its numerically impressive battalions (51 infantry battalions alone at the beginning of 1921) were filled largely with young and poorly trained soldiers, while even its more experienced officers were slow to abandon the techniques learnt in the First World War and adopt counter-guerrilla tactics. For example, large scale 'drives' across country accomplished very little, since the guerrillas enjoyed superior intelligence and could simply merge into the native population which by and large sympathized with them. Only towards the end of the campaign, in 1921, did some sections of the British Army begin to gain the upper hand by creating mobile foot patrols capable of carrying out rapid surprise raids.

Though guilty of far fewer acts of indiscipline and sheer vengeance than the RIC and its Auxiliaries, the Army too was infected by the growing atmosphere of lawlessness. In November 1920 the military authorities made the remarkable admission, in an attempt to gain official approval for reprisals, that 'the troops are getting out of control, taking the law into their own hands, and that besides clumsy and indiscriminate destruction, actual thieving and looting as well as drunkenness and gross disorder are occurring'. In February 1921 even General Sir Hubert Gough joined the critics, noting in an article that the police in many cases and the soldiers in some had been 'guilty of gross acts of violence, without even a semblance of military order and discipline, and that these acts are not only never punished, but no steps are taken to prevent their recurrence'. In May the Commander-in-Chief in Ireland, Sir Nevil Macready,* warned the Government that so great was the stress and strain on both officers and men that unless a settlement had been achieved by October virtually the whole garrison would have to be withdrawn. The Commander of the tank corps, Colonel Elles,* reported to the CIGS that the Army in Ireland was itself 'besieged': it was a Gilbertian situation with the humour left out. Unless martial law was rigorously enforced and other severe measures adopted, Elles stated, the guerrilla operations would drag on and Britain would eventually have to admit defeat. Lloyd George and his Government were not prepared to seek 'victory' by such draconian measures.[17]

Field-Marshal Montgomery* was to recall in his *Memoirs* that in many ways the war in Southern Ireland (where he served as brigade major to the 17th Infantry Brigade at Cork), was far worse than the Great War: 'It developed into a murder campaign in which, in the end, the soldiers became very skilful and more than held their own. But such a war is thoroughly bad for officers and men; it tends to lower their standards of decency and chivalry, and I was glad when it was over.'[18]

Eventually Irish terrorism triumphed to the extent that, by the terms of the Treaty signed on 6 December 1921, Southern Ireland was granted 'dominion status'; but Ulster was excluded and remained part of the United Kingdom. All British troops were withdrawn from Southern Ireland in 1922 but the thankless task remained of protecting the Ulster border against IRA raids. When the Treaty with the Republic of Ireland was ratified 18 Irish battalions disappeared from the British Army but at least Britain seemed to have kept control over the vital naval bases.[19]

After four and a half year of total war it was only to be expected that there would be tremendous public pressure for a rapid run-down of Britain's unprecedentedly great armies which had been maintained by conscription since 1916. In the emotional atmosphere generated by the Khaki election campaign in November 1918, the Government appeared to overlook the awkward facts that several peripheral wars were still in progress and that an armistice was not identical with a peace treaty. It was conceivable that large armies would have to march into Germany to compel her leaders to accept unpalatable terms. Moreover the demobilization plan, which gave priority to the rapid revival of industry, paid too little heed to the problem of the troops' morale. The Government proposed to release the key or 'pivotal' men who could help business to re-establish itself. This solution, it was felt, would in turn create jobs to be filled by the veterans. Unfortunately the scheme had the fatal defect of leaving it to employers to ask for their key men. These were in many cases men who had joined up late in the war, particularly after the crisis of March 1918. It also discriminated against those who had never been employed but had gone straight into the Army.[20]

The scheme caused understandable bitterness, but there was also a natural if unrealistic expectation on the part of many of the soldiers that they would all be demobilized immediately after the Armistice. On 3 January 1919 2,500 troops refused to re-embark at Folkestone. Other ominous incidents followed.

Regimental officers dealt with some thirty cases of insubordination; two Royal Army Service Corps groups in London formed Soldiers' Councils; a soldiers' deputation marched to Downing Street; and at Luton the town hall was burnt down. Most disturbing of all, there was a fully-fledged mutiny at Calais from 27 to 31 January 1919.[21] Given these disturbances, the proliferation of Communist propaganda, and the threat of large-scale strikes, it is easy to understand why Sir Henry Wilson and others in authority took the possibility of revolution seriously.

Winston Churchill, who became Secretary of State for War and Air on 10 January, took prompt action to restore Army morale and discipline. Assuming full control over demobilization, he decreed that henceforth men would be released according to length of service, age, and wounds rather than domestic industrial considerations. Army pay was doubled in order to narrow the gap between military and civilian wages. Some 80,000 'young soldiers' still under training at home were to serve abroad for two years so as to hasten the release of veterans. Despite its unpopularity conscription was to be retained to keep conscripts in service until March 1920. According to Churchill's new scheme, approved by the Prime Minister at the end of January, demobilization of some 3½ million surplus troops would be carried out at such a rate that they could be absorbed into industry. The armies of occupation would be composed of those who enlisted after 1 January 1916, were under 37 years of age, and had fewer than two wound stripes. These measures brought about a speedy improvement in morale and discipline and the great armies of 1916–18 began to dissolve rapidly and peacefully. In November 1918 there was over 3½ million troops on the British establishment (i.e. excluding those paid for by the Government of India); that figure had been reduced in a year to just over 800,000 and in another year (November 1920) to 370,000. The traffic, however, was not all one way because as early as January 1919 the Army Council felt obliged to reduce the minimum age of enlistment from 19 to 18 on the chance of attracting young recruits. Churchill rightly took pride in the way he had handled the problem of demobilization and rebutted at length Lloyd George's charge that there had been unnecessary delays. On 17 October 1919 he reported to the Finance Committee of the Cabinet that the scheme had been completed: in the eleven months that had passed since the Armistice an average of 10,000 men had been discharged every day. It was true to say, he added, that the Army had 'melted away.'[22]

Given the extent of British involvement in the effort to reshape both Europe and the extra-European world after 1918, it is easy to understand why the opportunity was missed for a thorough reappraisal of long-term future strategy in the light of recent experience and drastically changed conditions. In addition to the problems already outlined there were other inhibiting factors. Britain's leading politicians were preoccupied with post-war treaties and domestic political issues until 1922. Furthermore, despite the advocacy of Churchill and others, no Ministry of Defence was created to co-ordinate the organization and policy of the armed services; a revived Committee of Imperial Defence being the best acceptable substitute. The armed services, recently increased to three by the establishment of the Royal Air Force on 1 April 1918, each faced their own acute difficulties and were at odds on some vital issues. In practice the very survival of the RAF remained in doubt for several years because of the opposition of the two senior services. The Royal Navy emerged triumphant from the war to face the possibility of a crippling construction competition with the United States. The RAF, fighting for its life, exaggerated its claim to a unique role as an independent bombing force. The Army experienced no clear transition to peacetime duties in November 1918 but immediately found its manpower and other resources stretched beyond the limit to deal with crises at home and in Ireland, the occupation of enemy territory, and a sudden vast expansion of imperial policing duties.

One consideration, however, dominated all others where the post-war armed services were concerned: the urgent need for rapid and drastic financial economies. During the war Britain had lost heavily in overseas investments and had suffered setbacks in the face of American and Japanese competition. After the war she was handicapped by the slow recovery of her former European customers, notably Germany, while simultaneously facing an irresistible public demand for higher levels of personal consumption. Given the prevailing belief in rigorous government retrenchment it was inevitable that the armed forces should feature among the prime targets in an economy drive.[23]

There was, however, one brief and fleeting attempt by the War Office to preserve a peacetime Army organization, which took account of the enormous problems encountered in expanding from the small Expeditionary Force of 1914 to the mass conscript army of 1916–18. A Committee on the Organization of the After War Army was set up under the chairmanship of Lieutenant-General Sir Alexander Hamilton-Gordon on 12 April 1919 and reported on 26 July. Its fundamental assumption was that 'the organisation of the country for general mobilisation in war is of paramount importance among its military requirements, and it is therefore the principal function of the Regular Army to furnish the framework of the national organisation both for training in peace and for mobilisation in war.'

In the Committee's view a small regular expeditionary force could be improvised at short notice for minor wars, but the pre-war concentration of regular units at home in the Expeditionary Force supported by the Territorial Force as its second line had not constituted a suitable basis for a great war and should not be preserved:

> A system of peace organisation which concentrates the greater part of the trained regular personnel in a few regular units, which results in the mixture in all non-regular units of men of unequal physical standards and widely differing ages, and which provides no mechanism for expansion beyond units maintained in peace, cannot enable the whole manpower of the nation to be utilized . . . should another grave emergency arise.

The Committee recommended a field army of 20 divisions, each capable of throwing off a second division in the later phases of general mobilization. With the addition of a revived Guards Division this would constitute an army of 41 divisions. The national army could be formed either by a system of compulsory home service in peacetime or by voluntary service, in which case it envisaged an annual intake of 150,000 recruits.[24] The reasons why the recommendations of this high-level Committee were still born will quickly become apparent.

From August 1919 onwards British defence policy was broadly based upon the initially secret and subsequently notorious Ten Year Rule. Only an outline sketch of the origins and development of the Rule need be offered here since it has been thoroughly described by recent historians of British defence policy between the wars.[25] There is still disagreement as to the allegedly harmful effects of the Rule during the period of its operation from 1919 to 1932, but this need not concern us at this stage.[26]

Throughout the early months of 1919 discussions between ministers about future national defence policy were dominated by the paramount need for economy in the Service estimates. The Admiralty's building programme in particular seemed to raise the greatest immediate problem and when estimates of over £170 million were proposed the Chancellor of the Exchequr expressed 'profound shock'. The Secretary of the Committee of Imperial Defence, Sir Maurice Hankey, consequently drew up a memorandum for the Prime Minister which his biographer regards as the probable origin of the Ten Year Rule.[27] Hankey stressed that 'non-productive employment of man-power and expenditure, such as is involved by naval, military and air effort, must be reduced within the narrow limits consistent with national safety'. Simultaneously the Treasury circulated a memorandum asking for a cut in Service allotments from the total of £502 million for 1919–20 to a little more than one fifth of that figure for 1920–1. These issues were further discussed at a Cabinet meeting on 5 August 1919 when the Prime Minister suggested that a review of specific naval duties in the near future should be drawn up. The Admiralty circulated a paper to Cabinet members pointing out the advantages if it could assume a period of ten years of immunity from war with a great power or combination of powers, but added that five years would constitute a safer basis for planning since, *inter alia,* knowledge of American and Japanese building plans covered only the next five years. Astonishingly, this detailed naval paper was ignored when the Cabinet met to lay down the financial guidelines for future defence policy on 15 August.[28]

The main directives laid down by the War Cabinet to the Service Ministers at this meeting were:

> It should be assumed, for framing revised Estimates, that the British Empire will not be engaged in any great war during the next ten years, and that no Expeditionary Force is required for this purpose. . . .
> The principal functions of the Military and Air Forces is to provide

garrisons for India, Egypt, the new mandated territory and all territory (other than self-governing) under British control, as well as to provide the necessary support to the civil power at home. . . .
In framing estimates, the following maximum figures should be aimed at: Royal Navy £60 million.
Army and RAF £75 million.[29]

Since his biographer claims that Hankey was essentially 'the originator of the Rule', and since in his later years (and particularly after his retirement in 1938) he was apt to denounce its prolongation to 1932 with the wisdom of hindsight, it is interesting to record that as early as December 1923 Hankey (who, if anyone, should have been clear about the origins of the Rule) suggested that there had been confusion about its purpose from the outset. Writing to a War Office official, Hankey remarked that the decision had been taken at a Cabinet Committee on Finance in the Prime Minister's room on 11 August 1919. There were present besides the Prime Minister only Bonar Law, Austen Chamberlain, and Milner. The Foreign Secretary, Lord Balfour, was absent and there was no representative of any Service Department present; indeed, wrote Hankey, he did not know in what form the conclusions reached the latter. The belief, he concluded, was that the Cabinet had uttered a dictum to the effect 'no war for ten years'; the fact was that the Service Departments were to be asked to draw up fresh estimates for the following year on the assumption that no great war was to be anticipated within the next ten years.[30]

The significance of Hankey's letter is that it demonstrates that 'the Rule' originated in confused circumstances without the full participation of the Service Ministers or their professional advisers and at a time when the international situation was still in a state of flux. Even if the Rule was intended originally to apply only to the next year's estimates, as seems likely, it promptly assumed a permanent validity (as Hankey admitted in his letter) since it provided a guideline for the Committee on National Expenditure in 1921 and, with various modifications and extensions, remained in force until 1932.

From the standpoint of the early 1920s there was much to be said in favour of such a rule and little against it. Five years would have been more circumspect than ten, given the particularly blurred image in the kaleidoscope of world politics, but the basic facts remained: there was no major potential enemy (discounting the United States) against whom Britain need prepare for major war in the foreseeable future, while there were compelling economic and social reasons for draconian disarmament. As far as the Army was concerned, the Ten Year Rule only officially recognized what was day by day becoming a matter of fact: the great conscript force of 1916–18 was disappearing as fast as snow in summer and the remnant was reverting to a home and Imperial garrison based on long-term voluntary service and distributed according to the Cardwell system.

The Committee on National Expenditure of 1921–2 (commonly known by the name of its chairman Sir Eric Geddes as the Geddes Report or Geddes Axe) recommended drastic reduction of expenditure on all the armed services and in fact established standards of stringent economy for the whole decade. As regards future Army policy, the Committee accepted the full implications of the Ten Year Rule: the pre-1914 obligation to maintain an Expeditionary Force of six divisions for general service had gone; units stationed at home had now only to provide replacements for overseas garrisons (under the revived Cardwell system), prepare for minor expeditions, and ensure internal order. The Committee's main recommendations were:

1. Manpower could be reduced by 50,000 without affecting overseas service. This would involve the disbandment of 8 Cavalry regiments and 28 Infantry battalions.
2. Further savings could be made as a result of new arms (such as tanks) and the advent of the Air Force both as an auxiliary and as a partial substitute for troops on the ground.
3. There must be drastic cuts in ancillary and auxiliary services.
4. The Army estimates for 1922–3 should be cut from approximately £75 million to £55 million with further reductions the following year.

The War Office and the other Service Departments put up a reasoned opposition to these proposals and achieved some modifications. In some respects the Geddes Axe fell upon 'dead wood' as in its castigation of excessive staffs. Between 1922 and 1925, for example, the War Office staff was reduced from 4,114 to 2,561 without any marked decrease in efficiency. But in most respects the wielders of the axe were preoccupied with immediate savings rather than longer-term military efficiency. Twenty-two infantry battalions were disbanded as against the 28 recommended (including 5 Irish regiments and two battalions from surviving Irish regiments), and the cavalry was reduced—partly by amalgamations—from 28 to 20 regiments. The Geddes Committee also recommended that 9 battalions should be withdrawn from overseas garrisons and 7 were in fact withdrawn. The establishment of the reconstituted Territorial Army was reduced from 216,041 (in 1922–3) to 184,161 (in 1925–6). The Territorial Army was essentially for home defence, including anti-aircraft defence, since its members were not liable for overseas service. Ironically the recommendation from which the greatest savings might have resulted in the long run—the fusion of all three services and the unification of their auxiliary branches under a single ministry—was not adopted.[31]

It needs to be stressed that the economy measures signalled by the Ten Year Rule and the Geddes Axe were entirely in accord with the widespread public faith that the Covenant of the League of Nations obviated the need for national 'swords' or armies, and furthermore that general disarmament would soon follow. Few if any British diplomats or senior officers shared these illusions, but it was difficult to argue in the abstract against idealistic supporters of the League. Then, as later in the 1930s, pacifism and economy at the expense of the armed services tended to go hand in hand.

Although the Disarmament Conference at Washington in 1921 and 1922 concentrated mainly upon naval disarmament and arms control, there had also been entertained vague plans for air- and ground-force reductions. According to one plan drawn up by Lord Cecil to establish ratios in standing armies (excluding colonial troops and airmen) Britain would be allowed 90,000 troops and placed on a par with Holland, Spain, and Greece. The reaction of the General Staff to such suggestions can easily be imagined. 'In view of its commitments,' a general staff note warned in October 1921, 'the British Army is already on the lowest basis compatible with the execution of the task entrusted to it, and that any further reductions are out of the question. . . . From the Continental point of view the British

Army is almost negligible, and can in no sense be considered a menace to the peace of the world.' Except for the Guards battalions, combatant units at home were essential for maintaining the Cardwell system. Without conscription the Army at home could only raise an Expeditionary Force of two divisions until 1926 when more reserves would become available.[32]

From the end of the First World War until February 1922 professional responsibility for the Army lay in the hands of one of Britain's most exuberant, flamboyant, exotic, outspoken and even perhaps preposterous generals—Sir Henry Wilson. Wilson was the political soldier and fanatical Ulsterman *par excellence* and made no secret of his views. These proclivities, together with his belief in the Empire and his scorn for 'the frocks' as he contemptuously referred to politicians in general, have caused his once high reputation to plummet in recent decades. That his military judgements were always as suspect as his intemperate diaries suggest seems improbable. While it is unlikely that his standing can be fully redeemed from the adverse effects of his published diaries, a sympathetic appraisal will at least show that he held the highest post in the Army at a uniquely difficult period; that not all his predictions proved mistaken; and that in comparison with his successors as CIGS in the inter-war years he stands out as a forthright and combative spokesman for the Army's viewpoint. This is not the place for a lengthy survey of Wilson's performance as CIGS,[33] but the salient features of his *credo* must be sketched as an introduction to the shaping of Army policy in the early 1920s.

Wilson was first and foremost passionately committed to the preservation of the union with a united Ireland, not simply because he was an Ulsterman, but more importantly because he viewed the Union as being vital to the strategic interests of Britain and the continuation of the Empire. For men like Wilson and Carson Ireland was essentially an Imperial problem: to grant home rule to Ireland, or part of it, would be to precipitate the disintegration of the Empire. Wilson's conception of Imperial defence began with the security of the home base; for he believed, surely correctly, that the strength of the Empire derived more from Britain than vice versa. Hence the near-obsession in his diary entries in 1919 and 1920 with the overriding need to suppress Bolshevism in Britain and rebellion in Ireland rather than wasting scarce battalions in such peripheral tasks as supervising the plebiscite in Silesia or policing the Straits at Constantinople. Wilson felt that the War Cabinet, and Lloyd George above all, did not grasp this fundamental point, and he repeatedly castigated them to their faces as well as in his diary. The War Cabinet seemed incapable of applying his simple soldier's motto of 'govern or get out'. 'There is absolutely no *grip* anywhere', he complained in November 1919, 'Galloping *rot* has set in'. Reviewing that year in his diary he commented:

What a disappointing year. The Frocks have muddled everything, peace with our enemies, Ireland, Egypt, India, the Trades Unions, *everything*. They seem incapable of governing. To me personally the year has been wonderful . . . But the coming year looks gloomy. We are certain to have serious trouble in Ireland, Egypt and India, possibly even with the Bolsheviks.[34]

Apart from the security of the home base, including Ireland, Wilson's highest priorities—according to lists frequently recorded in his diaries—were Egypt and India; Mesopotamia usually ranked next; and Constantinople, Batum, Palestine, Persia, the Rhineland, and the plebiscite areas were placed bottom.[35] In a particularly anxious period in the spring of 1921, when he feared that a general strike in England would exacerbate the worsening situation in Ireland, he recorded his version of a heated interview with Lloyd George at Chequers:

I told him that if he would allow me to bring back 4 Battalions from Silesia, possibly the remaining 3 from the Rhine, 3 from Malta, 1 from Egypt and if possible 2 from Constantinople we ought to be able to hold both England and Ireland in the event of a Triple Strike, failing which i.e., the return of the above Battalions, I would only be able to hold England at the cost of losing Ireland. . . . I asked LG if he wanted to be P.M. of England or of Silesia, and I did my best to put my case before him which is the *dangerously* weak and narrow margin of troops on which we are running the Empire.[36]

Wilson's opinion of the Prime Minister reached its nadir in July 1921 when Lloyd George invited de Valera to London and told the CIGS he would have an opportunity to talk to him. Wilson allegedly replied that 'he did not speak to murderers' and would hand de Valera over to the police if he met him.[37] This may well have signified the end of personal relations between the Prime Minister and his chief military adviser; certainly in the closing months of his term as CIGS, which ended in February 1922, Wilson refused to attend Cabinet meetings and was represented by the Adjutant-General.[38]

Whether in the long run the Empire could have been preserved by the drastic combination of iron rule and ruthless withdrawal advocated by Wilson is very doubtful. Clearly he was right in thinking that the itch to take responsibility for other people's affairs, which to some extent he shared, had caused Britain to take on commitments at the end of the war which she could no longer shoulder either militarily or financially. But it was far from easy to decide which commitments could be safely written off and when. By the end of 1922, when Wilson was already dead—assassinated by fellow Irishmen—Lloyd George had at least achieved a temporary settlement in Ireland. The last British troops had withdrawn from Russia, Batum, Silesia, and Persia, and would soon be withdrawn from the Straits. Only a token force remained in the Rhineland which Wilson, as a notorious Francophile highly sympathetic to France's security problem *vis-à-vis* Germany, should have approved. In sum, nationalist opposition, the pressure of financial retrenchment, and sheer lack of troops were inevitably bringing about many of the withdrawals which he so stridently advocated as CIGS.

In the period immediately after the First World War the British Government appeared to be confronted with the stark choice of reducing its military commitments or retaining a large army to meet them. Although in fact the Army rapidly became 'the Cinderella Service' with enormous potential liabilities which it could not meet, this did not come about as the result of failure to present its case in the strongest terms. In June 1920, for example, Wilson wrote in a memorandum for the Secretary of State for War:

> Is it realised that at the present moment we have absolutely no reserves whatever (in formations) with which to reinforce our garrisons in any part of the world where an emergency may at any moment develop without warning? I cannot too strongly press on the Government the danger, the extreme danger, of His Majesty's Army being spread all over the world, strong nowhere, weak everywhere, and with no reserve to save a dangerous situation or to avert a coming danger.[39]

In the following month the General Staff presented a thorough and depressing review of the military liabilities of the Empire.[40] The salient facts which emerged were that in comparison with 1914 calculable liabilities had risen by 13 infantry divisions, 2⅓ cavalry divisions, and 26 RAF squadrons. Reinforcements which might be required for British overseas possessions amounted to nine divisions, four cavalry brigades, and five RAF squadrons. The Regular Army was already fully employed and could not be drawn upon for these reinforcements. The only savings in comparison with 1914 were in some of the garrisons of defended ports and home defence against invasion—both duties having been taken over by the Royal Navy—and in relinquishment of responsibility for the defence of South Africa. The General Staff summed up the net result:

> Before the war we had garrisons well-housed and contented, which proved more than sufficient for our needs, backed by an Expeditionary Force designated to fill two different and incompatible roles, for neither of which was it adequate. Now, owing to the greatly increased areas to be controlled, the general deterioration of the military situation outside Europe, and in the actual conditions of service, our garrisons are everywhere barely sufficient for our needs . . . and we have no reserves to meet emergencies. But for the increased strength of the Air Force the situation would be even more unfavourable.

Among the awkward questions which they posed was whether the League of Nations would reduce Britain's military liabilities in the future. In the Middle East they feared it would increase their problems since nationalist movements could appeal to the League against the injustice of imperial rule. The survey concluded gloomily:

> Wherever we look we find our garrisons beset by potential dangers which may far exceed their strength, and in the sum our liabilities are so vast, and at the same time so indeterminate, that to assess them must be largely a matter of conjecture. One thing only is certain, viz, that despite the temporary elimination of Germany, the problem before us is not less menacing than that for which we had to prepare prior to the recent war. That emergency could only be met by mobilising the manpower of the nation in support of the fighting services, and we should be well advised to retain the machinery for a similar expansion in the future.

Early in 1922 the Cabinet issued explicit instructions to the War Office that the main responsibilities of the Army in the foreseeable future were those of home security and Imperial defence. For the present the War Office should not provide for the contingency of another major national war, but rather should organize the forces stationed at home with a view to providing an Expeditionary Force for a minor war outside Europe.[41] The size and state of readiness of such a Force were largely determined by the operation of the Cardwell system, that is the need to keep at least as many battalions at home as on overseas service so as to provide a regular flow of replacements and reliefs. By the beginning of 1923 the distribution of units was becoming fairly settled after the immediate post-war emergencies. By far the largest and most important commitment continued to be the British component of the Army in India: no less than eight cavalry regiments, 45 infantry battalions, and 55 field batteries of artillery, a total of approximately 70,000 troops. The remaining overseas garrisons were the Straits—13 infantry battalions (soon to be withdrawn), Egypt six battalions, Iraq two battalions, and other colonies three (plus three native battalions). The garrisons in Northern Ireland (five battalions) and in the Rhineland (eight battalions) were counted as being on home service. Including these garrisons there were nine cavalry regiments and 53 infantry battalions at home.[42]

Wilson's successor as CIGS, the Earl of Cavan,* pointed out that the Army was considerably worse off than before 1914 as regards the peacetime organization of an Expeditionary Force because of a marked decrease in reservists. In 1914 there was an Army Reserve of 146,000 trained men and a Special Reserve of 55,000. Now (April 1923) there was only an Army Reserve of 76,000 and no special Reserve or Militia. The newly reconstituted Territorial Army was not available for overseas service in peacetime. Consequently the present available 'striking force' was the modest one of two divisions and a cavalry brigade which could theoretically be mobilized in 15 days and maintained in the field for up to four months. The skeleton striking force was equipped for operations in the Near East. However, as it would take five or six weeks to assemble shipping for the whole force, it would be over two months before disembarkation in, say, Iraq or India could be completed. This Expeditionary Force was designed in theory to be expanded to something more than double its size but the prospects for such an expansion, for a variety of reasons including lack of essential transport and stores, were remote.[43] The CIGS concluded his survey with a warning, echoed by the Secretary of State for War, Lord Derby, that uncertainty about such matters as conditions of service and the size and distribution of the Army had had bad effects from top to bottom. These ill effects were evident in administration, training, and above all in recruiting. Many parents were now doubtful about sending their sons into the Army as officers; there had, for example, been a considerable falling off in the number of candidates for Sandhurst and Woolwich.[44]

At least by 1923 the worst of the post-1918 upheavals were over and the Army was settling down again to the humdrum routine of home security and imperial policing. As Kipling had mordantly recorded for the pre-1914 era, the public had little interest in or sympathy for 'Tommy Atkins' once a great war was over, and the memories of 1914–18 were far more bitter and disillusioned than after previous wars. The post-1918 Army, lacking either the traditional esteem of the Royal Navy or the novel appeal of the Royal Air Force soon found itself to be the 'Cinderella' of the Services, criticized in the press, short of men, and dependent on obsolescent weapons and equipment. When Field-Marshal Sir William Robertson published some mildly critical articles in the *Morning Post* in 1924, Lord Cavan responded with the following pained remarks:

> Our great and threatening danger is that the Public see the necessity for a strong Air Force because they don't want to be bombed, and a strong Navy to escort food and the necessities of life to their shores, because they don't want to be starved, but they don't realise at all that neither Air Force nor Navy can operate without the protection of the Army. Consequently Governments are tempted to treat us as the unpopular sister, and we have to fight hard all the time.

Finance, he added, was by far his worst headache. The Treasury ordered the War Office to get inside a figure in its estimates but even after the estimates had been passed the Treasury constantly flatly refused to sanction expenditure on particular items.[45] Cavan's *cri de cœur* is supported by the statistics of the Services' budgets: for the Army's vote showed a steady decline every year between 1919 and 1932.[46]

Indeed, an observer in the 1920s could be pardoned for believing that Britain's great military contribution to the total war of 1914–18 had been speedily forgotten like a bad dream.

Not merely had the great armies themselves and the higher headquarters disappeared, but there seemed to be no inclination to profit from the dreadful experience by studying all the lessons ranging from tactics to civil and industrial preparedness. In particular, there was not any systematic attempt to grapple with the greatest strategic lesson of the war; that Britain's security was inextricably involved with that of western Europe.

And yet, rapid though the military retreat from Europe was in the early 1920s, the possibility of a continental commitment could not be entirely ignored for the future. The General Staff at least by implication recognized this in its strategic survey of July 1920 when it referred to the 'temporary' elimination of Germany, and Sir Maurice Hankey raised the same question more bluntly when he wrote in September 1920. 'it still seems inconceivable, after the amount of blood and treasure which has been spent in the last few years, that Great Britain could remain neutral and not go to the assistance of her late ally in the event of a further unprovoked attack by Germany'.[47] But for the moment this unpleasant vista was merely hypothetical: Germany was disarmed and impotent, while the shrinking British Army had more than enough commitments to occupy it overseas. With the Ten Year Rule becoming ever more firmly established as the authoritative guide to defence priorities it was hardly surprising that few senior soldiers were prepared to give serious thought to the unthinkable prospect of involvement in another great continental war. Indeed, when all the adverse conditions are taken into account, it is surely remarkable that the British Army did so much to remain in the vanguard of military development in the 1920s and early 1930s.

CHAPTER 2

The character and ethos of the British Army between the Wars

In a penetrating review of the Liddell Hart *Memoirs*, Michael Howard was prompted to ask the key question: 'what, if anything, did go wrong with the Army between the wars?' Beyond the obvious retort that nothing went wrong except that the Service was bedevilled by a pacifist electorate, a parsimonious Treasury, and chronic uncertainty over its role, Professor Howard suggested that there was still a case to be answered. There was ample evidence to suggest that the Army remained firmly geared to the pace of regimental soldiering as an agreeable occupation rather than a demanding profession; and that many officers, so far from wishing to adapt to social and technical changes, looked to the Army as a haven where they could escape from them.[1] This chapter will attempt to throw further light on these questions by an impressionistic discussion of some of the Army's chief characteristics and the atmosphere in which it existed. It concentrates almost exclusively upon the officers mainly because this study is concerned with military policy, but also because so few other ranks have published accounts of peacetime soldiering in this period. It is certainly not the intention to suggest that the Army can be identified with its officers.

The atmosphere after 1918 was profoundly hostile to the very existence and purpose of soldiering. In the words of Wavell's biographer, 'A naive pacifism was preached in schools, universities, cathedral pulpits and the Press; and it was taken for granted by all intellectuals that Regular officers were as bloodthirsty as they were cretinous.' The Army, accustomed by long experience to this kind of public reaction after a great war, withdraw into a self-conscious isolation. It resurrected a pre-1914 style of life apart from the outside world to an extent which later generations would find hard to understand.[2] The Armistice had hardly sounded before Private Frank Richards's commanding officer began to lecture his battalion on discipline: 'They must remember that they belonged to a Line Battalion, and discipline must revert back to its pre-War standard.' This meant endless drill and parading in *polished* steel helmets. As J. F. C. Fuller* gleefully commented, '90 per cent of the Army was at work scraping off the reality of war and burnishing up the war-tarnished conventionalities of peace'. There was even a proposal to restore the time-honoured red coat, the traditional colour of Mars and also allegedly of the costume of King Canute's bodyguard, but this outlay of £5 million was mercifully rejected by the Finance Branch.[3] As the horrific experience of the war receded, to be replaced by the manifold problems of peacetime soldiering at home and in the Empire, the feeling understandably grew that the unprecedented national military effort of 1914–18 had been a unique occurrence, even an aberration. No less an authority than the CIGS, Sir George Milne,* voiced this opinion when he told the Chiefs of Staff in 1926 that the war against Germany was 'abnormal'. Our normal wars, he said, started as small divisional commitments and we then have to reinforce up to a Corps. The Army was not even prepared for such a war as that at the present. 'Attempts had been made to prepare for mobilisation for another Continental war and considerable expenditure was being incurred in paying retaining fees to men who might be, but were very unlikely ever to be, required for any such eventuality.'[4]

In retrospect it seems astonishing that virtually no official attempt was made to garner the experience of the First World War while it was still fresh. No special War Office department or section was created to study its lessons—though there had been considerable advance planning for demobilization—nor was there a Royal Commission like the one that had gathered a mass of valuable evidence after the South African War. Indeed it was not until 1932, partly as a result of Liddell Hart's prodding, that a War Office Committee was set up to study the lessons of the war as embodied in the official histories. True, the war received almost obsessive attention in professional magazines such as the *Army Quarterly* (founded in 1920) and the Royal United Service Institution *Journal,* but that was no compensation for War Office inertia. There was, indeed, a unique opportunity to digest the experience of the war at the Staff College since both the directors and specially selected 'students' in the immediate post-war courses had come straight from command and staff appointments in divisions, brigades, and battalions. Even at Camberley, however, progressive students felt that the instructors were over-concerned with methods of winning the last war and insufficiently interested in new and progressive tactics and ideas—such as mechanization—for winning the next. It was obvious to a radically minded student like Martel* that trench warfare conditions would never occur again. Yet study was concentrated on the static Western Front operations to the neglect of the brilliant campaign in Palestine which pointed to the value of surprise, mobility, and speed in movement. After serving as an instructor at the Staff College from 1919 to 1923, specializing in the study of tank warfare, Philip Neame* was told, on arrival as an infantry brigade major at Aldershot, 'You are, of course, out of touch with modern military training.' In fact he saw little of modern training in the Aldershot division and suggestions in favour of partial mechanization put forward in his brigade training reports were invariably ignored. 'Our minds', he later recalled, 'were not encouraged to rise above somewhat out-of-date platoon formations and tactics, together with those curses of Aldershot of the years between the wars, the Aldershot Tattoo, the Horse Show and the Royal Review.' Already by 1921, Lord Gort,* who was avid to analyse and profit from the infantry's experience in the World War, was agreeing with Liddell Hart's criticism that all was far from well in Army training and doctrine. There was a definite tendency, he noted, to forget the lessons of the war and return to the old pre-war peace training routine.[5]

Two broad areas of war experience were badly neglected: the creation of large formations unknown to the small British Army in peacetime with the practice of command and staff work and the extended loyalties that this entailed; and the intense pressure to develop new instruments and techniques of fighting which had paid handsome dividends in 1918. Instead the post-war Army was simultaneously reduced to pre-1914 size and plunged without a break into world-wide garrison, occupation, and policing duties. Its imperial role was emphasized both by the clause in the Ten Year Rule specifically stating that no Expeditionary Force would be required for the Continent in the forseeable future, and by the restoration of the Cardwell system which Fuller, with pardonable exaggeration, described as 'that albatross which had then been rotting round our necks for fifty years.'[6]

It is impossible to gain a true impression of the Army's weaknesses between the wars without some discussion of the War Office itself. The War Office building, established in Whitehall after the South African War, suggests from a distance the possibilities of romance. In its historian's eloquent description.

Viewed from the bridge in St. James's Park on a misty morning of Spring the distant domes of the War Office roof are touched by the magic of sun and haze with the grace of the turrets of tall white castles, soaring up most royally from the streets of some city of high adventure. On closer approach the illusion is shattered. No atmosphere of romantic days lingers about this modern Department.

Descending to reality he adds that the War Office was traditionally the butt of Press and Stage as the home of all ineptitude, while to many a regimental officer it remained the *fons et origo* of an incredible mass of unnecessary rules.[7] It had acquired a deserved reputation for red tape and officialdom. When Sir Alexander Godley* became Military Secretary shortly after the end of the First World War, one of the first files brought to him was huge and thick and the last document had reached its 365th minute, written by Field-Marshal Sir Henry Wilson the CIGS: 'This correspondence has now reached a stage at which it reminds me of the old music hall song

Waltz me round once again, Willie,
Waltz me around and around,
Waltz me round once again, Willie,
Don't let my feet touch the ground!'

This anecdote corroborates Fuller's impression that Wilson had given up hope of getting any worth-while decisions out of the War Office and treated his final tour of duty there as an immense joke. Frederick Morgan* quotes the kind of exasperating example of the application of rigid rules that most officers encountered in some form. Posted back to England after a full six year tour of duty in India he had gained a place at the Staff College at Quetta. He was not allowed to transfer to Camberley but in order to take his place at Quetta was obliged to pay for the passage out and back for himself and family unless he was prepared to sign on for another six years in India. He chose the latter option. Later, in the early 1930s, the War Office struck 'Pug' Ismay* as 'hidebound, unimaginative, impersonal and over-populated', reminding him of the truth of Philip Guedalla's lapidary phrase 'There is an ineptitude about the War Office which it has never lost.' For a more balanced, though still critical, summing up, we may turn to Sir John Burnett-Stuart's* Unpublished Memoirs:

I have, as an individual, no personal grudge against the War Office. I served two four-year periods as a member of it, and knew it to be full of capable men and good fellows both on the military and on the civil side. But I always had the feeling, which was shared by many others of my generation, that there was something wrong with it. It was in itself too top-heavy; it was constantly immersed in detail which could so easily have been dealt with by commanders, in their different degrees, had reasonable powers and financial responsibility been allowed them; it was out of touch with the real Army, especially with the troops oversea; the civil side in particular never even saw the soldiers or commanders with whose requirements and difficulties they were so intimately concerned; the civil staff, also was not in cordial alignment with the military staff—as it was for instance, in the Admiralty; there was no close touch between the Army Council and G.O.C.'s-in-C of commands, who were never brought into collaboration, or even consultation, on matters of army or defence policy; and above all, it had no real military head: the C.I.G.S. was no more than 'primus inter pares', co-equal and co-ephemeral with the other military members.[8]

What most officers who served there recalled with particular distaste was the dominance of the Finance Branch. Thus Sir Ian Jacob remarked to the present author that the War Office civil servants were really an outpost of the Treasury who felt no responsibility for the Army's efficiency. He felt things were much better in the Air Ministry where the finance officers 'meshed in' with the Air Staff. What was particularly anomolous and a prime source of friction was that the War Office Finance

Branch could hold up expenditure on programmes actually approved by the CID and even the Cabinet. Writing after the Second World War, Martel remarks that the trouble, inefficiency, and unfairness that this power of veto on any expenditure down to the smallest detail had caused in the last thirty years was 'beyond description'. He cited the case of a bombed out hospital whose removal to new accommodation had been held up for months over a sum of less that £100. As he rightly pointed out, the War Office finance officials were really accountants: any business firm which allowed similar interference in its routine transactions would quickly go bankrupt. Fuller provides numerous hilarious examples of his struggles against these officials in the immediate post-war years. Rather than indulge in the Finance Branch's 'language of ritual', he found that the most successful tactic was to act first and negotiate afterwards. When the Finance Branch refused to settle a trifling bill for slides used to illustrate a lecture he threatened to send the following note to the photographer: 'I am commanded by the Army Council to inform you that there is not sufficient money in His Majesty's Treasury to meet this account. I have been requested to express to you the deep regrets of the Council for any inconvenience this may cause you.' He never saw the file again, but few officers possessed the nerve of a Fuller or the droll buffoonery of Henry Wilson.[9]

From what has already been said it may be gathered that the place of Secretary of State for War was not generally regarded as a 'plum' by aspirants to the highest Government offices. Indeed, there is no reason to believe that its reputation in the 1920s had improved since Campbell-Bannerman told Haldane in 1905 that 'Nobody will touch it with a pole', and Grey's earlier remark on the formation of the same Cabinet, 'If we enter it is not for pleasure's sake, and we must take the most beastly things. I will take the War Office.'[10] Occasionally, as with Haldane and again with Lord Hailsham (November 1931–June 1935), the Army was fortunate to get as its chief a politician of first-rate stature who could champion its interests with both ability and authority in Cabinet, but this brought the disadvantage, in Hailsham's case, that he was frequently employed on other Government business such as the Ottawa Imperial Conference in 1932 and the World Economic Conference of 1933. Moreover, there seems to be little doubt that Hailsham regarded his tenure as not much more than a stepping stone back to his previous appointment of Lord Chancellor. It is more typical that, after Churchil's joint tenure of the War and Air Ministries (January 1919–January 1921), both parties sent to the War Office politicians of the second rank in the 1920s in the persons of Sir Laming Worthington-Evans, Lord Derby, Stephen Walsh, and Thomas Shaw. Duff Cooper, though a true friend to the Army, might be put in the same category. As he himself sadly reflected, he had acquired little credit during his tenure of the War Office and, after falling foul of Neville Chamberlain, was astonished to be 'promoted' to the Admiralty in May 1937. He neatly illustrated the differing status of the two ministries: 'The First Lord has one of the finest houses in London, and a yacht in which to sail the sea. He knows also that in any encounter he may have with his colleagues he has the country on his side.' His successor, Leslie Hore-Belisha, was unusual in being an up-and-coming young minister who could aspire to higher office, yet ironically the War Office proved to be his nemesis.[11]

For obvious reasons the War Ministry tended to be unpopular with the public and Government alike since it represented great expenditure on destructive armaments. Very few ministers knew anything about strategy, and until the later 1930s the Cabinet seldom considered Army affairs other than to debate further reductions in its budget. Neville Chamberlain as Chancellor of the Exchequer was only expressing what many people felt when, in the mid-1930s, he described the Royal Navy and the Royal Air Force as 'deterrent' (i.e. defensive) instruments whereas he regarded the Army as an offensive or aggressive one.

The political heads of all the Service Ministries tended to have shorter tenures of office than the professional heads. In the inter-war period there were ten political occupants of the War Office (counting two spells by Worthington-Evans) as against six CIGSs. Cavan, Milne, and Montgomery-Massingberd* each served under three Secretaries of State for War, Wilson and Deverell* under two, and Gort under Hore-Belisha alone. In contrast to the brief tenures of the political heads of the War Office, continuity was supplied by the Permanent Under-

Secretary of State, who was a career civil servant and a member of the Army Council. The PUS was responsible for the preparation of all official communications of the Army Council and, as the Accounting Officer of Army Votes, Funds, and Accounts, was responsible for advising the Council on all questions of Army expenditure. As PUS from 1924 to 1939, Sir Herbert Creedy acquired vast experience and influence resembling that of Sir Maurice Hankey in the CID. Creedy was a model civil servant who, as far as possible, worked with rather than against the military members, but his financial responsibilities placed strict limits on his co-operation. Higham speculates that the actual order of power may have been civil servants, serving officers, and at the bottom ministers, but judgement must be reserved in the absence of any up-to-date studies of War Office administration.[12]

Business was administered by the Army Council† whose ex-officio president was the Secretary of State for War. There were two other ministerial officers, the Parliamentary Under-Secretary of State and the Financial Secretary. The former, who was usually drawn from the House of Lords, was responsible for all matters, other than training, affecting the Territorial Army, and the latter, in addition to finance, was responsible for the policy aspects of Army contracts. Of the four military members the CIGS as head of the General Staff was concerned with all aspects of military policy. The second military member was the Adjutant-General whose large area of responsibility covered recruiting, discipline, and medical services. The third military member, the Quartermaster-General of the Forces, dealt with all aspects of housing, movement of troops and stores, and transport generally; and the fourth military member, the Master-General of the Ordnance, was responsible for stores and the development of war material of all kinds. The PUS was the final member, and also served as secretary to the Council; he was the essential co-ordinating link between the Secretary of State and all branches of the War Office. The actual role of the PUS took on additional significance from the fact that formal meetings of the full Army Council, with all the machinery of printed précis, were extremely infrequent. For example, during Milne's seven years as CIGS, there were only 31 meetings spread out as

† See Appendix III.

follows: 5 in 1926, 6 in 1927, 6 in 1928, 3 in 1929, 2 in 1930, 6 in 1931, and 3 in 1932. In reality a great deal of Army business was conducted by regular but informal meetings of the military members and frequent meetings of two or more councillors to settle particular items of business. However, in times of emergency such as the Chanak crisis, the General Strike, the dispatch of the Shanghai Defence Force, or the financial crisis of 1931, the whole Council would meet informally at least once a day. Thus it is easy to imagine that Creedy, like Hankey covering the plethora of CID subcommittees, would be the only man to have a general grasp of all that was going on.[13]

According to 'Boney' Fuller's highly amusing if perhaps over-dramatized account, the Army Council during Sir Henry Wilson's time as CIGS was little more than that strange Irishman's performing troupe. Humming some such refrain as 'When I was a little Rifleman', Wilson would scrutinize the agenda, not with a view to solving problems, but to think out how best to extract from it a first-class dog-fight. Fuller reached the depressing conclusion that the whole object of Council meetings was to avoid reaching decisions. After Wilson's tomfoolery, the military membership of the Army Council during Cavan's tenure as CIGS (1922–6) was dominated by conservatives. Cavan himself had no experience of staff work and had no discernible views on strategic issues. He was opposed to serving officers publishing books on military subjects. The Adjutant-General, Sir Robert Whigham,* and the Quartermaster-General, Sir Walter Campbell,* were also conservative by temperament. Only the Master-General of the Ordnance, Sir Noel Birch,* was interested in technical development. It seems clear that during the whole inter-war period the Army Council, unlike the Board of Admiralty, did not develop a strong collective identity. Its military members remained essentially department managers, determined to maintain their own separate prerogatives, as Milne found to his cost when he unwarily attempted to represent his colleagues' views without first consulting them. The Army's lack of homogeneity was thus reflected in its highest representative body.[14]

Few officers looked forward to tours of staff service in Whitehall with any pleasure. Service in direct contact with troops had always been regarded, and indeed still is, as the essence of soldiering. Desk work with an office routine in central London was anathema to many officers, particularly as it reduced the opportunity for sport and open-air exercise. Ironside actually expressed relief when passed over for the post of Master-General of the Ordnance in 1930 as he felt unsuited to an 'office-stool' at the War Office. Sir Frederick Morgan described his term in Whitehall in the mid-1930s as a nightmare since he found there so little sense of urgency to prepare for the impending war. He cited as an example of the communal madness the delay in constructing an airfield at Gibraltar because it would entail demolishing a newly built cookhouse. Roderick Macleod put the Whitehall malaise into a broader perspective when he wrote to Liddell Hart in 1936 that there was too much routine work and too little scope for fresh thought, particularly for the lower grades of staff officer: 'Several of the G.2's when they go there are keen and energetic, with fresh and elastic minds, but several years routine kills their enthusiasm and originality, so that when they reach Director's rank they are stale and hidebound.' Macleod felt there was an urgent need to introduce more rapid promotion for abler men. As a general rule he believed the older officers to be unimaginative and slaves to system and routine. Too many were still obsessed by the last war. When he advised a young officer to study the operations of Alexander the Great, Genghis Khan, and Tamurlane, 'quite a good' senior officer had interjected that such military history was no better than fairy stories![15]

A source of festering discontent in the Army throughout the inter-war period was the system of promotion and the method of selection for senior appointments. The enormous inflation of the officer corps during the First World War, when nearly a quarter of a million commissions had been awarded, followed by the breakneck demobilization and reductions after 1918, inevitably caused a serious logjam. By the early 1920s the establishment of regular officers had settled at just over 14,000, which was very similar to the situation in 1913 except that the Army as a whole was slightly smaller. With a revival of pre-war regimental tradition and mess life, 'Ranker officers now began to wonder whether they could live up to the standards of peace-time soldiering, or whether to join in the rush to buy petrol stations, public-houses and chicken farms. . . . Men who had kept their nerve in the trenches lost it on the social front, and resigned.' On the other hand the traditional sources of regular officers were feeling the financial pinch and sent fewer of their sons to the Service.[16]

As a result of the Geddes Axe and successive cuts in the establishment many inefficient soldiers were removed from the rank and file but much dead wood was left in the senior ranks. In retrospect, Viscount Montgomery declared that the solution was 'an extensive use of weedkiller' in the senior ranks after a war to enable first-class young officers who have emerged during the war to be moved up. This unfortunately did not happen to the necessary degree after 1918.[17] Rather than a purge of senior officers (major-general and above), two main solutions were adopted: reversion to substantive rank for long periods and extensive use of the half-pay system whereby most officers had to mark time in semi-retirement (sometimes more than once) for periods ranging from one to three years. Some idea of the immensity of the problem may be suggested by the fact that four and a half years after the Armistice more than two hundred officers were waiting for vacancies to command battalions, quite half of whom had already commanded brigades in the field for over two years.[18] A few individual cases will illustrate the frustrations and difficulties caused by these two expedients.

After the Armistice Archibald Wavell* served as brigadier-general at Middle East headquarters and took on the additional duties of chief of staff when Major-General Sir Louis Bols* returned home ill. In the summer of 1920, however, he rejoined his regiment, the Black Watch, as a major (and brevet lieutenant-colonel) commanding a company. It took Wavell, generally recognized in the Army as a most thoughtful soldier and an outstanding military trainer, ten years to work his way back to his wartime rank of brigadier. Even then he was one of the favoured since less than one full colonel in ten could hope for further promotion. Another officer who had an outstanding career in the First World War was the late Brigadier Bentley Beauman.* Starting the war as a subaltern commanding a platoon he served throughout in or near the front line and finished as one of the youngest brigadier-generals in the Army; indeed, he even held temporary command of a reduced division in Italy after the Armistice. Thereafter he reverted to his substantive rank of captain, well down the captains' list in the South Staffordshire regiment. In 1936 he was unjustly passed over for promotion to major-general, a rank which he might well have attained in 1919 had the war continued. Philip Neame had won a Victoria Cross on the Western Front and ended the war as a GSO1 with the temporary rank of lieutenant-colonel. His permanent rank was still only that of captain in the Royal Engineers. After four years (1919–23) as a GSO1 instructor at the Staff College he stepped down to an appointment as brigade major and did not again reach the grade of GSO1 until 1932, fourteen years after he had first attained it during the great battles of 1918. Yet by his own admission he was one of the fortunate few, in that his brevet lieutenant-colonelcy was speedily confirmed. He met officers at the Staff College who had commanded infantry brigades with great success in the war only to revert from brigadier to captain. After the Staff College course several returned to their units as company commanders to serve under battalion or regimental commanders who had been through the whole war at home or in some job at a base. This kind of anomaly not surprisingly caused resentment. As Neame comments, 'This is not the way to bring our best military talent to the top, or to produce for our Army Generals young and active enough for the strain of active service.'[19]

The problem of having too many officers qualified for available appointments of the appropriate grade was mitigated by the unsatisfactory compromise of half-pay which in fact, when shorn of perquisites including a soldier servant and all staff and other allowances, meant a reduction not by half, but by nearly two-thirds. Wavell, who endured two lengthy intervals on half-pay, was fortunate in two respects: he and his entire family could live in his father's house; and his skill with the pen kept him mentally alert and gainfully occupied. He thought an occasional sabbatical from peacetime Army routine highly desirable but considered that it ought to be made financially possible to travel or take some civilian post. He regarded the system as iniquitous in that, while on half-pay, an officer would receive less than the pension he would have been entitled to, had he retired. The worst aspect of the half-pay system, however, occurred when the victim was uncertain whether he would be given another appointment. As General Sir Douglas

Brownrigg,* who later as Military Secretary helped Hore-Belisha to abolish the system, pointed out, these periods of uncertainty were particularly nerve-racking since they tended to occur when officers were financially stretched to pay the expenses of their children's education. Ironside,* who endured a long and stultifying period on half-pay before being appointed QMG in India in 1933, complained to Liddell Hart of the system of 'ghosts' in the Army in India which complicated an already confused promotion list. These were senior officers who in reality had retired but left their names on the list during a terminal period on half-pay. He also cited several cases of officers who were doing over two years on half-pay, and one case three years, before returning to active service.[20]

What made matters worse was that fewer officers than before 1914 could exist on their private means. Some critics felt that the precarious nature of the military career encouraged officers to play safe rather than voice critical views which might jeopardize their promotion prospects. Field-Marshal Sir Philip Chetwode* made the point in 1937 that:

> 9 out of 10 officers are very poor and are not allowed to supplement their exiguous pay in peacetime. They know the British Public demand victims for partial failure in war—and having got a wife and family and perhaps a son at school—very naturally play for safety in war . . . So the cavalryman with money who does not care a damn for Lloyd George or the critics and does what he thinks right, *not what he is ordered to* comes to the top, i.e., my noble self.

Major-General L. H. R. Pope-Hennessey was another senior officer who endorsed Liddell Hart's impression that in the First World War men with private means (such as Earl Cavan) had been willing to criticize superiors whereas impecunious senior officers (such as Deverell) had not.[21]

It may well be felt that, though regrettable, the exceedingly slow promotion prospects aggravated by periods on half-pay should have been accepted with less fuss since everyone was in the same boat. Unfortunately, however, this was not the case; for promotion prospects were well known to differ considerably between the various corps and regiments. In this respect the sweeping and bitter indictment by the Editor of the *Army, Navy and Air Force Gazette,* Captain J. R. Kennedy, in his rather hysterical book *This, Our Army* (1935) was right on target. The most obvious anomaly was that, whereas promotion in the Artillery, Engineers, Tank Corps, and Army Service Corps took place within a single list for each corps, in the 22 cavalry and 136 infantry battalions there was a completely separate list for each individual regiment. These groups were independent of each other. How could there be any uniformity when the Artillery promotion group number was 1,659, the Engineers 824, the Signals 378, the RASC 388, the Infantry 27, and the Cavalry 23? To complicate matters further in some corps but not in others subalterns were automatically promoted captain after a certain number of years if not elevated sooner. Characteristically, however, there was no uniformity about automatic promotion: the periods laid down were 11 years for Engineers, 13 for Artillery, and 20 for the Signals. No such terms had been laid down for the Infantry, Cavalry, or Tank Corps. In 1932 a War Office Committee chaired by the Under-Secretary for War, Lord Stanhope, discovered that 359 subalterns had over eleven-years service.

As regards the worst sufferers, subalterns with 16 and 17 years service, criticism reached such dimensions that as a consequence of the Stanhope Committee's findings a Royal Warrant was issued giving an increase in pay of two shillings per day to subalterns with more than thirteen-years service. It did not need Captain Kennedy's angry polemic to spell out the harmful effects of such a deadening and unrewarding career on young officers. But, as he proceeded to demonstrate, periods spent in the middle ranks also varied considerably in the different regiments and corps. Thus, for example, whereas on average (according to a table published in 1932) Irish Guards officers spent only 6.3 years as a senior lieutenant, 16.8 as a senior captain, and 18.3 as a senior major, a Signals officer would spend 10, 16.3, and 23 years in the equivalent ranks. Promotion in the Artillery was notoriously slow—the average periods being 13.11 as a subaltern, 19 as a captain, and as many as 29 years as a major. In the most handicapped corps officers were reaching senior regimental rank at an age which effectively debarred them from further promotion. Kennedy's analysis of the list of officers promoted lieutenant-colonel in 1933 and 1934 showed that the Guards were clearly the best off. Three officers under forty were promoted to the command of regiments and three only just over that age—the average age being about forty years and five months. Cavalry came next with an average of forty-three years and three months, Engineers followed with forty-four years and one month, while the worst off were the Gunners with forty-eight years and five months. Another way of viewing these anomalies was that there were infantry subalterns who were older than Guards commanding officers; Gunner captains were promoted major at approximately the age that Guards' majors were promoted lieutenant-colonel; and it took another decade before the Gunners reached the rank of lieutenant-colonel.[22] Just two examples will suffice to show the system in practice. Sir Frederick Morgan was commissioned a second lieutenant in the Royal Field Artillery in July 1913 and served throughout the First World War, later achieving a p.s.c. at Quetta, yet he remained sixteen years a captain and had completed nineteen years service before he was promoted major. Promotion in the Royal Tank Corps was also deplorably slow for distinctive reasons. As a new and small corps it had a meagre number of senior appointments of lieutenant-colonel and above on the establishment and, to make matters worse, when the Royal Tank Corps was officially formed in 1923 all existing senior appointments were renewed for a further three years. Finally, there was an influx of officers from other corps in the early years which had the effect of pushing subalterns, many of whom had been with tanks from the start, down the list. Horace Birks* was one of these. In the early 1920s he went down about a hundred places on the lieutenants' list and remained a subaltern for nearly fourteen years, even after he had graduated from the Quetta Staff College. Yet, as he recalled in old age, his progress up the ladder was probably faster than average![23]

At the other end of the promotion ladder large doses of 'weedkiller' were not applied to the senior staff officers and commanders of 1918 vintage, many of whom had reached the top comparatively young and were allowed to fill the highest appointments on the principle of 'Buggins's turn' well into the 1930s. In a different but equally fitting figure of speech, Montgomery remarked that 'They remained in office for too long, playing musical chairs with the top jobs but never taking a chair away when the music stopped.' In other words, after reaching the top senior officers moved horizontally from appointment to appointment until they reached retiring age, being succeeded on each lateral move by men only a shade less senior. Here again the half-pay system was a menace to younger officers since it enabled their seniors to hang on in limbo until suitable posts were vacated. Milne's two extensions of his term as CIGS to give him a record total tenure of seven years set a deplorable example in this respect, however defensible on other grounds. Though the establishment might think it in bad taste, Captain J. R. Kennedy certainly displayed courage in showing in detail in the *Army, Navy and Air Force Gazette* precisely how the game of musical chairs was working in the late 1920s and early 1930s as officers aged sixty and over were shuffled between home commands, the War Office, and India. He was not afraid to name names pointing out that Sir Cecil Romer,* Sir Percy Radcliffe,* Sir Francis Gathorne-Hardy,* and Sir Alexander Wardrop* had all been given an extension of service after more than twenty years in high rank. Surely, he asked rhetorically, they had had their share of the good things of the Army, and ought to make way for younger men. For lack of opportunity in the form of large-scale manœuvres they had not been tested in command for many years; few were sufficiently flexible in outlook to take kindly to new mechanized formations. When, in May 1933, General Sir Cyril Deverell was transferred from Western Command (where he had spent only two years) to Eastern Command, Kennedy pointed out that in effect this gave him an extension of four years. True, he had a brilliant record in the First World War but it was seventeen years since he had become a divisional commander, he was nearly 60 years old and could only hope for the further appointment of CIGS—which in fact he attained in 1936. His retention, therefore, Kennedy concluded, was more in his personal interest than that of the country. He aptly instanced Sir Edmund Ironside as a younger and more dynamic commander of proven ability who was being kept too long in the wings.[24]

It was of course asking a lot of men who had served their country well to retire before they were obliged to; it was the system that was at fault. Sir Alexander Godley frankly admitted his good fortune in receiving a Corps command in the Army of Occupation of the Rhine which, with home commands to follow and the Governorship of Gibraltar at the end, after a period on half-pay, prolonged his career by about ten years. Ironside, who was extremely critical of Godley, also felt it was retrograde of Milne to allow Sir Ronald Charles* to serve continuously for nearly nine years at the War Office as successively DMO and I and MGO. As he had previously been at Woolwich for three years, Charles had been away from active soldiering for eleven years. Certainly a few of the senior officers of First World War vintage who were given extensions which took them into their sixties remained physically fit and mentally active, but too many, as Ironside's correspondence and the Liddell Hart Papers show, did not. Colonel (later General Sir Harry) Knox* showed himself to be a 'complete die-hard' (in Martel's phrase) at the Staff College immediately after the First World War, being steadfastly opposed to mechanization and all new-fangled tactics. Ironside described him as 'A typical obstinate North of Ireland man . . . Very conservative and slow in the uptake.' Yet he survived to become Adjutant-General until eventually retired by Hore-Belisha in the purge of November 1937. In 1934 Brigadier Beauman was depressed to find the GOC.-in C. Northern Command (Wardrop) and his divisional commander (G. W. Howard)* both elderly and rooted in the tactics of the Boer War in which they had distinguished themselves. They both criticized Beauman in front of other officers for stressing tactics designed to minimize casualties, and at an officers' conference Howard remarked that heavy casualties must be accepted in modern war. He added for good measure the cliché, 'You can't make omelettes without breaking eggs.'[25]

Although some able men doubtless had their careers usefully prolonged by the operation of 'Buggins's turn', grounds for suspicion exist that Fuller was not the only brilliant but difficult soldier who was allowed to leave the service prematurely.[26] Furthermore the actual process of qualification and selection for higher commands was open to criticism. As Roderick Macleod suggested in a thoughtful critique of the orthodox career pattern, three types of officer were required in modern war: the regimental officer, essentially a physical type of man who need not be brainy but must be brave and determined, have the confidence of his men, and be skilled in minor tactics; the staff-officer type, good at detail and skilled in producing clear, concise orders; and lastly the commander, a mental type of man with an agile and flexible mind possessing—among other skills of leadership—the ability to get on with statesmen and allies. It was unusual to find all three types in the same individual yet in the British Army no one could be a staff officer unless first reported a good regimental officer, and very few achieved commands who had not proved able staff officers. 'Hence', Macleod concluded, 'we rarely get good commanders, and few men rise to high command until their mental powers are on the decline, or atrophied by much routine and detail.' The obvious solution was to separate the different types early in their careers and develop their abilities accordingly. Ironside, a gifted commander of men who was on his own admission ill-suited for the post of CIGS to which he was appointed on the outbreak of war in 1939 (succeeding Gort, another commander who was not at his best in staff work), voiced the more specific criticism that by 1930 it was not the surviving commanders of the First World War (C. J. Deverell, G. D. 'Ma' Jeffreys, T. G. Matheson,† and himself) who were being considered for the highest appointments but rather the senior staff officers from the war period such as W. Hastings Anderson, Harington, and Montgomery-Massingberd‡ who had never been tested as leaders in battle. As Ironside remarked bitterly on hearing that an officer he rated highly (H. K. Bethell)§ was not to be promoted: 'A long peace gets rid of those who were promoted for fighting, and we get men who have never done any . . . Fighters are often a nuisance in peace and the glib-tongued gentleman comes into his own.'[27]

There is ample evidence that the generation which should have risen to hold the top appointments in the late 1920s and early 1930s was kept waiting too long and as a result became frustrated and lost some of their zeal. The passing years also inexorably took their toll as hearts weakened and girths thickened. Ironside's correspondence with Liddell Hart contains numerous references to formerly brisk and energetic soldiers who were going off physically; and in 1933 Martel

† In 1918 they had commanded the 3rd, 19th, and Guards divisions respectively, while Ironside commanded 99th Infantry Brigade.

‡ Chief Staff Officers of 1st, 2nd, and 4th Armies respectively.

§ In 1918 Bethell was the youngest divisional commander on the Western Front (66th division) at 38. The Official Historian, Brigadier Sir James Edmonds, attributed his rapid promotion to his belonging to Haig's old regiment, 7th Hussars.

called Liddell Hart's attention to the number of sick men in top commands including Chetwode, Montgomery-Massingberd, and Radcliffe. As for morale, even some of the keenest officers began to despair that the Army would receive sufficient funds or produce the inspired leaders, which together could convert it into a viable instrument for modern war. It seems likely, for example, that Fuller had virtually abandoned hope of radical improvement before his premature retirement in 1934 for, as he wrote to Liddell Hart two years later, 'For some time now I have lost interest in our army, for I am of the opinion that there is no intention of modernising it.' Burnett-Stuart, whom many discerning critics believed to be the best choice for CIGS in succession to Milne, was depressed to find on returning from Egypt to take up Southern Command in 1934 that the situation was even worse than four years ago: 'the ranks are more depleted than ever, the equipment and armament practically unchanged . . . and many of the troops disgracefully housed'. In 1936, after a long correspondence with Liddell Hart about the state of the Army, he wrote: 'I don't like soldiering much really, and I profoundly distrust conclusions drawn from history. What I really like is poetry, and shooting partridges, and heraldry, and dry fly fishing and things like that. So I am now going away for a few days.' Even Wavell, the most enthusiastic and ingenious trainer of troops in the interwar period, began to find the daily routine of home soldiering so wearisome that in 1937 he confided to one of his staff that he felt he was getting stale and expected to be retired in the near future. Dill,* a sick man with a wife also in poor health, and Ironside, frustrated by being kept waiting too long, were among other talented soldiers who were probably past their best by 1939.[28]

Throughout the 1920s and 1930s Liddell Hart used his influential position as a military correspondent to press for the promotion of younger, more dynamic, and progressive officers. The various lists of promising officers located in his papers show that he (and his informants) were fine judges of 'form' since most of those he tipped for success (Wavell, Brooke,* Montgomery, Pile,* and others) vindicated his confidence in them in the Second World War while very few, who had an opportunity, failed.

Within a month of Hore-Belisha's advent to the War Office

in May 1937 Liddell Hart was urging on him, amongst other subjects for reform, that officers ought to reach command of a battalion at least by the time they were forty; become full colonel by forty-four; and major-general between forty-eight and fifty. In order to make this possible it would be necessary to reduce the retiring age of lieutenant-generals and major-generals from sixty-seven to sixty, and sixty-two to fifty-five respectively. When he computed the ages of those officers holding senior appointments he was surprised to find that on average they were considerably older than their predecessors in 1914. For example, the average age of the holders of the four first-class home commands had been fifty-five in August 1914 whereas in August 1937 it was sixty-two. The average age of the commanders of the five regular divisions was 54 years and 4 months in 1914 and 55 years 3 months in 1937. When critics argued that the more relevant statistic was the age on appointment to the various commands, Liddell Hart did his sums again and demonstrated that on this criterion comparative youth was even more on the side of the 1914 group: for example, age on appointment of the holders of the four chief home commands in 1914 was 53 years while in 1937 it was 58 years 11 months. The figures were almost identical for the four military members of the Army Council in 1914 and 1937 (i.e. 53 in 1914 and 58 in 1937). Liddell Hart emphasized that conditions of mobile mechanized warfare required younger rather than older commanders.[29]

The first positive sign of Hore-Belisha's intention to transform conditions for higher appointments was his purging of the Army Council in November 1937. Deverell and Knox, aged 63 and 64 respectively, were replaced by Gort who became CIGS at the very early age of 51 and Sir Clive Liddell* who became Adjutant-General at 54. Several other appointments followed the same pattern. Meanwhile Hore-Belisha had the whole question of promotion explored by a committee under the chairmanship of Lord Willingdon and following its report the Minister announced far-reaching proposals in July 1939:

> The normal age-limit for generals and lieutenant-generals was reduced to sixty; for major-generals, to fifty-seven; and for colonels, to fifty-five. The tenure of command and staff appointments was reduced to three years. The half-pay system was abolished. Promotion up to the

rank of major, instead of depending on the hazard of a vacancy, was to be by time: to captain after eight years' service, and to major after seventeen.

By these reforms Hore-Belisha and Liddell Hart earned the gratitude of subsequent generations of officers. In particular, though the reforms did not go as far as Liddell Hart wished, they greatly improved the career structure by ensuring, for example, that every competent officer could at least reach major's rank and do so younger than most officers hitherto. In August 1938 the *London Gazette* listed promotions for 2,000 officers—more than a quarter of the subalterns and captains in the combatant corps. It was also a major improvement to abolish the system of half-pay which Ironside bitterly described as 'a miserable dole designed to enable the War Office to keep up a cheap pool of senior officers.'[30]

Unfortunately, in some respects the short-term results of these reforms were disappointing. For example, thirteen general officers were promptly retired under the new age limits because posts could not be found for them, but even older officers holding appointments were not affected. The average age of potential corps commanders in August 1939 was three and a half years lower than in 1937 but still four and a half years higher than in 1914. The five divisional commanders and the mobile division commander in August 1939 were also a year and a half older than their predecessors in 1914. Worse still, there was no sign that the Army hierarchy had overcome its rooted dislike of specialists or its habit of forcing square pegs into round holes. Nowhere was the flagrant disregard for experience and special knowledge more obviously displayed than in the selection of the commander of the Mobile Division and the mis-employment of the handful of senior mechanized experts. Nor was any officer with experience in mechanization appointed to membership of the Army Council though this was a crucial area of development. Perhaps the unkindest cut of all for Liddell Hart was the way in which he was cold-shouldered by some of the officers, such as Gort and Adam* (the newly appointed DCIGS), whose advancement he had done so much to secure.[31]

When everything possible has been said in mitigation of the Army's inefficiency in the inter-war period, it is still difficult to deny the essential truth of Brigadier Beauman's severe judgement: 'Looking back, I cannot help feeling that the higher direction of the Army between the two wars was on the whole deplorable.' Allowing that they are somewhat partisan sources, the Liddell Hart Papers and the *Memoirs* derived from them display a recently victorious Army going through a depressing period which would have been more understandable had it suffered a humiliating defeat. Vendettas with petty origins—such as Burnett-Stuart's feud with Montgomery-Massingberd and Gort's quarrel with Broad*—festered over the years. Milne, despite what is argued by his defenders, certainly harboured grudges against those who had crossed him such as Fuller. Hobart's* involvement in divorce proceedings adversely affected his career many years after the event. Liddell Hart has exhaustively chronicled the establishment's stubborn resistance to long overdue reforms. Fuller, Liddell Hart, J. R. Kennedy, and other journalists occasionally levelled excessive and unfair charges but their targets, including Cavan, Milne, Knox, Montgomery-Massingberd, and Deverell, showed themselves hypersensitive to criticism.

Against all its critics the Army hierarchy raised the watchword of 'loyalty' which was repeated like an incantation by, for example, Montgomery-Massingberd to justify his animosity towards Fuller. Loyalty to superiors, to the regiment, or to the Army as a whole was a praiseworthy quality up to a point, but it is hard to resist the feeling that it was carried to excess in an attempt to suppress unwelcome criticism. As Michael Howard noted in reflection on the Liddell Hart *Memoirs*, those who urged the overriding need for 'loyalty' sought to make the Army a sanctuary to be jealously guarded against interference from the outside world of journalists, reformers, and politicians. Thus Deverell, in reprimanding Hobart, remarked that 'The Army must stand together and show a solid front to the politicians', while Gort displayed an appalling reluctance to 'upset people in the Clubs'.[32] These reactionary attitudes were, one senses, gathering to a very unpleasant head under the Hore-Belisha regime in the years immediately before the Second World War.

It would be wrong to convey the impression that the outlook of the officer corps between the wars was entirely characterized by a fond attachment to the past and despondency about the future. By general agreement a significant number of the ablest survivors of the First World War in the junior ranks—regimental officers and lower-grade staff officers—did learn the main lessons of that bloody, ill-managed conflict. There can be little dispute that when this generation, including Montgomery, Gort, Dill, Alexander,* Hobart, Wavell, Slim,* and Pile reached positions of authority in the Second World War they showed that they had profited from the mistakes of their predecessors. They saw, for example, the need to evolve more sophisticated tactics to gain ground with the minimum of casualties; to carry out imaginative and strenuous peacetime training; and, not least important, to develop closer understanding and trust with the soldiers they commanded. That these men did evolve higher standards of leadership based on a far more professional attitude may be seen from their biographies (Collins's study of Wavell is a good example) and from their contributions to the leading journals such as the *Army Quarterly* and *RUSI Journal*. Also, with very few exceptions, these zealous professionals displayed their particular interests in voluminous correspondence with Liddell Hart, that catalyst of so much of the progressive thinking of the period.

Operating as these men did like yeast within a somewhat stodgy officer corps, it is hardly surprising if some of them displayed a narrow and almost fanatical concern with professional matters. Thus Beauman recalled Dill as a man of high ideals, exceptional capacity for work, and a devotion to his profession that was almost startling in its intensity. It might be said that even in peacetime his profession occupied at least nine tenths of his thoughts and energies. Ironside was more critical. 'Dill', he wrote in 1931, 'is unimaginative, knows little of the world. Too hard driving. Thinks more of tactics than strategy.'[33] Similarly Gort's commander in the Shanghai expedition, Sir John Duncan,* wrote home to his wife: 'He is a bit too intense for peace-time soldiering. He is a very fine soldier and extremely able, but he is in a class by himself and works himself to death. It may be the result of his domestic troubles [Gort's wife was unfaithful], but if he was like this before I can quite imagine his wife leaving him.' Gort's popularity as Commandant of the Staff College declined when he suggested that officers might use their leisure hours more profitably by joining the Flying Club than by following the Drag.[34] Bernard Montgomery was perhaps the most ardent of all the officers of the 1920s who were determined to correct the faults of leadership they had recently witnessed in France. Until his unexpected marriage in 1927 he seemed absolutely devoted to his profession but this happy event brought a widening of interests and social contacts. Then, after his wife's tragic death a decade later, he again immersed himself with almost monastic dedication to studying war and perfecting the training of his brigade.[35] While it was a minor tragedy that the slightly older group including Burnett-Stuart, Chetwode, Karslake,* and Kirke* missed their chance for important commands in the Second World War, it was perhaps just as well that Montgomery and his peers (including Brooke and Alexander) were too junior to be commanders-in-chief at the outset of the war. Gort, Wavell, and others inevitably paid the price of dismissal or relegation to the wings for Britain's traditional unpreparedness for war.[36]

We now come to what is arguably the single most important facet in any general consideration of the British Army's character and ethos between the wars; namely the regimental system. Although the word 'Army' has been used throughout this study as a convenient shorthand expression, it belies the complexity of British military organization. Sir John Fortescue's apophthegm still retained much of its validity, or rather regained it after the First World War: 'The army was, and within my own lifetime continued to be, not an army at all, but only a collection of regiments.' Many officers have proudly described the significance of the regimental system for non-initiates, few more graphically than Major L. I. Cowper in his RUSI Gold Medal prize essay for 1924. In the Regular Army before 1914, he pointed out, the regimental tradition counted for everything and it had been invaluable during the war. In practice, however, the regiment of two or more battalions was too diffuse as a focus of loyalty; the basis of *esprit de corps* often narrowed down to the battalion.

But small-minded and parochial as some of the manifestations of *esprit de corps* might appear, it was realised that the very foundation of regimental life and efficiency depended on it and every possible means was taken to increase and foster it. Every recruit was instructed in regimental history. He lived in an atmosphere of tradition and moulded his life and conduct in accordance with what was, or was not, done in the Regiment. His barrack room was named after some Regimental victory . . . the glorious past of the Regiment was constantly before him and officers and men alike could not escape from the responsibility of their inheritance. Instead of, and more difficult to break than the tie of blood, was the tie of the Regiment . . . A magazine told news of past and present members of the Regiment, their wives and children. Old Comrades Associations were an annual opportunity for meeting; and should a little capital be needed for a start in life, the Aid Fund would provide it; if killed in action a man's name was recorded in the Regimental Chapel—alive or dead he belonged to his Regiment.

In the First World War, Major Cowper added, loyalty and sense of identification had been stretched as far as the division and some had hoped to see it extended to the Army as a whole. It was his belief, however, that no unit larger than the regiment could command unselfish service and suppression of personal ambition: regimental *esprit de corps* had fully revived after the vast expansion of the First World War and the regiment must provide the basis for expansion in any future great war.[37]

Modern students of the role of the regimental system tend to endorse Major Cowper's enthusiastic claims. Thus John Keegan concludes a brilliant essay with the conviction that the regiment is 'the most significant of Britain's military institutions, the principal vehicle of the nation's military culture, if one may so describe it, and a factor by no means without significance in the country's political and social history'. An American sociologist, Maurice Garnier, who studied the relationship between the regimental system and Sandhurst for his doctorate in the late 1960s, inclined to the view that regimental separatism had probably been inevitable and perhaps even desirable in a very class-conscious society: 'It may in fact be that, historically at least, an organisation which would have forced highly different individuals to interact closely (and be dependent on each other in battle) might not have been able to fulfil its goals.' In other words the regimental system may have been the most efficient way of getting the British Army to do its job. He also noted that the lack of obligatory Army standards left the regiments considerable scope for different requirements regarding their officers and methods of training. This sort of system, he warned, is usually resistant to change and might not adequately meet the needs of 'a post-industrial democratic state'.

John Keegan paints an attractive, if slightly over-romantic, picture of the modern regimental system emerging from the Cardwell reforms of the 1870s like a large, comfortable Victorian family. Like these families he sees the regiments 'extending their circle of kinship, friendship and acquaintance into the civil society which surrounded them, not only at the social level of the officers but down to the grassroots'. In addition to strong ties of sentiment and comfort, however, he believes that units of regimental size (600 to 1,000 men) have a particular tactical value which is 'enhanced by stability and its by products: reputation, corporate self-image, tradition—especially traditions of loyalty and courage'. Given these virtues it is not surprising that, beginning in the 1870s, he perceives something resembling 'a protracted infatuation between the British officer and his regiment'.[38] Less romantically, Michael Howard has described the regimental system as a perfect vehicle for an *emigration intérieure*—a way of life which comfortably insulates Army officers from a society with which they have little sympathy. He sees the institution's value mainly in political terms:

> The regimental system may isolate the military but it also tames them, fixing their eyes on minutiae, limiting their ambitions, teaching them a gentle, parochial loyalty difficult to pervert to more dangerous ends. It may be an obstacle to full professional efficiency; but it is perhaps a barrier to much else as well.[39]

In the inter-war period the regimental system's restricting and stultifying effects were more apparent to would-be military reformers than its constitutional value as a barrier to military despotism. Captain J. R. Kennedy was a most virulent critic who saw it as the chief obstacle to a single Army list for promotion. He pointed out that the Royal Navy and Royal Air Force both attained a high level of efficiency without a regimental system; indeed, even in the Army it was only the infantry and cavalry which placed overriding emphasis on regimental autonomy. Against the traditional arguments, Kennedy argued that the regimental system maintained differences in uniform which created unnecessary expenses and administrative problems, prevented a free exchange of officers between regiments and arms, and perpetuated 'an attitude of mind not consistent with modern tolerance, modesty and intelligence'. In the absence of a wider Army tradition it was a factor for disintegration rather than integration. Though he did not use the word, Kennedy also perceived that the regiments resembled more or less expensive 'clubs' catering for varying degrees of wealth and social status. Then, as later, regiments were defined as 'good', 'not very good', 'smart', or otherwise on criteria which had little, if anything, to do with their fighting efficiency. 'Good' regiments, as he observed, were often those whose officers could indulge in expensive outside habits or absent themselves for long periods of unofficial leave. It was wrong, he argued, for part of the Army to be turned into a sort of social playground. Recent students of the regimental system like Garnier, Keegan, and Simon Raven agree that subtle distinctions have survived the many disbandments and amalgamations since 1945. They also broadly agree on the 'pecking order'.[40]

The promotion question, which obsessed J. R. Kennedy, was only one manifestation of the general problem that the regimental system tended to perpetuate established procedures and exacerbate the difficulties of radical changes in organization. Colonel George Lindsay was a severe critic on those grounds. In particular he felt it was a great mistake in 1926 even to contemplate re-arming existing units of infantry or cavalry with tanks, armoured cars, or even machine guns. It was simply asking for trouble to continue and extend the regimental system ('innumerable small packets each with different traditions and ideas') in the new arms. In 1932 Lindsay,* now a brigadier, suggested to his divisional commander that the narrow and semi-autonomous world of the infantry regiments severely impeded the development of professional thought:

> The day is past when it suffices for an officer to be a good regimental officer, a good sportsman and a practical soldier; the value of these qualities good as they are, will be negligible in the next war unless combined with a degree of knowledge hitherto considered unnecessary. Such knowledge is not to be picked up casually by virtue of ordinary military routine, hunting or playing games; it requires properly organised instruction by competent teachers, such as cannot in my opinion be given by infantry battalions as now organized in 'penny packets'.[41]

Short of a really drastic assault on the regimental system, which not even Hore-Belisha was bold enough to attempt, the main hope of expanding officers' horizons and loyalties lay with the Staff Colleges at Camberley and Quetta. But together these could barely accommodate one officer in ten of the appropriate rank. This at least meant a healthy competition for places but it imposed a low ceiling of regimental soldiering over the unlucky majority who tended to resent overtly ambitious colleagues who strove to get their names on the regiment's Staff College list. There were also a few commanding officers left of the old school who regarded it as tantamount to desertion for regimental officers to seek to advance their own careers by leaving the regiment.[42]

The regimental system undoubtedly possessed many virtues. It permitted a distinctive officer class to form and perpetuate a subtly differentiated variety of tribal groups, and extended families or clubs which were small enough for the officers to form a close-knit society and to look after their men in a paternalistic way. Next, the system reinforced strong constitutional safeguards against officers taking an excessive interest in politics. Finally, according to numerous accounts, the system provided an admirable instrument for the building up of high military morale in peacetime and sustaining it under the most adverse conditions in war. Indeed John Keegan remains an unrepentant champion of the regiment as the 'perfect, self-enclosed forum wherein "heroic" leadership can operate'. In his view 'the only currency of unchallengeable value which circulates in an army is a reputation for courage; that reputation can scarcely be earned outside a fighting regiment'.[43] Nevertheless, despite all these assets the regimental system lay at the root of the malaise of the inter-war Army in the effects it had of narrowing horizons and obstructing reform. Correlli Barnett is surely right in holding this rigid system responsible for some of the British Army's shortcomings in the early stages of the war in the North African desert in 1940 and 1941.[44]

It remains to attempt to capture something of the pervading atmosphere and ethos of the inter-war Army. The stereotype Army officer of these years was the cartoonist Low's Colonel Blimp. The Army was easy game for the caricaturists and critics. A modern humorist, E. S. Turner, neatly encapsulated popular jibes against soldiers who could do no right: 'they acted as scabs in strikes, they desecrated beauty spots, they sat on the Rhine swilling beer and costing the taxpayer millions. Wherever they were, whatever they did, they were hidebound. That was the adjective which was now inseparably coupled with the word military.' The officers of course had their answers to these sweeping criticisms. As Burnett-Stuart wrote angrily to Liddell Hart: 'All the Army's work is done in an atmosphere that is not only unsympathetic, but definitely antagonistic. . . . all press criticism of the Army Command is either contemptuous or hostile, and incredibly ill-informed'. Ironside wrote the following riposte in 1933:

I am afraid that all this pacifism has brought the military forces into disrepute. Nobody wants to hear that they are efficient for fear that we may be accused of being militaristic. . . . I am afraid that there has come an end to most progress in the Army for years to come. The precious years when we might have done something have gone. My fear is that our experience will be allowed to die before it is used again. That is always the way in peace. We go back more and more to the martinet parade-officer, who delights in getting as many men as possible into as small a space as possible and then in drilling them by word of mouth . . .[45]

Another view was that, quite apart from the pacifism and demands for disarmament, peacetime soldiering was by its very nature ineffably dull and tedious. Soldiers were not to blame for this fact, though some of their remedies were unimaginative; it was simply their lot to endure until the next war came along to liven things up. Several retired officers who served in that period have urged the author to underline the sheer boredom of much peacetime soldiering. Exercises helped pass the time but they only took place during the summer season at home and the winter in India. Thus Major-General James Lunt sees what to the civilian may seem an excessive preoccupation with games, hunting, and other open-air activities rather as essential ways of enlivening a dull routine. As an example of the simplicity of soldiering in that era he instanced an exercise in picket posting on the Indian frontier on which the commanding officer's only comment was that bayonet scabbards were frayed and should be seen to. Fuller derisively described the mobilization of the 1st Division at Aldershot in 1931 as reminiscent of 1899 with 5,500 horses, 740 horse-drawn vehicles, and the old horse ambulances of the Boer War period. Even imaginative trainers like Fuller and Wavell found it difficult to take such exercises seriously since the cumbersome horse-drawn force was all too obviously a sitting target for aircraft. In the same year Burnett-Stuart gently took Liddell Hart to task for not realizing how inevitable it was that 'a soldier's life must produce some hardening of the mental arteries. Nor how the military superstructure tends to suffocate the most buoyant spirit.'[46]

Fortunately for the majority of Army officers, there was compensation for professional frustrations in the remarkable amount of leisure they enjoyed. To a very great extent the Army was run by the NCOs: the instruction, 'Carry on Sergeant-Major', epitomizes the real authority enjoyed by these men. Armies have become adept over the years in filling in the time when they are not actually fighting or training to fight and memoirs give a good idea of what the officers did in the inter-war period. Judging by the space they allotted to them—under titles such as *Big Game, Boers and Boches*[47] (the order is interesting)—the outstanding peacetime memories of many officers were wrapped up with sports, games, and killing all manner of birds and beasts.

Perhaps what most strikes the modern reader—apart from the sheer amount of free time available—was the extent to which this was a horse-dominated way of life. General Sir Alexander Godley, who incidentally had a fox-hound embossed in gold on the covers of his memoirs, was by no means expressing sentiments exclusive to the cavalry when he remarked, while chairing a lecture at the RUSI in 1927, that 'the best of all combinations that this country has always so successfully produced is the man and the horse working together in a partnership and harmony to which there is no equal'.[48] At the Staff College riding in the Drag Hunt was compulsory for all officers. Brigadier Stephenson recalls this as something of a cult with tremendous prestige attached to the appointment of Master of the Drag. When he attended the course in 1931–2 Sir Ian Jacob thought there was an absurd emphasis on the Drag; Henry Maitland 'Jumbo' Wilson* (then GSO1) only had time for leading members of the Drag. Daily riding at Camberley was thought to be essential to shake up the livers of chairborne officers. Hobart thought it deplorable that as late as 1938, after their regiments had been mechanized, cavalry officers were all allowed two free chargers each by the War Office.[49]

Lieutenant-Colonel M. C. A. Henniker's *Memoirs of a Junior Officer* are particularly valuable in this context since he concentrates entirely on the inter-war years. He recalls, for example, that in 1924 riding was one of the most important subjects taught at 'The Shop' (Woolwich). Gunners and sappers were still mounted officers and good horsemanship remained almost synonymous with military proficiency. He would have endorsed General Godley's sentiments because he believed that horses forged an invaluable link between officers and men, who rode together in work and play. At Aldershot, in Henniker's charming phrase, 'we soldiered with the jingle of harness in our ears', and a ride before breakfast was *de rigueur*. At the end of 1928, when he sailed for India, it still seemed to him that the League of Nations would prevent another war, so that '*the arme blanche*, chivalry, polo and hunting, would go on for ever'.[50]

Godley's *Memoirs of an Irish Soldier* are ostensibly concerned with his military career but accounts of soldiering, as in other generals' recollections, frequently veer off on to other matters: 'the racing was great fun'; 'the golf links were only about a mile from my back-gate' and on the intervening ground he and a colleague once shot twelve brace of partridges in an hour; 'our annual horse show was a great event . . .' and so on. When he was GOC.-in-C. Southern Command he hunted with fifteen different packs and filled in his spare time with 'wonderfully good days' shooting pheasants, partridges, duck, snipe, and grouse.[51]

Colonel (later Lieutenant-General Sir Philip) Neame, VC, who was outstanding among the Army's many fine all-round sportsmen, devoted nearly a half of his memoirs, *Playing with Strife* (admittedly written when a prisoner of war in Italy and therefore perhaps especially nostalgic), to big-game shooting in India and many other parts of the world. At the Staff College just after the First World War, besides the Drag Hunt he played a good deal of first-class hockey and also rode regularly in point-to-point races. One winter at Aldershot, the happy owner of four horses, he determined to do twelve-days hunting in a fortnight but was foiled by fog not military duties. At this same period he spent long summer leaves shooting partridges, pheasant, deer, and grouse in Scotland. He also competed at Bisley in rifle and revolver shooting and in 1924 was a member of the British Empire rifle team in the Olympic Games at Paris. Every winter he indulged in one of his favourite sports of skiing which he combined with mountaineering with some of the outstanding climbers of the day. Unlike Burnett-Stuart, who was devoted to the sport, Neame does not appear to have been a fisherman, nor, unlike Martel who was Army welter-weight champion on several occasions, did he box.[52]

If possible the part played by games and hunting in Army service in India was even greater than at home. When Henniker joined the Bengal Sappers and Miners at Roorkee in 1929 he found that not a single officer in the regiment owned a motor car. Three interests alone possessed their minds: soldiering, polo, and shooting. Henniker proudly recalls that for the next six years he too had no other interests. Polo was virtually obligatory—partly because the Commandant evaluated officers by their willingness to play, but also because on a small station everyone had to play to make up the numbers. According to Freddie Morgan, his Colonel at Jhansi studied inscriptions in the local cemetery to discover which was the least lethal pastime. Of sports that could be indulged in by officers alone he found that pig-sticking had caused fewer fatalities than polo or big-game hunting. Accordingly Morgan did a great deal of pig-sticking, though he was also a keen cricketer. In 1929 he was posted to 70th Field Battery at Lucknow where the battery commander, Major J. I. D'Arcy, was one of the old type of sporting, horse-coping Irishman. D'Arcy's proudest possession was his Game Book, in beautifully tooled leather binding with gold embellishment, in which he had recorded every round fired since his earliest youth and 'the stupendous tonnage of blood shed'.[53]

These sporting accounts, which could easily be extended, bear out the impression that the pre-1939 Army was very much more a distinctive way of life than it has since become. For one thing such prodigious slaughter of birds and animals for amusement is less fashionable today and few Army officers enjoy quite so much leisure. It is at least a relief to record that few memoirists attempted to justify their pleasures on professional grounds, i.e. that riding would give them an 'eye for country' in the military sense or that shooting animals would improve their aim in war—in modern war officers do not normally fire at the enemy anyway. Martel makes a case that games and particularly boxing enabled those who played them to keep calmer and steadier when they first came under fire; but against this must be set the loss of several promising officers, notably Major-General C. P. 'Guffin' Heywood,* as a result of riding accidents.[54]

Several Army officers showed awareness that their Service was not popular with the public. This was perhaps hardly unexpected in the aftermath of a great and costly war whose hoped-for benefits seemed increasingly illusory as the 1920s wore on. But there was in the 1920s a marked shortage of young men from the landed gentry to fill the 650 new commissions available each year. Moreover, whereas before 1914 an average of 80 university graduates were commissioned each year, by 1924 the figure had fallen to 12. Colonel Wingfield, in his RUSI lecture, thought the most important reason for the shortage of candidates was the public impression that 'the profession of officer in the army does not call for high qualities, and does not recognise ability to anything like the same extent as other professions'. 'No one', he added, 'would attempt to make officers into bookworms, and any such attempt would certainly not succeed, but you cannot do away with the idea that the fool of the family is good enough for the army.' He felt that there must be greater rewards, such as accelerated promotion, for industrious and able officers.[55] Field-Marshal Sir Philip Chetwode, though a conservative on mechanization, showed acute awareness of what would now be called the Army's poor 'public image'. Like Colonel Wingfield he believed the public to be under the misapprehension that even half-wits would make suitable officers, and he attacked Liddell Hart for unintentionally strengthening this attitude by his frequent criticism of the high command. Yet Chetwode's farewell address as Commander-in-Chief in India at the Quetta Staff College in October 1934 was surely the most devastating indictment of the military profession by a high ranking officer in the inter-war period. He was not happy about the present officer either in the British or Indian armies: 'I do not think that, as a class, they have improved in general education, or military instinct and leadership, since the War . . . if anything, the contrary is the case.' He believed there were just as many acute brains in the Army as in any other profession but they were not sufficiently used. Moreover, constant 'crabbing' by civilians had caused the officers to retire rather smugly into their purely military shells and to ignore the trend of thought and events in the civilian world around them. This encouraged 'a supercilious narrowness of outlook in every direction'. The military environment with its paper exercises was admittedly depressing but officers must acquire the habit of work and study.

> I am horrified, as I travel up and down India, at the number of officers I find, senior and junior alike, who have allowed themselves to sink into a state of complete brain slackness. Their narrow interests are bounded by the morning parade, the game they happen to play, and purely local and unimportant matters.
>
> I have found men all over India who evidently scarcely read the papers, and are quite unaware of the larger aspects of what is going on in India around them, and still less of the stupendous events outside this country that are now in process of forming an entirely new world.

He was glad that promotion examination papers were not published since they would reveal that many officers could not even express themselves clearly in the simplest language, let alone with any style or distinction. War, he continued, echoing Clausewitz, is largely a province of the imagination but few officers allowed much play to this faculty: 'It would almost seem that it is a crime to do so, or to be one inch outside "sealed pattern" and regulations. The longer I remain in the Service, the more wooden and the more regulation-bound do I find the average British officer to be'. He concluded with a plea to his audience of Staff College students to be original in thought and prepared to take risks:

> I am rather afraid that quite a number of the average Staff College students aim at being a correct, methodical, 'sealed pattern' staff officer, ground out to pattern by the Quetta and Camberley mill. Am I altogether wrong in thinking that, to many Englishmen, to be independent in thought, to have imagination, to go outside the obvious, to be different to others, is to be almost un-English, or even that more frightful crime 'not sound'?[56]

Several of Liddell Hart's military correspondents made criticisms which testified to the essential truth of Chetwode's indictment. Thus General Sir Cecil Romer remarked: 'Of course the ordinary British regular officer does not read much, in fact he reads nothing unless he is more or less forced to, and then he naturally goes to the garrison or regimental library . . .' Romer's experience was that Territorial Army officers bought military literature more freely than their regular colleagues. Ironside likewise thought that most senior officers became wound up in the routine of their daily work and did not make time to read; he regarded Chetwode as an outstanding exception of an independent-minded senior officer who read voraciously. Another notable exception to the charge was Wavell, who not only read very widely but was constantly trying out new methods to stimulate the officers under his command to independent thought. Wavell was a great believer in the practical value of studying history provided it was done in an imaginative way, for example by taking a particular situation and trying to get inside the mind of the man who made a decision. He was all too well aware of the military tendency to treat so-called principles of war as holy writ which acquired magic powers by constant incantation. He satirized such 'nursery-book principles' in amusing doggerel:

Be good and you will be happy.
Be mobile and you will be victorious.
Interior lines at night are the general's delight.
Exterior lines in the morning are the general's warning.

As he expressed it himself, he was a determined advocate of getting away from the 'barrack square' training and the 'barrack square' mind as far as possible.[57]

Unfortunately senior officers like Chetwode, Romer, Wavell, and Ironside were the exception rather than the rule. In too many units 'shop talk' or indeed any kind of intellectual effort beyond the rigid framework of the regulations and daily orders was positively discouraged. Only a few mavericks like Fuller and Hobart, or genuine eccentrics like Wingate, got away with it, but such dedicated professionals were seldom popular with their fellow officers. Brigadier Stephenson recalled a colleague in India, Major Majendie, who was greatly alarmed to discover that his son wrote poetry. Sir Ian Hamilton had similarly suffered for his literary associations before the First World War, such unsoldierly interests being considered in a most damning expression—'unsound'. Judging by their correspondence some officers virtually confined their study to the Army List.

In short the life of the average army officer between the wars was within a fairly narrow and unintellectual world; as the memoirs of the period reveal the emphasis was predominantly on the 'hearty' as opposed to the aesthetic or intellectual side. One disturbing consequence of Ironside's period on half-pay in 1932 was that he had time to meditate on these matters: 'The whole show', he informed Liddell Hart, 'has got frightfully parochial. As one looks at things from outside one can see it. I hope I was never so parochial when I was in command. The longer one stays outside the service the less does one want to come back to its pettiness.'[58] A significant manifestation of this parochialism is that, apart from official visits, British officers displayed little interest in military developments in European countries or signs of having read articles in foreign military journals. Where was the British equivalent of Guderian eagerly translating and circulating *avant-garde* articles from Britain, France, and other countries? Hence there should be no cause for surprise that British Army officers failed to appreciate the extent of the French Army's decline or the Wehrmacht's rapid development in the later 1930s.[59]

Though hard to document, one gets the distinct impression that the Army was also a narrow world in the social sense that officers erected barriers against outsiders. Major-General Charles Broad remarked in 1939 that the Army had never been so full of cliqués.[60] Montgomery-Massingberd was a landed Lincolnshire gentleman who moved in 'county' circles. In Sir Henry Karslake's opinion, Burnett-Stuart was 'an awful snob' in that, at the Staff College, he refused to 'know' anyone but members of the Rifle Brigade and Guardsmen. Snobs looked down on Deverell and even spread the rumour that he was an ex-ranker. Several British officers shared the fashionable anti-Semitism of the period as the Pownall diaries and Liddell Hart's correspondence with Colonel G. S. Hutchison reveal. This prejudice found few targets within the officer ranks but Hore-Belisha provoked comments on his racial origins and traits which can only be described as vile.

The Army's sexual taboos were far from clear cut and uncertain in their effects on transgressors. Extra-marital affairs or other misdemeanours were sometimes winked at and condoned provided they took place outside the regiment. Divorce was not necessarily a lasting stigma yet Hobart's handicapped him for years and influenced his removal from his command in Egypt in 1939. Sir Ronald Adam gained a vacancy at the Staff College because the officer next above him on the entry list lost his place as a consequence of applying for damages in divorce proceedings. It was clearly a world like that of the public schools in which ignorance of what was or was not 'done' could have serious consequences for an officer's career. Finally, as noted in the chapters on mechanization, tanks corps officers were sometimes looked down on by the horsy set as mechanics or tradesmen because they wore oily overalls and worked with machines. One gets the impression that Martel was highly exceptional even among technical officers who reached general's rank in actually relishing the 'nuts and bolts' aspect of his profession.[61]

Although the Army's character between the wars was greatly influenced by external circumstances such as political indifference and lack of money for new weapons and equipment, nevertheless it seems reasonable to maintain that the Service remained primarily responsible for its own style of life and morals. Like most armies at most times it was conservative but with a strong element of the reactionary apparent in its deep-rooted reluctance to adapt to both technological developments and changes in the society in which it lived. The Army's profound attachment to horses, for example, though admirable in terms of sentiment, was professionally costly in a world increasingly dominated by the petrol engine. In the officers' attitude to their men and in terms of leisure activities, pay, and career prospects the pre-1939 Army was much more of a distinctive world than it has since become. Perhaps this was most evident of all in the continuing near-autonomy of the regimental system with its attendant strengths and weaknesses. Thus, in answer to Michael Howard's question with which this chapter began, no single thing 'went wrong' to account for the Army's manifest deficiencies between the wars: there was simply no sufficient shock—not even the Hore-Belisha reforms—to shake the Army out of its traditional way of life and habits of thought. When, or indeed if, this shock eventually occurred must be studied by historians and sociologists of the Army in the years after 1945.

CHAPTER 3

The Role of the Army in the Locarno era, 1924–1932

Although, in approving the Ten Year Rule, the Government had tacitly accepted in 1919 that there was no risk of Britain becoming involved in a major war in the immediate future, it was still necessary to establish guidelines and priorities for home and overseas defence. Indeed, rapidly decreasing defence estimates and the emergence of a third Service in the form of an independent Royal Air Force rendered action imperative.

After the First World War Britain appeared to be directly vulnerable to enemy attack for the first time in her history—from air bombardment. The daylight raids on London in 1917 made a powerful impression on a Committee of the Imperial War Cabinet composed of Smuts and Lloyd George. Their conclusion, that in future air operations might become the principal form of warfare, was underlined at every opportunity by the Air Staff under its first chief, Sir Hugh Trenchard.* In 1921 Trenchard's arguments convinced a Cabinet Sub-Committee on Defence, chaired by Lord Balfour, that defence against air attack was 'the most formidable problem now before us'. In August 1922 the Cabinet approved of Air ministry proposals for the creation of 23 squadrons (14 bomber and 9 fighter) with the main objective of retaliation against an aggressor, which at that time could only mean France. A further step was taken the following spring in the setting up of the Salisbury Committee with the general brief of examining the relationship between the three Services and arrangements for co-ordinating national defence policy, and the particular task of laying down 'the standard to be aimed at for defining the strength of the Air Force for purposes of Home and Imperial Defence'. The Committee recommended creating a home defence Air Force of 52 squadrons designed to deter any aggressor by the threat of inflicting upon him unacceptable and inescapable destruction. The Army reluctantly accepted that the control of this force should remain with the Royal Air Force—whose continued independent existence now seemed more assured—but the naval representatives 'flatly denied that air power would make the slightest difference to war at sea'. This inter-service dispute reflected the Salisbury Committee's failure to fulfil its wider objective. The Committee rejected the proposal to create a Ministry of Defence with all three Services subordinated to a single minister, and left the unenviable task of reconciling inter-service disputes to a new Sub-Committee of the Committee of Imperial Defence composed of the three Chiefs of Staff.[1]

As regards the relationships between the older Services, the Army did not dispute the pre-eminence of the Royal Navy in the vital task of maintaining sea supremacy as the basis of the system of Imperial Defence, but found its resources taxed to the utmost to fulfil its routine peacetime commitments. These were: to provide adequate garrisons and defences for the strategic ports at home and abroad; to supply the British component of the garrison of India; to secure adequate local security for British colonies, protectorates, and mandates; to maintain the internal security of Great Britain and Northern Ireland; to provide an occupation force for the demilitarized zone of the Rhineland; and to organize an Expeditionary Force from the remaining troops at home in order to meet any overseas emergency.[2]

The drawbacks of the Cardwell system, which required at least an equal number of infantry battalions at home to supply drafts to those serving overseas, became even more obvious than they had been before 1914, not only because of the extension of British responsibilities, but also because of intensification of nationalist activities throughout the Empire, particularly in the Middle East and India. As a moderately progressive military reformer, Major B. C. Dening, argued in 1928: 'To break away from the Cardwell system will cause an upheaval in the Army as has not been known for half a century, for it will affect every branch of the organisation, administration and training for war of the forces.'[3]

In what one scholar has described as 'the poisonous atmosphere in Service relations' in which the early meetings of the Chiefs of Staff Sub-Committee took place,[4] it would have been unreasonable to expect the Service leaders to discuss joint planning for war against specific enemies unless clearly directed to do so by their political superiors. Indeed, the CIGS vetoed a proposal by Lord Salisbury, approved by Lord Curzon the Foreign Secretary, that the COS should examine possible wars against France and Japan without bringing this potentially controversial matter before the CID.[5] It needs to be explained that Sir Henry Wilson's successor as CIGS was an amiable but unimaginative Guards officer whose unpublished memoirs are appropriately entitled 'Recollections Hazy But Happy'. Cavan had achieved prominence in the last months of the First World War as commander of the Allied Armies in Italy but he had spent most of his service career as a regimental officer. He had not attended the Staff College, had no previous experience of the War Office, and modestly admitted that Sir Henry Rawlinson* ought to have succeeded Wilson. Cavan described himself as 'a soldier and fox-hunter'. As the Army's first representative on the COS he was a tyro in comparison with his two formidable colleagues Beatty and Trenchard.[6]

For its part the Foreign Office understandably proved most reluctant to supply the COS with a graduated list of potential enemies. Hankey noted that this caution sprang from 'a general timidity about nearly all politicians in handling war plans at first hand. When I used to go to them and say I thought we ought to be considering our plans for war with X they would say "Supposing it leaked out" etc.'[7] When, in 1924, Hankey asked the Foreign Secretary, Austen Chamberlain, on what political assumptions the departments should base their preparations for war the latter replied that he was against formal discussion of the subject at the CID and the less he himself knew officially the better. He agreed with Hankey that a war with Japan or, alternatively, with France was possible. Neither was at all probable but they offered the best criterion by which to judge our defence arrangements.[8]

War with France would be essentially a problem for the

Royal Air Force, and with Japan for the Royal Navy. The General Staff agreed that there was no question either of Britain landing troops on the Continent to fight the French or of invading the Japanese islands. In this context Cavan's otherwise astonishing memorandum for the COS dated 17 January 1924 becomes more intelligible. The CIGS concluded his survey with the assertion that: 'Under existing world conditions we require no plans of campaign (except for small wars incidental to our Imperial position) . . . We must concentrate on Imperial defence. There is no need to try and justify our existence by wasting our time and energies in the compilation of elaborate plans for wars against hypothetical enemies.' We need to know, he continued, who will be our allies and who will be allied with our enemies. 'Our experience in the late war has shown us that our great difficulty will be not so much to decide what operations to undertake as to how to prevent the numerous operations certain to be proposed by amateur strategists in high places from being undertaken.'[9]

The British Army's increasing preoccupation with Imperial defence in the 1920s does not mean that the question of the Continental commitment was ever entirely forgotten, much as many servicemen and more civilians might have wished it to be. For one thing, the tiresome French would not let us forget the recent past. 'Next time, remember', said Marshal Foch to Lord Cavan, 'the Germans will make no mistake. They will break through into northern France and will seize the Channel ports as a base of operations against England.' He also shrewdly remarked to Cavan that Britain could not keep her Empire firm and secure unless she kept the Rhine door locked. Frenchmen felt obliged to harp on this theme because France had failed to obtain either permanent occupation of the Rhineland or treaties of guarantee by both Britain and the United States to come to her assistance immediately in the event of unprovoked aggression by Germany. But in any case the basic principles of British strategy—to maintain a balance of power in Western Europe and to prevent a hostile power from occupying the Low Countries and the Channel ports—still seemed to be valid after the First World War. Indeed it could be argued that the advent of air power made them even more crucial than in the past. In practice, however, the emotional revulsion provoked by the war of attrition and its political concomitants of pacifist idealism, internationalism, and faith in disarmament tended to obscure basic strategic issues. As the official historian of Grand Strategy observes:

> Unfortunately, however, the very nature of most of the fighting in that war tended afterwards to distort debate about the correctness or otherwise of the strategic principles on which the campaigns of the war had been planned. The slaughter and filth of the trenches left a legacy of passionate hope, indeed belief, that such a war would never be fought again; while the more reasoned arguments of those who disagreed with the Western strategy which the Allies had followed seemed only to justify that hope.[10]

The views of the General Staff and of the Chiefs of Staff Committee on the Continental commitment were clearly expressed in a series of memoranda in 1924 and early 1925 concerning a proposed Geneva Protocol whose chief purposes were to outlaw 'aggressive war' and to provide for compulsory arbitration to determine whether 'aggression' had occurred. The Chiefs of Staff strongly opposed the Protocol on several grounds, including the vagueness of its terminology and the extension of unspecified commitments, but at the same time they accepted the General Staff's arguments in favour of a defence pact with France (and Belgium), provided certain limitations were observed. The General Staff had pointed out that Britain could not bind herself regarding the number of forces to be maintained in peacetime nor allow the French to dictate to us. Anticipating later arguments about 'limited liability', they recognized that the pact could not be limited to one or more of the Services—'Should the future unfortunately bring occasion for putting the pact into force, Great Britain must enter with all her forces available at the moment and must be prepared to expand these forces as necessary to meet the needs of the case.' They insisted that the commitment must be strictly limited to the defence of France and Belgium and must exclude Germany's eastern frontiers. It must also be tripartite since Belgian security was as important to Britain as French.[11]

The view that Britain's security was inextricably bound up with France's was even more forcefully and eloquently stated in a General Staff note dated 26 February 1925.[12] Anticipating Baldwin's famous phrase by some years, the note proclaimed:

> For us it is only *incidentally* a question of French security; essentially it is a matter of British security . . .
>
> The true strategic frontier of Great Britain is the Rhine; her security depends entirely upon the present frontiers of France, Belgium and Holland being maintained and remaining in friendly hands . . . the General Staff would once more emphasize the fact that 'French Security' spells 'British Security', that French morale is at present very low, even in the higher military circles, and that to anyone who can look ahead, with French eyes, this depression is easy to understand . . . The more frightened the French are the more tiresome they become, and they will block every move unless we can allay their fear. It is curious that Englishmen seem to be least able to realise the greatness of their own country, or to understand how much to a Frenchman . . . the support of the British Empire means.

A pact would not really extend Britain's obligations, the note concluded, because she already had a garrison in the Rhineland. What it would achieve would be to show Germany and France that she would meet her obligations, and to reassure France that she would continue to stand by her after the safeguards had gone. Hankey admitted that he was converted to the need for a pact with France and Belgium though he had hitherto shared the British public's instinctive dislike of any continental commitment. He saw the necessity to stress to the public that the aim was to exclude Germany from the southern shores of the Channel. 'People have not forgotten the air raids.'[13]

The General Staff also made plain in 1925 that its mistrust and apprehension of Germany remained undiminished. Though temporarily cowed by defeat, Germany would reassert herself:

> The General Staff have no fear of France; their only fear is *for* France. There are other dangers to civilisation beyond Germany, and the sooner Germany can be brought to range herself on the side of western civilization the better the chance that civilization will have of maintaining herself against those dangers

'But Germany's conversion', they added 'must be begun under discipline and in the knowledge that the first class Powers can and will prevent her trying to reassert herself by resort to war.'

Not surprisingly, the Royal Navy endorsed these General Staff views, particularly in so far as they concerned the security of the Channel ports. The Air Staff was initially doubtful, apparently taking the potential danger of an air attack by France seriously. But by the beginning of 1925 the Services (and the Foreign Office) were united in their dislike of the proposed Geneva Protocol and their support for a defence pact with France and Belgium.[14]

As early as 13 February 1925 Austen Chamberlain put to the Committee of Imperial Defence (CID) Stresemann's proposal that Germany as well as France should be included in a multilateral guarantee of Germany's western frontiers. Admittedly, said Chamberlain, it was hard to see why the French (and Marshal Foch in particular) were so preoccupied with their security at present but it was necessary to look ahead to the German generation of 1960 or 1970 who *would* be able to attack France. The ensuing discussion is worth quoting for the light it throws on British suspicions of France and reluctance to accept a bilateral pact. Suspicion towards and dislike of France made the inclusion of Germany seem all the more welcome. Balfour declared himself to be angry with the French: 'I think their obsession is so intolerably foolish that I do not feel I am a fair judge of that. They are so dreadfully afraid of being swallowed up by the tiger, but yet they spend their time poking it.' He did not believe that British public opinion could be driven to accept a definite commitment to France when there was no apparent danger. L. S. Amery made a point which would remain pertinent in the 1930s: that Britain and the Empire should guarantee the Belgian and Luxembourg frontier and leave the Rhine frontier to France. The French knew that a general promise from us could not be relied upon—it would depend on the circumstances—whereas Belgium and the Channel ports had always been a vital interest. At another discussion of the same subject a few days later Trenchard remarked: 'I do not think you should tie yourself by a pact to a country which in fifteen years is going downhill continuously, a country which is antagonistic and has piled up all this feeling against Germany. By doing that you automatically make Germany a certain menace for the future.' Cavan at this and later discussions spoke up strongly for Germany's inclusion in the pact. Presumably with the Soviet threat in mind, he remarked that 'it was essential to the future security of Europe that Germany should take her place alongside the Western Powers.' There was no new danger in theoretically undertaking to support Germany against France because France would never dare attack her if it would entail war with Britain also.[15] Both the COS and the CID approved the including of Germany in a multilateral pact.

The Locarno Treaties were signed on 16 October 1925. The contracting parties Belgium, France, Germany, Great Britain, and Italy guaranteed the frontiers between Germany and France and Belgium as fixed by the Treaty of Versailles. Once a violation of one of the relevant articles of the Treaty had been established by the Council of the League of Nations, each contracting party bound itself to come to the help of the victim 'as soon as the said Power has been able to satisfy itself that this violation constitutes an unprovoked aggression'. The ambiguities in these terms were apparent to the negotiators and were to have important consequences later. What constituted 'an unprovoked act of aggression', and did 'the said Power' refer to the victim of an attack or the guarantor coming to its aid? The British negotiators and Government interpreted the terms with the intention of maintaining their traditional freedom of action. In short, Britain would decide if a 'flagrant violation' had taken place, and would interpret this in the strictest terms as an actual invasion of French or Belgian territory. Austen Chamberlain revealingly told the CID that he regarded the Treaty as a reduction rather than an extension of British liabilities. Needless to say, no specific military forces were promised by the guarantors in the event of a breach of the Treaty. For the French this was naturally not good enough: now and later in the 1930s they wanted automatic guarantees (to include interference in the demilitarized zone of the Rhineland) which the British refused to give. The German reoccupation of the Rhineland in March 1936 was to prove that French fears were justified. Locarno also had an unfortunate effect in Britain in so far as it was seen as a positive step towards European security through the reconciliation of France and Germany rather than as a political gesture without the essential backing of military power.[16] Moreover, in assuming even these nominal obligations, Britain was acting alone. At the Imperial Conference of 1926 the Dominions politely but firmly expressed their wish to remain uncommitted. As Michael Howard succinctly put it: 'If the Foreign Office was alarmed at guarantees which could not in the event be fulfilled, the Dominions were still more alarmed at Britain giving any guarantees at all.'[17]

It might have been supposed that signing the Locarno Treaties would have led to a reappraisal of the role of the Army, and in particular to the preparation of an Expeditionary Force capable of intervening in a continental war. But this did not happen, despite a pious reminder from the Foreign Office that 'The more the nations of Europe become convinced of our readiness to fulfill our guarantee, the less likelihood there will be that we shall be called upon to do so.' Instead, in the first of what became a regular series of annual reviews of Imperial defence policy, the Chiefs of Staff in 1926 bluntly stated the actual assumptions on which the armed forces were established:

> The size of the forces of the Crown maintained by Great Britain is governed by various conditions peculiar to each service, and is not arrived at by any calculation of the requirements of foreign policy, nor it is possible that they ever should be so calculated. Thus, though the Expeditionary Force, together with a limited number of Air Force Squadrons, constitute the only military instrument available for immediate use in Europe or elsewhere outside Imperial territory in support of foreign policy, they are so available only when the requirements of Imperial Defence permit.
>
> It follows that, so far as commitments on the Continent are concerned, the Services can only take note of them.
>
> The despatch of our small expeditionary forces to a Continental theatre of war can never be more than a pledge of our readiness to fulfil our guarantees. The capacity to fulfil those guarantees will be assessed by the completeness of the framework for military expansion, and by our preparations for the industrial mobilisation necessary to keep a national army in the field. . . .

In discussing military policy in detail, the Chiefs of Staff remarked: 'Neither the size of the Regular Army nor that of the Expeditionary Force has any relation to the size of foreign armies. The size of the Regular Army is therefore conditioned by the number and strength of the garrisons maintained overseas . . . [and] cannot be calculated by the requirements of foreign policy . . .' Michael Howard refers to this first Annual Review as a 'brutally frank statement' of the Chiefs of Staff's own list of priorities, and to their views on the continental commitment as a 'remarkable declaration of military independence'.[18] But it was surely the Chiefs of Staff's duty to point out the contradiction between foreign policy and military strategy? According to the Ten Year Rule the Army was specifically instructed not to prepare an Expeditionary Force for a major war, while at the same time annual reductions in the Army estimates made it increasingly difficult to meet even minor Imperial emergencies. It is not too cynical to suggest that the COS were putting the Army's limitations 'on the record', knowing that if a continental crisis should arise the politicians would expect an Expeditionary Force to be ready to meet it. Churchill's criticism of the unreadiness of the Expeditionary Force in 1927, to be discussed later, shows that politicians were indeed expecting to have their cake and eat it.

In fact the gulf between politicians and service chiefs was not so great as the COS's blunt statement in their Annual Review might suggest. Indeed, their review went on to describe the ultimate goal of foreign policy as the 'liquidation of its continental commitments'. The Locarno Treaties greatly simplified the problems of Imperial defence because, with a friendly France, 'the Rhine becomes in fact . . . the strategic frontier of Great Britain on land'. There was therefore less urgent need to prepare home defences against either a sea or air attack, and the Territorial Army could be reduced. More men, money, and material could be devoted to the defence of the main line of communication from Britain through the Mediterranean to Singapore and the Far East.[19]

The Army's own view of its priorities was made even clearer at a meeting of the Chiefs of Staff on 27 May 1926. The new CIGS, Sir George Milne, remarked that the 1914–18 war with Germany was 'abnormal' and that the Army was now 'completely out of date'. The COS agreed that Britain's forces and armaments should be governed by the needs of Imperial defence and not swollen by other needs (i.e. such as might arise from the League of Nations, Versailles, and Locarno). Later, after a typical wrangle over the role of the Air Force, Milne declared that the Army was not able to take cognizance of Japan as a possible enemy. 'The priority in regard to Army commitments was India.' On 8 July 1926, in a note for the guidance of the Expeditionary Force Committee, Milne spelt out the practical implications of these assumptions: a continental war is of extreme improbability; preparations must be directed towards a sea voyage and operations in an undeveloped country, and it is therefore unnecessary to have more than a small proportion of the Expeditionary Force ready to take the field at short notice; one should aim to raise a mixed force of about one division with some cavalry and tanks.[20]

As Milne's note reveals, the Army's main concern in the middle and late 1920s was the defence of India and, in so far as it visualized the possibility of war with a major power, that power was the Soviet Union. It is easy to ridicule the Army for atavistically returning to the Victorians' 'Great Game' on the North West Frontier, but in fact their anxiety accorded with that of the Foreign Office. In 1926 at the discretion of the Cabinet, Sir William Tyrrell circulated a Foreign Office memorandum to the CID and the COS Sub-Committee. The main purpose of this review was to forestall Admiralty preparations in the Far East. To further that end, the Foreign Office noted that they had 'no hesitation in stating that their policy should be based on the assumption that Russia is the enemy, not Japan.' In 1927 Austen Chamberlain informed the CID that, 'from the political aspect, there was no prospect of our being called upon at an early date to implement our guarantee under the Locarno Pact. The danger point, if one existed, was undoubtedly *vis-à-vis* Russia.'[21] When on 5 July 1928 the CID discussed a Treasury proposal adopted by Churchill to put the Ten Year Rule on a moving day-by-day basis, Austen Chamberlain in a full survey of the international situation remarked that apart from uncertainty about Russian policy he would be content to rely on the continuing validity of the Ten Year assumption. Though it was doubtful whether Russia was capable of offensive operations at present, she constituted the greatest danger to peace. Russian aggression against Afghanistan would most concern Britain: the safety of India might be at stake. At a meeting of the Chiefs of Staff Sub-Committee on the following day the CIGS questioned the advisability of stating in so many words that the Expeditionary Force should be organized with a view to a war in Afghanistan. Hitherto it had always been organized for general purposes, and in Milne's opinion a reserve to meet Middle East emergencies was at least as important as preparing for war in Afghanistan.[22]

Meanwhile the Chiefs of Staff had examined the problems posed by the defence of Afghanistan in 1926 and 1927. Their conclusions were generally pessimistic, though in their opinion the integrity of Afghanistan was still as vital to British security as when Balfour made a policy statement in 1903. They believed Soviet designs on India to be the same as those of the Tsarist era, but now more likely to be pursued by insidious methods. If force were employed Britain could not send out reinforcements in time to save Afghanistan. They could not envisage a war between Russia and Britain only but in such an unlikely event the British Army could have no real effect on the situation in Asia. Subsidiary operations elsewhere would not at all reduce the forces needed in Afghanistan, and would also necessitate conscription. The most useful ally would be Japan but, they concluded, it was not easy to see how Britain could bring effective pressure to bear on Russia.[23]

In all their discussions of a possible war with Russia in defence of Afghanistan, the General Staff and the Chiefs of Staff assumed that ample time would be available (and conscription introduced) in order to prepare the enormous reinforcements they deemed necessary.[24] Indeed this may have been an attractive planning option precisely because of the time factor. The manpower problem was indeed formidable. In 1927, for example, the CIGS pointed out that the reserve situation was much weaker than before 1914. In addition to existing reserves, approximately half a million men would have to be recruited and trained in the first year of war in order to send 11 divisions to India as reinforcements in a war against Russia. In their annual review for 1928 the COS noted that war in Afghanistan would involve operations in an underdeveloped country with the bases of the opposing sides several hundred miles apart. The arrival of the Expeditionary Force would therefore be much slower than if the enemy were nearer to our gates. We could not exert our full strength to meet an emergency in the Far East before 1937 and 'some years must elapse before we could provide adequate opposition to a Russian aggression in Afghanistan'.[25]

In 1929 the nightmare of a full-scale war with Russia on the borders of Afghanistan began to fade and to be replaced with other preoccupations. On the one hand increasing doubts were expressed about the political reliability of the Indian Army because of 'Indianization' and the spread of nationalist propaganda. In 1929 India erupted in a series of internal upheavals and frontier operations which were to keep the British forces there fully occupied until the mid-1930s.[26] On the other hand a more realistic note was sounded in Foreign Office evaluations of Russian intentions and capabilities. Thus, in preparing their annual review for 1929, the COS were advised that Russia was in such a dreadful economic state that she was unlikely to contemplate war with anyone. Her policy was thought to be more and more to embarrass us over our colonies in the Far East. The General Staff graphically incorporated these views into their review of the world situation in 1929:

> It must be remembered that in Russia today money and food are short, discontent is spreading, and the morale of the army is doubtful. In such conditions, though it is impossible to exclude entirely a resort to war as a gambler's last throw, the situation of the Bolshevik leaders would have to be desperate indeed to induce them to run the risk that out of a war might arise a military dictator, who would sweep away the Communist regime.[27]

The Middle East constituted one of the Army's most important commitments in the inter-war period and a source of increasing difficulties from 1929 onwards. And yet, as Elizabeth Monroe has written, in spite of these vicissitudes, 'Britain remained paramount in the Middle East, unchallenged by any power of equal magnitude, and able to maintain order thanks to its security, and aura of empire, and its ability to summon reinforcements from Malta or India in case of need'. Britain successfully delayed the day of reckoning until after the Second World War mainly through a mutually advantageous alliance with the conservative ruling class of kings, pashas, and rich merchants; but also because her 'itch to administer maladministered peoples' conferred tangible benefits. In such dependencies as the Sudan, the British Colonial Civil Service brought 'the kind of economic gain which while breeding no gratitude, produces a grumbling tranquillity'.[28]

By 1928 the Mediterranean and the Near East, excluding Aden, absorbed 13 infantry battalions and one additional battalion was required to supplement the Malta garrison. This was quite a small force in comparison with the Indian garrison and, in terms of numbers alone, goes some way to justify Elizabeth Monroe's comment that 'the British remained supreme in the Middle East without a vestige of military effort between 1922 and 1929'.[29] The Army's 'effort' would, however, have been much greater but for what both its champions and detractors referred to as 'air substitution'.

The Air Ministry made its first venture into the traditional 'imperial policing' role of the Army early in 1920 in Somaliland where, with minimal ground support, the RAF speedily demoralized the Mullah Muhammed's Dervishes. At a total cost of just £77,000 this was surely one of the cheapest wars in modern history. Trenchard's faith in air power was fully vindicated and in 1922 Churchill transferred the responsibility for maintenance of law and order in Iraq to the RAF. This experiment proved so successful both in terms of pacification and in economy of ground forces that in the next seven years the Air Ministry was also given control of Palestine, Trans-Jordan, and the Aden Protectorate. The various methods of air control were also successfully employed on several occasions on the North West Frontier.

It might have been expected that the Army authorities, hard pressed to maintain overseas garrisons while still attempting to raise an Expeditionary Force from units at home, would have welcomed air substitution, particularly as it applied mainly to desert areas where it was hazardous and expensive to maintain troops. Had the inter-service rivalry for the lion's share of a diminishing budget been less intense, or had the RAF been a long-established service like the Royal Navy rather than a new and ambitious upstart, then perhaps the Army's attitude might have been more co-operative. In fact there is abundant evidence that from the first the Army reacted with hostility to what it regarded as unjustified encroachment in its own preserve. There was a justified fear that 'saving' of Imperial garrisons would result in a call for further reductions in establishments; there was resentment at command of ground forces being conferred on an RAF officer, as occurred in Palestine; and there was conviction—justified for Palestine but less so elsewhere—that air control simply would not work.[30]

Years of bickering in the Chiefs of Staff Committee on the issue of air substitution came to a head in 1927 when the General Staff firmly resisted Air Ministry pressure to take over responsibility for Aden. The CIGS, Milne, was incensed by a suggestion of Churchill, as Chancellor of the Exchequer, that the Services should 'tender for the job', pointing out that questions of establishment were outside the jurisdiction of the Chiefs of Staff Committee; the strength of the Aden garrison was a matter for the Army Council who were not prepared to discuss it. Milne complained that when he had asked for air support 'he never contemplated that this arrangement should be . . . used as a lever to reduce the infantry garrison of Aden'. On this occasion, as in most disputes with the junior service where its own interests were not directly threatened, the Royal Navy, in the person of Admiral Beatty, supported the Army. This was consistent with the Admiralty's line in the far more acrimonous air-*versus*-gun controversy over Singapore where the naval case was that air forces were impermament and unreliable in coast defence. When Milne and Trenchard failed to settle the Aden dispute privately, the issue was referred to the Cabinet which decided in favour of the RAF.[31]

In 1929, however, even John Slessor* was later to admit that Trenchard overplayed his hand when, in what was irreverently referred to as 'Boom's last will and testament' he proposed that the RAF should be made responsible for the defence of the Sudan, East and West Africa, the Red Sea and the Persian Gulf, the North West Frontier, and Coast Defence throughout the Empire. The most controversial of these proposals concerned India where, the authors of the paper argued, the addition of only five or six squadrons would permit the disbandment of between 25 and 30 battalions and 10 batteries—a saving of some £2 million per annum which could be used to improve the equipment of the Field Army. The proposals regarding the Persian Gulf and Coast Defences generally also antagonized the Navy. Slessor, one of the authors of the paper, heard a naval officer remark 'with almost apoplectic contempt: "Aircraft! Good God—Aircraft! I'd rather have *one gun* at Famagusta than all the aircraft you could produce."' The paper as a whole caused a rare storm. 'It was as though someone had suggested substituting a motor-cycle rally for the Derby.' The proposals were defeated by the combined opposition of the War Office, Admiralty, Colonial Office, and India Office.[32]

Returning to the Army's responsibilities in the Middle East, the one potentially explosive area which defied all political and military attempts to 'muddle through' was Palestine. In addition to the idealistic and emotional commitments of influential groups in Britain to both the Arab and Zionist causes, it is well to remember that strategically the stability of Palestine and Sinai were regarded as essential to the defence of the Suez Canal and as an important link in Britain's air communications with India and the East. Most diplomats concerned with Palestine in the 1920s would probably have settled for a compromise settlement of the Arab–Jewish problem (as difficult as squaring the circle), but British Zionists cherished more romantic visions. Colonel Richard Meinertzhagen, for example, hoped that Zionism would 'eventually dominate the Middle East from Sinai to Syria and east to Iraq or even further, constituting a healthy state and a corner stone in the British Commonwealth'.[33]

Until the grave inter-communal disturbances of 1929, it looked as though Britain might escape the consequences of her confused and contradictory policies towards the Jews and Arabs in Palestine. This illusion was based on the fact that Arab nationalism there was still largely dormant, while most Jews emigrating from Europe preferred the United States. In 1927 more Jews actually left Palestine than entered it. When rebellion broke out in 1929, started by an incident between Jews and Arabs at Solomon's Temple, the British garrison had been reduced below the minimum necessary to preserve order. Indeed Britain was censured in a report to the Permanent Mandates Commision of the League of Nations for not maintaining more troops in the country. A single RAF squadron supported by two companies of armoured cars were responsible for the whole of Palestine and Trans-Jordan and the armoured cars were all in Trans-Jordan when the troubles began. To most commentators, then and since, this emergency, and the greater one which began in 1936, proved that the RAF had overstated its claims for air control. It could protect Palestine from external attack across the desert but was largely impotent to deal with civil disorders in urban areas such as Tel Aviv and Jerusalem.[34]

Even when due allowance is made for the fact that at this stage the disturbances were entirely inter-communal and not directed at British forces or property, British response to the 1929 crisis was remarkably prompt and effective.[35] Within hours of the emergency being proclaimed a small advance party of troops had been ferried from Egypt to Jerusalem by air while the body of three battalions and an armoured car squadron promptly followed by rail and within a few days were reinforced by nearly a thousand sailors. The crisis revealed however that British political control had essentially depended on bluff, and after the 1929 disturbances died down a minimum garrison of two infantry battalions had to be retained.

It is unnecessary here to follow the bewildering twists and turns of British policy towards Palestine in the 1930s. The essential point is that after the emergency of 1929 Britain rapidly lost control of the situation and began to vacillate, thus encouraging both Arabs and Jews to step up their claims. The garrison was reduced to trying to hold the ring while British policy, in Elizabeth Monroe's words, 'began simply to register trouble, instead of controlling it'.

From 1932 onwards Nazi persecution led to a rapid increase in the number of European Jewish immigrants and this ominous development virtually ruled out any hope of a peaceful settlement. The campaign of violence and murder which looked like getting completely out of hand in 1936 was aimed much more directly at the British. Despite her preoccupation with the Italo-Abyssinian war, Britain increased the garrison to the equivalent of a division and at the height of the emergency, in August and September 1936, sent out a further ten thousand troops from England. Thus at the peak of the crisis the equivalent of two divisions were engaged in policing duties in Palestine. By January 1937 the garrison had been reduced to about seven battalions but there was to be no real lessening of tension before the outbreak of the Second World War.[36] The strategic consequences of this large and disheartening military commitment at a critical stage in the development of the European situation will be discussed later.

Apart from the Palestine emergency of 1929 and the almost continuous communal disorders and frontier incursions that kept the Indian garrison on its toes, China provided the stiffest test in the decade of Britain's ability rapidly to provide a military expedition to complement diplomacy. The imperialist powers holding privileged concessions in China had been anxiously watching the complex fluctuations of the civil war, and in particular the dangers posed by the northward progress of the comparatively well-disciplined and united Cantonese

Army commanded by Chiang Kai-shek which reached the Yangste at Hankow in September 1926. The Cantonese Army was confronted by a northern group led by Chang Tso-lin, the ruler of Manchuria, and including the Army of Sun Chuan-fang who nominally controlled the provinces outside the lower Yangste and was therefore responsible for the security of the international concessions in Shanghai. This city, the centre of Western commercial interests in China, faced not only the alarming prospect of direct attack from the anti-foreign Cantonese Army, but also the scarcely less disturbing influx of a horde of undisciplined soldiery in the event of a battle between the rival warlords. On 5 January 1927 an international crisis arose when the British Concession at Hankow was overrun by a mob including a number of Cantonese troops. The British residents suffered a few casualties but mostly found a safe refuge on board ships at the river port. The Concession was occupied. It seemed only a matter of time before the foreign enclaves at Shanghai suffered the same fate but with far greater losses of life and property.

On 17 January the British Government authorized the dispatch of the Shanghai Defence Force with the following objectives:

(*a*) To secure the safety of the International Settlement at Shanghai, denying entrance into it of any Chinese force, organised or disorganised; thus providing a place of refuge where the lives of British nationals would be safe.
(*b*) To bring home to the Chinese that any further attempts to wrest concessions by force would not be tolerated.
(*c*) To protect British property so far as it could be done without aggressive action or without forming detachments which would involve further dangers.[37]

The strength of the force represented a division shorn of a considerable amount of its guns, vehicles, and heavy equipment. Of the three infantry brigades comprising the understrength division, one was to be supplied from India and the other two from troops in the Mediterranean and home stations. Aircraft for reconnaisance and a few armoured cars but no tanks were included. The Indian 20th Brigade embarked at Bombay on 27 January and on the following two days the British component of the 13th and 14th Brigades sailed from Southampton. This prompt departure ensured that the first transports from India would reach Shanghai by 15 February, and those from England about a week later. On the whole this improvised mobilization was a testament to close liaison between the War Office, the Board of Trade, and the Admiralty. Units which existed only on paper in peacetime had to be formed and supplied with transport. The Commander and Staff had to be hurriedly appointed (much as Sir Ian Hamilton and his Staff were appointed and dispatched to the Dardanelles in March 1915), and had no chance to see their troops until arrival. Again as in the Dardanelles expedition, ships were not always stowed so as to ensure that articles came out at the other end in the order required, nor were components always in the same ship.

In military terms the outcome was an anticlimax. By the time the main contingent, commanded by Major-General John Duncan, arrived, the Cantonese Army had been defeated and was in full retreat. The main duty of the Defence Force was to hold an outpost line or cordon and regulate civilian traffic through it. Apart from occasional sniping and a few vain attempts by armed parties to break through the cordon, the only really dangerous activity involved the rescue parties which went outside the cordon line to bring in Europeans in charge of missions, hospitals, and similar establishments. Tactically the armoured cars proved valuable in patrolling the few roads that existed but the Defence Force was fortunate not to suffer from its complete lack of tanks.[38]

In his review of recent developments affecting Imperial Defence Policy in 1928, the CIGS mentioned that the sudden need to dispatch such a comparatively large force to China had come somewhat as a surprise. Together with the need to reinforce the Palestine garrison it had had the effect of drawing Britain's meagre reserves eastward from home and Mediterranean stations. Although the bulk of the Shanghai Defence Force was speedily withdrawn it was deemed necessary to retain a permanently increased garrison of one Indian and seven British battalions, two battalions stationed at Singapore and six in China. Milne made it clear that his chief anxiety in the Far East was not so much the security of British property and nationals in China from internal disorder as the need to deter Japan from attacking our possessions. While fully accepting that this was primarily the Navy's responsibility, Milne was particularly anxious about the land defence of Hong Kong. 'The capture of Hong Kong', he wrote, 'would deprive us of a Naval base, the loss of which might well result in the impossibility of our obtaining a decisive result in any subsequent operations we might wish to undertake.' He proposed to double the garrison of Hong Kong (from two battalions to four) specifically 'to provide a material deterrent against attack by Japan'.[39]

By the late 1920s the War Office and the General Staff were becoming increasingly worried about the Army's deterioration in numbers and equipment and its inability to meet possible commitments. Their repeated warnings make depressing reading now and, as Austen Chamberlain remarked at the time, were only tolerable because of the apparently peaceful state of the world. The Army Estimates were reduced every year until 1932 and this was reflected in the steady decrease in the number of troops budgeted for on the home establishment. Thus, for example, between 1922 and 1926 the total Army Estimates were reduced by nearly £20 million, more that £12 million of which was achieved by cuts in effective services (as distinct from non-effective services which included military pensions and half-pay for officers). The total establishment of the Army declined from 231,062 in 1922 to 207,537 in 1931, though it must be borne in mind that recruiting sometimes failed to produce the full number provided for.[40]

In his memorandum on 'The Present Distribution and Strength of the British Army in relation to its duties' in 1927, the CIGS painted a gloomy picture of the Home Army as evidenced by the unpreparedness of the Expeditionary Force compared with 1914. The sudden need to dispatch 17 battalions to the Far East at the beginning of the year had exposed a disturbing lack of reserves. It had left only 56 battalions at home (including 10 Guards battalions and those in the Rhineland) as against 80 overseas. Milne was still—like Wilson before him—seriously worried about home security; after all, no less than 36 battalions had been called out on emergency duty during the General Strike in May 1926 and that number could easily be doubled. The CIGS's nightmare was Communist-inspired subversion at home coinciding with a major crisis overseas. 'It is quite apparent', he concluded, '[that] if the Expeditionary Force is removed from England to prosecute a war which is unpopular with any appreciable portion of the industrial community, the residue of regular infantry units left in England will be totally inadequate to provide the necessary backing to the police in maintaining internal order.'[41]

The CIGS was understandably furious when the Chancellor of the Exchequer criticized this report in the CID on the grounds that 'the Expeditionary Force had been cut down to 5 Divisions, of which the last two could not take the field until 5 months after the outbreak of war, whereas in 1914 we had 6 Infantry Divisions and a Cavalry Division capable of taking the field within a month'. Churchill found this astonishing in view of the fact that the War Office staff had doubled compared with before the war. Milne replied correctly that the size of the War Office staff was irrelevant to the preparedness of the Expeditionary Force. The deficiencies in the Expeditionary Force were due solely to lack of resources and money. 'The War Office could only organize what they had. It was a question entirely of manpower and reserves: these did not exist because of the way the Army had been cut down in strength of men and material.' In a later memorandum further rebutting the Chancellor's criticisms, the Secretary of State for War, Sir Laming Worthington-Evans, pointed out that the readiness of the Expeditionary Force was also affected by the Ten Year Rule which the Cabinet had recently extended. The Government had laid down that the Expeditionary Force should be designed for an extra-European war in a distant theatre with the corollary that there would be considerable time to organize shipping after mobilization had been ordered. This vital factor rendered a comparison with the cross-Channel service in 1914 highly misleading. The present schedule, he concluded, was for the mobilization of one division and part of a cavalry division after two weeks at the least and a further four divisions after six months. Many units in the later contingents (particularly the 4th and 5th Divisions) would have to be formed after mobilization, i.e. they did not exist in peace-time. These included 1 Battalion (RTC), 3 Field Brigades (RA), 1 Light Brigade (RA), and 2 Field Companies (RE). The only sense in which the state of the Expeditionary Force could be considered satisfactory, the Secretary of State for War concluded, was that it was based on the actual forces available and was not a paper scheme.[42]

The tendency on the part both of the Government and its professional strategic advisers to play down the likelihood of European military commitments in the near future and to stress the urgent needs of Imperial defence probably reached an extreme in 1930. In their annual review for that year the Chiefs of Staff remarked that in the past year the centre of gravity of the defence problem had shifted away from Europe towards the Middle and Far East. They laid particular emphasis on the point that Britain's forces were *not* designed to meet her commitments under the Locarno Treaties: plans had not been called for and none had been made. They concluded that 'This country is in a less favourable position to fulfil the Locarno guarantees than it was, without any written guarantee, to come to the assistance of France and Belgium in 1914.'[43]

While the Chiefs of Staff collectively tended to neglect the potential menace of a secretly rearming Germany, the same cannot be said of the General Staff. In 1925, for example, the CIGS informed the CID in a somewhat chauvinistic style that the General Staff's mistrust and apprehension of Germany remained undiminished. 'They regard the German nation as a primitive people, scientifically equipped. . . . vigorous, prolific and unscrupulous, combining the height of modern efficiency with the mentality and brutality of the Middle Ages.'[44]

When Milne became CIGS, he made a practice of submitting careful annual estimates of German military strength and potential as well as forecasts of her future military development. If anything Milne's survey tended to underrate Germany's clandestine accumulation of war material and weapons. He was particularly concerned about Germany's reserves of semi-trained manpower in militaristic organizations such as the Stahlhelm and the patriotic associations which provided a disturbing contrast to the undermanned and inadequately trained Territorial Army.[45]

Though hardly alarmist in tone, Milne's reports were not well received. In May 1929, for example, the Foreign Office circulated its own memorandum on the military situation in Germany which ridiculed the General Staff's views. The Foreign Office argued that the Weimar Republic was anti-militaristic and would provide a bulwark against a revival of Prussianism. The Chancellor of the Exchequer, Philip Snowden, discounted Milne's review for 1930 because it was 'based on slender evidence'; while the Prime Minister, Ramsay MacDonald, was content to remark non-committally that the German situation required 'careful observation'.[46]

Valuable support for the General Staff's suspicious attitude was supplied by Hankey. As early as 1928 he tried to have Germany accepted as the 'probably enemy' of the newly created Principal Supply Officers Committee (a Sub-Committee of the CID), but the Chiefs of Staff would not agree. Early in 1931 Hankey wrote to Sir Herbert Creedy, Permanent Under-Secretary at the War Office, that the strategic centre of gravity was no longer moving eastward, if indeed it had ever done so, and was now starting on a return journey. 'If there is a danger today it is, in my view, in Europe, and more especially in Eastern Europe, rather than in the Far East or Afghanistan.' The inference he drew was that the ten years' peace assumption was beginning to look shaky.[47] By 1931 the manpower, equipment, reserves, and manufacturing capacity of all three Services were so unsatisfactory that the Chiefs of Staff felt obliged to question the political assumptions underlying the Ten Year Rule. As the official historian of *Grand Strategy* with undue caution comments, 'The state of the Army was, perhaps worst of all.' 'The Army is pared to the bone', declared the CIGS and, he added bitterly, 'the only reproach that has ever been levelled against us at Geneva is that we have disarmed too much, and that our army is so small that it is incapable of fulfilling our international obligations.'[48]

The Services' growing disquiet about the Ten Year Rule was given powerful impetus by the Manchurian crisis in 1931.[49] It was clear that all British possessions in the Far East were vulnerable to Japanese attack and also that there were no grounds for believing that the anxiety would be transitory. The Chiefs of Staff accordingly used their annual review for 1932 to pose a trenchant challenge to the continuation of the Rule. They began by asserting that the Ten Year Rule had had the effect of undermining all the Services' ability to carry out their vital tasks. As regards home defence, for example, all the naval bases and ports had obsolete defences and there was 'nothing approaching a bare margin' in defence against air attack. If the Expeditionary Force were to be committed to operations under the Locarno Treaty only one division could be sent in the first month and three more to arrive piecemeal in the first four months. Such a contingent could only have a moral effect on the campaign. Even for the defence of India or our Eastern possessions such a slow rate of mobilization would place us in a very difficult position.

The Chiefs of Staff recognized that even without the Rule financial considerations would have operated, but 'they would not have had behind them the same unanswerable argument against even really urgent proposals'. Not restricting themselves to purely military aspects, they declared that they found it hard to believe that funds to relieve the most glaring deficiencies could not have been found. For example, between 1924 and February 1932 £700,000 had been spent on public works including roads, to relieve unemployment, whereas even one per cent of this amount would have made a significant difference to defensive arrangements. In fact the assumption of ten years of peace had proved an insurmountable barrier to the execution of any policy in Imperial Defence, however urgent might be the necessity. One of the most serious consequences of the Rule had been the run down of the arms industry to such an extent that the country was worse placed than in 1914; yet, they suggested, expenditure on armaments could nearly all be made in Britain where a considerable proportion would go to the wages of skilled workers who were now drawing unemployment benefit.

They ventured even further on to political ground in asserting that British public opinion had not been educated or encouraged to understand the need for defence preparations. After all military preparedness was not inconsistent with a peace policy. 'With the encouragement of the State', they added darkly, 'an intensive propaganda of a different kind has been carried out in the schools, universities, churches, press and, through the wireless broadcast, in the homes of the people. This propaganda has tended to discourage personal sacrifice for the purposes of national defence.' One effect of this propaganda was that recruiting for the Army was difficult despite the high level of unemployment. In sum, they contended, there was a general ignorance of the facts and an unjustified spirit of complacent optimism which could not be remedied while the Ten Year Rule prevailed. At present Britain's defensive arrangements were in a state of ineffectiveness unequalled by any foreign military power. They concluded with three recommendations: first, that the Ten Year Rule should be cancelled; second, that a start should be made in providing for purely defensive commitments, with priority for the Far East; and thirdly that a decision should not be delayed until after the outcome of the Disarmament Conference. 'Recent events in the Far East are ominous. We cannot ignore the Writing on the Wall.'

The Treasury remained unimpressed by this swingeing attack. It noted that neither militarily nor financially could Britain contemplate a war in the Far East. It made no mention of Germany at all and thought that the only threat to Britain and her line of communications was posed by France with whom war was exceedingly unlikely. The Ten Year Rule was no more than a working hypothesis to relieve the Chiefs of Staff from preparing to meet very remote contingencies or ones which were '*beyond the financial capacity of the country to provide against*' (italics in original). It was a matter of balancing risks and in the Treasury view at the present time financial risks were greater than any other that it could estimate.[50]

When the COS Annual Review was considered by the CID on 22 March 1932, its general strategic, and political analysis was accepted. Indeed the Foreign Secretary, Sir John Simon, regretfully admitted that 'the ten year assumption was a dangerous one'. The Cabinet confirmed the Review the following day but with two significant provisos: its acceptance must not be taken to justify increased expenditure on defence without regard to the prevailing financial and economic crisis; and furthermore the subject was so closely connected with the issue of disarmament that it needed further exploration. In the event this was to mean a delay of eighteen months before even a serious 'stock-taking' of the Services' worst deficiencies was undertaken. When due allowance is made for the unprecedented economic depression and the hopes placed on the impending Geneva Disarmament Conference, the official historian's sober reference to the 'almost unbelievable tardiness' of the Government in accepting the practical implications of the Chiefs of Staff's warning is surely justified.[51]

Most students of British defence between the world wars have criticized the Ten Year Rule, referring to it as 'notorious', or, as 'odious and secret'.[52] The general consensus of opinion is that while there was much to be said for some such broad guideline in the years immediately after 1918, it was a mistake to confirm the Rule in 1928, and put it on a moving basis so that the assumption of ten years' peace was pushed into the indefinite future. The most serious charge is that the Rule was unduly prolonged to 1932 long after, in the Chiefs of Staff's phrase, the writing had begun to appear on the wall.

The basic and ultimately unquantifiable problem is how much of the Services' unpreparedness in 1933 (i.e. when the Rule ceased to apply) was specifically and definitely the result of the Rule and how much would have resulted, even without it, from such considerations as Britain's domestic, social and economic problems, her over-extension in foreign commitments, and the prevalent belief in disarmament and international arbitration of disputes. However, though these considerations were indeed instrumental in the forming of the Ten Year Rule in 1919, the Rule in itself gave the Treasury the whip hand and convinced the Defence Departments that even essential requirements could not be met. All three Services had specific programmes—such as the Singapore Base, defended ports, a metropolitan airforce of 52 squadrons, and the Expeditionary Force which all suffered delays and deficiencies as a direct result of the functioning of the Rule.[53]

The greatest drawbacks to the concept of a Ten Year Rule only became fully apparent after its demise. Ten years is an extremely long time in terms of international relations, but a comparatively short time for a largely disarmed and pacific democracy to rearm for a major war against more than one potential enemy. It is hard to understand how supporters of the extension of the Rule from 1925 onwards can have deluded themselves on the two vital questions: would Britain's potential enemies be so considerate as to allow her ten years to rearm once the warning signal had been accepted; and would she have the will power and industrial capacity to make the tremendous effort required in time?

CHAPTER 4

The Defence of India and the Cardwell system

Although this study is primarily concerned with the British Army at home, the problems that the Army encountered in preparing for a possible war in Europe cannot be appreciated without some account of the influence exerted upon it by the Indian Army and the British Army in India.

The main political feature of the inter-war period was the rapid growth of Indian nationalism and agitation for a greater Indian share in government. Significant concessions to 'native opinion' were made by the Montagu–Chelmsford reforms in February 1921. These included the creation of a Legislative Assembly of which nearly three-quarters of the 146 members were elected, and a Council of State of which over half of the 61 members were elected. More important still, the reforms established a convention that three out of the eight members of the Viceroy's Council should be Indians. Henceforth, although Indian representatives were elected on a very restricted franchise and the Viceroy retained the final say in major matters of policy, Indian opinion had more and more to be taken into account.

The two components of the armed forces in India totaled nearly 250,000 men in the 1920s. The purely British element of just under 60,000 troops consisted of 45 infantry battalions, five cavalry regiments, eight armoured car companies, and 69 artillery batteries. The Indian Army proper, composed of native soldiers commanded largely by British officers holding Indian Army commissions, totaled approximately 190,000 men formed into 100 active and 18 training battalions of infantry, 21 cavalry regiments, 18 mountain artillery batteries, and numerous ancillary units of pioneers, engineers, and signallers. The two forces were kept separate at the regimental level but brigaded together, a brigade normally consisting of one British and two or three Indian battalions. The high command and staff positions were shared among officers drawn from both armies.

Though recruited and trained in Britain, units of the Regular Army when serving in India were wholly supported by Indian taxes. They were under the political control of the Government of India and were ultimately, via the Viceroy, responsible to the Secretary of State for India and Parliament.[1] Whether the British troops temporarily stationed in India were maintained purely for the defence of the subcontinent, or whether they could be regarded as imperial forces with wider responsibilities, was to become an increasingly controversial issue during the inter-war period.

Since the 1870s units of the British Army in India had been maintained by the Cardwell system. Indeed, though Edward Cardwell had several aims in mind when introducing his celebrated reforms, it is hardly an exaggeration to state that his basic problem was how to provide a permanent garrison for India, comprising almost half of the British Regular Army, on a basis of voluntary enlistment. Before the introduction of the Cardwell reforms a far larger proportion of the Army was stationed abroad than at home. Moreover, once a particular unit was sent overseas it might be posted from one garrison to another for periods of twenty years or more, so that soldiers ran a considerable risk of virtually permanent exile. Not surprisingly this acted as a deterrent to recruitment.[2] Further drawbacks to this haphazard method of garrisoning the Empire were that there were insufficient troops at home to form an Expeditionary Force in an emergency, while the premium placed on long service prevented the creation of a worthwhile reserve. Cardwell's reforms were ingeniously interrelated to solve these various problems. By withdrawing British garrisons from the self-governing colonies he first created an approximate balance between units at home and abroad in order that the former should supply regular drafts to the latter and periodically replace them on overseas service. Brigade depots were also created to associate regular (linked) battalions with the auxiliary forces in particular areas and so to improve recruiting by fostering local pride. Finally, and not least important, Cardwell introduced short-service enlistment, initially of six years with the Colours followed by a similar period in the Reserve. This Reserve was designed to make Army service more attractive while at the same time creating a pool of trained men on the continental model. Although these, and Cardwell's other reforms, at least introduced a definite system where there had been none before, they never operated as smoothly as he intended. A series of imperial crises and minor campaigns before the South African War entailed that in practice it was never possible to keep anywhere near an equal number of battalions at home. Consequently units at home were increasingly hard pressed to maintain regular drafts; they were unable to train properly and degenerated into understrength training battalions for their sister battalions overseas. In the 1890s a leading military critic, Colonel G. F. R. Henderson, aptly described the home battalions as 'squeezed lemons'—the real Army, he added, was only to be seen in India. To aggravate the problem, annual recruiting figures often fell below the minimum necessary for the system to function. This in turn led to a lowering of physical standards in recruiting and pressure on soldiers to sign on for life service. In sum, late Victorian Governments were attempting to square the circle by expecting an underpaid and underprivileged Army raised by voluntary enlistment to garrison a world-wide Empire on a short-service basis. Several of Caldwell's successors, notably H. O. Arnold-Forster after the Boer War, attempted, but with no success, to remedy these drawbacks before the system was placed in abeyance in 1914.[3]

When the Cardwell system was resurrected after the First World War Fuller described it as an 'albatross' round the Army's neck. Most would-be reformers, including Ironside, Hobart, and Lindsay, agreed with him that it constituted a formidable obstacle to change since it permitted so little scope for experiment. The familiar defects soon reappeared: thus after 1921 the balance tilted increasingly on the side of battalions overseas so that between 1922 and 1928 the disparity was never less than 14 even though the six battalions in the Rhineland and some short-tour battalions in the Mediterranean, including the Occupation Force in Turkey, were counted as on 'home service'.

Thereafter the balance was almost restored until the Abyssinian War, closely followed by the Palestine rebellion, upset it irrevocably and the imbalance again slipped to 14 battalions. In these circumstances the Army at home was strained to the limit to provide drafts to maintain the strength of overseas garrisons so that the Expeditionary Force, as we have seen in other chapters, had little reality beyond War Office lists.[4]

As one of the Army's indefatigable advocates of reform, Major B. C. Dening, gloomily noted in 1928, 'seemingly everything in the Army is dependent upon the Cardwell system', including the troops' terms of service and regimental *esprit de corps*. The training and equipment of the home Army must not become too different from its overseas counterparts, and changes of establishments or equipment which would interfere with the draft-finding capacity of units 'could not be tolerated'. To break away from the system, Dening predicted, would cause an upheaval such as has not been known for half a century. India, he correctly perceived, was the principal *raison d'être* of the system, while within India military thinking tended to be dominated by the traditional problem of the North West Frontier: 'We thus have a situation in which the greater portion of the British Army is regulated by the conditions prevailing on a portion of one of the frontiers of one of the Empire's constituent parts.'[5]

The system frequently came under attack in professional periodicals such as the *RUSI Journal*, but the critics' alternative suggestions were not taken up by the War Office. In a particularly frank exposé in 1927 Captain Appleton pointed out that, contrary to sentimental myth, the majority of recruits in most regiments were not drawn from the 'home areas', and indeed regiments very rarely served there when at home. The system was too rigid in peacetime and anyway would have to be abandoned in event of major war. His solution was to form groups of regiments linked with Territorial Army battalions and served by a large depot which would relieve the individual regiments from the onerous duty of supplying overseas drafts. Dening admitted that a thorough reform would cause convulsion but argued for a compromise solution which would result in less disorganization than if changes were delayed until the outbreak of war. He would retain about 60 infantry battalions on the Cardwell system, while gradually mechanizing 66 units which in time could also become interchangeable. In a prize essay in 1928, which must have met with some official approval, Captain J. Keith Edwards argued that the present military organization, which prevented effective intervention on the Continent, could be fatal to Britain's interests. The Cardwell system was breaking down in practice in that units at home were being trained and equipped differently from those in India where, for example, the mechanization of first-line transport had a lower priority. His solution resembled the ill-fated scheme upon which Arnold-Forster's reforms had foundered in 1903–5; namely to raise separate continental and colonial armies, the first on really short service to create a reserve and the second to serve seven years with five in reserve. The main stumbling block would be recruiting for two separate armies. More typical of the War Office attitude was the lecture given by Colonel G. N. Macready* in 1935 with the CIGS Montgomery-Massingberd, in the chair. After reviewing the problems which any radical changes in home organization and equipment would cause for India, he lamely concluded that the Cardwell system must be retained for the present.[6] Only under Hore-Belisha's prodding in 1937 did the War Office even scrutinize the system with a view to significant changes.

The role of India in British strategic thinking underwent a gradual but profoundly important change of emphasis in the inter-war period. Whereas historically the defence of India had been taken to include internal security and protecting the frontiers—above all the north-west—against external attack, from the 1920s onwards the notion steadily grew that India should contribute to the general defence of the Empire in a more coherent and systematic way than in the nineteenth century.[7] On the one hand the latter policy seemed a natural sequence to India's massive contribution to the imperial war effort in the First World War, when 285,037 British troops from the Army in India and over a million Indian native soldiers had been posted overseas and her entire contribution to the war had been paid for by the Government of India. Such an extension of responsibilities also seemed logical in view of Britain's increased imperial burden and her diminishing capacity to shoulder it. On the other hand most Indian nationalists were vehemently opposed to the employment of Indian troops outside the subcontinent. For quite different reasons the Government of India was reluctant to accept that the Indian establishment carried any surplus troops who could be employed overseas on imperial duties. Lastly, the eyes of the Indian General Staff tended to focus somewhat exclusively on the problems posed by Afghanistan, with whom there had been war involving no less than 340,000 British and Indian troops as recently as 1919, and the perennially aggressive frontier tribes.

Though the Afghan invasion of 1919, and the accompanying rising in the Punjab, were easily defeated after a month's fighting, they exercised a profound effect on Indian strategic thinking in the 1920s. Henceforth Indian military planners feared a concerted threat from internal disorder, tribal unrest, and renewed war with an Afghanistan now prompted and supported by the Soviet Union. Without great distortion the whole inter-war period can be viewed in terms of the gradual reconciliation of these discordant views of the Indian Army's priorities—traditional frontier defence or broader imperial commitments.

The issue of India's future contribution to imperial defence was raised as early as 1919 by a committee under the chairmanship of Viscount Esher which took the view that, as a result of the First World War, there had been an eastward shift in the strategic balance of empire. India would have to bear more of the burden of defence in the Middle East and Asia. This suggestion was bitterly opposed by the Government of India and in March 1920 the Indian Legislature voted to repudiate the report. In the immediate post-war period, Indian forces provided the bulk of the enormous garrison in Egypt and the dismembered Ottoman Empire, but the Indian battalions were withdrawn from Istanbul early in 1922 and from Egypt and Palestine in 1923. The last Indian troops left Basra in 1928.

Esher also failed in his attempt to make the armed forces in India less independent of the War Office by giving the CIGS control over the appointments of the Military Secretary at the India Office and the Commander-in-Chief in India. Not surpisingly these proposals were disliked by both the India Office and the Viceroy.[8] While the Government of India never denied that it would have to reinforce British defences overseas in event of a major war, it was not prepared publicly to acknowledge this responsibility in peacetime. Significantly the British Government always bore the cost whenever Indian troops were sent overseas during the inter-war period.

A CID Sub-Committee on Indian Military Requirements in 1922 reached the main conclusion that 'While the whole of the resources of Britain will in the future, as in the past, be available to support the Government of India in maintaining British supremacy in India if it is seriously threatened, it is the recognised duty of India to provide for her own defence against external and internal dangers in all but the gravest emergencies.' The Indian Army, it stressed, could not be treated as if it were absolutely at the disposal of His Majesty's Government for service outside India. India should not be required to maintain large permanent garrisons overseas. Units for this purpose must be surplus to establishment and paid for entirely by Britain. The Committee took a conservative view on troop levels, endorsing the opinion of the Commander-in-Chief, Lord Rawlinson, that there was no case for reducing the number of British or Indian troops. Rawlinson reported that the present total establishment (1921) of 227,901 (compared with 233,507 in 1914) was barely sufficient to maintain internal security. Against external aggression the Indian Army was strong enough only to occupy either Kandahar or Jalalabad: it could not take Kabul without large reinforcements from Britain. The Committee also supported Rawlinson's view that there should be no question of reducing troop numbers in consequence of improvements in arms and equipment. Nor, finally, should the proportion of British to Indian troops be altered. The ratio had moved somewhat in the Indians' favour since the severe 'holding' regulations introduced after the Mutiny and now stood overall at 1 Briton to 2.41 Indians.[9] In sum, this authoritative Committee offered little prospect that India would be prepared to carry out a drastic review of her defence doctrine and forces with a view to playing a larger role in imperial strategy. Lord Rawlinson broached the far-sighted proposal that an Imperial Reserve Force should be created in Asia at Britain's expense, but the War Office, in view of the cuts in expenditure it was then suffering, evinced little interest. Rawlinson's sudden death in March 1925 temporarily ended the discussion.[10]

Before examining the major inquiry carried out by Lord Birkenhead's Committee in 1927 it is necessary to convey some impression of conditions in the British Army in India in the 1920s. In comparison with the fervent discussion of new weapons, equipment, and tactics in Europe as a result of the First World War, the Indian Army struck most newcomers as a depressing backwater still living in the atmosphere of the Victorian era. The First World War had bequeathed little to the Indian Army in the way of either new equipment or ideas. Not merely was money lacking for such essential innovations as lorries and light tanks, but there was a strong tendency among senior officers to insist that new-fangled machines were no substitute for traditionally armed infantry. Thus General Sir Andrew Skeen,* an expert on mountain warfare, laid down during his four years as Chief of the General Staff that no modern instruments of warfare were to be introduced into schemes or manœuvres. The younger officers were, on the whole, greatly interested in new methods, but only a few of their seniors, such as Chetwode, offered any hopes of innovation.

The real curse of Indian service, apart from the climate, was internal security since it entailed cutting up battalions into small detachments with no opportunities for realistic training or access to new equipment. In Ironside's opinion a battalion was almost useless as a military force after three or four years on such tedious duties which, he said, put a premium on turnout, barrack inspections, and cookhouse sanitation. Normally 22 of the British battalions were engaged in internal security duties but by 1938 the number had risen to 28. British tactics in hill fighting, Ironside thought, had not changed 'since the year one': there was a reluctance to admit that a few light tanks or armoured cars supported by aircraft could revolutionize the painfully slow progress of columns which had to throw out pickets to cover almost every yard of movement. In the interval, at the end of the 1920s, between the running down of mule transport cadres and the delayed acquisition of six-wheel lorries, manœuvres were actually carried out with bullock trains reminiscent of the Mutiny days. Ironside found he had to try out the lorries quite separately from the cavalry because if horses were out no one wanted to look at motors. Even then two regimental cavalry officers asked if they need attend since they had remount inspections! There was a rather complacent tendency among senior officers to regard the Army at home as existing solely for the benefit of India. 'The tail', as Ironside put it, 'wants to wag the dog.'[11]

Tank enthusiasts serving in India, like Colonel Karslake and Lieutenant Birks, believed that tanks and armoured cars would be worth their weight in gold in the less hilly southern region of Afghanistan, yet Karslake found military thinking at Quetta backward as regards mechanization and Birks described the subject as 'dead as a dodo': traditional doctrine held that tanks were useless in frontier warfare.[12]

There was, however, a more optimistic view which entertained greater hope for the modernization of the Army in India if only it could be supplied with up-to-date equipment. Thus Martel wrote to Liddell Hart from Roorkee in 1929: 'Army in India in no way the dud show that people at home suggest—a real live show in many ways though short of equipment.' He felt that there was great scope for mechanization generally and thought Chetwode and Ironside were doing splendid work opening people's minds. He urged repeatedly that what India needed was a good light tank for open warfare. Medium and heavy tanks provided a poor gun platform in rough ground and were too cumbersome for rapid flank manœuvres. As an instructor at Quetta Staff College in 1932, Martel and his students worked out a plan for taking Kandahar in two days with light tanks and aircraft: the official plan required 70 days! The force would then advance to attack the Russians on the river Helmand. By 1932 India had received two companies of light tanks and a third was added the following year. These Mark II light tanks proved of great value when first used in India in the Mohmand operations in 1935. Even Martel's enthusiasm was tempered, however, for he ended his letter on the bold Quetta scheme with the remark: 'The Air Force is a good show out here; I wish the Army was as progressive.'[13]

The virtual autonomy enjoyed by the Army in India *vis-à-vis* the War Office and the Army Council was unfortunate because of the encouragement it gave to the preoccupation with frontier warfare. Like the home Army it suffered a succession of financial cuts and squeezes, culminating in 1931 when officers' and other ranks' pay was reduced by 10 per cent. Its administration was inefficient in parts, if not downright corrupt. Though the Army in India did begin to receive motor transport vehicles in the late 1920s and a handful of light tanks in the early 1930s, it could with some justice regard itself as a poor relation in comparison with the Army at home—ill-equipped though that force considered itself to be. The survival of a large number of horsed cavalry regiments in India (five British and 21 Indian as late as 1936) was merely one of the more prominent problems in the growing incompatibility of the two armies as theoretically interchangeable units in the Cardwell system.

Before this and other problems affecting the role of the Army in India came to a head, however, the CID Sub-Committee's inquiry into the defence of India in 1927 provided what was virtually the last airing of the traditional preoccupation with a possible Russian attack through Afghanistan.

Though Lord Birkenhead, the Secretary of State for India and Chairman of the Committee, had expressed the view in 1926 that Soviet Russia constituted a threat to the subcontinent (one Bolshevik slogan was allegedly 'from Dublin to Delhi'), it is doubtful if many people seriously contemplated a Russian invasion of India through Afghanistan. Balfour, for example, made his scepticism plain during the inquiry. The Committee accepted in fact that Russia was not at present bent on aggression and her army was a doubtful instrument for such a difficult operation.[14] Nevertheless she had signed a treaty with Afghanistan in 1921 which she was exploiting to the full, notably by supplying that country with 18 pilots and 11 out of its 13 aircraft. In 1925 there had been a serious diplomatic crisis when Russian forces occupied an island in the river Oxus. More ominously, Russia was spreading anti-British propaganda among Afghanistan's border tribes and was trying to foment Indian opinion against the British. A fundamental assumption throughout the inquiry, rather against contemporary evidence, was that Afghanistan would be friendly to Britain and hostile towards Russia. In these conditions, the Committee reported, it was still in Britain's interests (as it had been before 1907) to oppose overt Soviet aggression across Afghanistan's borders: a Russian crossing of the Oxus or occupation of Herat would constitute a *casus belli*. While the Indian Government and its forces would be responsible for dealing with minor dangers—

localized threats from Afghanistan and the frontier tribes—the forces of the Empire would have to be mobilized if there were a major war with Russia. More significant than this general declaration, however, was the detailed discussion of alternative military plans and forces available.

Sir George Milne, the CIGS, believed that Russia could initially concentrate some 30,000 troops at her two railheads of Termez and Kushk Post and could eventually maintain eight divisions from each. He thought Russian strategy would be to take Kabul and try to forestall the British and Indian forces on the line of the Hindu Kush. It was agreed that at present India could raise a maximum field army of four divisions, four cavalry brigades, and six squadrons of aircraft: an inadequate force to defeat the Russians and one which could not be reinforced from the internal security units. Nothing therefore could prevent the Russians occupying the northern part of Afghanistan; the question was whether they could be driven out with Afghan assistance.

In the light of this information the General Staff in India adopted the cautious view that the best plan would be a defensive on the line of the Helmand. As they pointed out, the role of the Army was to defend the subcontinent against Afghanistan and the frontier tribes and not against Russia. Their forces were too weak to defend against Russian attack and they doubted whether Britain could spare sufficient reinforcements.

The CIGS and CAS, Sir Hugh Trenchard, remarkably in close agreement for once, deplored this defensive strategy and advocated an offensive in both the northern and southern sectors to expel the Russians from Afghanistan. Air forces would play the major role at the outset to check any Russian attempt to 'rush the Hindu Kush' or attack Kabul, and the main offensive would be launched—after about six months—by bombing aircraft supported by a mechanized army. (A leisurely build-up by both sides was expected since they would have to lay railway track and improve roads as they advanced.) Milne, making the bold assumption that the British Government would immediately introduce national service when the crisis began, reckoned that 19 divisions would be available from home after a year. It would, however, take three months to transport the first three divisions and a cavalry division from Britain to India. Questions

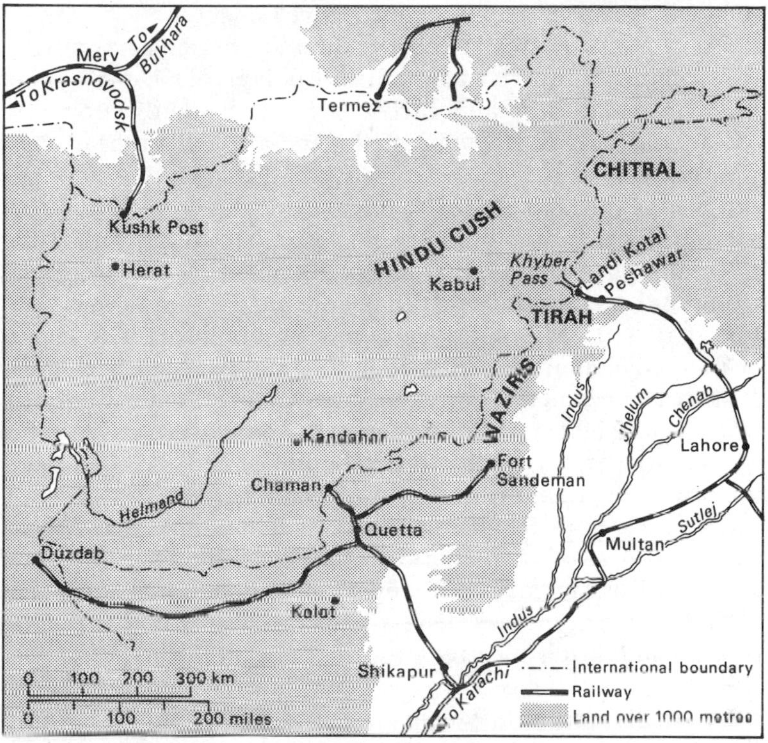

Map 1: Strategic railways on the borders of Afghanistan in the 1920s

from Committee members revealed a staggering gap between exiting forces and this grand conception. Trenchard admitted that the RAF in India was at present utterly unsuited to play the part he had sketched for it, while Milne confesed that the Army in India had not yet even properly studied the use of mechanized forces. Milne seemed to be unduly influenced by the projected mechanization of the British Army 'to which he had just given a great impetus'. He was well aware of the defects of the Army in India: it had no tanks or anti-aircraft artillery and the chronic shortage of transport would delay mobilization even of the Field Army of four divisions. It would, he accepted, take many years to render the Indian Army efficient for a major war yet, as the Committee were authoritatively informed, nearly a third of the total Indian revenue was already being spent on defence and the Indian Government was under increasing political pressure to reduce the defence budget.

Confronted by this sharply conflicting professional advice, the Committee sought the impartial opinions of Field-Marshals Earl Haig and Sir Claud Jacob,* who both stoutly supported Milne and Trenchard against the Indian General Staff. The Committee consequently approved the offensive strategy (known as the 'Blue Plan') while writing euphemistically that the CIGS's plan was by no means complete. It also ruled that for planning purposes it must be assumed that conscription would not be introduced at home during the first year of war, but that 250,000 volunteers could be obtained. The report evaded any definite statement on the vital issue of whether the British Government should make a financial contribution to improve the efficiency of the Army in India, confining itself to the remark that the Indian forces should be prepared adequately for war with Afghanistan and the frontier tribes. The crucial, but scarcely realistic, assumption was maintained that Britain would send reinforcements on a massive scale in the event of war with Russia. An accompanying memorandum by the Chiefs of Staff argued that no subsidiary operations in another theatre of war could bring effective pressure to bear on Russia.[15]

The report of the Birkenhead Committee, with its traditional preoccupation with the defence of the north-west frontier against Russia and its assumption that the whole of Britain's Regular and Territorial armies would be availble if there were a major war with the Soviet Union over Afghanistan, was rapidly overtaken by events. On the one hand the despotic reformer the Amir Amanullah, who was suspected of leaning too heavily on Soviet aid, was overthrown in 1928 and replaced by the more conservative and pro-British Nadir Shah. In 1931 the Indian General Staff abandoned the ambitious Blue Plan regarding operations against Afghanistan bequeathed by the Birkenhead Committee, and replaced it with a more modest 'Pink Plan'. This concentrated many more troops on the lines of communication and renounced a possible advance to Kabul. Also, another difference to the Blue Plan, offensive operations would take place initially either along the northern line (towards Jalalabad) or the southern line (towards Kandahar), but not both—due mainly to the lack of sufficient motor transport. By the mid-1930s, as threats from other directions became more ominous, both the Foreign Office and the Chiefs of Staff agreed that Afghanistan was reasonably secure; they felt that Russia would probably seek to increase her influence in the region by subversion and propaganda rather than by armed force. On the other hand, India's progress towards self-government, accompanied by communal disturbances and diminishing revenues, meant that a fundamental reappraisal of the size and cost of the British garrison in India could no longer be avoided. These considerations together led to renewed attention to the wider issue of India's potential contribution to Imperial defence.[16]

Consequently in the early 1930s, the India Office found itself under pressure from various directions. The War Office argued that India should pay more for its British troops by covering the cost of their training in Britain and even part of the cost of the British Army Reserve since it might be used on India's behalf. By contrast between 1925 and 1934 Indian expenditure on defence fell steadily and so compelled cuts in establishments and equipment. (The British garrison for example, was reduced from 57,080 in 1925 to 51,669 in 1930.) There was in fact a strong case for reducing the British garrison in India as the policy of Indianization of units (specifically of the 4th Division) began to take effect, because the proportion of British troops had always been kept artificially high since the Mutiny by the principle of 'holding'. Yet the Commander-in-Chief in India vehemently opposed any reductions, arguing that the present garrison was fully stretched dealing with Congress disorders and the disturbances in Kashmir, Bengal, and Burma. The Army in India refused to believe that substitution of air forces was the answer and in any case the RAF could not spare additional squadrons.[17]

While accepting the Commander-in-Chief's advice that any reductions would increase the risk of disorder, the Government of India noted that the decline of income due to falling revenues and devolution of resources to provincial governments would compel further reductions unless Britain could contribute financially to the defence of India. The Indian middle and lower classes were becoming dangerously restive because they bore a painfully heavy burden of taxation but could see only 'an extremely meagre standard of expenditure on beneficent activities'. It must be said that Indian politicians had some justification for their hostility towards the General Staff: they were not even informed, much less consulted, about their country's military requirements.[18]

In December 1933 the British Government took the momentous decision to make an annual contribution of £1.5 million to Indian defence. A month later Lord Hailsham, Secretary of State for War, in effect asked the India Office for a *quid pro quo* in the form of a division in India earmarked as an Imperial reserve. Though the Commander-in-Chief in India and the Viceroy were opposed, Sir Samuel Hoare at the India Office reluctantly accepted Hailsham's suggestion. By 1937 both the Commander-in-Chief and Viceroy had become sympathetic towards the idea of creating an Imperial reserve in India; the Viceroy (Lord Linlithgow) in particular was sensitive to the growing Japanese threat. But Indian consent depended on finance: as the Viceroy put it bluntly, 'You have the money—we have the men.'

Meanwhile in 1936 Hailsham's successor, Duff Cooper, accepting that India was advancing on the road to self-government, abolished the 'holding' policy and cut the Indian establishment by 9,000 British troops.[19] Thus when Hore-Belisha entered the War Office in May 1937 the situation was ripe for a radical reappraisal of Indian defence organization and strategy. The British Government had at least accepted a token financial commitment to maintain British forces in India, while on her side the Government of India was at last moving towards acceptance of the view that Indian defence should be considered in the broader context of Imperial strategic requirements.

Hore-Belisha's determination to carry through a radical reorganization of the British Army at home immediately involved him with the complexities of the Cardwell system and the imperative need to reduce the garrison in India. He soon encountered the obstinate opposition of the CIGS, Deverell, who on the basis of his twelve years in India declared that no reductions were possible. When invited to submit an analysis, Deverell simply presented an old paper, drawn up by Sir Philip Chetwode the C.-in-C. in India, in favour of maintaining the traditional garrison and a covering note to say that he could not better Chetwode's arguments. Deverell's inflexibility undoubtedly contributed to Hore-Belisha's decision that he must be removed from office. Significantly, among the stumbling blocks to Army reorganization which the War Minister listed in a note to the Prime Minister on 1 November was 'The elimination of the India obsession, which refuses to allow objective examination of the proper disposition and organisation of our Imperial Forces, and assumes that the India commitment is fixed for all time on unchanging traditions and that it must govern the pace and the capacity of development of the rest of the Army.'[20]

Meanwhile Hore-Belisha's confidence that the Cardwell system could be changed was fortified by the memoranda which Liddell Hart prepared for him during the summer of 1937 and which considered Indian defence in the light of the numerous threats facing Britain and her Empire. Liddell Hart discounted the possibility of a Russian invasion of Afghanistan, and rode his hobby horse to the effect that improved means of mobility in the form of railways, motor transport, and air transport would enable fewer troops to carry out internal security duties more effectively. 'A small number of troops who arrive on the scene when the first sparks are struck may avert a conflagration which a much larger number, arriving later, may hardly be able to extinguish'. He did not only advocate a reduction of the British garrison of 57,000 but stressed that such a large commitment was only justified if a considerable part of it could be treated as an Imperial strategic reserve. This might consist of one armoured mobile division and two infantry divisions.[21]

Unfortunately for Hore-Belisha, the War Office Committee which he set up under the Financial Secretary, Sir Victor Warrender, proved an extremely damp squib.[22] Judging by its report, the Committee, which was set up on 8 June 1937 and reported on 8 August, confined itself to a study of the 'nuts and bolts' of the Cardwell system without challenging its continuing viability or taking account of the ominous atmosphere of the day and the possibility that the Army might soon in a state of utter unpreparedness be precipitated into a major war. It was characteristic of the Committee's conservatism that Liddell Hart's memorandum was mentioned but largely discounted on the grounds that he had not discussed terms of enlistment, the period of service overseas, or minor details of organization on which the whole system would depend. It was not impressed by his suggestion that the size of infantry battalions might be reduced and men replaced by machines: men, it affirmed, were still more valuable than machines in countries such as India and Palestine. The aversion to radical change was also apparent in its comment on Liddell Hart's proposal that specialized divisions should be organized for specialized warfare. In the Committee's opinion it would not lead to economy and was unsound strategically. With a medium-term enlistment, the Committee reported optimistically, there would be no need for specialist training because there was ample time for the average man in the ranks to learn any form of warfare which might be required. It had not, the Committee protested, approached the problem 'in a spirit of hide-bound prejudice', but none of the alternative schemes it had examined seemed more likely to meet Britain's complex needs than the Cardwell system.[23] 'Indeed', the report concluded, '. . . short of the perfect scheme, which hitherto has failed to emerge, the Cardwell system, despite its weaknesses, still has much to commend it, and it is questionable whether we should not be in a worse plight than we are today were we working under any of the alternative systems which we have had under review.' The main recommendations were that more units of Indian troops should be raised for garrison duty in India and the Empire; that special units should be formed at home to meet abnormal situations overseas; and that the terms of service should be modified in the hope of attracting more recruits. It failed to confront the obvious, albeit thorny problem, of recommending a drastic reduction of the 45 British infantry battalions in India and Burma. Nor did it explain how the Army at home could be mechanized yet remain interchangeable with units of an un-mechanized Army in India.

Shortly after the Warrender Committee reported, Hobart informed Liddell Hart that his paper on Army reorganization had been bitterly resented in the War Office 'as having come from outside and being thrust on them by the Secretary of State'. Several of Liddell Hart's contacts, such as Haining,* the DMO, were outraged at his interference. Hobart also told Liddell Hart that Burnett-Stuart had done their prospects of reform no good by reassuring Hore-Belisha that the Cardwell system was basically all right, though a bit too rigid. Having shot this bolt in vain the War Minister was obliged to defer his second attempt at radical reorganization until he had purged the Army Council. As Director of Military Training, Hobart found his work blocked at every turn by the Cardwell system and India's Mutiny mentality i.e. insistence on maintaining the garrison strength of eighty years ago. He felt that only a really big man would be prepared to insist on these two being altered and he would need a lot of drive and a new Adjutant-General (someone other than Knox) to get the War Office to alter the system. Hore-Belisha soon found that Knox's successor, Liddell, was not the man for this tough assignment and in 1938 he was again rather pathetically asking Liddell Hart's advice on a suitable Adjutant-General to change the Cardwell system.[24]

The Government's adoption of a policy of limited liability in December 1937 gave Hore-Belisha additional leverage because he was able to convince his colleagues that it was impossible to reorganize the Army at home for its new role without changing the organization and size of the forces in India. Even so, as the Liddell Hart *Memoirs* and Pownall diaries make clear—from opposite sides of the fence—he had to struggle hard through January and early February 1938 to get the General Staff to agree to a sufficiently strong memorandum. Pownall, though agreeing that Britain was overinsured in India, got the impression that Hore-Belisha did not realize that the Army there was not his responsibility.[25] Liddell Hart, while repeating his general arguments of the previous year, now stated bluntly:

> India's own needs for defence and internal security could be met by nineteen battalions out of the present forty-three. The remaining twenty-four are locked up capital unless they can be used to reinforce the Middle and Far East in emergency. Indeed, so long as the Cardwell system is maintained they are worse than superfluous, since not only are they preserved in a form that does not meet the conditions of modern war, but a similar number of units of the same type have to be maintained at home.[26]

Hore-Belisha hammered home two related points in his forceful memorandum dated 10 February 1938. First, the Government of India had accepted certain commitments to dispatch forces overseas to discharge Imperial tasks (including Egypt, Aden, Singapore, the Anglo-Iranian oilfields, and the possible reinforcement of Hong Kong and Burma): it was time to take a definite decision to create an Imperial strategic reserve and to locate part of it east of the Mediterranean basin (i.e. in India).

Secondly, the Army in India must be reorganized and modernized, including a reduction of establishments.[27] In March 1938 the CID approved Hore-Belisha's proposals in principle and set up an interdepartmental committee, including representatives of the Air Ministry and the Indian General Staff, to consider matters of issue between the War Office and the India Office. Its chairman was the recently appointed DMO and I, Major-General H. R. Pownall.

Pownall's diary entries reveal that, apart from the air aspect, the British and Indian General Staffs found themselves in close accord. All were agreed that the Indian Army must be modernized with one division definitely held as a general strategic reserve for use anywhere in the Empire—most probably at Singapore or in the Middle East. India was prepared to give up four British battalions which would be used to create a Middle East reserve in Palestine (three battalions) and bring Malta up to its full quota (one battalion). But Pownall realized from the start that everything would hinge on finance since the Indian delegation declared they had nothing extra to spare while home defence expenditure had already topped its ceiling of £1,570 million.

Archibald Rowlands,* financial adviser to the Defence Department in India and a member of the Indian delegation, privately informed Liddell Hart that the General Staff in India would take a reasonable attitude towards withdrawal of some units and modernization of others. Thus it was generally admitted that 18 cavalry regiments were superfluous and two were to be converted to light tanks. India was also willing to replace animal transport by trucks, keeping mules only for the frontier. Rowlands took the view that if the British Government met the cost of general modernization, Indian politicians would not seriously resist the use of part of the forces for Imperial purposes. Shortly before returning to India in August, Rowlands emphasized that finance was the vital consideration: 'India, with a total central revenue of only £65 million, just cannot find the capital for any large scheme of conversion of troops into armoured mobile units.' Contrary to the Indian delegation's expectations the British Government showed a marked reluctance to put up the money. Nevertheless, Rowlands agreed with Liddell Hart that there was scope for a moderate reorganization.

He did not believe that the Cardwell system should be allowed to constitute a fatal obstacle to the creation of mechanized battalions at home which could not be balanced by a similar number in India.[28]

The Air Ministry representative, Group Captain Slessor, felt that the Indian delegation was asking far too much in expecting Britain to pay for the modernization of both the Covering Troops and the Field Army without giving a larger role to air power. They offered no proposal to reduce the staggering disparity between expenditure on land forces (approximately 93 per cent of the Indian defence budget) against only 7 per cent for the air force. Although air forces were earmarked to play a major role in a 'minor war' against Afghanistan, there was not a single fighter plane in India and only one battery of AA guns; yet the mechanization programme included 22 cavalry regiments and 32 artillery batteries. As Slessor recalled in his memoirs: 'We were quite unready to admit that India had the sovereign right to make as big a mess as she chose of the employment of the R.A.F. in India . . . especially when she was now turning to us for additional help.'[29]

The Pownall Committee's report argued that, whereas the threat to India's north-west frontier had diminished, other potential dangers to Britain and her Empire were increasing, and might lead to a crisis in which Britain would simply be unable to meet all the numerous calls on her armed services and resources. India must recognize that she had a wider role to play in Imperial defence, particularly in the Middle East and at Singapore while, conversely, the report hinted without going into detail, India required financial assistance to modernize her forces.

The Pownall Committee's conclusions may be summarized as:

1. India should reduce her establishment by four British battalions, to be used elsewhere by the War Office.
2. She should provide an Imperial reserve of one division located in India.
3. An increase of four RAF squadrons and one and a half Bomber Flights was necessary if India was to contribute to the air defence of the Middle and Far East. The Air Force in India should be modernized.

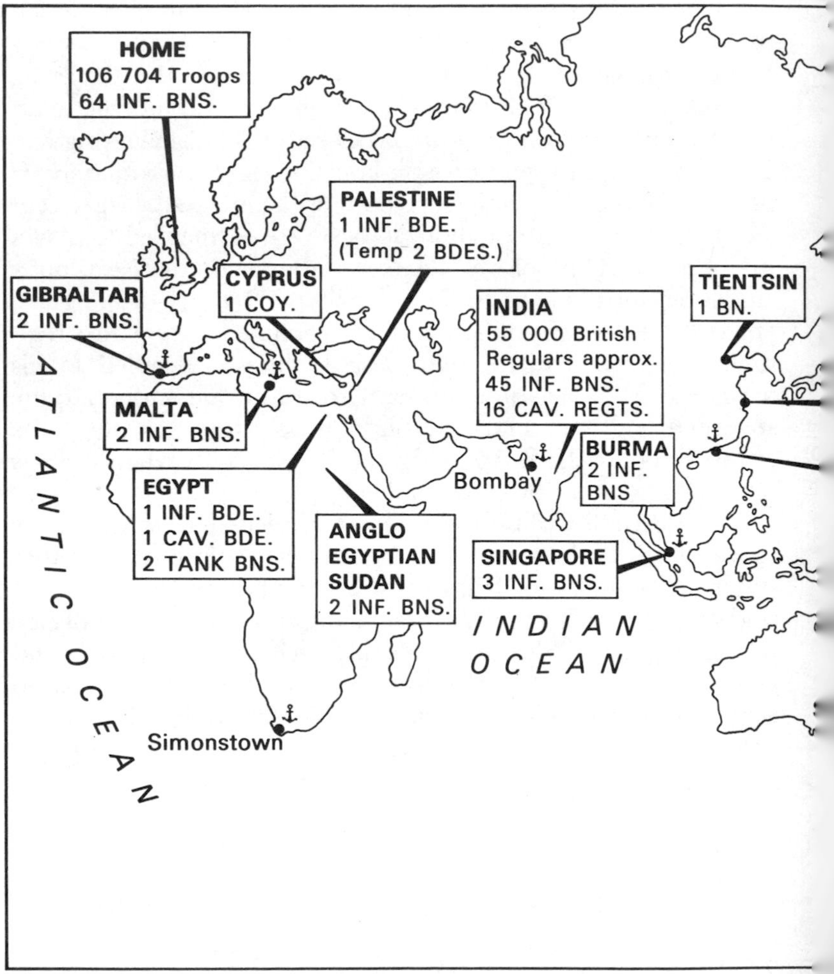

Map 2: Distribution of British Troops, 1 January 1938
Source: W033/1502, Memorandum by Secretary of State for War, 10 February 1938

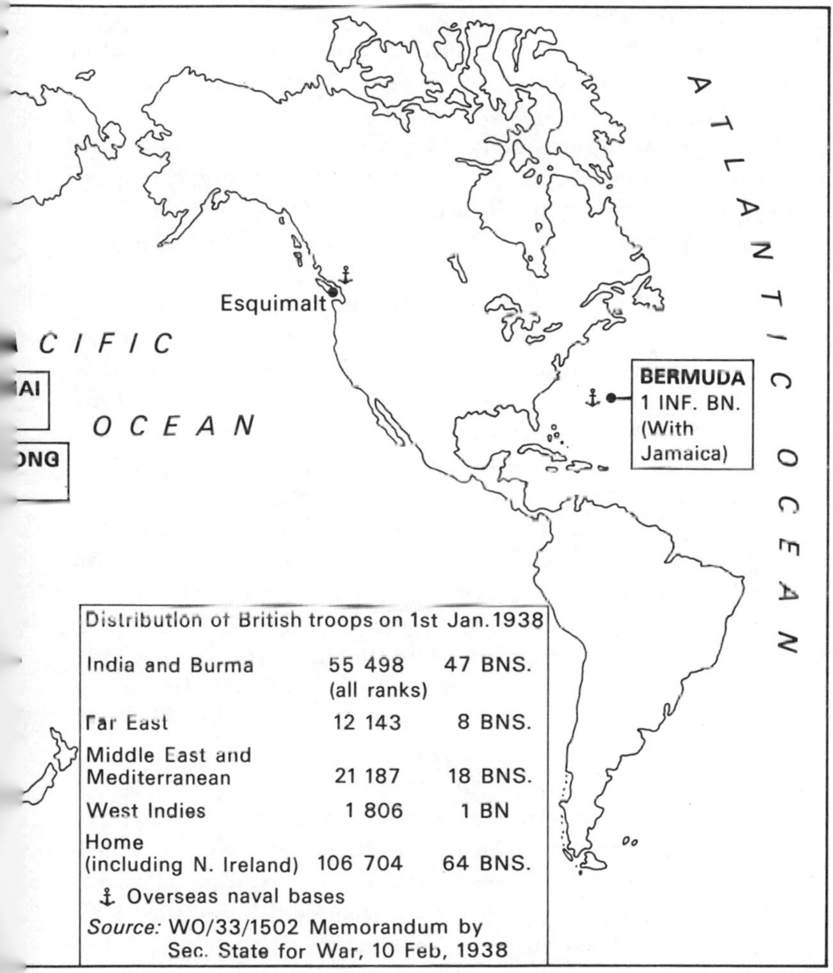
Esquimalt
CIFIC
AI
OCEAN
ONG
ATLANTIC OCEAN
BERMUDA
1 INF. BN.
(With
Jamaica)
Distribution of British troops on 1st Jan. 1938
India and Burma 55 498 (all ranks) 47 BNS.
Far East 12 143 8 BNS.
Middle East and Mediterranean 21 187 18 BNS.
West Indies 1 806 1 BN
Home (including N. Ireland) 106 704 64 BNS.
⚓ Overseas naval bases
Source: WO/33/1502 Memorandum by Sec. State for War, 10 Feb, 1938

4. The Imperial reserve division should be completely modernized and the remainder of the Army in India modernized on a lower scale.
5. Indian defence policy should be more closely coordinated with Britain's.[30]

Almost simultaneously an unofficial Indian military committee on modernization, inspired by General Auchinleck,* was making similar proposals and was urging in particular that India should develop her capacity to manufacture munitions and weapons, and that the forces should be thoroughly reorganized to fulfil five functions: frontier defence, anti-aircraft and coast defence, external defence, internal security, and a general purpose reserve.[31]

The Chiefs of Staff's discussion of the Pownall report, which they substantially approved, brought out additional misgivings to those of Slessor about the Indian Army's commitment to modernization of the forces there. When, for example, Lord Gort, the CIGS, mentioned that the British Army at home would soon have 25-pounder guns whereas the Indian Army still had 18 pounders, Sir Ivo Vesey* (CGS in India) admitted that stocks of ordnance and engineer stores were inadequate even for war with Afghanistan. Even more revealing, when the CAS, Sir Cyril Newall,* asked why it was necessary to keep 16 horsed cavalry regiments in India costing more than the whole of the air forces there, Vesey replied that at least nine should be retained and it would be costly to mechanize the other seven. Sir Robert Cassels,* the C.-in-C. in India (described by Rowlands as having a simple mind but quite a reasonable man apart from his passion for cavalry), was averse to any 'snap' decision on the reduction of cavalry regiments. In general Vesey was reluctant to admit that India could assist modernization by abolishing unnecessary units. For example, Pownall told the COS that, in addition to the four British battalions, his Committee had recommended the withdrawal of two Field Artillery Brigades but that India was unwilling to release them. On the air side the COS were informed by the Air Officer Commanding-in-Chief in India that India did not consider she needed any further aircraft in the next five years because bombers would be employed in fighters' roles. On the all-important question of costs, Vesey warned that Indian opinion would resent any increase in the military budget, but he painted a rosy picture of what India could do if Britain made available £30 million and met recurring costs of £4½ million per annum which, he pointed out, was less than two per cent of Britain's projected rearmament programme. The COS left this question to the Cabinet. In their accompanying comments on the Pownall report, they emphasized that they had not been convinced of India's need to retain 16 cavalry regiments and eight brigades of Field Artillery. Neither the Army nor the Air Force in India were at present in any shape to discharge their Imperial commitments. Early action was essential to place India's defence organization on a more up-to-date footing. But, they insisted, the situation in India should not be restored at the expense of Britain's own rearmament programme.[32]

In protracted ministerial discussions during the summer of 1938 the British Government displayed a predictable reluctance to foot the bill for modernizing the Army and Air Force in India.[33] When confronted, however, with the Indian Government's attitude of 'no money then no Indian forces for Imperial purposes', it was obliged to make concessions. The Chancellor of the Exchequer agreed to increase the annual subsidy from £1½ million to £2 million and to contribute £5 million towards the cost of modernizing the Imperial reserve division. The much larger question of the cost of general modernization was deferred pending the exhaustive report of a committee under the chairmanship of Lord Chatfield, set up in the late summer of 1938.[34]

After familiarizing itself with all aspects of the defence of the subcontinent, the Chatfield Committee sailed for India at the end of October and spent the next three months based in Delhi but visiting the frontier and inspecting factories and installations. It also heard the evidence of a great number of senior officers, government officials, and Indian politicians.[35] The Committee presented its report in February 1939 but it was not taken by the Cabinet until June by which time impending war in Europe overshadowed even the urgent problems of Indian military reorganization.

The Chatfield Committee's report underlined the main conclusion of the Pownall Sub-Committee: the Russian threat to Afghanistan had waned and the menace to India now came from Italy and Japan. In an understatement it remarked that Britain could do less to defend India than previously. Consequently, although the north-west frontier could not be neglected —40,000 regular troops had been engaged in operations in Waziristan as recently as 1937—India should take a larger share in the protection of her sea communications in Eastern waters and the strategic points vital to her security. In effect the Committee refused to accept that there was any distinction between Indian and Imperial interests in defence—a bold assumption in view of India's progress towards self-government. Its chief conclusion was:

> The general principle that we would put forward . . . is that the forces maintained in India should be adequate not merely for the narrower purposes of local defence, but also to assist in ensuring her security against the external threats that we have described; and further, that India should acknowledge that her responsibility cannot in her own interests be safely limited to the defence of her land frontiers and coasts.

The report recommended that the whole Army in India must be modernized though not necessarily all to the same high standard as the Imperial reserve forces. To assist modernization the traditional threefold division of the Army into Field Force (four divisions and four cavalry brigades), Covering Force (the equivalent of three divisions on the frontier), and Internal Security Troops (approximately 43 infantry battalions and seven cavalry regiments) should be abolished. The new organization should comprise Frontier Defence troops, Internal Security forces, Coastal Defence, External Defence, and a General Reserve. The greatest innovation lay in the last of these new groups: it would include a 'highly mobile striking force' composed of cavalry light tanks, cavalry motor units, infantry, and artillery and be capable of launching a rapid counter-offensive against the Afghan army. With the North West Frontier guarded by a mechanized force, such as Milne had dreamed of in 1927, more units could be freed for external defence. The External Defence troops should be organized in brigades as it was unlikely that they would need to fight as a division.

Now at last the Committee had recommended the kind of large-scale reductions which Hore-Belisha and the Pownall Committee had pressed for in vain: one cavalry regiment and six infantry battalions should be brought home, and three Indian cavalry regiments, four companies of sappers and miners, and 14 Indian infantry battalions should be disbanded. These disbandments should be spread over four years to reduce the effects of unemployment. On the all-important financial aspect, the Committee recommended that while the Government of India should bear ordinary maintenance costs and, perhaps, the additional costs of External Defence troops when used overseas, Britain should bear the bulk of the initial modernization costs which it estimated at £34 million to be spread over five years.[36]

Ironically, by the time the COS considered the Chatfield report on 12 May 1939 a European war seemed so likely that the Committee's far-reaching recommendations for the withdrawal or disbandment of units from India appeared risky. The COS consequently recommended that no unit should actually be disbanded without further consideration. They added that two British battalions from India and one from Hong Kong were urgently needed in the Mediterranean to restore the balance of the Cardwell system which had been badly disorganized by the Palestine rebellion. One battalion formerly on the Indian establishment was henceforth to be stationed permanently at Aden, and India was to be asked to supply an additional battalion for the reinforcement of Singapore. The COS further recommended that priority for the £5 million allocated by the British Government for modernizing of the Army in India should be given to the external defence forces.[37]

In June 1939 the Cabinet agreed that Britain must shoulder the bulk of the financial burden of £34 million recommended by the Chatfield Committee: three-quarters should be made available as a grant and the remaining quarter as a loan free of interest for five years. Two major advantages were expected to accrue for Imperial defence as a whole: a considerable reservoir of trained troops organized in brigades, and a new manufacturing capacity for armaments and munitions east of Suez.[38]

Clearly these decisions came too late for any real progress in the modernization of the Army in India to be made before the outbreak of the Second World War. Indeed it was weaker and less prepared for war in 1939 than in 1914 with a total of 205,038 British and Indian troops as compared with 269,954 in 1914. As for up-to-date equipment, as late as February 1939 there was still only one anti-aircraft battery in the whole of India. The Indian forces fell far short of being able to fulfil the internal and external roles envisaged for them by the Chatfield Committee. They could, however, be employed—as they had for the past hundred years—as 'the milch cow of the Empire' as Chetwode put it in 1935. Since it had become increasingly doubtful whether the Royal Navy would be present in force to protect troop transports in Eastern waters after the outbreak of war in Europe, it was prudently decided to dispatch reinforcements overseas from India before the Empire found itself at war with Japan or Italy. Accordingly, between July and September 1939, these reinforcements sailed from India: one British and two Indian battalions with ancillary troops to Egypt; one Indian battalion with a detachment of anti-aircraft guns to Aden; one British and two Indian battalions to Singapore; and one battery of mountain artillery to East Africa.[39]

On the political side the advent of war transformed the situation from both the British and Indian viewpoints. In 1940 the British Government undertook to pay virtually the whole cost of India's contribution to the war, thus going far beyond what the Government of India had asked for in the inter-war period. Indian opposition to the use of Indian forces for Imperial purposes also predictably diminished after the outbreak of war, though the course of the war itself contributed enormously to the momentum of nationalist opposition to British rule.

This chapter has attempted to explain the connection between the Cardwell system and the defence of India. Most military reformers regarded the former as an obstacle since it complicated the process of mechanization; militated against the creation of an Expeditionary Force in peacetime; and prevented a radical redistribution of imperial garrisons in response to changing strategic conditions. India, which its 45 British infantry battalions and five cavalry regiments, clearly lay at the heart of the problem; indeed some Indian authorities believed the provision of their garrison to be the whole purpose of the Cardwell system. Only a drastic reduction of British units in India, such as was recommended by the Chatfield Committee, could tip the balance in favour of units at home. Yet the British forces in India were not paid for by Britain and were not under the control of the

War Office or the Army Council. Given the unending duty of frontier policing, escalating periodically into outright warfare (as in the operations in Waziristan against the Fakir of Ipi in 1937), the growing problem of inter-communal violence, and the rise of nationalist disorders, it was understandable that the Government of India should tend to regard the internal responsibilities of its forces as all-important and should oppose any weakening of the 'holding' principle or the withdrawal of British units. On the other hand, it may fairly be argued that the British military authorities in India were excessively pre-occupied with Afghanistan and the Russian presence on its further borders, that they were overly suspicious of and luke-warm towards the Indianization of units, and were slow to see that to some extent machines (particularly aircraft and armoured cars) could be substituted for troops. With the notable exception of Lord Rawlinson, senior soldiers in India were also slow to realize that not only for Britain's sake but in India's own interests, part of her large garrison must be earmarked for an overseas role in view of the growing Japanese and Italian threats to the Far East and Mediterranean respectively.

It is no exaggeration to say that the financial aspect dominated the discussion of these interrelated problems throughout the inter-war period. Since, until 1933, the British garrison in India was maintained entirely by Indian taxes, it was very reasonable for the Government of India to argue that they must be employed primarily for purposes of internal security. This attitude was strengthened, in a period of diminishing revenues and devolution to provisional legislatures, by Indian demands that a larger slice of the defence budget be diverted to social purposes. The British Government gradually came to accept that if it wanted an imperial strategic reserve in India it must be prepared to pay for it. But this raised the much larger issue of who would finance the modernization of all the forces in India, including the small air force and navy. Until the very end of the 1930s it seemed inconceivable that in view of its limited defence budget and fiercely competing priorities in home defence, the British Government would foot the bill, but on the eve of the Second World War it agreed to do so. As a corollary, following the recommendations of the Pownall and Chatfield Committees endorsed by the Chiefs of Staff, Indian defence matters were to be more closely co-ordinated and controlled from Whitehall than ever before. While this was an entirely logical development in the light of the three-pronged threats to the British Empire in Europe, the Mediterranean, and the Far East, it was nevertheless somewhat ironic that India should be belatedly drawn into the framework of Imperial defence just when active pressure for the British to quit India was becoming irresistible. However shakily and anachronistically, the Cardwell system also survived until the rapid post-war disintegration of the Empire it had been created to garrison.

CHAPTER 5

Mechanization: the first phase, 1918–1932

Mechanization has rightly been regarded by military historians as the most important criterion for assessing the British Army's adaptability and openness to new ideas during the inter-war period. Unfortunately this complex issue has often been treated too narrowly and too much from the standpoint of the leading proponents of tanks and armoured warfare, Fuller and Liddell Hart the most notable among them.[1] Although their voluminous writings provide compelling evidence of how things appeared to the progressive pro-mechanization school, they do not in general adequately display the full range of problems—such as financial restraints and uncertainty about the Army's role—which handicapped the political and military authorities at the War Office. Thus the popular notion of a handful of military radicals obstructed by a phalanx of reactionary Blimps has become deeply rooted, as is the corollary notion that the former group's ideas about *blitzkrieg* were avidly adopted by Germany in the 1930s with disastrous results for the Allies in 1939–1940. Although there is enough truth in this caricature to make it plausible, the actual explanation of Britain's failure to retain her lead in the 1930s as the pioneer of mechanized forces must be seen in a wider context that embraces domestic politics and the international strategic situation. Access to the official records and to a wide range of private papers for the inter-war period now permit scholars to reappraise the struggle for mechanization from a less committed standpoint than that occupied by its leading advocates.[2]

By the end of the First World War the tank had proved its value, in battles like Cambrai (November 1917) and Amiens

(August 1918), as the mobile answer to static defences based on successive lines of trenches protected by dense barbed wire entanglements and covered by machine guns. A few visionaries, Colonels E. D. (later Sir Ernest) Swinton and J. F. C. Fuller in particular, saw independent fast-moving tank formations as the means to restore strategic mobility and gain decisive results through deep thrusts into the enemy's rear areas, but the war ended before such revolutionary prospects—embodied in Fuller's 'Plan 1919'—could be put to the test.

In reality most of the heavy tanks in existence at the end of the war were 'military mastodons', too cumbersome, slow, and vulnerable for the exciting operations sketched by Fuller. As Colonel Martel, himself an enthusiastic supporter of tanks, was later to point out, the anti-tank gunner enjoyed a great advantage in 1918, since the tank commander rarely realized his danger until the gun had fired the first and often fatal shot. According to Martel tank casualties rose as high as 50 per cent in battles towards the end of the war. Even concentrated machine-gun fire could put them out of action. Fuller's 'Plan 1919' envisaged really fast tanks which would be employed independently to pass through the enemy's lines and attack his headquarters and communications. Thus, while the heavy tanks pummeled the enemy's body in frontal attacks, the fast tanks would drive a pin straight into his brain. The general specification for this fast tank, known as the Medium D, was prepared in July 1918. It was to be capable of crossing any natural obstacle likely to be met; to weigh not more than 20 tons; to travel at 20 m.p.h. on the level and to carry enough oil and petrol for a circuit of 200 miles. Some models would be armed with a machine gun and others with a 6-pounder gun. Not least significant in this remarkable project, Lt.-Col. Philip Johnson, a member of the Chief Mechanical Engineer's staff at Tank Corps Headquarters, was set to study the possibility of giving the Medium D the ability to float and swim across rivers or water obstacles. The first of three models actually produced before the Armistice attained a speed of 28 m.p.h. on good level going, and repeatedly swam across the river Stour near Christchurch; but, as Martel admits, there were radical troubles: 'we had tried to aim at too high a specification in one step'. The ending of the war not only checked research on this revolutionary model but also cast into limbo, at least as far as official doctrine was concerned, the strategic role for which it was being developed.[3]

In the inevitable run-down of the Army immediately after the end of the war each branch naturally sought to emphasize its successes and minimize its failures so as to ensure for itself the largest possible role in the future. The cavalry, which appeared most vulnerable to the charge of obsolescence, argued that the Western Front was an aberration and stressed its impressive achievements under Allenby in the open warfare in Palestine culminating in the capture of Damascus. Though the Tank Corps was open to the argument that it was the product of the unexpected trench stalemate, it had better reason than the cavalry to be enthusiastic about its future potential. Between 1916 and 1918 its rise had been dramatic: 'From a figment of the imagination, it had become a force of twenty battalions and twelve armoured car companies.' Nevertheless, its unique contribution tended to be muffled in the aftermath of war by the orthodox catchphrase that success was due to 'the co-operation of all arms'. So far from being a forward-looking doctrine, this argument was really a conservative smokescreen intended to preserve the precedence of the traditional arms. In short, tanks were regarded as an auxiliary to the infantry. Even Major-General Elles, Commander of the Tank Corps, surprisingly subscribed to this orthodoxy. Thus in practice the 'co-operation of all arms' implied adjusting the speed of all supporting arms to the pace of the infantry rather than accelerating the infantry's speed of movement to that of the tank. This was not unreasonable as long as tanks could move only four or five miles an hour and were subject to numerous mechanical faults; but by the summer of 1918 the Medium C (or Whippet) with a speed of 8 to 12 m.p.h. was in action and the much faster Medium D was on the horizon.[4]

The tendency to see the tank merely as a temporary expedient to solve a particular problem of trench deadlock was evident in the immediate post-war years among senior officers who had not witnessed the new arm's achievement at first hand. Sir Louis Jackson, a distinguished sapper general, gave this view respectability in a lecture on the 'Possibilities of the Next War' at the RUSI in November 1919: 'The tank proper was a freak.

The circumstances which called it into existence were exceptional and not likely to recur. If they do, they can be dealt with by other means.' Though many cavalry officers naturally regarded the tank with apprehension and some with overt hostility as a dangerous rival, few went so far as General Sir R. G. Egerton (Commander of III Indian Army Corps in Mesopotamia in 1918), whose admiration for the horse bordered on the mystical:

if we turn to the introduction of mechanical transport into the Army to replace the horse, and look into the faces of individuals who deal with the horse and the faces of men who deal with the machine, you will see in the latter what, I might almost call a lack of intelligence! Many of us remember the old hansom cab driver and the bus driver, cheery men who seemed to enjoy driving their horses. Now, what you see is a hunched-backed man leaning over a wheel looking like Cerberus. I consider that the horse has a humanising effect on men, and the longer we can keep horses for artillery and for cavalry the better it will be for the Army, because thereby you keep up the high standard of intelligence in the man from his association with the horse.[5]

It needs to be stressed, however, that the views of the vast majority of officers who thought seriously about the likely nature of future war fell well short of Fuller's visionary radicalism on the one hand and Egerton's horsy antedeluvianism on the other. Indeed, a glance at such professional periodicals as the *RUSI Journal* and the *Army Quarterly* in the 1920s will reveal a wide spectrum of views with a concentration on the middle ground of cautious progressiveness. We may delineate at least five categories of attitudes on mechanization, excluding those —probably many—who simply did not think seriously about their profession but regarded the Army merely as a pleasant and socially acceptable way of passing a few years.[6]

First were the revolutionaries who believed with Fuller that the tank was an invention of overwhelming importance which would dominate future land warfare. The older arms, if not actually superseded by it, would become its auxiliaries. These views were naturally congenial to a small band of progressive officers most of whom became members of the Royal Tank Corps, the most influential being Lt.-Col. Charles Broad, Major Frederick 'Tim' Pile, and Major Percy 'Hobo' Hobart. Although these and a few less well-known officers shared a similar confidence in the future of the tank, they did not necessarily hold identical views on every aspect of organization and tactics.

The second category may be styled reformers; they supported a thorough revision of tactical doctrine but neither their ends nor their means were as drastic as Fuller's. Notable in this group were Colonel George Lindsay who commanded the armoured car units in Mesopotamia after the First World War and later became Inspector, Royal Tank Corps; Colonel Henry Karslake, a gunner who became a Brigadier-General in the Tank Corps in 1918; Major B. C. Dening, a regular contributor to the military journals; and Major Giffard Martel who remained in the Royal Engineers and in 1925 built his own one-man 'tankette'. What characterized such officers, in Dr Winton's words, was the combination of 'a strong desire for basic change with a sense of tactical balance and a realisation of the constraints imposed by circumstances'.

The third, and very large, group may be termed progressives. These were thoughtful officers who appreciated the tactical shortcomings revealed in the First World War but were largely content to work for improvement in their own arms or areas of experience. They included a few really senior commanders of First World War vintage such as Generals Rawlinson, Milne, and Chetwode, and some relatively senior officers such as Burnett-Stuart, Ironside, and Harington. The majority, however, were Lieutenant-Colonels and Majors in 1918 who rose to high command in the later 1930s and in the Second World War. They included Wavell, Montgomery, Gort, Alan Brooke, Dill, Auchinleck, Alexander, and Slim. Most of these officers remained sceptical about the ideas of the mechanized warfare advocates until at least the later 1920s, and while some of them, like Burnett-Stuart, Ironside, and Wavell, became converts to mechanization they never shared the enthusiasm of Fuller, Pile, or Hobart.

The fourth category, who may be termed conservatives, were not opposed to mechanization *per se* but disapproved of the concept of independent armoured formations. They emphasized the tank's vulnerability to artillery fire, its logistical and mechanical limitations, and the threat it posed to orthodox tactical doctrine. On the other hand they welcomed tanks as infantry-support weapons and accepted, with varying degrees of enthusiasm, that the transport of the traditional arms should be gradually mechanized. The rudimentary level of mechanization in the 1920s, applied to both tanks and transport, gave the conservatives powerful arguments for caution, but their failure to grasp the potential of a new style of warfare imposed an increasingly irritating brake on the revolutionaries and reformers in the 1930s. Their insistence on merely grafting the new on to the old created a number of anomalies which were to become more and more apparent in succeeding years.

The fifth and final category—excluding the utterly indifferent—were the true reactionaries like General Egerton and Brigadier Neil Haig, the Field-Marshal's cousin, who declared in the *RUSI Journal* that 'the cavalry will never be scrapped to make room for the tanks', who were probably rather rare, at least in making their social prejudices public. These officers, pathetic or admirable depending on one's viewpoint, were opposed not merely to the tank but also to the mechanization of transport. Such attitudes, if Liddell Hart is to be believed, reflected a deep-rooted snobbery towards the technical side of the profession. Thus officers in the technical branches were sometimes referred to as 'blokes', implying they were not 'gentlemen' in the full military sense of the term, while other ranks with technical qualifications were designated 'tradesmen'. Reactionary officers echoed, or elaborated upon, Rudyard Kipling's disparaging remark at an early mechanized exercise 'It smells like a garage and looks like a circus.'[7]

As a newly constituted arm, originating under the unlikely sounding umbrella of the Heavy Machine Gun Branch, tanks were ill-placed to withstand the rapid and draconian run-down of establishments that occurred immediately after the war. To make matters worse most of the existing types appeared unsuited to the main military duties of Imperial policing and peace-keeping. Instead of slow-moving tanks 'There was a gap in the military ecology which the armoured car comfortably fitted.'[8]

It was only after considerable delay and a determined struggle by its few supporters in the War Office, notably Colonel Fuller, that the Royal Tank Corps was formally established on 1 September 1923. There were to be only four battalions on a scale of one per each division, but not forming an integral part of the division. Headquarters, with tank driving and maintenance schools, were established at Wool in Dorset, with the battalions located at Aldershot, Catterick, Tidworth, and Lydd. Colonel C. N. F. Broad developed the tank gunnery school at Lulworth Cove. When financial considerations caused the abandonment of work on the admirable Medium D in 1919, it was replaced by the less elaborate Vickers (Medium) Tank. Originally regarded as a stopgap, the Vickers (Mark II) made it debut in manœuvres at Aldershot in 1923 and remained the staple British model for the next decade. It could cross a six-foot gap, travel up steep slopes and cross most natural obstacles except that, unlike the Medium D, it was much too heavy (twelve tons) to float and 'swim' across water. It was armed with a 3-pounder gun in a revolving turret permitting all-round fire, and two machine guns. Although mechanically a remarkable achievement in its day, it was not well constucted for combat. The machine guns could not fire frontally and there was no place from which its commander could control operations. Wireless sets were not yet widely available or very reliable. Even with these limitations, in the absence of specialist anti-tank guns, the Vickers dominated the battlefield in the mid-1920s.

There was now a real prospect of being able to move a force a hundred miles in twenty-four hours, turning the enemy's flanks and cutting his communications. This naturally encouraged progressive theorists like Fuller, but equally caused conservative officers to feel apprehension for the morale and future role of the other arms. In the early exercises the Vickers tank performed similar tasks to those of the former cavalry division: scouting ahead, accompanied by lorry-borne infantry, or attacking a defended position from the flank. As these tasks left the main infantry body to advance unprotected against concealed machine guns, a need was felt for a large number of small cheap tanks to assist the infantry in open-warfare conditions. Martel, though he was too modest to say so in his books on the history of tanks, began the quest in 1925 with his privately built 'tankette'. The hope at that time was that by making a small reduction in infantrymen the War Office would be able to afford large numbers of small, fast, and cheap tanks. At about the same time the first steps were taken to design an experimental heavy tank which could be mass-produced in wartime if there were a recurrence of siege conditions.[9]

In the first half of the 1920s there was also a great deal of thought and experiment applied to military transport. In this sphere changes in civil life clearly abetted the aims of the advocates of mechanization; for motor vehicles were rapidly replacing the horse in both private and commercial transport. By 1927 nearly two million motor vehicles were licensed in Britain; long-distance lorries were competing with the railway freight car; and working horses were becoming scarce. Horse-drawn vans and omnibuses were on the way out. Unfortunately the variety of fully tracked and half-tracked vehicles with which the Army experimented had little or no commercial appeal. Hence from 1923 the Army relied increasingly upon a 30-cwt six-wheel cross-country lorry which, because of its uneconomical cost per ton-mile, was adopted by only a few commercial firms.[10]

Before turning to examine the development of the first experimental forces in more detail it is necessary to underline the important point that the Army's difficulties were due at least as much, if not more, to the political and economic climate in the 1920s as to conservatism within its own ranks. Although ideological pacifism was not so common as many military men believed, the public undoubtedly manifested a war-weariness and what Liddell Hart aptly termed 'passivism' which affected the Army more than the other two Services. Nevertheless, there was a general understanding in Parliament that the need to man overseas garrisons by the Cardwell system made it impossible to make further significant reductions in numbers of troops or drastic changes in organization. On the other hand, only the imminent prospect of involvement in a major European war would have justified the development of armoured forces.

Nor was mechanization ever a sharp issue. A few Labour extremists who saw the tank as a symbol of aggressive militarism were offset by their more moderate colleagues who regarded the horse as an outmoded relic of upper-class society. On the Conservative side ex-cavalry officers stressed that horses had performed well in suitable conditions in the Great War and that mechanical vehicles were too unreliable to replace them. Others favoured mechanization in principle but feared that the excessive cost of new equipment would have an adverse effect on the other arms. Since Parliament never debated mechanization as a distinct issue it is difficult to generalize about political attitudes beyond saying that the consensus in both major parties favoured gradual, cautious, inexpensive modernization which fell far short of the policy advocated by Fuller and Liddell Hart.[11]

One of the Army's greatest difficulties in mechanizing is most clearly seen in the passionate commitment to financial retrenchment which characterized Governments of all colours throughout virtually the whole of the inter-war period. Following the general guidelines recommended by the Geddes Committee, the Army Estimates decreased from just under £94 million in 1921 to £42½ million by 1926 and went on falling steadily year by year until 1932. The annual allocation for the purchase and maintenance of all army weapons and war-stores in the decade between 1923 and 1933 averaged only £2 million which was considerably less than the sums allocated to the other two Services. 'The effects of the stringency', in the words of the official history of *British War Production*, 'were all but crippling.' While Treasury control was not such an unmitigated evil as is sometimes suggested, its actual method of operation did militate against innovation, or indeed changes of any kind. Briefly, each year the War Office added the costs of existing forces and commitments to those of newly planned programmes, compared this total with the lump sum suggested by the Treasury, and then attempted to make the necessary reductions. These draft estimates were then closely scrutinized by the Treasury and compared with the previous year's, the guiding principle being that every increase or new item had to be explicitly justified. Memoirs abound with instances of penny-pinching and protracted arguments over trivia which this system often entailed. Moreover, it meant that savings in one area could not be automatically credited to additional expenditure in another. Furthermore, Treasury sanction was required for any expenditure not provided for in the Estimates, and money left over at the end of the financial year automatically reverted to the Exchequer. This system made for strict house-keeping and accounting but it had serious disadvantages; it allowed virtually no flexibility, set too much emphasis on precedent, and did not provide for continuity in the kind of research, trials, and experiments essential to the development of mechanization.

As the CIGS, Lord Cavan, complained to Sir William Robertson in 1924, the War Office was *ordered* by the Treasury to get inside a particular figure, but even after the Estimates had been passed the Treasury now constantly refused to sanction some particular item. In his memoirs he recalled that when he pressed for wireless sets for the Army he was told flatly that no money was available; and his recommendation that £100,000 be spent on tanks was abused in the House of Commons as a profligate waste of public money. His whole period as CIGS was a struggle for existence.[12]

As with the case of 'Plan 1919' during the First World War, the theories of the mechanized warfare enthusiasts continued in the immediate post-war years to outstrip both official doctrine and existing capabilities of tanks and other vehicles. Fuller, through a variety of bold and unorthodox lectures, articles, and books, continued to be the chief spokesman of the revolutionaries.[13] In his prize-winning essay for the 1919 RUSI competition on 'The Application of Recent Developments in Mechanics and Other Scientific Knowledge to Preparation and Training for Future War on Land', he asserted that the tank could completely replace the infantry and cavalry, while artillery in order to survive would have to develop into a kind of tank. He estimated that it would take five years to reorganize the Army into mechanized divisions and another five to overcome prejudices and vested interests. On 11 February 1920 he gave a lecture at the RUSI on 'The Development of Sea Warfare on Land and Its Influence on Future Naval Operations', in which, with a dazzling display of imaginative crystal-gazing, he developed the analogy of tanks as the battleships of a new era of fluid land operations. Although in the ensuing discussion one speaker suggested that the development of anti-tank guns would cause the tactical advantage of swing towards the defence again, the general reaction was extremely favourable. Indeed, Fuller's biographer regards this occasion as in many ways the peak of his influence and acceptability. The opposition was soon however to 'gather strength and break like an angry wave upon the Whitehall beach'.[14]

In all accounts of the development of mechanized warfare Fuller's name is rightly linked with that of Liddell Hart. Though Liddell Hart later claimed with reason that when the two first met in June 1920 he was already moving towards the 'revolutionary' position on tanks, the contemporary evidence leaves no doubt that Fuller was then the more advanced thinker and had completed the conversion of his young admirer whose pioneering tactical theories had hitherto been primarily concerned with infantry. Fuller was, after all, the senior by seventeen years and had seen far more of warfare—in South Africa and the First World War—than Liddell Hart who had volunteered in 1914 and experienced only a few weeks as an infantry subaltern at the front in 1915 and 1916. Indeed, with uncharacteristic humility, Liddell Hart frankly admitted in 1928 that up until then he had been the junior partner. In fact through frequent meetings and a voluminous correspondence the two helped each other to refine and develop their ideas. Fuller was the bolder, more dynamic, and original thinker; whereas Liddell Hart was more balanced, tactful, and less extravagant as a military polemicist. In the present writer's own words, 'in the 1920s Fuller may be described as a blazing comet, while Liddell Hart was a less brilliant but steadier star'. Two main differences between the two pioneers' thinking on mechanization may be discerned at this stage. First, Liddell Hart advanced more detailed and realistic plans for the gradual conversion, in four stages, to a 'New Model Army'. Even so, though he showed where reductions could be made to save the funds he calculated to be necessary, he by no means allowed for the rigid restrictions imposed by the Treasury system. Secondly, though giving precedence to the tank, he always stressed the need for infantry (or 'tank marines') as an integral part of the mechanized force, whereas for the most part Fuller relegated infantry to a strictly subordinate role of protecting lines of communication and fixed bases.[15]

Fuller, to pursue the image of the blazing comet, threatened to burn himself out in a professional sense in the 1920s, reacting with increasing stridency and tactlessness to what he regarded as obstruction from an unreceptive War Office. As his biographer shrewdly notes, military policy, especially where technology is concerned, is almost always made within the establishment which appears to be largely impervious to popular or political clamour, except occasionally through Parliament. Even the question of mechanization was ultimately a political matter so that Fuller's proselytizing activities unavoidably took on a quasi-political tone. This became more apparent from 1923 onwards as frustration—and a widening concern with war as a political and social phenomenon—led Fuller to suggest that, since democracies were incapable of taking the necessary actions to secure national survival, a more authoritarian system might be necessary. As his biographer notes, Fuller's abrasive style 'achieved the object of advertising his message but not of selling it'. It needs to be stressed that, though Fuller was sometimes excessively outspoken, given his comparatively junior rank, and did not trouble to conceal his contempt for fools, he was nevertheless sorely provoked. Thus, to cite but two examples, in 1923 the CIGS, Lord Cavan, forbade Fuller to publish his Staff College lectures entitled 'The Foundations of the Science of War'. Cavan was opposed to serving officers publishing books and was able to enforce this policy so long as Fuller remained at the Staff College. Fuller also aroused an obsessive hostility on the part of General Montgomery-Massingberd who was later to exert a baneful effect on his career. What seems most to have angered Montgomery-Massingberd was Fuller's 'disloyalty'. In several tirades to an unsympathetic Liddell Hart, he attacked Fuller's publications (admitting on one occasion that he had not read the book he was criticizing and had no intention of doing so), and expressed the view that 'For a soldier especially . . . character is more important than brains. If you can combine both so much the better, but if you can't then character every time.' Fuller was well aware of such emotional opposition, as his correspondence with Liddell Hart reveals, and it led him to adopt an increasingly contemptuous outlook towards the Army hierarchy.[16]

In September 1925 the Army carried out its first large-scale manœuvres since 1914. A tank battalion was attached to each side and one of the purposes of the three-day exercises was to try out the new concepts of mechanized warfare. The results were disappointing. On the first day, for example, the infantry of the improvized 'Mobile Force' de-bussed nearly ten miles from their jumping-off position and arrived too late to have any effect, while the horse transport became entangled with the troop carriers. The manœuvres as a whole revealed the lack of an official operational doctrine. As Colonel Henry Karslake, then on the staff of Southern Command, wrote to Liddell Hart: 'We are not making the effort to produce a really mobile fighting force, merely mechanizing transport to move infantry more quickly.' What was needed was a brigade of light one-man or two-man tanks to enable the armoured force to break through the defensive crust and attack vital localities in the rear. This was discouraged at that time.[17]

The outcome of the manœuvres was not however entirely negative. The Secretary of State for War, Sir Laming Worthington-Evans, who had already evinced more interest in modernizing the Army than his predecessors, attended the manœuvres with Fuller as his escort and guide. In his Estimates speech in March 1926 Worthington-Evans announced his intention to form 'a small mechanized force of all arms' for experimental purposes at one of the major training centres. Since Britain was ahead in this sphere, he stressed, there was no justification for uneconomic haste. In fact more than a year would elapse before the Experimental Mechanized Force was formed in May 1927.[18]

In the interval, prospects for a truly progressive policy of mechanization were considerably enhanced by the advent in February 1926 of Sir George Milne as CIGS in place of the cavalry-loving Cavan. The new CIGS entered office with the reputation of being cautiously progressive but, more to the point, he had accepted the suggestion of Liddell Hart and made Fuller his Military Assistant. This was an unusual appointment: the post was usually occupied by a more junior officer; Liddell Hart had specifically suggested that the occupant take on the new role of 'thinking ahead'; and Fuller was notorious throughout the Army as a 'military Bolshevik' fanatically committed to mechanization. Whether Milne had fully grasped what he had let himself in for may be doubted. The balance sheet of his seven-year term of office is still the subject of controversy, but it is clear that he had an unfortunate tendency to embark audaciously on new projects only to turn cautious in the face of opposition. As Fuller commented in retrospect: 'Could one have turned him mentally upside down, what a superb CIGS he would have made!'[19]

On 13 November 1926 Milne organized an impressive demonstration at Camberley for the Cabinet and Dominion

Prime Ministers which was designed to bring out the possibilities of future mechanized warfare. Every available kind of mechanized vehicle took part, including a prototype of a 30-ton 'Independent' tank which was intended to form the core of an armoured force capable of carrying out independent strategic thrusts. Heavy rain converted the area into a quagmire but this only served to underline the advantages of tracked over wheeled machines. Although too much should not be read into a set-piece demonstration, here were displayed all the tactical elements of *blitzkrieg,* including self-propelled guns and aircraft swooping on the defenders' position in synchronization with the ground attack.[20]

There is no need to describe here in detail Fuller's fateful decision to decline the opportunity to command the Experimental Mechanized Force which was formed at Tidworth on Salisbury Plain early in 1927. His overt objection was that as presented to him, the command of 7th Infantry Brigade would involve too much of a distraction in the way of overseeing the routine administration of the Tidworth garrison, but he allowed Milne's understandable failure to respond to his conditions to provoke him to the point of threatening to resign from the Army. Though he was persuaded to withdraw from this extreme step, the command was given to an orthodox infantryman, Colonel R. J. Collins,* and Fuller lost for ever the splendid chance to put his theories into practice. It was, as his biographer remarks, 'probably the worst decision of his life'. He had badly miscalculated in trying to extract conditions from Milne, and one can only suspect from his correspondence, that it was the 'showdown' for which he had long been hankering out of bitter disillusionment with his military superiors. The tragic irony of the affair was that Fuller effectively committed professional suicide on a comparatively trivial issue; had he quietly accepted the command he could easily have freed himself from routine drudgery and devoted the bulk of his time to the mechanized experiments.[21]

This unfortunate episode had a further sequel. More than six weeks elapsed after Fuller's resignation before the War Office announced, on 21 April, that Colonel Collins had been transferred to command 7th Infantry Brigade. From this bald statement and other inside information, Liddell Hart gained the impression that the War Office was back-tracking from its stated intentions: instead of a properly constituted experimental force it now looked as though there was to be merely an infantry brigade with some mechanized units occasionally attached. Consequently, on 22 April he published an article in the *Daily Telegraph* entitled 'An Army Mystery—Is there a Mechanical Force?' This bombshell, followed by a similar challenge in the *Westminster Gazette*, promptly had the desired effect of causing Worthington-Evans not only to confirm the War Office's intentions but also to list the units of the mechanized force.[22] Here was a striking example of Liddell Hart's successful use of the Press to affect Government policy. He paid a price in the loss of privileged access to the War Office. Milne was incensed, while Montgomery-Massingberd wrote patronizingly to say that he had harmed his prospects as a journalist by opposing the system. In ample compensation Fuller praised him warmly for outmanœuvring the War office, and after the trials Martel wrote: 'I think that the formation of a proper mechanized force was largely due to your efforts.'[23]

Though the value of the experimental manœuvres in August 1927 was limited by the miscellaneous nature of the assembled tanks and vehicles and by the cautious orthodoxy of the brigade commander, Colonel Jack Collins, the event nevertheless was an important landmark in the development of armoured forces. Liddell Hart's contemporary accounts for the *Daily Telegraph*, summarized in his *Memoirs*, probably underestimated the problems which even a more dashing commander would have experienced with such a motley assortment.

In the first phase Collins sought to establish a method of movement which could be applied to fast-moving armoured cars and light tanks, slower-moving medium tanks and even slower tractor-drawn artillery, and infantry transported in six-wheeled lorries or half-tracked carriers. His difficulty was exacerbated by the lack of a system of radio communications to enable the commanders to talk among themselves and co-ordinate their actions. His solution was to distribute the brigade into three groups 'fast', 'medium', and 'slow' according to their vehicles' road-speed, but unfortunately this did not coincide with their cross-country capability. Liddell Hart referred in his report to the extreme vulnerability of the 'serpentine column' which coiled over a distance of thirty-two miles and frequently became congested at bottlenecks. He added that these march exercises 'came to look like an attempt to drill a mechanical menagerie into a Noah's Ark procession, and more fitted to fulfil a sergeant-major's dream than a vision of mobile warfare'.

When the brigade went on to attempt more advanced operational tests, Collins seemed to progressives like Liddell Hart, Fuller, and Pile to be obsessed with the security of his force and to neglect the impact which its mobility could have on the enemy by threatening his flanks. Hence the joke became current that the Force had adopted as its motto the banker's rule: 'no advance without security'. In the final phase of tactical exercises there was no sign that Collins or any of his subordinates envisaged a role for the armoured force of wide strategic manœuvre designed to throw an enemy off balance; it was simply an additional limb to be attached to a conventional division or corps carrying out careful limited advances like those in the latter part of the Great War.

The only bright spot, from this viewpoint, was the imaginative handling of the reconnaissance group of armoured cars and tankettes under the command of Colonel F. A. Pile. In a demonstration specially arranged for Winston Churchill on 31 August, Pile's light force, with the fanatical tank commander Major P. C. S. Hobart also taking part, provided a glimpse into future possibilities by carrying out a high speed encircling manœuvre. Burnett-Stuart's 3rd Division was paralysed by the superior mobility of a force of tanks and armoured cars less than a third of its size.[24]

On 8 September the CIGS addressed the senior officers of the Mechanized Force at Tidworth. Milne took as the text for his 'sermon' I Corinthians chapter 14 verse 8: 'For if the trumpet give an uncertain sound, who shall prepare himself to the battle?' Although Liddell Hart was given the complete text of the address and published a summary of it two days afterwards in the *Daily Telegraph,* he was later, in his *Memoirs,* to exaggerate the contrast between Milne's stirring call for mechanization and the disappointingly slow progress that actually ensued. Realizing that his audience included several journalists, Milne took care to stress in his introductory remarks that progress was likely to be slow: finance was strictly limited; armoured cars had

had to be dispatched to China; and vehicles had to be thoroughly tested before orders could be placed. 'What you have worked on this year', he remarked, 'is only the germ of an idea that wants expanding. I myself, and most of the senior officers of the Army, cannot expect to see a great expansion in our time.' Moreover, although he called for a complete change of outlook in preparing for future war, and mentioned that there would be armoured, as well as infantry and cavalry, divisions, he also warned that an armoured force might be quite unsuitable for warfare in some parts of the Empire. He had been a little nervous about the experiment but it had gone well. Even these cautiously progressive remarks were too much for Major-General Harry Knox, the Director of Military Training, who, on reading Liddell Hart's report, declared 'It is not authentic'. Knox also allegedly lamented to a Royal Tank Corps officer, 'If they mechanize anything more, we shall have no Army left.' Liddell Hart believed that it was Knox who persuaded Milne not to issue the full version of his address to the Army.[25]

Milne was right to stress that the 1927 exercises were an encouraging beginning to what was bound to be a slow process of mechanization. Even armoured enthusiasts were aware of serious limitations and defects. The absence of an effective anti-tank gun, for example, lent an air of unreality to the proceedings. The best infantry anti-tank weapon was then the Swiss Oerlikon 20 mm machine-gun, which could penetrate only one inch of armour at 200 metres, but the Army possessed few of these. Colonel Karslake stressed the need for a good anti-tank gun capable of giving the tanks close support. The 3.7-inch howitzer was ineffective, while the self-propelled Birch gun, of which only a few existed, was surprisingly not developed. Instead the infantry had to make do with variously coloured flags which, as Burnett-Stuart remarked, tended to 'breed like guinea pigs or rabbits'. In 1929 the War Office issued the rather pompous instruction that 'Commands are authorized to use dummy guns instead of flags if the transport can be provided, but the flag must be retained to represent the gun when the transport is not available. Commands will take steps to see that absurdities in tactical handling do not occur in the use of these flags.'[26]

Another glaring weakness was the slowness of the light tanks available which could not keep up with the Vickers, let alone race past them. Thus when attacking commanders had to make an artificial division by giving the small light tanks a start while the faster medium tanks followed behind to give covering fire. Early in 1928 a War Office Research Committee approved plans for a two-man scout tank which would be bullet proof, fully tracked, and capable of up to 40 m.p.h. on roads, but lack of money held up production.[27]

One of the most intractable problems was the inability of horsed cavalry to co-ordinate its movements with armoured cars, tanks, half-tracks, and lorries. Winston Churchill as Chancellor of the Exchequer, supported by Worthington-Evans, urged a large-scale reduction of cavalry regiments (of which 12 out of 20 were stationed at home) but was successfully resisted by a Cavalry Committee chaired by Montgomery-Massingberd. As late as 1928 the War Office was trying to find a suitable short lance of the pig-sticking type for adoption by the cavalry. Churchill's efforts did at least secure the conversion of two cavalry regiments (the 11th Hussars and 12th Lancers) to armoured cars beginning in 1928, but eight years then elapsed before the War Office decided to motorize or mechanize a further eight cavalry regiments. Only in 1937 was the wholesale conversion of the remainder of the cavalry agreed upon.[28]

The last specific criticism of the 1927 exercises concerns Army–Air co-operation. Most of the advocates of mechanized warfare stressed the tremendous possibilities of close air support and local RAF officers tended to be helpful. In particular Wing Commander Trafford Leigh-Mallory,* who was in charge of the School of Army Co-operation at Old Sarum at that time, gave the experiment his full support. In addition to the normal roles of air reconnaissance and artillery observation, his squadrons also put in a number of spectacular low-level attacks in conjunction with the tank assault. At a higher level, however, the Air Staff, under the dominant influence of the CAS Sir Hugh Trenchard, regarded any such diversions as a threat to the RAF's independent bombing doctrine. Consequently squadrons were assigned to Army support with the greatest reluctance and Army overtures to secure closer co-operation were vigorously opposed. On one occasion the Air Ministry warned the War Office against allowing Army officers to encourage Air

Force officers to violate official Air policy. Indeed it is fair to say that despite the significant contributions made by British writers to the theory of *blitzkrieg*, the inter-war period (and indeed much of the Second World War) was chiefly characterized by lack of close co-operation between the RAF and the Army.[29]

That official War Office policy was to proceed extremely cautiously with mechanization was underlined at the annual Staff College Conference of senior officers in January 1928. When Fuller, Elles, and other progressive officers pressed for the development of an experimental 'New Model' Division designated specifically for a European war, Milne endorsed the reply of the new Adjutant-General, Sir Walter Braithwaite,* that finance would not permit the Army to develop two different kinds of division. The CIGS declared that six years (the period mentioned by Fuller for the gradual creation of the new division) was far too short a time for the programme he had in mind. Since it was necessary to take several million pounds off the Army Estimates he and the Army Council preferred a gradual development of all divisions, including the horsed cavalry division, with tanks attached as necessary rather than the more rapid creation of a special division with its own tanks. Worthington-Evans confirmed that this was War Office policy in his speech on the Army Estimates on 8 March. Neither the civil nor the military authorities were prepared to carry out drastic reduction of units; they preferred to retain the forces in being while striving to save money to devote to research, new weapons and vehicles. Thus the 1928 Estimates contained an increase of £60,000 for vehicles and fuel in a total of £1,085,150 but an increase of only £4,000 for animals and forage in a total of £732,600.[30]

For its exercises in 1928 the Experimental Mechanized Force, renamed the 'Armoured Force', had the important new advantage of 150 wireless sets.[31] These were issued to all armoured cars and a complete company of tanks. But the Force was strictly no more 'armoured' than the miscellaneous force of the previous year, its only additional vehicles being some six-wheeled lorries and a few half-track carriers for the 3.7-inch howitzers. Indeed the 1928 exercises were seriously inhibited by lack of suitable tanks and vehicles. Only 16 light tanks were available, which lacked turrets and were armed only with machine guns. The slow Vickers Medium with its demanding maintenance requirements was becoming obsolete. Admirable replacements were designed but lack of money prevented their development beyond a few prototypes. As for infantry transport, the half-track and six-wheeled lorries were both inadequate for cross-country movement in company with light and medium tanks.

The most successful aspect of the 1928 exercises appears to have been the demonstrations specially arranged for Staff College students and Members of Parliament. These set-piece displays doubtless helped to popularize mechanization and gain support, but they also had unintended harmful effects. The repetition of pre-arranged performances within the narrow confines permissible for public viewing probably militated against trying out new tactical ideas. Certainly the main exercises followed an unimaginative, stereotyped pattern which disappointed all the more progressive supporters of mechanized warfare. For the final exercise, in what looks like an official move to prevent the superiority of the Armoured Force from demoralizing the traditional arms, the opposing sides were levelled up. Burnett-Stuart's 3rd Division was strengthened by the addition of mobile units including a company of tanks and a company of armoured cars, whereas the Armoured Force was weakened by having its light tanks placed under control of 2nd Cavalry Brigade. In contrast to the previous year when the 3rd Division had been routed by the Mechanized Force, this time neither side gained a clear advantage and the exercise ended in stalemate.[32]

At the end of the trials Milne made the rather surprising decision to disband the Armoured Force so as to concentrate instead on the mechanization of infantry and cavalry units. In announcing plans for this dispersal in the House of Commons on 27 November, Worthington-Evans claimed that the experiment had 'fulfilled its purpose. Valuable experience was gained which is enabling us to extend the experiment.' It seems clear that budgetary considerations were uppermost in the Secretary of State's mind. Milne's innate caution, on the other hand, seems to have been strengthened by Montgomery-Massingberd's overt opposition to the continuation of the mechanized experiment. In his unpublished memoirs the latter claimed that he had thrown a spanner into the works to safeguard the morale and training of the cavalry and infantry. In his view it had been a mistake to pit an entirely new formation based on the medium tank against older formations in order to prove its superiority.

What was wanted was to use the newest weapons to improve the mobility and fire power of the old formations . . . What I wanted, in brief, was evolution and not revolution . . . I discussed this question very fully with Lord Milne who was then C.I.G.S. and as a result the 'Armoured Force' as such was abolished and a beginning was made with the mechanization of the Cavalry and Infantry Divisions.

This claim was corroborated by Colonel Pile in a conversation with Liddell Hart on 28 November 1928. According to Liddell Hart's record, 'The disbandment of the Armoured Force was due to Montgomery-Massingberd (GOC.-in C. Southern Command) and as David Campbell* (GOC.-in-C. Aldershot Command) tended to support him, Milne gave way to their views.' Pile added that the infantry components of the Armoured Force would return to their ordinary duties, while the self-propelled guns would be tried in an anti-aircraft role. Burnett-Stuart, then commanding 3rd Division, felt that as his superior officer, Montgomery-Massingberd (who disliked him anyway because of their antipathetic temperaments), resented the fact that for the mechanized experiment Burnett-Stuart was directly responsible to the CIGS. Under Montgomery-Massingberd the whole atmosphere of Southern Command changed: 'the slightest attempt to get a little ahead of the existing training instructions was nipped in the bud; and it became more popular to think of the last war rather than the next one'.

This verdict was not quite fair to Montgomery-Massingberd who was at least looking ahead. His vision of the next war was that in the first six months at least the British Army would have to fight with cavalry and infantry and should therefore study how to support these two arms with tanks.[33] In his *In the Wake of the Tank* (1931), Martel actually credited Montgomery-Massingberd with the progress in mechanization made in 1928, but admitted privately to Liddell Hart that he named senior officers in this way on several occasions merely out of tact. Pile's gloom at the disbandment of the Armoured Force was lightened by the hope that Milne intended to revive it in the more suitable training conditions in Egypt after a year's suspension.[34]

Senior officers in fact varied considerably in their reaction to Milne's decision. Conservative officers like Montgomery-Massingberd and Braithwaite were primarily concerned to protect the morale and ensure the modernization of the traditional arms; whereas at the other extreme tank enthusiasts like Lindsay and Broad had virtually lost hope in the Armoured Force so long as the methodical Jack Collins remained in command. Between them stood Burnett-Stuart, well-aware of the material limitations and defective direction of the Force, but confident that the infantry would in time adjust to tanks and that another year's training would greatly benefit the tactical handling of armoured formations. Milne's greater sympathy for the conservative case is understandable: he was constantly confronted with the need for increased economy; overseas commitments stretched the available conventional forces to the limit; and, above all, he was responsible for the whole Army, not just the mechanized portion. Nevertheless, it is regrettable that he failed to maintain continuity in the evolution of mechanized forces, particularly since the impending economic crisis was to make it harder than expected to reassemble the dispersed units.[35]

After the intense interest generated within the Army by the mechanized experiments of 1927–8, the next two years were comparatively uneventful. A general election in the summer of 1929 returned a Labour Government dependent for survival on Liberal support in the House of Commons. Though the new Secretary of State for War, Tom Shaw, resisted a Labour back-bench motion to reduce substantially the Army's strength, he proved to have no mind of his own on military issues. On mechanization in particular he maintained Worthington-Evans's policy of gradual change within the narrow confines set by Philip Snowden's strict economic conservatism as Chancellor of the Exchequer. At the War Office senior soldiers were most impressed by the penetrating intelligence and open-mind of the new Financial Secretary, Emanuel Shinwell, whose habit of asking 'Why?' kept the officials on their toes. Liddell Hart reposed considerable hopes in the new Secretary of State for Air, Lord Thomson,* who had been a brigadier in the Regular Army. Soon after the Labour Party's return to power, in July 1929, Thomson asked Liddell Hart to put his views on mechanization on paper so that he could take them up with the Prime Minister, Ramsay MacDonald. Liddell Hart submitted two bold memoranda outlining plans for the reorganization of the Army at home and in India. The keynote was that the desired goal of mechanization could not be achieved without a drastic reorganization including the reduction of some existing units, notably of cavalry. Thomson had enough to occupy him at the Air Ministry and does not appear to have had much success in persuading his colleagues. On 30 November 1929 Lord Thomson told Liddell Hart that the Cabinet felt it could not break its contract with the men ('and still less with the officers') so that a nominal reduction of infantry battalions without making troops redundant would not save money in the short run. Liddell Hart gained the impression from this conversation that the 'real Cabinet objection to saving by mechanization is, first, no instant profit and, second, it throws men out of employment, i.e., Army is regarded really as an extension of the dole . . .' A War Office scheme to expand the Royal Tank Corps to three brigades came to nothing in 1929, largely because there was intense opposition to the necessary disbandment of four infantry battalions. Lord Thomson's death in the crash of the new airship R 101 on 5 October 1930 further diminished the prospects of Army reorganization in the interests of mechanization.[36]

The Labour Government inherited the Army Estimates for 1929–30 passed under the previous administration. Although the Army's budget had been cut by approximately £500,000, the total amount spent on vehicles increased by nearly £150,000 while that spent on animals decreased by £40,000. Although the modest programme for the provision of new tanks was substantially unchanged, there was certainly to be no expansion, nor were any infantry battalions to be reduced. For the tank specialists the prospects were depressing. As Brigadier George Lindsay, Inspector of the Royal Tank Corps, informed Liddell Hart in January 1929, the new 16-ton tank was excellent both mechanically and in fire-power. Only three models existed but it was hoped to produce eleven more so as to create a section in Egypt and one at home. But only one was allowed in the coming year and that had been achieved out of a surplus on the experimental vote. According to Lindsay, Broad was so depressed he felt like giving up his post and taking to a quiet life. All the mechanized warfare enthusiasts deplored the decision to tie the tanks to an infantry brigade.[37]

The lessons of the two-year experiment of the Armoured

Force were discussed at the Staff College Conference in January 1929 which set the tone for that summer's exercises. Brigadier Collins, who opened the discussion, tended to stress the difficulties rather than the potentialities of an armoured force. The drawbacks he listed included the difficulty of protecting a semi-armoured force on the move; problems of supply and maintenance; the hazards posed by different types of ground; and vulnerability to concentrated air attack. Colonel Wavell, by contrast, speaking from an infantryman's viewpoint, emphasized the moral effect which a highly mobile force could exert, especially when the infantry felt powerless to hit back. Milne concluded by reassuring the assembly that the armoured force was not dead altogether:

> It has served its term, and while we are considering possible establishments we are trying out other experiments . . . What we are aiming at, at the present moment, is the proper organization of four basic formations—the Cavalry Brigade, the Light Armoured Brigade, the Medium Armoured Brigade, and the Infantry Brigade. Once we have got the four properly worked out and properly equipped it will be the task of our successors to bring them together and form them into higher organizations.

It was clear, however, that by putting infantry reorganization first, Milne and his colleagues were postponing a thorough programme for the creation of armoured divisions to a distant date. The Director of Staff Duties, Major-General Bonham-Carter, actually mentioned in his address at the Conference that it would take ten or fifteen years to organize the Army for war on modern lines.[38]

The 1929 trials may be summarized briefly. They were primarily intended to advance the mechanization of the conventional arms while developments in armoured warfare lay dormant. Even these objectives were hindered by the stereotyped nature of the tactical exercises set by unimaginative commanders, the unavailability of suitable vehicles (particularly insufficient light tanks), and the narrowness of the objectives themselves: 'While it can be argued that these experiments were necessary to modernize the infantry and cavalry, the paltry results seem to have justified neither the effort expended nor the dispersal of the Armoured Force in 1928.' The one bright spot of the 1929 exercises was that they demonstrated the feasibility and importance of radio/telephone control within the tank battalion.[39]

Early in 1929 Worthington-Evans announced that Milne had been given an extension of two years as CIGS in order to secure continuity in military policy. Milne had shown a sound grasp of wider strategic issues in the COS Committee, and had accepted the need to operate within the narrow confines permitted by the Government's overriding concern with financial retrenchment. Whether his extended term was in the best interests of the Army as a whole may be doubted. Colonel Tim Pile certainly thought not and painted a depressing picture of the War Office towards the end of 1929. According to Liddell Hart's notes Pile reported:

There has been an atmosphere of gloom in the War Office for the last three months. Much friction between Milne and the political chiefs who will not listen to his arguments, although Shinwell is the most open to reason. Partly due to ineffectiveness of Milne himself and his chief subordinates. Milne is really 'gaga' now. Milne is always having to argue a case put up to him by his juniors which he doesn't fully grasp and doesn't know whether he believes in. All the General Staff directors are dud. Charles thinks that guns suffice. Boham-Carter* has no initiative. Gillman* is hopeless as Master-General of the Ordnance. Among the heads of that department Peck* alone has character, and he has made an impression on Shinwell. In consequence, as the General Staff will not cut existing units, money is to be saved on the Estimates . . . by cutting new equipment.

'There is', Liddell Hart noted, 'no chance of providing any of the new 16-ton tanks this year. Peck and Pile sought to secure the manufacture of 4, and (War Office) Finance advised them to put up the case on the ground of providing work at Woolwich Arsenal, but General Staff would not back them.'[40]

Later in 1930 Pile, on his own initiative, managed to get an order approved for three 16-ton tanks (costing £15,000 each), sixteen light tanks, and twelve tractors. All this had been done, he proudly told Liddell Hart, out of £60,000 saved on the maintenance vote, and even then he had had difficulties in obtaining Milne's consent.[41]

The Army Estimates for 1930 were in fact only reduced by £45,000 but the amount spent on the vote for tracked vehicles fell by £221,000. A workable model of a light tank was now available but the money was lacking to produce it in quantity. This was ironical in view of the fact that £150,000 had been spent *in advance* on machine-gun carriers in the previous budget. These financial considerations may have influenced Milne's decision not to re-establish an armoured brigade in 1930. As a result of the lack of new vehicles, the low strength of the infantry units, and appalling wet weather, the 1930 manœuvres were even less significant than those of 1929. Further practice in controlling tank movements by radio was probably the most positive outcome, though the goal of a radio in every tank in 1931 was deemed too expensive by the Treasury.[42]

The most important event in the development of mechanization in 1929 occurred neither in the engineering workshops nor on the manœuvre grounds but in the publication of the first manual to give official recognition to the concept of mechanized warfare. This was Colonel Charles Broad's booklet, *Mechanized and Armoured Formations,* but familiarly known in the Army as the 'Purple Primer'—from the colour of its covers rather than from the suggestion of any purple prose in its contents. Indeed, the preface stressed the manual's provisional nature, suggesting that its chief purpose was to encourage officers to study mechanization in the lengthy period which must elapse before armoured forces could be produced. Nevertheless the booklet exerted an important influence on the development of British armoured doctrine in the 1930s besides being carefully studied in Germany.

At the core of Broad's thinking lay the belief that tanks should be used primarily to exploit their fire-power and shock action in attack and that they were best employed independently. Broad had emphasized this view to Liddell Hart shortly before drafting the manual because he felt Liddell Hart, like so many contemporaries, was too preoccupied with mobility. 'Surely', wrote Broad in response to Liddell Hart's proposal that a cavalryman should command the Armoured Force, 'the whole object is superiority of fire—with cavalry you will get nothing but shock—weapon training and building tanks as gun platforms will go to glory'.[43] Consequently, though Broad envisaged the Army of the future as organized along somewhat traditional lines in cavalry divisions, light and medium armoured formations, and infantry divisions, he made it clear that the medium armoured brigades were to provide the strongest formations, or spearheads, with the main role of independent attack as distinct from co-operating with infantry and cavalry. Broad's sketch of armoured forces used to break through an enemy's front lines, sever his lines of supply and communication, and create chaos in the rear areas was reminiscent of Fuller's 'Plan 1919', and an accurate forecast of the use of armoured divisions in the early campaigns of the Second World War. This was truly visionary or prophetic writing since no complete armoured brigade had yet been formed anywhere.

Broad realized that in both theoretical and practical terms armoured formations were most vulnerable in the problem of supplies. Brigadier Collins had made the first tentative steps in the 1927–8 experiments to work out servicing and supply arrangements but the subject was still in its infancy. The boldest attempt to analyse the problem to date was contained in a lecture at the RUSI in 1929 by Colonel D. C. Cameron, an RASC officer. Cameron made the crucial observation that mechanized forces could not 'live off the land', nor should they be tethered to a railhead. With remarkable prescience he sketched the concept of establishing large stocks of supplies behind the advancing mechanized forces with a fleet of mechanized vehicles to ferry them to the forward units.[11]

The Purple Primer was not without its contemporary critics. Though generally favourable to Broad's progressive views, Liddell Hart felt that he had not sufficiently stressed the potentiality of armoured forces for long-range thrusts into the enemy's rear areas, the shock effect of using tanks at night, and the importance of combining low-flying air attack with tanks. Most important, Liddell Hart regretted Broad's neglect of 'tank marines', i.e. specially trained infantry in armoured vehicles. On this subject the Primer merely stated 'Under certain conditions, one or more infantry battalions carried in buses may be attached to mobile formations.' No doubt this attitude was partly influenced by the tank enthusiasts' determination not to be smothered by the conventional arms; but there was also the consideration, which Liddell Hart acknowledged, that it was better to aim at a homogeneous force instead of the miscellany of tanks and transport in the 1927–8 trials that were widely different in pace both on the road and across country.

Martel largely supported Liddell Hart's criticism and argued that what was really wanted for the mobile force was large numbers of medium tanks co-operating with mechanized artillery and infantry carried in lorries. It was essential for all arms to train together and get to know each other rather than, as Broad envisaged, expecting a tank brigade to co-operate with normal formations with whom it had not carried out any training. Martel later went further, however, in suggesting that preparation for war should have been carried out on a light-tank basis in the hope that large-scale production of medium tanks would be produced when the imminence of war loosened the purse strings. In fact, what the Germans actually did in the later 1930s. He argued that it was better to train with a large number of inexpensive light tanks rather than rely on more expensive medium tanks which were only available in small numbers.[45]

The favourable reception of the 'Purple Primer' contrasted sharply with the lull in the actual development of mechanized forces following the expectations raised by the experiments of 1927–8. The most depressing setback was the indefinite postponement of Broad's draft five-year plan designed to produce four tank brigades by 1935. Milne had originally encouraged the idea but Broad gained the impression that the CIGS would not force it through against the opposition of his colleagues. As he wrote to Lindsay, then in Egypt, on 7 November 1930:

> I have very little to tell you except a tale of woe. Our R.T.C. reorganization is turned down on the grounds that it would make the Army more efficient and they say the Government would not have that at any price. I think myself that the C.I.G.S. is getting worn out with all the opposition and political uncertainty and is more or less done as far as getting anything out of the present people goes.

While it was probably too much to expect a fundamental reform of Army organization, given the demands of overseas defence and financial stringency, it should have been possible to graft four or more armoured brigades on to the existing system. Even this possibility was to be ruled out for several years by the slump of 1931.

Thus Liddell Hart exaggerates only slightly in depicting the situation at the end of the 1920s in terms of the struggle of a mere handful of tank enthusiasts against the indifference or actual obstruction of the majority of the senior officers at the War Office. From the exceptions among these, the progressives suffered a serious loss in the sudden death, towards the end of 1930, of the Quartermaster-General Sir Hastings Anderson, who was widely tipped as a future CIGS. As for the tank enthusiasts, Broad was in charge of planning war-organization under the Director of Staff Duties from the Spring of 1927 until early 1931. Pile entered the War Office in August 1928 as Assistant Director of Mechanization in the MGO's Department and remained there until October 1932. George Lindsay was Inspector of the Royal Tank Corps from 1925 until September 1929, assisted by Major F. E. Hotblack* who was a GSO2 in the Directorate of Military Training.[46] These comparatively brief tours of duty lasting three or at most four years were designed to give officers a refreshing variety of staff and command experience but the system had the serious disadvantage that it was rarely possible for the same officer to see a technical project through from its first conception to the final issue of new equipment to the troops.

The year 1931 probably marked the nadir of the Army's fortunes in the inter-war period. Although, in the 1920s, it had existed in a political environment at best indifferent and at worst hostile, it had at least known what to expect. But from 1931 onwards both the domestic and international scenes became increasingly inimical to the Army.

The Army was a prime sufferer from the extraordinary financial crisis which faced the Government in 1931. Britain's export trade declined by 30 per cent during the year; the number of men unemployed rose from just over one million to well over two million, and a very serious budget deficit seemed unavoidable. In these circumstances the May Committee on National Expenditure, while recognizing that the armed forces were fully stretched, recommended large cuts in pay rates, capital expenditures, and operating funds. Though given only a few days to respond, in August 1931, the Army Council put up a well-reasoned opposition. The CIGS particularly objected to cuts in pay and educational allowances which he deplored as a policy of penny wise and pound foolish; the reductions would break pledges and undermine efficiency to achieve only paltry savings. Nevertheless, the War Office representations were rejected by the Cabinet. The latter required a temporary reduction of £2 million and a further permanent reduction of just under £2 million. As a result the Army Estimates for 1931–2 fell to their lowest total in the inter-war period of just under £36 million.[47] Among the consequences, expenditure on all military schools, ordnance factories, and research was to be cut by 10 per cent. All building projects were to be halted and there was to be no large-scale training for the regular Army. As Pile expressed it to Liddell Hart, 'The financial stringency was awful!' The CIGS would hope to keep mechanization where it was but there was no prospect of an advance. But, he added philosophically, it might easily have been far worse. He was glad that Milne was getting another year's extension as CIGS.[48]

Milne's second extension, giving him an unprecedented seven-year term as CIGS, enhanced his position of authority in the Army Council virtually to that of Commander-in-Chief. Unfortunately his fellow Army Councillors, who all took office early in 1931, were collectively less impressive than their predecessors. Lieutenant-General Sir Felix Ready* became QMG replacing the late Hastings Anderson, General Montgomery-Massingberd succeeded Braithwaite as Adjutant-General, and Major-General Charles succeeded Gillman as Master-General of the Ordnance. More seriously, Milne surrounded himself with a new team of conservative General Staff directors who tended to be anti-mechanization. According to Pile, who had to work with them, 'The last lot of General Staff directors—Charles, Bonham-Carter, Elles—at least paid lip service to it [mechanization]. But Bartholomew* (DMO and I) is unobtrusively yet dangerously "anti". Peck [Director of Mechanization] described him as "the real danger to mechanization". Vesey* [DSD] knows nothing of the modern army. . . . Elles [DMT] has failed to get a move on and talks of slower tanks' (i.e. for co-operation with infantry). Pile summed up as follows: 'There is no plan in mechanization . . . the War Office tendency is to motorize not mechanize.' Indeed Major-General S. C. Peck, who had held the office since its establishment in 1927, was the only enthusiastic advocate of mechanization in an influential position in the War Office in 1931, and when he was placed on half-pay in June 1932 his successor, Major-General

Alan Brough* possessed neither the vision nor the technical ability to fill his shoes.[49]

Nevertheless, despite these formidable handicaps, the summer of 1931 witnessed what Liddell Hart was later to describe ecstatically as 'the most influential tactical experiment in the British Army since Sir John Moore's training of the Light Brigade at Shorncliffe Camp in the early years of the previous century'. He was referring to the temporary assembly, for the training season only, of the first tank brigade under the direction of Brigadier Charles Broad. Broad's force, styled 1st Brigade Royal Tank Regiment, consisted of 2nd, 3rd, and 5th battalions RTC and one light battalion. The technical significance of the brigade was that, unlike the Experimental Force of 1927–8, it was composed entirely of tracked vehicles, even though the improvised light battalion was equipped only with Carden-Loyd machine-gun carriers representing light tanks. There was an additional innovation in that each company of the tank battalions comprised a section of medium and a section of light tanks—thus proving that the two could work together. Montgomery-Massingberd's transfer to the War Office had at least the beneficial by-product of bringing a much more progressive chief to Southern Command in the person of Sir Cecil Romer.

Between April and the end of August Broad supervised section, company, and battalion training in order to evolve a drill that would enable the brigade to manœuvre as a unit. Here the ability to communicate was all-important. Each tank had six coloured flags to operate a simple two-letter code system for visual signalling between tanks. Some sections had radio sets in each tank but others had wireless control down to section commanders only and therefore relied entirely upon flags within the section. Broad was more concerned with establishing control at this stage than with attempting anything elaborate in the way of tactics, and by the end of the summer, despite difficulties with the individualistic Hobart who commanded 2nd RTC battalion, he was able to manœuvre the whole brigade of 180 tanks in immediate response to his orders on the wireless. In September, after a fortnight working together on Salisbury Plain, the brigade put on a brilliant unrehearsed display for the Army Council by moving several miles across the featureless terrain in a thick fog. Broad's gamble paid off for 'as the fog lifted and the sun came out, the phalanx of tanks rolled into sight and at Broad's orders paraded and wheeled non-stop with an almost inhuman precision. It was breathtaking in its apparent simplicity, [and] unforgettable as a spectacle.'[50]

To the mechanized warfare enthusiasts these culminating exercises on the Plain proved the 'controllability' of an armoured brigade, which paved the way for the development of a new mobile style of warfare. Liddell Hart was later to assert that an armoured brigade 'was the only kind of formation that could . . . be controlled and manœuvred on the modern battlefield'. Cavalry formations would be checked by modern firepower and infantry formations would take too long to assemble and deploy.

Yet the very success of this all-tank experiment only added anxiety to the other arms who feared a take-over bid by the Tank Corps. These apprehensions, though exaggerated, were fuelled by Hobart's fanaticism and tactlessness. Even so committed a tank supporter as Martel was later to regret that the 'all armoured' idea had been pushed too far at the expense of co-operation with the other arms, whose support would be essential in conditions less congenial to tanks than Salisbury Plain.[51] In any event Milne again appeared willing to allay the fears of the conservatives by deciding at the end of the exercises not to form a permanent tank brigade in 1932. Liddell Hart listed this decision among the cons in weighing up Milne's regime but added, 'Owing to the failure to produce more tanks even the formation of one Tank Brigade would mean all the divisions would be entirely denuded of tank support.' The explanation given to the Press was that such a step had been deemed unadvisable in view of the forthcoming Disarmament Conference, but the extreme financial squeeze provides a more plausible reason. As Colonel Kenneth Laird,* the new Inspector of the RTC informed Lindsay, the real reason was that suitable quarters did not exist on Salisbury Plain to house the men and equipment of an entire brigade.[52] Whatever the true explanation, momentum was once again lost after a brief period of promise.

Although Milne's term as CIGS extended beyond the period covered by this chapter to February 1933, this is a convenient point to comment on his regime especially from the viewpoint of mechanization. In terms of his sound strategic contributions in the Chiefs of Staff Committee and his dealings with ministers and War Office officials during a period of acute economic depression it is possible to rate his achievements very highly.[53] His defenders can also legitimately point out that, given the guiding principles of the Ten Year Rule, to which compulsory financial reductions were regularly added, no soldier in his place could have done much better.

On the other hand, critics like Liddell Hart pointed out that he left the proportions between the different arms almost exactly as he found them; namely four tank battalions to 136 infantry battalions with only two of the 20 cavalry regiments converted to armoured cars. Moreover, after a promising start he had generally refrained from appointing dynamic radicals like Fuller to positions of influence, preferring instead safe men who could be relied upon to steer the Army through its leanest years with the minimum of disturbance. There is ample evidence to show that Milne became tired and depressed by his thankless role at the War Office. Pile's critical opinion has been noted earlier and Sir Samuel Hoare (Secretary of State for Air 1924–9), told Liddell Hart in October 1929 that 'Milne had become an old man—mentally and physically. Milne was speechless at the Conference and could not put his case forward. He [Hoare] had even had to help him out.' Fuller's views must be taken with caution since he tended to be scathing about senior officers generally and had personal reasons for animosity towards Milne. He described the CIGS to Liddell Hart (in November 1932) as 'a cad', and listed his faults as 'secretive, suspicious, vindictive' to which another officer present added 'and conceited' with which Fuller concurred. He remarked that Milne had done no more in seven years, than Cavan ('a gentleman' whom the soldiers trusted). Milne could not tolerate any directors of ability around him. Martel confirmed this impression in a letter to Liddell Hart in January 1932: 'I have talked to a lot of people at the War Office and I agree now with you. There is a definite retrograde atmosphere at WO and if we don't buck up and get a move on we will deserve to lose more to the RAF.'[54]

While some of these comments underestimated Milne's difficulties, it is hard to resist the conclusion that it would have been better for the Army and his own reputation had he left the War

Office in 1930. Even so this verdict must be tentative because it is uncertain who would have succeeded him. Anderson who was favoured by some 'insiders' died in 1930, while another favoured candidate, Sir Charles 'Tim' Harington, was also past his best in Hoare's opinion. There were progressive candidates of sufficient seniority like Burnett-Stuart or Romer but the earlier elevation of Milne's eventual successor, Montgomery-Massingberd, would have not been an improvement.

Nevertheless, despite all the difficulties and handicaps discussed in this chapter including public apathy, acute financial stringency, excessive caution at the War Office, and uncertainty over the Army's role, Britain in many respects was still the leading pioneer in mechanization at the end of 1931. It is to the following period, 1932–9, that we must now look in order to understand how this advantage was allowed to slip away and why Britain was almost completely lacking in armoured forces on the outbreak of the Second World War.

CHAPTER 6

Mechanization: the second phase, 1933–1939

The years 1933 to 1936 saw a loss of momentum in Britain in both the production of new types of tank and the development of armoured formations. In the later 1930s, confronted with rapid German rearmament in which mechanized divisions were prominent, Britain opted for the gradual mechanization of the traditional arms as distinct from expanding the Royal Tank Corps. By 1938 satisfactory progress was being made with various experimental tank models but comparatively few modern tanks were actually being issued to the Army. Even the first Mobile—or Armoured—Division was not expected to be ready to take the field until the middle of 1940. Thus, when Britain went to war in September 1939, her small Army had been almost completely converted to motor transport but she was sadly lacking in anything resembling the German Panzer division, six of which took the lead in the conquest of Poland. The ironical aspect of Britain's loss of the lead in the theory and practice of armoured warfare has been stressed by several historians—that outstanding practicioners of *blitzkrieg* like Guderian later acknowledged their indebtedness to British theorists and mechanized experiments.[1] The object of this chapter, after charting the rather depressing course of mechanization in Britain between 1933 and 1939, is to assess the reason for this decline, in order of priorities.

The War Office's decision to continue a very cautious programme of mechanization in 1933 was mainly influenced by the financial situation. The total Army Estimates for that year, nearly £38 million, represented an increase of nearly £1½ million over the previous year, but the total to be spent on vehicles,

£885,000, showed no marked increase. Lord Hailsham, the Secretary of State for War, stated that the only mechanization projects for the year would be the conversion of one more artillery brigade and a continuing quest for a four-wheeled cross-country vehicle. The 1933 training programme saw the revival of training of the Territorial Army, which gave its morale a much needed boost, the concentration on 'small-war' situations in divisional exercises and the use of tanks in the infantry-support role to the exclusion of tank brigade manœuvres. 'What', asked Captain J. R. Kennedy rhetorically, 'is the use of treating manœuvres as being a potion made up of a little cavalry, a little infantry, still less artillery, a few tanks, an odd aeroplane and some old slogans, all stirred with rain and mud into a cold mixture which we know will ruin our national digestion, if not poison it completely?' The new CIGS, Montgomery-Massingberd, has been criticized for basing doctrine and training in 1933 on the assumption that the Army's primary mission, now and in the foreseeable future, was to police the Empire but this seems unjust in the light of Cabinet and CID attitudes to a Continental military commitment.[2]

It must be admitted, however, that if Montgomery-Massingberd was not the almost criminally incompetent reactionary depicted by his bitterest critics, he was certainly not an enthusiastic supporter of tanks and armoured warfare. Liddell Hart's gloomy prediction to Hankey before Montgomery-Massingberd's appointment proved generally accurate:

> Thus in trying to foresee the results of his tenure of office I anticipate that he will not favour, still less initiate, steps towards the necessary reorganization of the Army; that he will be antipathetic to the extended use of tanks, and also of air-craft; that he will discourage, if not penalise, independence of view and freedom of speech among the younger officers; that he will endeavour to check critical examination of the history of the war. . . . What I fear most is that his regime will lead to influential posts being increasingly filled with officers who are either unprogressive or skilled in hiding their opinions at the expense of the more constructive minded.

As regards the fortunes of individuals, Liddell Hart was also correct in believing that the new CIGS would make no effort to prevent Fuller's retirement, would harm the prospects of Burnett-Stuart and Ironside, and enhance those of the arch-conservative Knox.[3] Towards the end of Montgomery-Massingberd's period of office Duff Cooper (himself no radical on questions of cavalry and tanks) told Liddell Hart that the CIGS had recently urged him to provide two horses for each officer in the cavalry regiments that were to be mechanized and, astonishingly, to provide horses for the RTC which had never had them. He had even used the hoary argument that hunting taught quickness of decision. Duff Cooper was also amused at the CIGS's 'loyalty complex', but remarked pityingly that the 'poor old man' would soon be going.[4] To correct what too often resembles a caricature, however, General Sir Charles Bonham-Carter thought that Montgomery-Massingberd had been the best CIGS since the war in putting the Army's case in Cabinet discussions. More surprisingly, Hobart more than once expressed admiration for him. General Sir Henry Karslake, who admittedly detested Burnett-Stuart, reported that Montgomery-Massingberd was well regarded during his time in Southern Command. Martel was another who thought that Burnett-Stuart was guilty of deliberately provoking the CIGS.[5]

Despite the lack of opportunity for independent exercises in 1933, tank battalions played a prominent part in both the 1st and 2nd Divisional manœuvres, demonstrating the inability of existing infantry formations to deal effectively with armoured units. At the end of the training season came the momentous announcement of the permanent formation of the Tank Brigade under the command of Brigadier P. C. S. Hobart who, for economy's sake, was asked to combine this demanding appointment with that of Inspector of the Royal Tank Corps. Hobart at once consulted Lindsay (commanding the experimental 7th Infantry Brigade) and Broad about a 'charter' for the Tank Brigade whose principles would have to be adhered to 'even if the C.I.G.S. drops dead'. Hobart was determined to break free from the restrictions imposed in the 1933 training season of close co-operation with infantry. 'We are surely on the right lines', he wrote to Lindsay, 'if we divorce the Tank Brigade from all "frontal attack" *close* co-opn problems', though he accepted that these must be provided for by the eventual assignment of a tank battalion to each division of the Field Force. His main ideas for RTC policy were succinctly expressed:

1. Preservation of the Tank Brigade and all it stands for;

2. Completion of a 6th RTC battalion as the nucleus of a second Tank Brigade to be formed in Egypt;
3. Expansion of the RTC.[6]

The essence of his ambitions for the Tank Brigade was contained in his training directive: 'A Tank Brigade may be employed on a strategic or semi-independent mission against some important objective in the enemy's rearward organisation . . . The Tank Brigade should avoid strength and attack weakness . . . In addition it must be capable of more intimate co-operation with the other arms where the situation demands such action.' More specifically, in 1934 he hoped to develop the manœuvrability of the brigade; practise co-operation with the RAF; test methods of supply and maintenance; and aim to move 70 miles a day or 150 miles in three days.[7]

The Tank Brigade began to assemble on Salisbury Plain in the spring of 1934. It comprised initially the 2nd, 3rd, and 5th battalions RTC whose companies each consisted of sections of five medium and seven light tanks. A new light battalion made up of tanks drawn from the existing battalions was not ready until June. An important new feature was that the brigade's transport made it self-contained in fuel, food, and ammunition supply for several days, thus permitting independent operations against an enemy's communications.

The Tank Brigade on the move must have been an awe-inspiring sight, for Hobart used a dispersed formation with both frontage and depth of about ten miles. It was found that the brigade could move at 8 m.p.h. covering 60 or 70 miles a day with only about five per cent casualties from breakdowns. A remarkable feature was that Hobart continued the exercises at night with the loss of only about one mile per hour. The key to his success was that all orders, even within companies, were given by radio-telephony. He insisted that communication between tanks on the move was practicable; and also that the RTC could manage its own signals. Under his inspiring leadership all officers quickly became proficient in using the wireless, even if some had to forfeit their hours of leisure when they were accustomed to play tennis. He also stressed the great potential value of tank and air combination, undeterred by the meagre allotment of only one flight of reconnaissance aircraft and one flight of fighters. Though his fervent belief in the independent action of armoured forces entitles him to be regarded as one of the earliest prophets of *blitzkrieg*, he failed to convince even many moderately progressive officers that an armoured force could operate miles behind an enemy's front without being checked or destroyed. Indeed, as Liddell Hart later implied, one needed to be a visionary to discern the future triumphs of *blitzkrieg* in the tank exercises of 1934:

One had only to see the brigade on the move to realize that, as regards equipment, it was very far from being a complete force that could be dispatched on active service. Not only were the medium types still of the old pattern, but the close-support tanks were simply the same machines theoretically adapted to the other role—by giving the gun-barrels an upward tilt and a touch of white paint. And although a considerable improvement had been made in the petrol-tank capacity of the light tanks, these were still a mixed collection.[8]

Between December 1933 and August 1934 Hobart and Lindsay worked out a number of technical details for a combined exercise in which the Tank Brigade and 7th Infantry Brigade would co-operate under Lindsay's overall command. Unfortunately their fundamental differences over future armoured organization remained unresolved. In many respects they shared a common vision. Both regarded the Tank Brigade as the decisive offensive arm; both saw the need for a reconnaissance force of armoured cars; both accepted the need for anti-tank and anti-aircraft protection of the Tank Brigade's base and both saw the need for auxiliary units. The root of their disagreement lay in their ideas about the scale of these auxiliary or supporting forces. While Hobart felt that these should merely be small attachments to the Tank Brigade, Lindsay believed that the Tank Brigade itself should be incorporated into a mechanized division. In short, Lindsay laid for far more stress than Hobart on the need for large-scale support by artillery, engineers, signals, and other ancillary units. Thus, while it is an exaggeration to describe Hobart's ideal formation is an 'all-tank army', he certainly did place more emphasis on tanks than did Lindsay in his notion of a Mobile Division. As one of Hobart's most ardent devotees, Colonel Eric Offord, later recalled: 'We didn't want an all-tank army, but . . . what could we do? The infantry were in buses, they couldn't come with us. The artillery were . . . obstructive. They never put the rounds where you needed them, and when you called, it always came too late.'[9]

In retrospect the culminating exercise of the 1934 training season involving the employment of the experimental Mobile Division was to acquire a portentous significance which it did not really have at the time. Indeed, it was to be seen as the crucial turning-point after which the prospects for the creation of armoured forces with the role of deep strategic penetration became increasingly bleak. This later verdict was unjust to Hobart but even more so to Lindsay, neither of whom regarded the exercise as the decisive trial of their ideas. There was the general disadvantage that the Tank Brigade and 7th Infantry Brigade would only come together for a week in September; thus the commanders and staffs would not have trained as a team and the improvised division would be deficient in transport and equipment. In addition there was a particular handicap: a horsed cavalry brigade was utterly unsuited to reconnoitre ahead of tanks when the objective was as much as a hundred miles from the starting point. The cavalry's lack of speed, armament, or endurance for such a task was demonstrated at a Southern Command map exercise in February 1934 after which Lindsay drew up a paper for the CIGS emphasizing that, while the Mobile Force was worth trying out that year, it could not be an adequate test for want of a mechanized reconnaissance unit and suggesting that three cavalry regiments be motorized for that role in 1935. Lindsay warned prophetically that since commander, staff, signals would not have worked together until the day of the execise there was a grave risk of mishandling which might put back further progress for at least a year.[10]

From the viewpoint of the enthusiasts it was essential that the Mobile Force should be shown to advantage in the culminating exercise, but this was by no means the primary objective of the director and chief umpire, respectively Burnett-Stuart and Wavell. Burnett-Stuart in particular felt that the traditional arms needed to have their morale restored and that some of the tank zealots needed to be taken down a peg or two. These sentiments became widely known before the exercise. Although Liddell Hart later went perhaps too far in suggesting that Burnett-Stuart deliberately sabotaged the Mobile Division's chances, he was not far out in his verdict that 'if the scheme had been primarily designed to cramp the Mobile Force, it would have been hard to contrive anything more ingenious'.[11]

The Mobile Division's task was to carry out a long-range raid against a cluster of closely-grouped objectives which lay behind the enemy's lines near Amesbury. The enemy consisted of 1st Infantry Division and the 2nd (Horsed) Cavalry Brigade under the command of Major-General J. C. Kennedy.* The Mobile Force had to start from an assembly area west of the Severn and this entailed a detour and a very long trek before reaching the defended obstacle of the Kennet and Avon Canal. The distance was feasible for the new light tanks and for the bus column, but too long a stretch for the old medium tanks without allowing for a prolonged pause for maintenance work. Lindsay was also warned that the Mobile Force must be ready to fight a major battle immediately after the raid. As Lord Bridgeman later remarked, this was like telling a jockey to go all out to win the Derby but to be ready to ride in the St Leger immediately afterwards. To handicap the Mobile Force still further, Burnett-Stuart directed that it could not move until 2 a.m. on the first day (19 September), thus allowing it only four hours of concealed movement before daylight.

Lindsay's first idea was to advance on a wide front with several mixed columns. Armoured cars, light tanks, and infantry would dash forward to seize bridgeheads across the Kennet and Avon Canal on the first day, while the medium tanks followed at a more leisurely pace in time to attack at dawn on the second day. Hobart, however, vetoed this plan mainly because he was averse to splitting up the Tank Brigade. Lindsay's second plan involved an extended march to get around 1st Division's flank by moving at night and lying up by day for maintenance work. The attack in this scheme would not take place until the third day. When Burnett-Stuart warned Lindsay against risking a spectacular failure he withdrew the plan. His third and final scheme amounted to making the best of a bad job. The infantry would move up independently to seize the canal crossings on the first day and the Tank Brigade would follow in a single bound the following night. This had two disadvantages: it revealed the direction of the Tank Brigade's attack twenty-four hours in advance, and it left the details of the final phase to be worked out later.

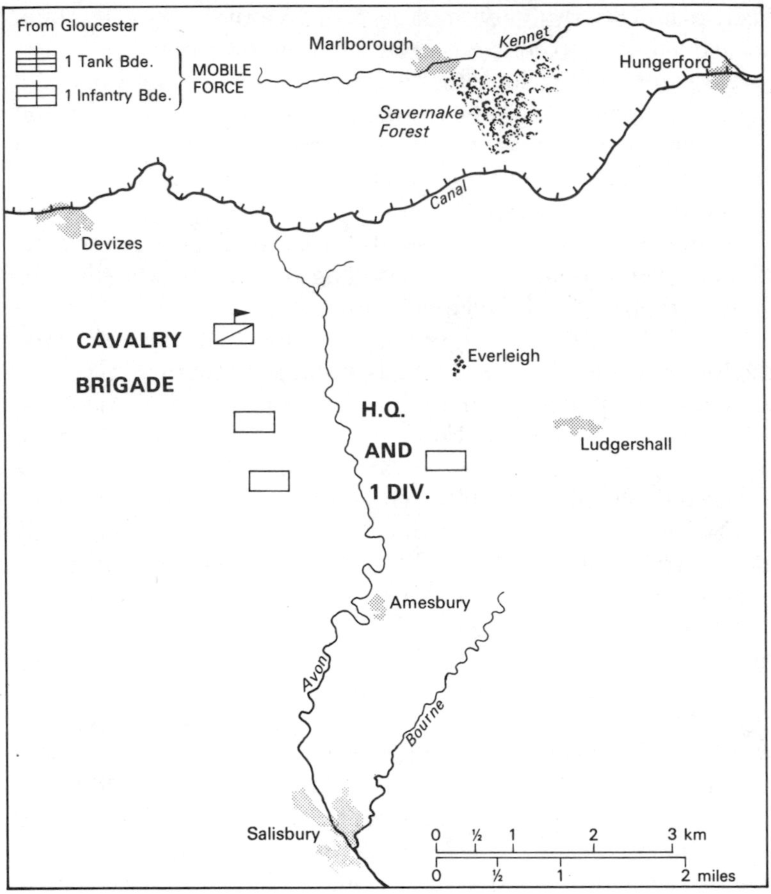

Map 3: Disposition of forces, training exercise September 1934
Source: J. R. Kennedy, *This, Our Army*

To add to the handicap of his lack of a close rapport with Hobart, Lindsay suffered from a series of umpiring decisions—imposing road blocks, air attacks, and other delays—which made his task impossible. His infantry force successfully occupied a bridgehead across the canal at Hungerford but was heavily attacked from the air while awaiting the arrival of the tanks. When these took refuge in a well-concealed laager their position was betrayed by a throng of sight-seers and officers' wives so that the place resembled Piccadilly in the rush-hour.

Hobart felt that the whole exercise had become a farce and refused to take his part seriously. On the afternoon of the second day Burnett-Stuart directed Lindsay to withdraw his forces, but in the meantime Kennedy had boldly sent the motorized elements of the 1st Division round behind the Mobile Force to set up road blocks and cut off its retreat. Once again the umpiring staff intervened in favour of the infantry forces. Despite all these difficulties, in the most successful part of what had become a fiasco for the Mobile Force, Lindsay and Hobart saved their force by splitting it into several columns which by-passed Kennedy's obstacles.

In his criticism of the exercise Burnett-Stuart tried to strike a balance. While on the one hand he admitted that he had designed the exercise partly to bring out the Tank Brigade's limitations, on the other hand he cautioned against exaggerating its failure. He praised Kennedy for his bold counter-offensive, but pointed out that he had been the beneficiary of some unrealistic umpiring decisions. Ironically, he criticized Lindsay's final plan for being too concentrated and direct, and sketched an alternative very similar to Lindsay's original scheme which had been thwarted by Hobart's non-co-operation. Hobart's keenness was praised but the Tank Brigade was criticized for too complacently assuming it was invulnerable to counter-attack and for its excessive ideas of logistical support. Burnett-Stuart's ominous conclusion was that, while the Tank Brigade was not intended simply to shepherd infantry into the fire-zone, its primary role was nevertheless tactical rather than strategic: it should concentrate its future training on actions near the main battle rather than on independent missions.[12]

Hobart's reactions, in a long letter to Liddell Hart a few weeks after the exercise, were remarkably restrained. Though it had been a complete 'frame-up' to raise the morale of the infantry and cavalry, he felt that such a boost was necessary; indeed, 'from the big point of view much good has been done, and there has been a great restoration of confidence in those two arms'. 'I think', he added, 'the Powers were confident that the morale of the Tank Brigade would be unshaken whatever they did. And I think they were justified in that confidence.' In a sympathetic analysis of the obstacles put in Lindsay's way, Hobart noted that he had been denied his only two real options:

either to send his light battalion on a long detour via Romsey whilst the bulk of the Brigade attacked in the north-east via Everleigh; or, better still, simply march to Devizes and cut off 1st Division from its main Army. 'The only interesting thing thereafter was the ease with which we got away.' Though this had been an anticlimax after the Tank Brigade's training, it was really important that the other arms' morale had been raised. 'Enfin,' he ended cheerfully, 'the Tank Brigade is rather like that determined lover who La Rochfoucald (was it?) wittily pointed out will always defeat the smug husband, because he is always thinking of approach and attack whilst the husband trusts to the fancied security of safeguards.'[13]

Though Hobart was excessively sanguine, in the immediate aftermath the Mobile Force's failure seemed no more than a temporary setback deliberately contrived in the interests of the Army as a whole. Thus one may question Liddell Hart's later judgement that it was largely responsible for impeding the development of armoured formations at the very time when Germany was beginning to create its armoured forces. It is doubtful whether Britain would have been able to match Germany armoured division for armoured division even if the Mobile Force exercise had been a complete success. Liddell Hart was, however, right to stress that the apparent defeat of a mobile force by an infantry division seriously affected the judgement of a host of senior officers who had come down from Whitehall to witness the experiment. They jumped to the superficial conclusion that as this exercise had ended in frustration, any such operations would be impracticable in war. In short, a strong reaction set in against the concept of using a mobile armoured force for long-range strategic strokes. The permanent formation of a mobile division, though not abandoned, was deferred until the following year, by which time the unlucky Lindsay had been posted to India on promotion to Major-General.

The General Staff also began to move towards the idea that the role of the future Mobile Division would closely resemble that of the old horsed Cavalry Division. The significant decision was made to convert the 3rd Hussars to light tanks in 1935, which constituted a first step towards the mechanization of cavalry in preference to the expansion of the Royal Tank Corps.

Moreover, in November 1934 it was made clear that no additional Tank Brigades would be created until the country became considerably richer. An important subsidiary decision was that one battalion of slow and heavily armoured tanks was eventually to be provided for close support duties in each infantry division. In short, by the end of 1934 the hopes of the armoured warfare enthusiasts were already being undermined by two developments: the mechanization of the cavalry to form a Mobile Division, and the assignment of infantry tanks to the close-support role.[14]

In sharp contrast to the strategic potential of tank forces emphasized in the 1934 manœuvres, the CIGS's directive for training in the following year laid down that the Tank Brigade was to be confined mainly to actions in or close to the main battle. There was also the lingering belief that tanks and horsed cavalry could work together. As Hobart, still commanding the Tank Brigade, ruefully commented to Liddell Hart: 'In view of the alarm caused in many bosoms by the "independent action" of the tank brigade and "the way these dam [*sic*] tanks are always trying to get away from the Army" we are to be tied more closely' (to the infantry). He felt that it would have taken two more years of practice to develop the technique of penetrating deep into enemy country, 'however', he wrote bitterly, '"Jock" Stuart labels this conception as fantastic . . .' The operation particularly suggested to him was a frontal attack by the Tank Brigade on an enemy in position without the co-operation of infantry, but with such artillery support as could be obtained. Hobart avoided 'committing hari-kari in this way' but felt that Southern Command (i.e. Burnett-Stuart) still hankered after it. In addition to these restrictions, the Tank Brigade's equipment was far from satisfactory. The thirteen-year old medium tanks were now hopelessly antiquated and less than two dozen Mark V light tanks were available. There was still no really efficient wireless set. Though Hobart felt that Burnett-Stuart was a major inhibiting factor, the latter too was disturbed that 'Aldershot' had returned to trench warfare. 'I am bored with my job,' he wrote to Liddell Hart. 'There is no Army left to do anything with—nor would I be allowed to do it if there was.'[15]

Despite these handicaps, Hobart managed to put on one

exercise, in July 1935, in which he demonstrated an armoured force's ability to carry out a strategic advance by moving dispersed and by entirely discarding its long tail of transport vehicles carrying ammunition, fuel, and food. Guderian almost certainly studied reports of this exercise, so it may not be too fanciful of Liddell Hart to discern here the origins for the idea of the former's advance through the Ardennes in May 1940. A further achievement in 1935 was the light-tank battalion's demonstration of the feasibility of night operations. On the debit side, though Hobart accepted the need for close support from artillery, he did not press for the adoption of a powerful tank gun firing high-explosive shells. Then, at the end of August, the Tank Brigade was broken up so that its four battalions could masquerade as infantry tanks for the Corps exercises which pitted 'Eastland' against 'Westland'. These Army manœuvres, the largest for a decade, focused attention on the renovation of the infantry divisions in preparation for a possible European war. From then onwards, as Liddell Hart records in his *Memoirs*, even the more thoughtful soldiers 'became so concerned with the prospects of getting fresh equipment for their own arms that they took less interest than previously in the progress of armoured forces and new operational techniques'.[16]

In 1935 Montgomery-Massingberd, supported by the Army Council, took the momentous decision that the RTC should not be expanded at the expense of the older arms. Instead the infantry should gradually be motorized and the horsed cavalry regiments converted into mechanized units. In 1936 a start was made with the conversion of five cavalry regiments to light trucks and three to light tanks. The following year Deverell decided to mechanize the whole of the cavalry. Similarly at the end of 1935 it was announced that 28 infantry battalions were to be converted into mechanized machine-gun battalions and that the transport of all infantry battalions as well as that of the divisional artillery was to be changed from horses to motors. This policy of gradually motorizing and mechanizing the whole Army bore fruit in that the Field Force of 1939 was entirely equipped with track and motor transport—in advance of all other armies at the time. But this was achieved at a high cost in terms of the delay in forming armoured divisions with an offensive fighting capability. The contrast with Germany's commitment to the rapid formation of armoured (Panzer) divisions in the late 1930s which led to the disastrous outcome in May 1940 has often been underlined, not least by Liddell Hart. Unfortunately, such critics did not unequivocally stress the need for British armoured divisions for a European war at the time when the Army's less ambitious policy of modernization was being formulated.[17]

At this time, however, the programme met with the approval of such a cautiously progressive supporter of tanks as Colonel Martel. In the second (1935) edition of *In the Wake of the Tank,* he predicted that 'For a long time to come, and perhaps for ever, the greater bulk of all armies will be normal formations and not armoured troops'. Rather than arouse bitter opposition by drastic changes, he was in no doubt that the right method was to modernize existing arms instead of forming new ones, i.e. an expanded RTC. He envisaged the Army of the future as divided into mobile and combat troops: tank brigades would play a vital part in the former in reconnaissance and controlling enemy movements, while the infantry would assault the harassed and, it was to be hoped, half-defeated enemy on the battlefield.[18] By contrast the leading RTC advocates of mobile armoured formations were angered and depressed. Thus Tim Pile argued that the right programme would be to produce another Tank Brigade. 'That is the only show in our Army worth a damn . . . They all forget that the infantry is still completely unprotected. We will again see hordes of soldiers driven forward against machine guns. Tanks—*fast* tanks are the only answer.' He felt the worst aspect of the War Office's programme was that it was wholly defensive. Even if the infantry tank was given to the Army the only result would be a reversal to the war of 1916. Pile remained an out-and-out advocate of speedy tanks.[19]

Hobart was even more critical. He thought it was right to mechanize the cavalry but an error to give them tanks, which should all be manned and controlled by the Royal Tank Corps. As its commander he not surprisingly deplored the relegation of the Tank Brigade to infantry-support duties for the second year running in 1936. The Brigade was already less efficient than in 1934. What he most feared was 'the spoiling of this potentially wonderful instrument of war, because no one at the top realises what it could be, and what could be done with it'. At the end of

1936 he reported gloomily to Liddell Hart that things were going from bad to worse. He was to be put on half-pay and the formation of the Mobile Division was shelved indefinitely. 'So Passchendaele has really triumphed and we're definitely back to static war and frontal attacks. And the Old Men wonder why the British people have too much sense to enlist.' He concluded that Burnett-Stuart was being 'absolutely defeatist and despairing' about tanks and was checking the progress which Montgomery-Massingberd had started.

Hobart was depressed too by the failure to provide new vehicles and equipment. On the 1st Tank Brigade signals exercise in September 1936, for example, he had only just acquired eight decent wireless sets (200 were needed). He had only a few old 2-man light tanks because most of the new equipment (and trained officers) had been sent to Egypt and the cavalry now had priority. Slowness of production was partly to blame but the War Office directors of mechanization did not know what they wanted. He wanted to teach tanks to fight at longer ranges but the light tanks' anti-tank machine guns could only penetrate at 500 yards—on an optimistic estimate—and even then might not achieve a knock-out.[20]

Although the Royal Tank Corps and their supporters naturally deplored the decision to mechanize the cavalry, from a wider social viewpoint it was a major accomplishment for which Montgomery-Massingberd should take credit. As Dr Winton points out, he was one of the few soldiers who could have done it without raising a major controversy. Though a gunner himself, his long association with the cavalry and similar social outlook identified him as one of it own. Consequently, when he decreed that they must say goodbye to boot and saddle they were prepared to bow to the inevitable. Winton is also probably right to insist that Montgomery-Massingberd had no real alternative but to mechanize the cavalry in lieu of expanding the Tank Corps. The wholesale disbandment of a Corps with immense social prestige would have created a tremendous furore in a Service whose morale was already appallingly low. In the event there was little overt cavalry opposition to the changes though the commanding officer of the Scots Greys indulged in political lobbying in a vain effort to avert the mechanization of his own regiment.[21]

As might have been anticipated, however, the cavalry accepted unavoidable changes in its methods of transport and armament with a minimum of change in its professional and social outlook. Pile thought it was folly to force the cavalry to mechanize while allowing officers to retain their chargers. 'The proposal to form a cavalry tank school at Weedon shows that they have come into the Army to hunt'. Major-General Horace Birks (RTC) was later to recall that his Corps held cavalry regiments in contempt because when they did start to mechanize 'they did it with one eye on bales of fodder instead of getting down to the tank side'. 'They were frightened of losing their horses and their hunting and so on which one can understand because it meant a lot to those people.' Interestingly Birks thought cavalry took much more readily to armoured cars than to tanks.[22] Cavalry officers could still be found to stick up for their arm's unique qualities and continuing relevance. Thus Major-General Howard-Vyse* in a heated controversy in *The Times* generated by Liddell Hart wrote: 'In our old cavalry regiments, on the other hand, successes and failures in innumerable wars, greatly reinforced by a constant association in peace with that comparatively swift animal the horse, had resulted in quickness of thought and an elasticity of outlook which are almost second nature.' Deverell, as CIGS, told Liddell Hart that he was mechanizing divisional cavalry regiments, despite protests, because horses could not keep up with motorized infantry and carry out reconnaissance in time. 'Burnett-Stuart was apt to forget this in claiming that they could see over walls!' Captain J. R. Kennedy concluded a pungent criticism of the cavalry mystique with the hope, probably vain, that 'officers may no longer be required to make themselves ridiculous by putting on spurs to dine, to dance, or to attend mechanized parades'.[23] While it seems clear that the cavalry, by and large, was reluctant to change its mental outlook, in fairness it must also be noted that there was a good deal of prejudice against them in the other arms, particularly the RTC, which made adaptation even harder.

It may be appropriate to break the sequence here to question the characteristic British compromise by which the cavalry were 'associated' rather than amalgamated with the RTC in the summer of 1939 to form the Royal Armoured Corps. This uneasy marriage was the predictable outcome of a War Office Committee chaired by a Guardsman, Lieutenant-General Sir Bertram Sergison-Brooke,* in 1938. According to Hobart this Committee put far more emphasis on cavalry spirit, regimental tradition, and the type of officer it draws than on tanks and the RTC. It recommended that officers remain in separate regiments but the men would enlist in a single corps to be trained wholly by the RTC. Hobart saw this as a dilution of the RTC and a threat to the efficiency of the Tank Brigade. In the event all units of the RAC retained their old designations, distinctions, and badges. Units of the RTC became battalions (later regiments) in the new Royal Tank Regiment. Personnel were eventually to become interchangeable but the pace was not to be hurried.[24]

By the mid-1930s Britain was not only losing the lead in doctrine and field experiments with mobile armoured formations; she was also falling behind the more progressive European armies—notably those of Germany and Russia—in the production of modern tanks. In the first half of the 1930s as has been shown, the War Office's inability to find funds for the production of more than a few experimental models provides a major explanation for Britain's comparative decline. The War Office was also badly handicapped by its almost total dependence on the firm of Vickers-Armstrong for tank designs. Thereafter the increasing doubt thrown on the Field Force's continental commitment militated against increased expenditure on tanks, even when the purse strings were loosened. In 1937 the Army Estimates were boosted by an additional defence loan to just over £82 million. The proportion to be spent on wheeled and tracked vehicles also increased to 9.2 per cent of the total (£7.6 million) as compared with 2.6 per cent in 1934, 3.9 per cent in 1935, and 6.3 per cent in 1936. During the same period, 1934–7 inclusive, the annual amount devoted to animals fell from 1.15 to 0.25 per cent.[25] Anti-aircraft guns and air defence generally received a much higher priority than tanks. Accordingly, there was little expansion of production capacity. When the swing towards 'limited liability' reached its furthest point in the Cabinet's review of priorities in December 1937, the estimated saving on tanks would exceed all other Army economies added together. It is not therefore surprising that Deverell,

Gort, and other leading soldiers felt that Liddell Hart was undermining their case for an improved Army including a prompt supply of modern tanks. In 1937 the Army actually underspent its vote on warlike stores by nearly £6 million. What is unusual is Liddell Hart's apparent failure to see any connection between the acceptance of 'limited liability' and the decline in emphasis on tanks.[26]

In the event, lack of agreed designs and inadequate production capacity meant that Government cuts in the numbers of tanks to be permitted were not in fact as significant as they seemed. Thus infantry tanks were to be reduced from a target of 833 to 340 and medium tanks from 247 to nil, but even the final designs for the latter were not expected until mid-1939. The War Office sensibly ordered types which could be more easily produced in the near future; for example, Hore-Belisha planned to offset the short-term loss in medium tanks by increasing orders for cruisers from 350 to 585. It is clear, however, that in the late 1930s the War Office was caught without agreed designs for different types of tank to perform specific tactical tasks which could be mass-produced as soon as factories could take orders.[27]

The Army's low place in the pecking-order should not conceal the fact that its own technical experts in the field of tank design and production were very disappointing. Responsibility for the delays in re-equipment lay primarily with the Master-General of the Ordnance, Sir Hugh Elles. Duff Cooper had originally considered him to be the ablest member of the Army Council but he had severely reprimanded him before leaving the War Office, having come to the conclusion that he was lacking in grasp and lazy though impressive in appearance. Simarily Major-General John Kennedy thought him 'a nice fellow' but 'a poseur and a flat-catcher'. Karslake and several other senior officers expressed critical views on Elles. In Liddell Hart's view:

> Elles was sceptical of the independent armoured force idea, and more inclined to believe that another war, if it ever came, would begin where the last war had finished, with the tanks leading and aiding the infantry attack as at Cambrai and Amiens. While he saw the value of a fast light tank in a cavalry fighting–reconnaissance role, he was mainly concerned to produce a new tank fit to work closely with infantry in the assault.[28]

Elles's weakness as MGO was not offset by Brough and Studd,* respectively Director and Assistant Director of Mechanization in the vital period 1932–6. That period was marked by inertia and shortsightedness; a variety of experimental models were designed and tried in a desultory way, but all proved unsatisfactory, and much time was wasted in trying to correct mechanical faults. There was a deplorable reluctance to appoint expert engineers to this Department, but the arrival of such an expert, Major-General A. E. Davidson,* in 1936 to replace Brough made a big improvement.[29] Even more significant was the selection of Martel as his assistant, after eighteen years outside the War Office as an outstanding but unofficial expert on tank designs and performance. It was Martel's great achievement, related in detail in his memoirs, to secure the American Christie tank, with its admirable suspension, as the prototype of the British Cruiser after being greatly impressed by the use the Russians had made of it on his visit to their manœuvres in September 1936. Martel's drive and ingenuity in overcoming the various obstacles put in his way, first by the Americans and then by the War Office, suggests what might have been done earlier by more energetic and knowledgeable predecesors. But even Martel, supported by Hobart as DDSD (Armoured Fighting Vehicles) from March 1937, failed to make headway in that year with plans for a new medium tank.[30]

By 1937, therefore, the War Office had embarked on a policy of producing three different kinds of tanks (with variant models) to fulfil different roles: the light tank and armoured machine-gun carriers for reconnaissance purposes; the cruiser or medium tanks for Armoured Divisions; and the heavy infantry tanks (later called 'Matildas') for the assault on defensive positions.[31]

The Mobile Division, whose establishment had been approved as long ago as 1935, was actually due to be formed on 1 October 1937 and the question of who should command it became a major issue. War now seemed imminent and the advocates of armoured warfare felt that it was essential that one of their members, preferably a tank corps officer, be given command, whereas most senior officers at the War Office tended to close ranks against what they regarded as a take-over bid by a small group of difficult, ambitious radicals susceptible to the dangerous influence of Liddell Hart.[32] The latter provides a link to another aspect of the controversy in which command of the Mobile Division became one of the fundamental differences between Hore-Belisha and the Army Council. In fact the appointment constituted a trial of strength between Deverell, supported by his senior colleagues, and the reforming War Minister.

The promotion of officers to the ranks of brigadier and major-general was controlled by a War Office selection committee consisting of the CIGS, the Adjutant-General, the Military Secretary, and the generals holding the major home commands. This committee made recommendations to the Secretary of State for War who had the final say.

Early in September 1937 Liddell Hart discovered that the CIGS, Deverell, intended to give command of the Mobile Division to a cavalryman, John Blakiston-Houston* whose chief claim to distinction was that he was an expert in equitation. Liddell Hart noted: 'it is like a man who has always kept horses, buying an expensive new car and engaging an expert chauffeur—only to turn him into the housekeeper, while turning his groom into the chauffeur without even troubling to teach him how to drive!' Hore-Belisha, however, was not impressed by Blakiston-Houston and initially favoured Broad. Other possible officers of sufficient seniority with experience in actual command of mechanized units were Major-Generals Lindsay (now exiled in Calcutta) and Pile (on half-pay since promotion), and Colonels W. M. Sutton (Commanding AFV School), M. Kemp-Welch (on half-pay), and P. C. S. Hobart (DDSD).[33]

Ironside's diaries throw an interesting light on the development of the controversy. By 26 October Lord Gort, the officer most directly involved as the recently appointed Military Secretary, was almost on the point of resignation. Gort was in the awkward position of trying to sell Hore-Belisha an unsound horse (i.e. Blakiston-Houston) which the minister was too astute to buy. Ironside inclined to agree with Hore-Belisha: Blakiston-Houston was, he felt, 'too bull-headed' and, according to the War Minister's report, 'could only slap his thigh and shout'.[34] As a compromise acceptable to the cavalry the Selection Board put up Alan Brooke (Director of Military Training), an excellent gunner and staff officer but with no mechanized experience. Early in November Hore-Belisha reluctantly approved

Brooke's appointment but only on condition that Hobart replaced Brooke as DMT. Pile was given the important new command of 1st Anti-Aircraft Division and thereby removed as a candidate for the Mobile Division. Pile felt that the latter command should have gone to an officer with mechanized experience who knew how to lead from personal knowledge. Brooke had never served 'in a mobile show' and had probably never sat in a tank with headphones on. In Pile's opinion he was a firm believer in the infantry attack well-supported by artillery —and was too rigid to change. Yet without a commander of great imagination and enthusiasm the Mobile Division would soon become the un-Mobile Division.[35]

Pile's misgivings were justified for when Brooke was transferred to the newly formed Anti-Aircraft Corps command in mid-1938, Gort (now CIGS), insisted on replacing him by another cavalryman Major-General Roger Evans,* formerly Household Cavalry and only recently appointed DDMI. This looked like a deliberate snub to the qualified Tank Corps major-generals and, unlike Brooke, Evans was not an outstanding officer. As Liddell Hart cryptically concludes, Evans took the division (by then renamed 1st Armoured) to France in May 1940 but he was never again employed in the field. The failure to appoint Hobart, or another Tank Corps officer, to the command of the Mobile Division proved fatal to the division's prospects as an armoured *striking* force as distinct from a substitute for the old cavalry *reconnaissance* division. In fact, given the Government's indecision over the Army's role even if it were to be dispatched to the Continent, Hobart was probably the only commander of sufficient vision and determination to preserve and develop the division as a striking force. In the event little was done between the end of 1937 and the outbreak of war to prepare the division for such a role: Britain went to war without a single effective armoured division or a coherent doctrine of armoured warfare.[36]

After the high point of the Mobile Force exercise in 1934 and the Army manœuvres in 1935, military training became less rather than more realistic as war approached. Thus in November 1937 Burnett-Stuart submitted a highly critical report on the year's training in which he asserted that 'there is no major unit and no formation in my command [Southern] which is fit to take the field against the troops of a first-class military power'. A vicious circle had been created: the Army could make no show of efficiency for lack of men and equipment; and men would not join an army which could not make an efficient showing. He cited the case of a Medium Artillery Brigade which could man only two guns for its biennial practice camp. Broad, too, found that year's exercises discouraging. A civilian friend in Essex told him that they never saw any soldiers and the Army 'seemed to have a lot of mechanical vehicles which they didn't quite know what to do with'! The lack of modern tanks tended to depress Britain's most likely potential ally and mystify her likely enemy as Burnett-Stuart later recalled:

We had many visitors to the Southern Command. General Weygand, with General Pagécy, spent the day seeing the Tank Brigade, and shook his head and went away, hoping that we really had something better than what he was shown. Later on General Field Marshal von Blomberg, with General von Stumpf and others, visited the Tank Corps centre at Bovington, where he was given an excellent luncheon; he too went away shaking his head, but hoping that we really had not anything better than what we had shown him, though obviously finding it difficult to believe it.[37]

Hobart, as Director of Military Training, was particularly depressed by training conditions and the War Office's unhelpful attitude to the Army's unpreparedness. In November 1937 he told Liddell Hart that training was blocked at every turn by the Cardwell system combined with the fanatically independent regimental system and the insistence of maintaining the Indian garrison of 80 years ago. He felt that junior officers would welcome a radical reorganization but the colonels would 'fuss madly'.[38]

It might therefore have been expected that Hobart would welcome the news, in July 1938, that he was to be posted to Egypt in September to organize and command the new second Mobile Division. His correspondence with Liddell Hart, however, shows that he felt that he was being shunted aside to an appointment which the War Office did not take seriously. What he frankly coveted was command of the Mobile Dvision at home. Why, for example, had he not been given a GSO1 or a proper headquarters staff? More seriously, without more tanks (tanks *with guns* as he emphasized) the Mobile Division would be a sham since there were only one and a half tank battalions in Egypt and three were needed for a brigade.[39]

Yet despite Hobart's understandable reservations Egypt had been the most promising area for the development of British armoured doctrine throughout the 1930s. The first pioneer of experimental work with armoured vehicles in Egypt was George Lindsay who was appointed GSO1 of British troops there in 1929. Lindsay practised the offensive–defensive method of war as recommended by Fuller and Liddell Hart. He also sought to bring out the value of paralysing the enemy by striking at his spinal cord—an essential water point on his line of communications. Two years later, when Burnett-Stuart accepted the Egyptian Command, Lindsay informed him that although physical conditions were ideal, the entire armoured forces there consisted of only 16 Vickers Medium Mark II and two armoured-car companies one of which (5th) was not officially recognized by the War Office. Nevertheless, in his three years in command there, Burnett-Stuart transformed Egypt into an exciting training area with the emphasis on mechanical experiments and positive thinking about armoured warfare. With the admirable selection of Pile as commander of the Canal Brigade (in 1932) Burnett-Stuart was able to stage imaginative exercises involving the co-operation of aircraft with ground troops, and night operations. Whereas in England, when on leave in 1933, Pile felt that the Army was 'marching down the hill again as hard as ever they can', in Egypt 'we really do soldier . . . and no nonsense of attacking machine-guns'. He particularly stressed the value he and Burnett-Stuart placed on night exercises: in April 1935, for example, his brigade carried out a splendid night crossing of the Nile for the benefit of the visiting CIGS.[40]

When the Abyssinian crisis in October 1935 caused additional mechanized units to be hastily dispatched from England to counter a possible Italian invasion, a Mobile Force was improvised around the nucleus of 11th Hussars and 6th Battalion RTC, which Burnett-Stuart had persuaded the War Office to establish in Egypt before his departure in 1934. To these forces were added 1st (Light) Battalion with a Medium Tank Company of the 4th Battalion from England. In overall command was Vyvyan Pope,* who had been specifically summoned from India by Hobart as a trusted man to take control in case of war.

In the event the Force returned to barracks without seeing action and woefully conscious of its mechanical unreliability. Nevertheless Pope's biographer believes that he deserves much of the credit for the basic experimental work which led to the British armoured forces' triumph over the Italians in 1940–1. Unfortunately, Hobart had achieved this rapid build-up of armoured units on the Egyptian frontier at a heavy cost to the Tank Brigade in England.[41]

Hobart himself arrived in Egypt at the height of the Munich crisis to form the Mobile Division in the face of a possible Italian invasion from Cyrenaica. He was allegedly greeted by the GOC.-in-C. Egypt, General 'Copper' Gordon-Finlayson,* with the brusque remark: 'I don't know what you've come for and I don't want you anyway'. Hobart's miscellaneous force comprised a Cavalry Brigade, a Tank Group, and a Pivot Group. The Tank Group—the only real striking element—consisted of the 1st and 6th Battalions RTC., the 1st still equipped with light tanks and the 6th having only two companies of mediums. Hobart's great achievements in the year he spent in Egypt were to weld this miscellany into a division ready for war (the famous 7th Armoured or 'Desert Rats') and to accustom it to operating in the desert. It was Hobart's tragedy that he fell foul of Finlayson who gave him an adverse personal report, and that the prejudice against him was inherited by Finlayson's successor, Lt.-General H. M. 'Jumbo' Wilson. Wilson called for Hobart's removal from command of his division in November 1939 and Wavell, recently appointed Commander-in-Chief Middle East, upheld the decision. Both reported that Hobart was suitable for a different type of appointment at home but he was to retire and become a corporal in the Home Guard before getting another chance to train an armoured division. Although Hobart was notorious for his prickliness of manner, outspokenness, ruthlessness in exercising his command, and fervent belief in tanks as an offensive force, it is difficult not to feel that he was removed from an important post at a critical time for insufficient reasons and thereafter deliberately denied a suitable appointment in which to exercise his outstanding talents.[42]

Hobart's failure to get command of the Mobile Division at home and his summary removal from Egypt raises the wider question of the War Office's curious handling of the careers of the leading advocates of armoured warfare. Pile and Hobart notably believed that 'they' (the War Office hierarchy) were out to thwart the tank exponents and Liddell Hart's writings tend to support their conviction. Ronald Lewin also writes of Lindsay, Broad, and Pile being 'carefully removed from any contact with tanks'. While it would probably be too definite to talk of an anti-tank conspiracy in the War Office and Army Council, there was an undeniable feeling, endorsed by successive CIGSs (including Gort), that they must be 'kept in their place' and not allowed to become the predominant influence in the more significant commands. Hobart expressed the sense of persecution when he wrote to Liddell Hart in 1936:

> Infantry tanks are not an uncomfortable idea to the Ivory Nobs: after all, they were used at Passchendaele. It's the Tank Brigade and the Mobile Division about which there is danger: and this damned 'upstart' R.T.C.—'great mistake ever forming it'. Both the C.I.G.S. and Adjutant-General have openly said so. I would be glad if you would burn this letter.[43]

It must be borne in mind, however that, although the leading tank advocates were a comparatively united group in comparison with the conservatives, there were marked differences of personality and doctrine among them. Thus, as was shown earlier, Lindsay and Hobart did not see eye to eye on the role of the Tank Brigade in the 1934 exercises. Martel was always primarily interested in practical engineering matters and held a balanced view of the position of armoured forces within the Army as a whole. Lindsay was a notable casualty following his eclipse in the 1934 exercise. He seems to have accepted his exile to Calcutta in 1935 comparatively cheerfully, but on his return to England in 1939 he retired from the Army, presumably because Gort (by then CIGS) held that he was finished. Though subsequently given command of 9th Highland Division during the war he did not see active service, nor did he exert any further influence on armoured tactics. Broad was another armoured expert whose talents were by no means fully exploited. Between 1937 and 1939 he served as major-general in charge of administration at Aldershot after Gort had opposed his appointment as QMG. It was a tragedy for the Army that Gort and Broad had quarrelled over a trivial matter. Broad subsequently held the Aldershot Command in 1939–40, and was finally GOC.-in-

C. Eastern Army India from 1940 to 1942. Most officers who worked with Broad, including Adam, Armitage,* Hutton,* and Karslake, thought him first class, but Karslake mentioned also his lack of tact, citing as an example that at Quetta he had agreed, but only at his daughter's request, to make an exception to his rule by allowing one RAF officer to visit his house. This attitude did not go down well with RAF officers at the Staff College.[44] Tim Pile is in a different category from Hobart, Broad, and Lindsay since command of the 1st Territorial Army Anti-Aircraft Division was widely regarded as a 'plum' appointment in 1937 and he was, after all, a gunner. He proved to be an outstanding success as an organizer, trainer, and inspirational leader of anti-aircraft forces. He was promoted General and appointed GOC.-in-C. Anti-Aircraft Command, a position he retained for the whole war. Nevertheless, it is evident from the Pownall diaries that Pile had bitter enemies on the General Staff. In this case the evidence suggests that Liddell Hart made the mistake of pushing an able protégé too ostentatiously, notably in pressing his claims to succeed Deverell as CIGS in October 1937.[45]

Finally, Martel's case is different again in that he was a Royal Engineer not a member of the Tank Corps and was not 'sent to Coventry' like Lindsay, Broad, and Hobart. Between 1936 and February 1939 he was successively Assistant Director and Deputy Director of Mechanization at the War Office, and was then given command of 50th (Northumbrian) Territorial Division. On 21 May 1940 he directed the improvised counter-attack at Arras in which two of his battalions co-operated with 1st Tank Brigade, but he does not seem to have made a favourable impression as a commander in this admittedly 'forlorn hope' action. In December 1940 he was appointed Commander of the Royal Armoured Corps but the post was abolished after he had become involved in disputes with Hobart. In 1942 he went to Moscow as head of the British military commision and retired at the end of the war.[46]

Thus, whether or not there was a definite campaign against them, pioncers of armoured tactics and doctrine were certainly not given the opportunities which they might reasonably have expected to command in war. In particular, Lindsay, Broad, and Hobart—after the outbreak of war—could legitimately feel that they had been unjustly pushed aside, especially given the lack of comparable tank specialists to replace them. It needs to be remembered, however, that the Liddell Hart–Hore Belisha purge in late 1937 caused several able officers such as Karslake to be prematurely retired and also that many good commanders, like Gort himself, were retired or placed in insignificant posts as a result of the inevitable shake up in the first year of the war.

In the year before its outbreak Britain was still experimenting with a variety of tank models but production problems were holding up supply. The least of these was in light tanks, the production of which had been increased from one a week in 1937 to eight in June 1938. However, armed with only heavy machine guns and protected by a mere 15 mm of armour, these were vulnerable to 2-pounder anti-tank guns. In June 1938 the light cruiser, which could do 45 m.p.h. across country, was still in the model stage but it was hoped that two could be produced per week by January 1939. The heavy tank weighing 28 tons was even further from production. Finally, two types of infantry support tank (code-named 'Matilda') were nearing the delivery stage. The smaller weighed only 9 tons and could only travel at 7–8 m.p.h. Forty or fifty were delivered by the end of 1938. The larger, an excellent model, weighed 23 tons, was armed with a 2-pounder main gun, carried a crew of four, and was expected to be ready in 1939. Most important, its armour of between 60–75 mm thickness could keep out a 2-pounder armour-piercing shell. The most urgent need was for a new medium tank to replace the obsolescent Vickers Medium for the mobile role in the Tank Brigade. By the end of 1938 two types (the A9 and A13) based on the Christie model were on order but few were expected until 1939. These were the prototypes of the later Crusader, the standard British medium tank in the armoured divisions in 1941 and 1942. It is noteworthy that British tanks were armed with nothing more powerful than the 2-pounder gun, a weakness for which critics held the armoured advocates responsible; for they tended to emphasize speed at the expense of hitting power. The 2-pounder gun could not deal effectively with anti-tank weapons and was moreover at a disadvantage compared with the 37 mm gun of the German Panzer Mark III (which could penetrate the British mediums' 30 mm of armour at 500 yards).[47]

That the Mobile Division remained little more than a conglomeration of units was due mainly to the Army's lack of a clear conception of its role. The relationship between the cavalry and tank components remained uncertain and mutual suspicions were not ended by their absorbtion in the Royal Armoured Corps in 1939. Two mechanized infantry battalions had also been formed but had not yet worked out precisely how to co-operate with tanks. Nor had the artillery worked out techniques for supporting rapidly moving tank forces.[48]

By September 1939 Germany had already created six Panzer divisions and by May 1940 she possessed 10. Admittedly these contained a large proportion of obsolescent Mark I and Mark II light tanks but the whole German approach differed from the British.[49] The Germans set out from 1935 to create armoured divisions and made no attempt to produce anything like the British tank brigades equipped with heavily armoured tanks for the support of infantry in heavy fighting. Although the Panzer division had far more unarmoured troops than the British, it contained a large proportion of obsolescent Mark I and Mark II light tanks but the whole German approach differed from the try divisions though most of the infantry divisions remained dependent on horse transport. Britain's loss of momentum in the second half of the 1930s is graphically illustrated by her tank situation in May 1940. Apart from 7th Armoured Division, still being formed in Egypt, the British Army had only two battalions of the Royal Tank Regiment in France and the Divisional cavalry regiments. The 1st Armoured Division was still assembling on Salisbury Plain and was not in a fit state to go to war.[50]

Several factors clearly contributed to Britain's loss of the lead to Germany in developing armoured formations in the later 1930s and her almost total incapacity to conduct armoured operations in Europe at the outset of the Second World War. Lack of money was evidently crucial in preventing the creation of large tank forces until the later 1930s, and thereafter the Army was still badly placed because of its low priority *vis-à-vis* the other Services and its inferior production base. Nevertheless, it was precisely when financial stringency was at its tightest in the early 1930s that Britain carried out her most progressive experiments with the world's first tank brigade. Another factor was military conservatism embracing such diverse elements as the cavalry's reluctance to mechanize, the inability of most senior officers to envisage strategic armoured operations, and a general unwillingness to push through radical reforms in a hurry. Parliamentary and public indifference—or overt hostility—towards the Army could be held to be a third inhibiting factor. Yet none of these considerations are so important as the question of the Army's role, which was a matter for high level political–military decision making. Unless a definite decision was made to the contrary, the Army's whole organization, recruiting system, training, equipment, and—not least—tradition were strongly oriented towards imperial defence. The Cardwell system did not permit the development of large armoured forces on the home establishment. The Tank Brigade was, 'in effect, an appendage to the British Army'; it could be retained only by maintaining an equivalent number of armoured-car companies overseas, but these were quite unsuitable for Continental war.[51] Critics were reluctant to face the awkward fact that, although imperial defence could be enhanced by mechanizing the infantry and cavalry, it was less suitable for larger armoured formations. Haldane had partly overcome the rigidity of the Cardwell system before 1914 by organizing his Expeditionary Force into divisions from the existing units at home, but he had taken care not to be specific about its likely destination. Contrary to what is often asserted, the pre-1914 Expeditionary Force was organized to meet *any* overseas emergency.[52] Haldane's successors in the 1930s suffered from two insurmountable handicaps: the transformation of European armies in terms of both fire power and means of movement. An army organized for imperial defence was simply no long suitable for the demands of modern continental war. This was the central dilemma to which the soldiers found no clear answer in the 1930s and which the Government avoided until its hand was finally forced in the spring of 1939.

Thus military conservatism and the predominance of the imperial defence mission clearly played a significant part in determining the form, doctrine, and size of Britain's armoured forces. The decision to mechanize the Cavalry rather than expand the Tank Corps meant that two-thirds of the Mobile Division consisted of light tanks manned by men from ex-cavalry regiments. Conservatives like Montgomery-Massingberd believed that the Mobile Division could cover the advance of the Field Force in a European war very much as the cavalry division had done in 1914; whereas Burnett-Stuart envisaged the Mobile Division performing a similar role but in an imperial war against a less powerful adversary. Few officers were as clear-cut in their thinking on this issue—or as outspoken—as Burnett-Stuart. To the chagrin of armoured warfare advocates like Hobart, Liddell Hart, and Fuller, the Mobile Division turned out to be primarily a reconnaissance and security formation, rather than a striking force capable of operating independently. Finally, though the Tank Brigade remained precariously part of the Mobile Division—despite Deverell's talk of removing it in 1937—it was an unwieldy instrument because of the imbalance between its infantry and tank components—a proportion of only two infantry to nine tank battalions.

Thus this account fully endorses the judgement that 'perpetual doubt about the Army's role in war was the most significant factor influencing its organization and doctrine in the inter-war years'.[53] It is ironical that Liddell Hart who did so much to pioneer tank development and armoured doctrine in the 1920s and early 1930s, and to a lesser extent Burnett-Stuart (whose influence inside the Army hierarchy was nevertheless important), should have undermined what little prospects there were after 1934 for the formation of armoured divisions by their well-publicized opposition to the Army's continental commitment. On this criterion—a clear perception, that is, of what was likely to be the Army's most crucial role and the elaboration of a Field Force best-suited to fulfil it—the soldier who emerges with by far the most credit is Hobart. He alone unequivocally declared that the European role was the most important and drafted his concept of armoured forces accordingly. Hobart's memorandum in October 1937 expounding and defending his views on the European role of the Army with particular reference to Armoured Fighting Vehicles (AFV) is so pungent and prescient that it deserves to be quoted at length. His concluding summary conveys a good idea of his approach:

The Western theatre will be decisive for us. Elsewhere, we have to accept risks. Air operations will severely curtail our first contribution to Continental operations. Not much more than static defence can be expected from Infantry formations against a first class enemy. Our allies already dispose of considerable defensive strength. The greatest threat from our point of view is a German drive to secure advanced air bases. German armoured formations, leading such a drive, can be countered by defence where it is ready, but only by armoured counter-attack otherwise. Our necessarily small contribution in the first phase must be of maximum value. In relation to the forces of our allies the greatest value we can provide is offensive armoured formations to assist to counter the German drive.

Therefore, we ought to organise a Field Force with a high proportion of armoured formations eventually. Meanwhile, the Field Force, such as it is in the present state of the Army and the rearmament programme, must be adapted as best it can be to its task. The Mobile Division, destined to be the first arrival in the theatre of operations, is at present unwieldy and is not offensively as effective as it might be. The Infantry formations, arriving later, can only be expected to contribute to defence in an already declared situation. We are expanding an uneconomical proportion of our resources, in the provision of lighter forces (mechanized Cavalry), to the detriment of the provision that we might make for a more effective offensive contribution.[54]

Pile reported to Liddell Hart that the CIGS had had Hobart 'on the mat' for what he regarded as a subversive memorandum. It was on this occasion that Deverell added that it did not matter if an infantryman or gunner commanded the Mobile Division. The Tank Corps might get their chance in two or three years' time.[55] Hobart, more than any other soldier or civilian, had the right to say 'I told you so' after the German triumph in France in May 1940.

CHAPTER 7

The Defence Requirements Committee and the role of the Army, 1933–1934

The first report of the Defence Requirements Committee and its adoption, severely modified, by the Cabinet in 1934 marks the watershed in British defence policy between the wars. The Committee was appointed less than a year after Hitler's accession to power in Germany, and its deliberations coincided with the failure of the Disarmament Conference at Geneva (though hopes in Britain for an agreement on armaments were by no means dead). Although the cancellation of the Ten Year Rule in 1932 by no means signified the beginning of rearmament, the DRC's investigation of the Services' worst deficiencies was a first tentative step in that direction. Moreover, by nominating Germany as the most dangerous potential enemy against whom long-term defence preparations should primarily be directed, the DRC called for a drastic revision of the Services' priorities and roles. At the same time, by delicate wording by the resourceful Hankey, the Services could claim that the overall 'imperial' balance was maintained. This chapter is less concerned with the DRC's findings as a whole, since these have fully been discussed elsewhere,[1] but more particularly with the role of the Army.

The DRC emphasized, and maintained against ministerial criticism, the vital importance it attached to the Army's being prepared to intervene promptly in a continental war. Yet behind a façade of unanimity the Chiefs of Staff were in reality seriously at odds about both the need for a military commitment on the Continent and the Army's ability to fulfil it. For a variety of reasons ministers were reluctant to accept such a commitment; indeed, several remained unconvinced that it was necessary. The outcome was a compromise whereby the continental role was upheld in principle while ministerial support and funds to prepare an Expeditionary Force were largely withheld. As a consequence an almost continuous debate on the role of the Army dragged on until near the outbreak of the Second World War and this had very serious effects on military doctrine, training, and readiness for war.

In order to understand the National Government's delay in dealing with the glaring deficiencies in the armed Services as revealed in the Chiefs of Staff's Annual Review of 1932, two main considerations must be borne in mind. First, the economic crisis was still held to outweigh the needs of defence in 1933. The role of the Treasury will be examined more fully in later chapters. Here we need only note that some of the more sweeping criticisms made against its officials were exaggerated or wide of the mark. True it lent powerful support to the National Government's rigidly orthodox reaction to the financial crisis of 1931: the insistence that confidence must be restored by a combination of reduced expenditure and a minimum of interference with the economy. With good reason the Treasury was worried by the balance of payments situation, and feared that if large-scale rearmament were attempted too quickly the country might be exhausted before war began. In 1934 Neville Chamberlain was expressing the orthodox Treasury view when he rejected the idea of a defence loan as a solution to the DRC proposals; but by April 1935 the Treasury was preparing to abandon financial orthodoxy in the light of the alarming evidence of the amount Germany was spending on rearmament. Recent research does not bear out the charge that its officials were unaware of the need to build up the arms industry, or that they put cost accounting before national security. On the contrary they were kept well informed about needs and new developments (such as radar), but they knew that industry would be quite unable to fulfil rearmament orders in the short term given the years of neglect by successive governments. Thus more ambitious plans without strict Treasury control of priorities would not necessarily have resulted in better-equipped forces by the late 1930s. Where the Treasury is open to criticism is in the remarkable degree to which it applied strategic conceptions of its own in determining defence priorities. In the period covered by this chapter its preoccupation with a return to financial stability was surely understandable. That real measures of rearmament were not contemplated until 1935 was primarily due to the Cabinet's reluctance to accept that external military threats were more serious than the domestic economic crisis. Thus, in explaining a small increase in the Army Estimates in March of that year, the Financial Secretary to the War Office, Duff Cooper, stated that the increased expenditure was not for any augmentation in the size of the Army or to improve its readiness for war, but merely to replace cuts made a year before 'in face of the danger of national bankruptcy which was then thought . . . to be even a greater danger than that of having inefficient fighting services'.[2]

The second obstacle to even considering the Services' worst deficiencies with a view to limited rearmament was the fervent hope placed in the success of the Disarmament Conference which assembled in 1932. It must also be remembered that when German claims for equality of status and French demands for security were quickly seen to be incompatible, British sympathies tended to lie with the former. To begin with, as Professor Gibbs observes, 'the under dog [i.e. Germany] was regarded as the symbol of disarmament, not the obstacle to it'. Germany was persuaded to return to Geneva at the end of 1932 but by the time the Conference reassembled in February 1933 Hitler had become Chancellor of the Reich, and Japan shortly afterwards announced her intention to resign from the League of Nations. The British Government, and in particular the Prime Minister, Ramsay MacDonald, made desperate efforts through the summer to keep hopes of multilateral disarmament alive by presenting new plans for phased reductions of armaments in which Britain would give a lead. These hopes were shattered, and the Conference doomed, when in October 1933 Hitler suddenly announced Germany's withdrawal both from Geneva and from the League of Nations. It was in this atmosphere of frustrated hopes for disarmament and a darkening international outlook that the Chiefs of Staff submitted their Annual Review for 1933.[3]

When they met to discuss their review on 20 June 1933 the

chairman, Admiral Chatfield,* pointed out that while the Far East remained a potential danger zone, the situation in Europe had deteriorated considerably because of the Nazis' rise to power. He regarded Locarno as our greatest commitment at that time but was confident that if we had to support France against Germany the French army with British help would be adequate, while the French air force would look after the air and leave Britain free to defend herself. The CIGS, Montgomery-Massingberd, was sure that Germany would rearm, whatever happened at Geneva, and would be troublesome five or ten years hence. The British Army he pointed out, was worse off than the Navy and it would take eight or ten years to complete mobilization arrangements. At present the Army could do nothing serious in the first six months of a European war. On the outbreak of war one division or possibly two might be sent out 'more as a token than anything else'. Sir Edward Ellington,* the CAS, was scarcely more optimistic in his discussion of the state of the RAF. Chatfield concluded by remarking that so far nothing at all was contemplated which would enable Britain to carry on a war against Japan. 'It was traditional British policy never to be ready and to be rather proud of it: we must stress that this attitude was now very dangerous.'[4]

Their Annual Review was presented in October 1933 and in it the COS emphasized that Germany had already started to rearm and within a few years would have to be reckoned with as a formidable military power. Although they thought German aggression in the near future more likely in the east than the west of Europe, they affirmed that it was vital to Britain's security that the Low Countries be not overrun by a great continental power. They warned futhermore that 'limited participation in a European war would not be feasible, and to commit a proportion of our slender military resources to the Continent would . . . be fraught with the gravest danger'. Thus, unless the Government was prepared to make the armed forces ready for continental war, military action, at any rate during the first six months, would have to be confined to a defence of the Empire overseas.[5]

In the light of this report and of similar warnings from the Foreign Office, the Cabinet decided on 15 November 1933 to lay down certain guidelines to replace the discarded Ten Year

Rule. Defence expenditure should be governed by the requirements of, in order of priority, the defence of British interests in the Far East, commitments in Europe, and the defence of India. No expenditure was to be incurred exclusively for defence against attack by the United States, France, or—it is interesting to note—Italy. Finally, a subcommittee of the CID should prepare a report with recommendations for a programme to make good Britain's worst defence deficiencies. This was the origin of the Defence Requirements Committee (DRC). Its chairman was Sir Maurice Hankey, secretary of the Cabinet and the CID, and the other members were Sir Robert Vansittart (permanent head of the Foreign Office since 1930), Sir Warren Fisher (permanent secretary to the Treasury since 1919), and the three chiefs of staff. The Committee worked fast and intensively and presented its report to the Cabinet at the end of February 1934.[6]

Personalities played an important part in the DRC and hence in shaping the broad guidelines of British defence policy in the ensuing five years. The dominant members were Vansittart and Fisher. Vansittart's virulent Germanophobia was already in evidence, while Fisher displayed an almost obsessive hostility towards the United States. Their combined strength was too much for the naval–imperial view (expressed by Chatfield and supported by Hankey) which contended that Japan was Britain's most likely major adversary. The DRC's report acknowledged the Japanese threat by recommending the completion of the Singapore base, but urged that Britain should seek to re-establish friendly relations with that power, even at the risk of offending the United States. Germany, by contrast, was 'the ultimate potential enemy against whom all our "long range" defence policy must be directed'. While war with Japan would be predominantly the Royal Navy's concern, Germany was primarily a matter for the Army and the Air Force.[7]

Among the Service chiefs Admiral Chatfield was the only outstanding personality; indeed, it might be claimed he was the only Service spokesman of first-rate ability on the COS Committee throughout the 1930s. Montgomery-Massingberd was an ageing unimaginative soldier in poor health and somewhat lacking in personality. Although a very experienced staff officer (he had made his name as Chief of Staff of Rawlinson's 4th

Army in the First World War), he was not a man of progressive or original views in matters of strategy and service doctrine. Nevertheless, the records show that he presented the Army's case clearly and sensibly throughout the DRC proceedings, an impression which is corroborated by the Secretary.[8] The same cannot be said for the CAS, Sir Edward Ellington, who had begun his career in the Army as an artillery officer and had learnt to fly only in his mid-thirties. The DRC's Secretary thought him 'extremely weak in discussion and his utterances most confused'. He created turmoil towards the end of the DRC proceedings by admitting that 19 squadrons earmarked for Army co-operation were not included in the RAF's agreed total of 52 squadrons though he had earlier maintained that they were. Colonel Pownall, whose diaries show that he was far from being prejudiced against RAF officers *per se*, found Ellington not only difficult to deal with but also 'a cheerless cove'. 'In eleven meetings I have never once seen him smile nor heard him make a cheerful remark to anyone. And the use of the word "good morning" is unfamiliar to him.'[9] Hankey's role was complex. Though his professional and personal inclination was strongly towards the Royal Navy and the defence of the overseas Empire, he repeatedly stressed the crucial importance of the Low Countries to Britain's security, endorsing the Army's view that an Expeditionary Force was essential to protect this interest.[10]

Contrary to what might have been expected, throughout the DRC proceedings it was the Chiefs of Staff who were the moderating influence while the civilians, whose role was presumably to restrain the impossible proposals of the services, were in fact the alarmist element, demanding quicker and heavier rearmament, whatever the price. Thus the COS rejected Sir Warren Fisher's proposal at the first meeting that they should state what was needed without regard to political and financial difficulties. This caution was well-grounded in bitter experience. Chatfield, for example, correctly predicted that their proposals would be cut by thirty or fifty per cent; he had little faith that the Government's attitude to defence expenditure had changed significantly since the abolition of the Ten Year Rule. Their experience during the term of the Rule had conditioned the COS to recommend 'rounded' programmes because they believed that if inter-service rivalries became too blatant all three would tend to suffer in the long run. Consequently they regarded a modest amount of rearmament almost as an end in itself rather than a means of carrying out a specific strategic policy. Thus it was a fair criticism that the 'balanced' proposals of the COS were unrelated to a wider strategic plan. Each department submitted its estimates to the DRC on the assumption that when whittled down and developed collectively over five years (the period agreed for remedying worst deficiencies), the programmes would provide a reasonable level of rearmament in comparison with the 'lean years' they had recently experienced. Fisher and Vansittart vainly urged the COS to be less self-denying, and pointed out that increased expenditure was of little value if it did not satisfy definite strategic priorities such as insuring Britain against air attack or providing a Territorial Army trained and equipped to reinforce the Expeditionary Force. In reply, Montgomery-Massingberd stubbornly maintained that the strongest Expeditionary Force the Army could field was one of four infantry divisions, a cavalry division, and a tank brigade. To bring the Territorials up to operational standard would be prohibitively expensive. When Vansittart urged that the sum of £250,000, which the DRC proposed to allocate to the Territorials, be trebled, the CIGS demurred. Ellington was even more self-denying over the target of 52 squadrons for home defence. This programme, which had been laid down in 1923, was designed to protect only London and south-east England against attack by France. The CAS agreed that an additional 25 squadrons would be required to protect the Midlands and the North against attack by Germany, but he was not prepared to press for them. 'Starved of resources for years, uncertain of their ability to recruit the necessary manpower and conscious of the lack of any armaments-base to make major expansion possible, the timidity of the Service Chiefs, pathetic as it now appears, is understandable.'[11]

The DRC's decision that Germany was the ultimate potential enemy led the Committee to lay special emphasis in its report on the Army's greatest deficiency, the absence of an expeditionary force capable of securing Britain's traditional interests in the Low Countries. The development of air power, it believed, made the Low Countries even more important to the defence of Britain than in the past:

Their integrity is vital to us in order that we may obtain that depth in our defence of London which is so badly needed, and of which our geographical position will otherwise deprive us. If the Low Countries were in the hands of a hostile Power, not only would the frequency and intensity of air attack on London be increased, but the whole of the industrial areas of the Midlands and North of England would be brought within the area of penetration of hostile air attacks.

The DRC saw the solution in recommendations remarkably similar to those of 1914: namely an Expeditionary Force of one cavalry division, four infantry divisions, two air-defence brigades, and one tank brigade with a full complement of ancillary units to be put into the field within one month of mobilization and maintained there in all essentials. This was but an essential first step. To support this force by contingents of the Territorial Army would require consideration when the needs of the Regular Army had been met. 'We believe', the report affirmed, 'that a force organized as above, and supported by appropriate Air Forces, would, as a deterrent to an aggressor, exercise an influence for peace out of all proportion to its size.'[12]

This notion of a small Expeditionary Force exercising a deterrent effect on the Continent was, it must be stressed, the considered judgement of the DRC as a whole. The Army General Staff's conservatism is, however, evident in the section of the report dealing with the organization of the Expeditionary Force. They sought a compromise between the completely unarmoured force of infantry and horsemen of 1914, and 'an extreme degree of mechanization' which would entirely replace the infantry by men in fighting machines. In view of Britain's world-wide commitments the complete mechanization of the Army was neither a possible nor a desirable measure. 'It would demand a highly specialized army trained and equipped for one contingency only, viz., war in a European theatre and on ground suitable for its employment.' Neither of the Army's traditional responsibilities, the provision of garrisons for naval bases and the protection of British interests in overseas territories, 'would be met by the creation of a highly specialized "robot" army at Home, even if that were the best system for a Continental war, itself a matter far from certain'. The object would be to create 'a partly mechanized force of high striking power, yet not so specialized as to be unadaptable to the general requirements of

Empire defence'. Experiments were now being made with medium tanks (weighing between 12 and 16 tons) but it was not yet possible to decide on the composition of the Tank Brigade. The cavalry component would be improved by equipping it with light automatics, mechanizing its first-line transport, and providing it with light cars for reconnaissance. No vehicle capable of replacing the horse was yet in sight. Montgomery-Massingberd successfully opposed Vansittart's criticism that there was insufficient mechanization on the grounds that a larger mechanized force was not justified and would upset the Cardwell system.[13] At an early stage in the DRC discussions Pownall warned Hankey that the vagueness of the CIGS's proposals for an Expeditionary Force would be challenged: 'there was a school of thought which dreaded the idea of an organization based on the division of 1918'.[14]

The DRC proposed to allocate the Army £40 million (nearly half the whole programme) to be spent over the next five years. This figure was calculated on what the War Office could actually spend, given the run-down of the arms industry, rather than on the Army's total needs. Pownall calculated that to produce an Expeditionary Force of four divisions 'and to do the Territorials properly too,—would mean about £145 million over five years'. He rightly called this 'an impossible figure, and dangerous too, for if it was presented ministers might well declare that the Army was too expensive and turn to the RAF who claim to get as good, or better results, at much less cost'. The Secretary of State for War was also well aware that an additional £30 million was required to implement the Defence of India Plan.[15]

Hankey's acute political sense, derived from his unique experience in defence matters, forewarned him to expect opposition to the DRC's proposals for a continental Expeditionary Force. As early as 25 January 1934 he had advised his colleagues on the DRC to discuss this matter very carefully; and after the Cabinet's reception of the report on 8 March he wrote to warn the concept's staunchest supporter, Vansittart, to expect trouble. After the Cabinet meeting Sir Samuel Hoare (Secretary of State for India) remarked to Hankey that Britain was preparing for exactly the same kind of war as the last. Hankey warned General Dill (then DMO and I) 'to have his gun loaded about the Expeditionary Force', and he also asked

Ellington to stick up for the report on that issue. 'Both [i.e. Dill and Ellington] stressed the importance of the moral effect of the Expeditionary Force and the bad moral effect of not having one to send.' Vansittart entirely endorsed this view but the 'moral effect' of a small and underequipped Expeditionary Force was not a proposition calculated to impress sceptical ministers acutely attuned to the mood of public opinion.[16]

It was significant that after two month's delay the Cabinet referred the DRC report to the Ministerial Committee on Disarmament (henceforth DC(M)) on 2 May 1934, and that a further three months passed before the Cabinet approved that Committee's amended version. Throughout this period the Government was much more concerned to keep alive hopes of disarmament than to face the prospect of rearmament.[17]

Colonel Pownall, secretary to the DRC, wrote an interesting diary entry at the first meeting of the DC(M): 'Chamberlain is going to be the trouble . . . he is under the impression that one can go into a war with limited liability, i.e., Air and Navy cut out all land contribution. Deadly dangerous. His ideas on strategy would disgrace a board school. A reference made in the form of a questionnaire to the C.O.S., all most elementary.' A few days later Pownall referred to the 'extraordinary system by which these big strategical questions, involving the whole future defence policy of the country, are discussed by Ministers without having the oral evidence and argument by the Chiefs of Staff'. In his opinion the CID was the proper statutory body for such discussions, but unfortunately the CID was largely becoming an instrument for stamping proposals put up to it by sub-committees.[18]

As Pownall's diary entry suggests, and Hankey had expected, it was the DRC's proposed Expeditionary Force for the Continent which aroused most controversy amongst ministers, and Neville Chamberlain who led the attack. Behind the Chancellor's ruthless logic lay an emotional revulsion against the trench stalemate of the First World War and a fear that, if the DRC's proposals were accepted, they would lead to a repetition of that stalemate. Since the French frontier with Germany was generally considered to be impregnable, argued Chamberlain, the key to the problem must be Belgium. If her frontier fortifications were strong Germany would be forced to attack by air and an expeditionary force would not be needed. If, on the other hand, her frontiers were not fortified, a British expeditionary force could not possibly prevent a German breakthrough. The solution for Chamberlain was to concentrate on improving the Navy and Air Force while leaving the Army to its extra-European rôle. Lord Hailsham, the Secretary of State for War, tried to counter these arguments by repeating the DRC's case for preventing the Germans from obtaining air and submarine bases in the Low Countries. Britain's aim, he urged, should be to establish a forward line as close to the Rhine as possible and for this a strong expeditionary force was needed. Chamberlain and Simon, however, remained unconvinced that an expeditionary force was essential to sustain this strategy. The DC(M) referred ten questions to the Chiefs to Staff of which four were crucial:

1. Could Britain land an Expeditionary Force on the Continent in time to prevent Germany from overrunning the Low Countries, or would the situation develop into a stalemate near the coast as in the Great War?
2. Even if Germany occupied the Low Countries and established bases there, could not Britain—assuming she had sufficient air power—make such an occupation untenable?
3. What did the French think about an Expeditionary Force from Britain? Did they want one, or would they rather have a strong air contribution, together with Britain's naval aid?
4. Would not Britain do better to contribute financially to the building of fortifications on the Belgian–German frontier?[19]

In their replies to this and later questionnaires from the DC(M), the Chiefs of Staff maintained a unanimous front, defending their original proposals for an expeditionary force with such cogency that the sceptical ministers could hardly disregard their expert advice. Yet behind the façade presented to ministers the remarkably detailed accounts of the COS proceedings recorded by Hankey and his colleagues of the CID Secretariat reveal acute and unresolved differences of opinion which were to have serious repercussions as the political controversy over the role of the Army persisted. Before discussing these conflicting Service views, however, the COS's unanimous answers to the DC(M) must be noted.

The COS continued to stress the vital importance of denying

the Low Countries to Germany as an advanced air base for an attack on Britain. They estimated that an air attack from the Low Countries would be initially 80 per cent stronger than if launched from bases in Germany. Moreover, they argued, France was mainly concerned with defending her own frontiers and regarded the Belgian frontier as less vital to her security than Britain did to hers. This was to remain a strong argument in favour of an expeditionary force. The COS insisted that the promise of air and sea support to our potential allies was not enough. The arrival of even small land forces would have an incalculable moral effect out of all proportion to their size as they had done in 1914, and this encouragement might well enable our allies to hold out long enough for reinforcements to reach them. The COS concluded that *for her own security* Britain must have an expeditionary force of five divisions ready for prompt dispatch to the Continent with reinforcements to be made available later if circumstances permitted.[20]

When the COS discussed their replies to the original DC(M) questionnaire on 4 May 1934, the disagreements were chiefly between Montgomery-Massingberd and Ellington with Chatfield playing the role of Socratic chairman, though clearly more in sympathy with the Army's than the Air Force's views of German strategy and the nature of a future war.

Montgomery-Massingberd opened the discussion by saying that, according to information supplied by Colonel Andrew Thorne,* the British Military Attaché in Berlin, the Germans were building an air force designed for close co-operation with their ground forces. Ellington flatly disagreed with this: according to air intelligence the Germans thought the French defences too strong and so would make a major effort to jump over them—by air. The CIGS said he understood that French strategy was to use their frontier fortifications to hold up the Germans for 6 or 8 weeks while they mobilized: they had no plan to attack through their fortifications and while they might attempt to occupy the Ruhr their policy was really defensive. If the French were unlikely to launch a preventive attack, Chatfield then inquired, could we assume that our role would be defensive? The CIGS thought it would be essentially the same as in 1914—to try and turn the scale by attacking the German flank so as to prevent their reaching the coast. However, his ideas about the Army's role were extremely vague; he was against tying the BEF to the French or the Belgians or to anybody else specifically: 'It ought to be put in at the best strategical position to pull its full weight.' Antwerp might quite possibly be the place where it would land. 'Colonel Thorne gathered that the underlying idea in Germany was to push forward the land forces as fast as possible in order to establish air bases closer to us.' Ellington repeated that his own information was that the Germans did not think a big advance on land was possible and were therefore concentrating on building up air forces. In answer to Chatfield's question whether an expeditionary force could get to the Low Countries before the Germans overran them, Ellington was doubtful if the Government would even allow the Expeditionary Force to sail until the German air threat had been sized up. Air attacks might well make the Channel ports untenable, particularly as accurate night bombing was now possible by means of parachute flares. Both the CIGS and CNS were sceptical. The former remarked that bombing of the ports would have to be pretty well continuous and anti-aircraft guns would make this extremely unpleasant by day. Chatfield pointed out that German bombing had hindered work at Dunkirk in the First World War but never entirely stopped it. In any case could the Germans spare enough aircraft to stop the Expeditionary Force if France were attacking her? Ellington replied with what sounds like a touch of sarcasm: 'If the Germans attached as much importance to the Expeditionary Force as Sir Archibald Montgomery-Massingberd, then he thought they certainly ought to try to stop it being disembarked.' The CIGS rejoined that he found it difficult to conceive of anyone directing German strategy in that way. In an extreme case, using Nantes instead of Antwerp, and provided the Expeditionary Force was largely mechanized, he thought the total difference would be about a week as a maximum before the force could be landed. In answer to further probing questions from Chatfield, he maintained his view that the Expeditionary Force *could* arrive in time (even if operating from the Biscay ports) and that its arrival would have an enormous moral effect. His trump card, and it was one which other soldiers would repeat when the Government veered increasingly towards 'limited liability', was to ask: supposing

Britain agreed on air and naval action only, could the Government guarantee that an expeditionary force would not be needed? Since the answer was patently in the negative the COS agreed to adopt the CIGS's paper in essentials as their reply to the DC(M).[21]

Several points here call for comment. First, Belgium did not announce her return to a policy of strict neutrality until 1936, so that in 1934 it was still reasonable to think in terms of direct, limited support to Belgium rather than indirectly via France. This was more acceptable strategically and politically than intervention in France which suggested a repetition of the pattern of events in the First World War. Even so, to be taken seriously, such a strategy would necessitate staff talks with Belgium and probably France also. Neither politicians nor service chiefs favoured such an overt acceptance of a military commitment. Secondly, despite the CIGS's reference to mechanized forces, he was clearly thinking in terms of a token force which would exert a disproportionate moral effect. This assumption appeared to absolve the General Staff from precise study of the composition and role of the Expeditionary Force. Finally, the CIGS's interpretation of German strategy turned out to be considerably more accurate than the CAS's, though not surprisingly neither foresaw the 'phoney war' of 1939–40 which gave the Expeditionary Force ample time to take up its position in France. It is clear from the discussion that the CIGS and CNS were drawn together by the belief that the CAS was exaggerating the role of air power. Indeed, when faced by Chatfield's question as to whether, given approximately equal air forces for bombing and fighter defence, the air war would not reach stalemate and 'tend to fizzle out as a result of mutual exhaustion', Ellington replied that after about a month a form of stability would be reached when both sides would have used up their resources and be reduced to making periodic attacks only. There was clearly some degree of common interest in the COS's unanimous defence of a land commitment to the Continent but it was not based upon sufficiently detailed plans to withstand the political battering which the idea would receive in the mid-1930s. But this was hardly the COS's fault, given the Government's unwillingness to accept a definite political commitment on the Continent.

At the end of June the Chancellor reported back to the Ministerial Committee on his proposed amendments to the DRC programme in the light of the economic and political situation. Chamberlain made three broad assumptions. First, that the financial situation was still so difficult that the DRC's proposals to meet the worst deficiencies in all three Services *pari passu* was impractical: ministers must decide on priorities. Secondly, he accepted DRC's nomination of Germany as the greatest potential danger and drew from it the conclusion that home defence must be given first priority. Thirdly, in his opinion the best defence was a powerful home-based air force which could serve as a 'deterrent', with the Army as a second or long-term line of defence. This last suggestion was of course very different from the DRC's proposal that the Army should be the *first* line of defence designed for rapid intervention in Europe to keep the German air force at a distance. Chamberlain justified a 'startling reduction' in the proposed deficiency expenditure on the Army from £40 million to £19 million partly on grounds of lower strategic priority and partly because he doubted whether the larger sum could be spent in five years.[22]

By general agreement Lord Hailsham put up an impressive, though largely unavailing, resistance to Chamberlain's proposals in the DC(M). Pownall noted that the Army was fortunate to have such a powerful advocate, while in July Sir Christopher Bullock, Permanent Secretary to the Air Ministry, told Liddell Hart that the Army's stock had risen on the need to have an expeditionary force, though its allotted sum had been cut because it had asked for too much. In October Bullock told Liddell Hart:

> Hailsham has strong pull in Cabinet, where he bullies them, and is getting his way over the Army. He was likely to get several millions extra to modernize the Expeditionary Force as the Cabinet accept the need for such a force, the chief ground being that we must use it to obtain elbow room on the Continent, either to bring [British] air bases nearer Germany, or to keep German aircraft at a distance from London.[23]

Though his arguments had a less persuasive effect on some ministers than Bullock believed, Lord Hailsham's case was impregnable on purely military grounds. First, he pointed out that the Army's worst deficiencies, which had accumulated through loyal observance of the Ten Year Rule, urgently needed to be remedied, whether or not a continental commitment was accepted. True, the extra speed of mobilization and higher standard of equipment and weapons would entail greater expenditure for a European war, but preparation for a non-European war would still be costly. It would take £30–40 million, for example, to implement the Defence of India Plan. Secondly, since the DC(M) had accepted the COS's expert advice on the vital importance of the Low Countries to British security, it could hardly refuse to prepare an expeditionary force which was said to be essential for this purpose.[24] Thirdly, if the Chancellor was basing his reduction of the Army's allocation partly on the grounds that Germany would not be ready to wage war in five years, thus permitting a slower rate than suggested by the DRC, why was the RAF's programme being not merely accepted but substantially increased? Was it not illogical to spend more on the RAF while simultaneously denying the money necessary to prevent Germany launching an air attack from Belgium? In fact, Hailsham claimed, 'The Army . . . was necessary in order that Belgium should be available as an air base for ourselves and not as an air base for Germany.' Hailsham concluded a recital of the Army's desperate shortages by remarking that it had been cast as 'a Cinderella of the forces'.

In reply the Chancellor denied that it was illogical to spend more on the Air Force. His idea was that the Air Force should serve as a deterrent. 'The Army, on the other hand, he did not regard as a deterrent; it only came into action if the deterrent failed.' The Army as the second line in defence must have a lower priority. He admitted that he was faced not only with the difficulty of finance, but that of public opinion regarding Army expenditure, which would be regarded as money spent on making preparations to take part in a war on the Continent. 'For political reasons alone, it would be very necessary to spread the Army expenditure over a considerable period in order to avoid criticism.' Several ministers, including J. H. Thomas, Simon, and Ormsby-Gore strongly supported the Chancellor's view, though Hailsham deplored the attitude that 'since the public demanded a large Air Force that should get priority' with only the left-overs for the Army. In a subsequent discussion of the DC(M) the Chancellor went even further in acknowledging the influence of public opinion on his revision of the DRC programme. Referring specifically to the Army he remarked, 'If we spend too much the Government could be turned out and a successor might do nothing at all. It was therefore a wise calculation to under-provide in some circumstances.'

Apart from Sir Bolton Eyres-Monsell's comparable struggle to maintain the Navy's share of the DRC programme, Hailsham was virtually playing a lone hand among the thirteen ministers who made up the DC(M). His lengthy exchanges with the Chancellor made little headway and the minutes suggest that he became rather irritated and despondent. This is confirmed by an eye-witness, Colonel Pownall, who noted on 17 July 'Hailsham in rather a sulky mood nowadays. The Army is indeed the Cinderella of the Services, and he doesn't like it.' It was on this day (17 July) that Hailsham's patience appears to have been stretched beyond breaking point. The Chancellor proposed that from the reduced total of £19 million for the Army's worst deficiencies no less than £6½ million should be spent on anti-aircraft defences at home. Hailsham retorted that if a reduced sum was to be spread over a longer period the Army could not be expected to be ready to fight in the meantime; so the War Office must be absolved from responsibility for the risks run. At this point Stanley Baldwin took Hailsham's part to secure a more reasonable compromise.[25]

The final decision of the DC(M),[26] approved by the Cabinet, was that the Army would get £20 million for its deficiency programme for the five years ending in March 1939. Of this total £12 million was allocated to the Expeditionary Force and the remainder was to be available for port defence (particularly Singapore) and for the ground defences of Great Britain. The only concessions won by Hailsham, with Baldwin's support, were that the reduced total should not be drawn upon for the extension of air defences to the Midlands and North of England, and that the Army's needs, like those of the other Services, should be reviewed annually. Pownall shared the almost universal consensus of opinion that air defence *deserved* top priority when he added to the diary note quoted above: 'He [Hailsham] has been given £20 million to play with up till March 1939, which is really not too bad—just half of what the DRC said would be needed to patch up deficiencies.'

The DRC report, amended by the DC(M) was presented to the Cabinet and approved on 31 July 1934.[27] Under the significant sub-heading 'Home Defence: Europe' the report confirmed: 'The Low Countries are vital to our security from the point of view of both naval and air defence, and in the opinion of the Government's technical advisers can only be defended by the provision of military forces to co-operate with other countries concerned . . .' And a later paragraph asserted: 'In deciding whether or not we should have an Expeditionary Force for use in the Low Countries, the question is not whether we should intervene, but whether we should be capable of intervention. We consider that, in the interest of our own defences, we should be capable of this.'

However, while there could be no doubt that a continental commitment for the Army had been accepted in principle, it was far from certain that the policy would be implemented. Several influential ministers, notably the Chancellor, had made plain their personal abhorrence towards such a commitment, while at the same time (and this was particularly true of J. H. Thomas) they lost no opportunity to stress the public's revulsion from the idea. This concern for what was alleged to be 'public opinion' reached its apogee in a remarkable exchange at a CID meeting in November 1934:

> Sir B. Eyres-Monsell [First Lord of the Admiralty] drew attention to the phrase 'Expeditionary Force' in a C.I.D. Paper. He asked whether the War Office could see their way to avoid the use of this expression, which, if used in public, would have a bad moral effect. Mr J. H. Thomas [Dominions Secretary] agreed that the expression 'Expeditionary Force' had unpleasant inferences in the public mind.
>
> The Prime Minister [Ramsay MacDonald] agreed, and asked that not only in public, but in all official papers the term 'Expeditionary Force' should not be used.[28]

The Chancellor also made it clear that fulfilment of the DRC programme would depend on the country's economic recovery and so it could not be guaranteed in advance. A further indication of the Government's unwillingness to accept the full implications of Britain's strategic interest in the security of the Low Countries occurred during the summer of 1934 when, after protracted discussion, a Belgian request that Britain should strengthen Locarno by giving an automatic guarantee that she would go to war if Belgium were invaded, was declined. This caution appeared inconsistent with Baldwin's startling remark in the House of Commons on 30 July 1934 that with the advent of air power, 'When you think of the defence of England you no longer think of the chalk cliffs of Dover; you think of the Rhine.' This left no room for doubt as to the identity of the potential enemy. True, explicit guarantee could hardly be given to Belgium without involving France, and this in turn would inevitably prompt a renewed request for staff talks. In short: 'The need having been admitted, the military means to satisfy it—judged by the standards of the Government's professional advisers—were then promptly denied.'[29]

Nevertheless, despite these continuing reservations, a continental commitment was once again becoming a definite possibility. Thus Liddell Hart, a sensitive instrument for recording changes of strategic emphasis, noted after a talk with Colonel Martel in September 1934 that 'the Director of Military Training is issuing instructions that the Army is to train for European warfare next year (and a best equipped Army)'. Similarly, at a War Office meeting in November to brief military correspondents on proposals for Army reorganization, Major-General C. P. 'Guffin' Heywood, Director of Staff Duties, opened by saying there was now a clear possibility that the Army might have to intervene on the Continent.[30] However, neither the War Office nor the General Staff looked on such a commitment with enthusiasm. In presenting the Army Estimates in the House of Commons on 17 March 1934, Duff Cooper played down the likelihood of an expeditionary force being sent to the Continent. Nobody could predict where the force would be used, and it therefore had to be capable of operating anywhere in the Empire: 'On Salisbury Plain or even on the fields of Flanders the tank is no doubt the most powerful weapon you can possibly use, but it is not necessarily the most powerful in the North-West Frontier, or in the swamps and ditches that surround the suburbs of Shanghai.' The General Staff, while they agreed that the Low Countries were vital to British security, were loath to make precise military plans. The CIGS held strongly that Britain's land forces 'should not be committed prematurely to a rigid, preconceived role as was the case prior to 1914: they should not be committed beforehand to the defence of any particular line. On the contrary their mobility and training should be exploited by regarding them as a strategic reserve for employment as circumstances may require.' The Expeditionary Force might be employed offensively or defensively, for example in attacking the flanks of a successful German advance in Holland, Belgium, or even northern France.[31]

Although the Cabinet had approved the DRC's main recommendation that Germany was the most dangerous potential enemy against whom defence preparations should be directed over the next five years, no serious military planning in fact resulted in 1934. One explanation was that the Locarno Treaty imposed impossible restrictions, if observed according to the letter, since it would entail the making of two sets of plans: one concerted with France, Belgium, and Italy against Germany, and the other with Germany, Belgium, and Italy against France. This restriction was, however, a pretext rather than a real obstacle: neither the Government nor the Chiefs of Staff showed the slightest enthusiasm for embarking on Staff conversations with Britain's most likely allies in a future war—Belgium and France. Another reason for the absence of serious planning was the Government's fear that such planning would result in demands for increased expenditure. Thirdly there was its contradictory attitude to the schedule for defence preparations: on the one hand it was feared that war might come before 1938; on the other hand the limit for meeting worst deficiencies was extended to 1942.[32]

But the Services' greatest handicap was probably their internal disagreement about the likely aims of German strategy. Both Montgomery-Massingberd and Chatfield felt strongly that Ellington was exaggerating the German air threat to Britain by placing it in a false strategic context. Ellington's ideas were 'alarming' because they left France out of the picture. As the CIGS remarked 'He could hardly conceive of any situation arising *vis-à-vis* Germany and ourselves into which France would not be drawn.' He also thought the CAS was guilty of exaggerating Germany's air superiority since Britain would be able to fall back on the United States for material and the Dominions for trained pilots. Even if Germany did concentrate on trying to knock-out Britain by air attack she would not be able to keep up intensive bombing for long because of the action which France and Belgium would be taking against her. The COS's debate on the German air threat dragged on into 1935, the CAS being in a minority of one in maintaining that Germany would concentrate at the outset of war on a knock-out air attack against Britain. Hankey argued that, from his knowledge of Germany's traditional belief in concentration, she was most likely to attempt a knock-out blow through Belgium. Montgomery-Massingberd agreed, and added that if Britain, France, and Belgium were ready, Germany would probably not risk an attack at all. Chatfield suggested that there were signs that Germany was now looking eastward towards Czechoslovakia, Russia, and the Baltic Provinces. The COS reports forwarded to the CID failed, however, to bring out these widely differing views which continued to characterize their discussions.[33]

The COS were not surprisingly at odds likewise on the more restricted question of how best Britain could help maintain the security of the Low Countries. While the CIGS urged the importance of keeping German bombers at a distance by holding the Low Countries, the CNS expressed doubt about the value of ground defences against air forces. The CAS proposed that the air component of the Expeditionary Force be sent to Belgium before the troops, but the CIGS understandably regarded this as risky. His view was that whether the date of readiness aimed at was 1938 or 1942 was irrelevant since all that need be decided in advance were ports of disembarkation and areas of concentration for an expeditionary force. One should avoid the mistake of 1914 of being tied to either a French or a Belgian plan. There should be alternative concentration areas for the support of Holland, Belgium, or France. He admitted he did not know the French plan but thought their probable area of concentration would be Namur. Also, an Expeditionary Force could support Belgian forces to the east or north, or the defensive sector of the Ardennes to the south-east. All that need be considered now, he concluded, was how to get the Expeditionary Force to some suitable concentration area and protect it on the way. The Joint Planning Committee was accordingly instructed to investigate staff problems connected with embarkation, transport, lines of communication, and concentration areas without regard to wider questions of strategy. Even these practical aspects of staff work could not be carried far without staff conversations with France and Belgium.[34]

The Chiefs of Staff do not appear in a very favourable light in their first attempts to grapple with the enormous problems of defence deficiencies in 1933 and 1934. It is a fair criticism that 'the strategic doctrine behind their D.R.C. programme was . . . vague and undecided' and also to some extent that 'the C.O.S. saw operations against Germany strictly in terms of their own Services and, for the most part, felt that their Departments would play the decisive role in war. They showed no sign of viewing the problem from a common strategic or even tactical, viewpoint.' Their experience with the Ministerial Committee in 1934 clearly showed the danger that if the COS could not agree on a common doctrine they would have one imposed from above by politicians who subordinated military considerations to those of finance and politics.[35]

On closer inspection, however, it is apparent that the COS and the defence departments were caught up in a vicious circle. Given the Services' recent experience of bitter internecine struggle for the lion's share of a shrinking defence budget; their tendency to pursue overlapping and complementary but not truly combined roles in Imperial Defence; and their unavoidably divergent approaches to the possibility of war with either Japan or Germany, it was surely unrealistic to expect them to agree upon a common strategic doctrine without a very firm political directive. Hankey clearly realized the difficulty and sought to solve it by a 'rounded' DRC programme designed to meet all three Services' worst deficiencies on the same time scale without deciding on strategic priorities. There were ominous signs in 1934 which would become even clearer when, in 1935, Italy joined Germany and Japan as potential enemies, that the Services could not possibly be prepared in the foreseeable future to meet all eventualities. The solution, if there was to be one, must be achieved in the sphere of foreign policy. It cannot be said that the politicians showed much understanding of the Services' problems in 1934. With the exception of the heads of the Service departments, ministers generally displayed a lamentable lack of understanding of strategic problems and repeatedly fell back on what financial considerations and 'public opinion' would allow.

Colonel Pownall's experience as secretary of the DRC did not enhance his respect for politicians' handling of defence issues. On 18 June 1934, for example, he noted:

The Chancellor's ideas of what constitutes Defence Requirements are, as to be expected, most unsatisfactory. That is natural from two Treasury civilians who have no knowledge of the subject and a Chancellor who is both obstinate and strategically under-educated. It is amazing how little these high ups know about the ordinary 'civics' of Empire which they should have learned at the preparatory schools.[36]

The best that can be said in defence of the ministers' criticisms and amendments of the DRC proposals is that they faithfully reflected the electorate's apparent unwillingness to see more spent on defence in general, and were moreover correct in assuming that money spent on home defences and the air force would win far more approval than money spent on capital ships or, worst of all, an expeditionary force for the Continent. In effect the Government sought a politically acceptable solution in 'window dressing' and put unfounded faith in a vague notion of 'deterrence' through air power. Hankey's 'rounded' programme of £75 million had been amended to one of only two thirds that size, and so altered in distribution that the air gained at the expense of the other two arms for reasons far from convincing on military grounds alone, however much they appealed to the general public. One can but echo the verdict of the official historian that the first deficiency programme ended 'on a note of bleak frustration'.[37]

CHAPTER 8

Towards a policy of limited liability, July 1935–May 1937

The DRC presented its second (or interim) report in July 1935 against a darkening international background. Japan had abrogated the London Naval Treaty after rejecting British proposals for a new agreement; her attitude remained menacing and she would soon be relatively at her strongest in the Far East; German expenditure on armaments was approaching £1,000 million a year; and—most seriously in the short-run—Italy's quarrel with Abyssinia threatened to destroy the Stresa front. Although it seemed unlikely that Germany would be ready to embark on deliberate aggression before 1942, the latest date which could reasonably be assumed for Britain's own security was January 1939. So great were the deficiencies of all three Services, however, that their only hope lay in a massive defence loan of the order of £200 million. Even with that amount, as Colonel Pownall remarked, 'working under peace conditions it will be *very* hard to get the Services right by 1942, the manufacturing capacity simply doesn't exist'. At the end of July 1935 the DRC was reconstituted as the Defence Policy Requirements Committee (DPR) and authorized to prepare a comprehensive third report in the light of the deteriorating situation. Despite the cautious terms of reference 'a sense of urgency was at last creeping in. Deficiency programmes were now passing into the stage of genuine rearmament.'[1]

As far as the Army was concerned, the outcome of the first and second DRC reports was a confirmation of the need to prepare the regular units at home which made up the Field

Force for possible intervention in a continental war. Although the Chancellor, Neville Chamberlain, had contested the wisdom of such a commitment and had succeeded in halving the sum allocated to remedy the Army's worst deficiencies over the period 1934–9, nevertheless the consensus of Service and political opinion upheld the vital importance to Britain of maintaining the Low Countries' security and also the need for land forces for that purpose. Thus, for example, in their Annual Review for 1935 the Chiefs of Staff emphasized once again the deplorable state of the Field Force which 'could only be mobilized gradually for a campaign in partially-developed countries'. To launch so small a force into war on the Continent, they considered, might well be disastrous. 'Nevertheless the integrity of the Low Countries is, with the advent of air power, of greater importance than ever in our history, and the Army must be prepared in conjunction with the French, to attempt to deny those countries to German invasion . . .'[2]

However, behind this façade of general agreement on the high priority to be attached to developing a field force capable of rapid intervention in a continental war, there lurked profound and widespread doubt and disquiet. These feelings were inspired chiefly by bitter memories of the trench deadlock in the First World War which had recently been freshly stirred up by a flood of 'anti-war' literature. In particular we should note the prevailing views that Britain had been inveigled into a total war, against her true interests, as a result of the pre-war staff conversations with the French; and also that the political aftermath had proved the four years of carnage to have been largely futile. As early as 1931 the influential journalist and military critic, Liddell Hart, was persuasively stating the case for a return to an allegedly historic 'British Way in Warfare' founded upon sea power and the instrument of blockade, associated with a policy of 'limited liability' towards any military commitment to the Continent.[3] In addition to the popular 'gut reaction' of saying 'never again' to a mass war of attrition like that of 1914–18 there were more sophisticated arguments, such as mistrust of the French, often coupled with the complacent assumption that they could look after themselves; or more attractive, the view that Britain could make an adequate contribution to collective security by giving priority in rearmament to the Royal Air Force and the Navy. This last consideration understandably appealed to the Services concerned for, despite the united front which the Chiefs of Staff almost invariably presented to their political masters, there was in reality profound and often bitter disagreement between them which rivalry for priority in rearmament tended to exacerbate.

The consequences for the Army were unfortunate in that the period from July 1935 to May 1937 witnessed a drift towards 'limited liability'. True, in this period controversy nominally centred on the wisdom of preparing the Territorial Army divisions as contingents to reinforce the Regular Field Force rather than on the principle of committing the latter to a continental war. In fact, however, the rearmament of the Field Force was greatly handicapped by prolonged controversy about its priorities so that eventually even its availability for support of a continental ally was thrown into doubt.

The outstanding advocate of limited liability among senior serving officers was Burnett-Stuart,[4] who was GOC.-in-C. Southern Command 1934–6 and considered by many to be a strong candidate for CIGS. In a note of a talk with him dated 26 August 1935, Liddell Hart recorded that Burnett-Stuart had come to watch the tank exercise in uniform with a fishing rod.[5]

He spoke scornfully of training our army for European warfare and of 'Battles of the Marne'. The War Office chiefs were thinking in terms of the last war. Yet we could not even perform our first duty—that of keeping up the Imperial garrisons adequately . . .

In his view, the role of an expeditionary force should be handed over to the RAF, which would be conducted without risk and without the entanglements which developed as soon as we landed troops on the Continent. The Army should be kept for its proper role, that of guarding the Empire and forming an Imperial Reserve.[6]

Burnett-Stuart boldly, and perhaps recklessly as far as his own career was concerned, disseminated these views among his fellow-officers and also made them public in several letters to *The Times*. In his Unpublished Memoirs written at the end of the Second World War, he wrote unrepentantly:

I knew that the despatch of an Expeditionary Force to France on the outbreak of war with Germany was still an integral part of our Defence policy, and I was convinced that to send the British Army to a Continental War in its then condition would be to condemn it to disaster. That we should align ourselves unreservedly by the side of

France was an obligation which we could not escape, but I could not make myself believe that the sacrifice at the commencement of hostilities of such an army as we had would help either of us . . .

My one and only reason for thinking as I did, was the state of the army; whatever the political, strategical or ethical arguments for the despatch of an Expeditionary Force, they must give way when faced with the fact that we had no Expeditionary Force fit to send. That seemed to me to be commonsense. But I could get no one to agree with me. I met three lines of counter-argument; either that I overstated the army's deficiencies, or that even a poorly armed and insufficiently trained force could at least dig itself in and hope for the best, or that I over-rated the strength and armaments of Germany. And always the argument of the effect on French morale. Nevertheless, I continued to the end obsessed by the iniquity of a policy which accepted for the army a most exacting and hazardous commitment, and at the same time denied to it the means of making itself fit to meet it.[7]

Many Army officers, faced with this terrible dilemma, echoed the sentiments of Burnett-Stuart and Liddell Hart in private correspondence, in their diaries, or in discussions at professional institutions. On the one hand few of them seriously believed that Britain could avoid military involvement should Germany launch an offensive in Western Europe; on the other hand they understood better than either politicians or the general public the utter unpreparedness of even the Regular Army for such an ordeal. For obvious reasons few serving officers were prepared to advocate publicly the preparation for total war with its logical concomitant of conscription.[8] It was understandable, if regrettable, that the 'one thought' of senior officers such as Generals Montgomery-Massingberd (CIGS) and Dill (DMO and I) was 'to postpone a war—not look ahead'.[9]

Whether or not 'public opinion' would have responded earlier to the need to meet German aggression by all-out rearmament if given more determined political leadership must remain a matter of speculation. Since the Press was largely Tory it could easily have been prompted to campaign for rearmament. It is noticeable that politicians invoked 'public opinion' in support of whatever policy they wished to pursue. Colonel Pownall, for one, thought that ministers in the DPR Committee such as Neville Chamberlain, Runciman, Eustace Percy, and Eden exaggerated the fear that public opinion would 'rise up in anger at the idea of the Territorials being sent to "another

Passschendaele"'. In January 1936 Pownall posed (in his diary) the harsh and unpalatable challenge which the Government proved unwilling to recognize until almost the eve of the Second World War:

There was a further and most dangerous heresy—the Chancellor's. That of 'limited liability' in a war. They cannot or will not realise that if war with Germany comes again (whether by Collective Security, Locarno or any other way) we shall again be *fighting for our lives*. Our effort *must* be the maximum, by land, sea and air. We cannot say our contribution is 'so and so'—and no more, because we cannot lose the war without extinction of the Empire. The idea of the 'half-hearted' war is the most pernicious and dangerous in the world. It will be 100%—and even then we may well lose it. We shall certainly lose it if we don't go 100%. In God's name let us recognise that from the outset—and by that I mean *now*. The Chancellor's cold hard calculating semi-detached attitude was terrible to listen to.[10]

Before the DPR Committee could present its third report in November 1935, Italy's overt aggression against Abyssinia caught Britain's defences in the Mediterranean unprepared and converted what was already a difficult strategic dilemma of a possible war with Japan and/or Germany into a virtually insoluble tripartite threat. Only a year or so earlier, when the political guidelines for the first DRC were under discussion, Italy had been included among those powers whose enmity, for planning purposes, had been considered inconceivable. Indeed, until the Abyssinian crisis broke, Britain had given little thought to the defence of her important line of communications through the Mediterranean. As the crisis developed it became even clearer that neither the British nor the French Government was willing to risk becoming entangled in war with Italy. Britain was determined not to act unless full French military support was certain and that was never the case during the crisis. The Chiefs of Staff Committee, in which Admiral Chatfield and Sir Maurice Hankey played a dominant role, strongly advised the Government to buy time and attempt to conciliate Italy.[11] One scholar has gone so far as to suggest that Britain could not defend Egypt or the Suez Canal, let alone fight in defence of the Covenant, and that Italy's military, air, and naval forces constituted a really formidable opposition.[12] This view appears to be contradicted by the COS's contempt for the Italians' fighting ability and their reassurance to the Government that if war did break out a favourable outcome 'could not be a matter of doubt'. Nevertheless, the Admiralty considered the fleet at Malta to be dangerously exposed to Italian air attack, while even the alternative base at Navarino on the west coast of Greece (referred to throughout the crisis as 'Port X') fell within the range of enemy bombers.

In fact the crisis not only exposed the weaknesses of all three Services in the Mediterranean theatre, but brought to the surface fundamental disagreements between them which were normally glossed over in the interests of avoiding unseemly squabbles in front of politicians. In particular, there was a prolonged and acrimonious quarrel over the tactical role of the Air Force, the CAS insisting that the bulk of available aircraft be allocated for attacks on northern Italy, while the CNS and CIGS vainly protested that priority must be given to the protection of the fleet and co-operation with the Army in the defence of Egypt.[13]

Although in discussions of a possible single-handed war with Italy the Army's role was clearly subordinate to that of the other two Services, being confined essentially to the defence of the Mediterranean bases and Egypt, the crisis of 1935–6 was to exert considerable influence on military policy for the remainder of the decade. Early in September three battalions were dispatched from England to reinforce Malta, and later in the month the DPR Committee decided to send an extra brigade to Egypt. Early in October Sir Miles Lampson, the High Commissioner for Egypt and the Sudan, became extremely alarmed (excessively so, according to Pownall) about a possible combination of internal trouble coupled with an Italian attack on Sollum whence Italian aircraft could bomb Alexandria and the British warships there. Two brigades in India were ordered to stand by but Baldwin, the Prime Minister, was against sending further troops from England as the effect on the public would obviously be bad. In November the War Office belatedly awoke to the fact that it had not prepared an appreciation of the Italian threat or sent draft instructions to the local commanders, who themselves had failed to produce a combined appreciation though invited to do so. As the likelihood of war with Italy receded and negotiations took place for the Italians to reduce their large Army in Libya in exchange for two British battle-cruisers being withdrawn from Gibraltar, the DPR Committee, prodded by the Foreign Secretary, Sir Samuel Hoare, decided to send out various mechanized units for the defence of Egypt against attack from Libya. These reinforcements included a battalion of light tanks, a company of medium tanks, and a mechanized brigade of the Royal Artillery. The local commanders would have liked to seize Tobruk but this would have required an extra division which could only be obtained by mobilization.[14]

Historians have rightly noted the salutary effect of Italy's challenge in the Mediterranean in finally alerting the British Government to the real extent of her disarmament and vulnerability, and thus preparing the ground for the first positive steps towards rearmament.[15] On a wider view, however, the repercussions of the crisis were adverse—even disastrous. Italy was added to Britain's potential enemies and good relations with France were severely strained. Moreover, Anglo-French preoccupation with the Mediterranean greatly facilitated Germany's bloodless, but flagrantly illegal, reoccupation of the Rhineland in March 1936. For the British Army, in particular, the crisis brought what proved to be a permanently increased commitment to defend Egypt and the Middle East, a burden which was to be exacerbated by the Palestine rebellion in 1936. Here was an already formidable Imperial commitment which henceforth might well result in a land campaign against Italy where the enemy would have great advantages in shorter communications.[16] It is easy to appreciate how advocates of limited liability towards Germany might come to envisage the defence of Egypt as an alternative role for the Field Force, and one more in keeping with its size and low state of preparedness.

The Third Report of the DRC was presented to the Cabinet on 21 November 1935 and was referred for further discussion to a Ministerial Committee (DPRC) presided over by the Prime Minister which completed its own report in mid-February 1936. The Cabinet received these reports at the end of February, in the main approving the recommendations of its Ministerial Committee. The essential details of the programme were presented to Parliament, in outline, in the Statement on Defence early in March.[17]

On the political front the DRC pointed out that the concept of collective security, if not quite defunct, was certainly moribund. Of Britain's three potential enemies Germany seemed to them the least likely to be accommodated by diplomacy. The DRC stressed that the whole nature of its inquiry and the issue of defence preparedness had acquired greater urgency since the previous year. The British public must be even more prepared to face the possibility of sudden attack. The report asserted once again that the Army's commitments should include occupation for Britain and denial to the enemy of an advanced air base in the Low Countries. If military aid to continental allies was to be effective it must be available within a fortnight of the outbreak of war. The aim in mobilization arrangements should be to disembark the Mobile Division and Air Defence Brigades on the Continent in a week and the remainder of the first contingent of the Field Force with the full complement of auxiliary troops—about 155,000 men in all—a week later.

The Committee ventured on to more controversial ground in recommending that, if the Field Force were sent to the Continent, it should be reinforced at intervals by contingents of the Territorial Army fully equipped for modern war. The schedule it suggested was the first contingent of four divisions to be dispatched four months after the outbreak of war; a second contingent of four divisions two months later; and a third contingent of four divisions after a further two. Thus the target to be aimed at eight months after the outbreak of war was five regular divisions and twelve Territorial Army divisions fully equipped and with the necessary complement of Corps and line-of-communication troops. The Committee recommended an initial outlay of £26 million to modernize all twelve Territorial divisions, but admitted that in the next three years (1936–9) limited production capacity would restrict rearmament to the first (regular) contingent of the Field Force.[18]

Colonel Pownall returned from a skiing holiday in Austria in mid-January 1936 to find the DPR (Ministerial Committee) already in full swing in discussing the DRC report. After two afternoons of 'wuffly discussion' he noted, Hankey had burst out that his Committee had done their best and produced a balanced plan: if others could do better let them try. The ministers consequently met alone, without even Hankey (a rare event), and substantially approved all the proposals for the RAF and the Navy in principle. In deference to expected public criticism of the Army proposals, however, they agreed to concentrate mainly on rearmament of the Field Force. The Territorial Army was to be modernized and steps taken to improve its recruiting, but its war reserves were not to be built up for the present; the question was to be reviewed in three years. Pownall's diary comment is interesting: 'This will make little odds as our productive capacity is inadequate to build up war reserves for the T.A. before then in any case. All this is eminently satisfactory and the Army should be very grateful to Hankey. They might well have been left out in the cold had it not been for his efforts both in the open, and under the rose, on its behalf.'[19]

Hankey fully deserved Pownall's tribute, not only for giving the Army's role special emphasis in the DRC report, but also for defending it against opposition in the Ministerial Committee. In this, Chamberlain's perennial questioning of the wisdom of a continental commitment for the Army received powerful support from the Government's chief industrial adviser Lord Weir,* who had been working at the Air Ministry since June and insisted on full membership of the DPR Committee. He boldly challenged the DRC report on the grounds both of supply and strategy. He dominated the discussion at the first meeting and asserted that the programme could not be completed in five years and that the object must therefore be to concentrate on the best deterrent force.[20] He was firmly convinced that air attack was now the major menace and should take priority in all questions of rearmament: 'This growing development of Air as a striking force has become a kind of shadow hanging over us all—the danger of an attack at home which might wreck the Empire . . .' Most authorities thought it would be difficult to defend a country against air attack yet, he had noticed, British official papers emphasized defence. What was needed, he urged, was a powerful air offensive and the build up of British striking air strength. Although in air matters Weir was clearly a follower of Lord Trenchard's gospel of strategic bombing, in his equally forthright attack on the Army's organization and doctrine he showed himself to be a disciple of Liddell Hart.[21] He argued that the speed of modern war invalidated the Army's outline plan for the defence of the Low Countries. If the second part of the Regular Field Force disembarked a fortnight after mobilization would it be in time? He thought not. German mechanized forces would attempt to encircle the Maginot Line and might well do so in less than a week. It would surely be a better investment to develop the Air Force at the expense of the Army? Weir dealt some telling blows in his criticism of the conservatism of military thinking on organization of units and tactics:

> The backbone of this Force is still to be infantry—who are to be brought up to date by mechanising only their transport—and by providing one Mobile Division to support them . . . That is, I suggest, thinking in terms of 1914–1918, and forgetting all the lessons which should be learnt from that experience. Our policy should be to assist Belgium and France in holding these advanced bases by the action of mechanised forces, and by aircraft themselves.

He was horrified by the principle that tanks were for the support of infantry. On that theory, infantry would still be 'the central arm': 'The last war started with that theory. As it went on it became more and more an artillery war supported by aircraft. The next war is likely to be a war of aircraft supported by tanks with infantry in very much smaller numbers for holding and mopping up.'[22]

Although Weir did not rule out the feasibility of modernizing the small Regular Army, he stressed that the RAF—in its offensive bombing role—should have priority. Another disadvantage of the Army was that it would require a far larger shadow armament industry than the RAF.

Chamberlain underlined Weir's doubts as to whether even the first contingent of the Field Force could arrive on the Continent in time, and also suggested that the RAF should be made the striking force, so reducing the Army's demands. Furthermore, he thought there might be undesirable public reaction if the Territorial Army was said to be preparing to take part in a future European war. Eden, too, stressed the difficulty of getting expenditure on the Army through the House of Commons and approved by the country.

Duff Cooper and Montgomery-Massingberd put up an impressive defence of the DRC proposals concerning the Army. They said they were not asking for an increase in the land forces, but merely to put the existing forces on a proper basis and provide reserves so as to avoid the disastrous mistakes of 1914. They accepted that it was impossible to build up the Territorial Army's war reserves over the next three years, but it was essential to have a clear policy for that force: the TA units surely had a right to know which contingents they would be in; their great fear was that they would be used as drafting units. The CIGS failed to answer Weir's telling criticisms of the Army's outdated emphasis on infantry, but he flatly denied either that any money could be saved by substituting air for land forces or that air power alone would decide the next war. Montgomery-Massingberd scored a neat debating point by noting that these questions had been answered in detail by the COS in a May 1934 memorandum which Lord Weir had clearly not read.[23]

The best defence of the Army's continental role was, however, formulated for the Prime Minister by Hankey in a memorandum of 15 January 1936. Hankey's case was essentially political rather than military and it remained valid throughout the tergiversations of the next three years. War can only be averted, he argued, by a combination which includes at least France and Belgium. They and others are not satisfied that aircraft alone can defend them against invasion and still look on armies and fortifications as their mainstay. 'If we have no efficient army they will feel that we do not mean business.' Without some aid from us France will not help Belgium, Belgium will collapse; London will be exposed to the worst horrors of aerial bombardment; and we shall not have an effective base from which to retaliate on Germany. Hankey ended with an eloquent appeal: 'In a word an efficient army, if only a small one, is essential to reassure our potential allies, to put heart into them to make the necessary effort, and to deter war; and, on the day of battle, to cover our offensive air forces.'[24]

Baldwin's solution to these sharply conflicting views has already been noted. He proposed that the War Office should be authorized to do all it could to modernize the regular contingent of the Field Force over the next five years. The recommendation for the later (Territorial) contingents should simply be held in abeyance for three years. Thus the Weir–Chamberlain opposition had successfully blocked the DRC's main proposals for the Army whose demands on industry were thereby cut. On the other hand, the continental commitment of the Regular Army was tacitly accepted but without any directive to the General Staff to reconsider the composition and tactical doctrine of the Field Force on the radical lines advocated by Weir. Thus Baldwin's solution, which was approved, 'hardly looks like a master-stroke either of statecraft or of strategy. It looks much more like a triumph of evasive action.'[25]

In retrospect the German reoccupation of the demilitarized zone of the Rhineland in March 1936 marked a crucial tilting of the military balance in Europe in Germany's favour. Indeed, it used to be widely held that it was the last opportunity for France and Britain to resist Hitler and perhaps strike a fatal blow at his domestic prestige. Now that most of the contemporary documents are accessible, however, this view is hard to sustain. What now seems most remarkable is how little British or French statesmen grasped that a vital strategic advantage was being surrendered and how utterly unprepared either country was to fight for it. Early in 1935, for example, the Cabinet had concluded, without taking advice from the Chiefs of Staff, that the maintenance of the demilitarized zone was *not* a vital British interest. When the subject came up again in the summer of 1935 in connection with a possible Air Pact, the same attitude prevailed and a government adviser summed up the popular view: 'Many people in the United Kingdom would say that Hitler was quite right. Still more would say that it was no affair of ours. Few would be ready to risk their own lives or those of their kith and kin, or to embroil the nation in a European war for this reason.'

Early in 1936 the new Foreign Secretary, Anthony Eden, asked the CID to evaluate the demilitarized zone from the viewpoints of the Army and the RAF. Rather surprisingly in view of Baldwin's famous remark that in the new age of air-power Britain's frontier now lay on the Rhine, the Air Staff view was that the zone was of negligible value as a barrier between Germany and her likely opponents: Britain, France, and Belgium. With the speed and range of modern aircraft, they argued, the zone represented little more than a few minutes' flying time and would make no substantial difference either for allied defence against or air attack on Germany. By contrast the General Staff's appreciation stressed the great strategic value of the zone, indirectly to Britain and directly to her likely allies—both from the defensive and offensive viewpoints. As regards defence: 'Germany would have to concentrate further back from an undefended than from a defended frontier, possibly east of the Rhine; this would not be such a serious disadvantage for mechanised forces as for others; but in both cases it would make it more difficult for the Germans to surprise the French before they had had time to man their fortifications at war strength.' As for the zone's value as an offensive springboard: 'If Germany wishes to stand on the defensive on her western frontier, the unilateral demilitarised zone is a weakness, since the Western Powers could mobilise and concentrate behind their frontier fortifications and attack, when ready, against a hastily perpared defence.' On the eve of the German reoccupation the Cabinet took the view that the only breach of the Locarno Treaty which could be considered 'flagrant' was the assembly of German forces in the zone with the obvious intention of actually invading France or Belgium. They had reason to believe, furthermore, that even the French would regard a simple reoccupation as only a 'qualified' breach of Locarno and therefore not a *casus belli*.[26]

There is no need here to discuss in detail the reasons why France and Britain failed either unilaterally or collectively to make any effective response to Hitler's *coup*. Britain lacked the two vital requisites of military strength and public support.[27] France, having failed to develop the mobile forces capable of mounting a rapid counter-offensive without general mobilization, as advocated by De Gaulle, proved impotent to make the prompt response which might have denied the zone to Germany without bringing on a major war. In Britain the Chiefs of Staff supported the Government's reluctance to become involved by urging that if there was the smallest danger of war with Germany Britain ought first to disengage herself from the Mediterranean responsibilities which had exhausted practically the whole of her slender reserves. Even if that could be done, the COS gloomily added, it would take two to four months before the Army and RAF units withdrawn from the Mediterranean could be reorganized at home. The CIGS's assessment was also predictably pessimistic. The Army could do nothing without mobilisation, he asserted: 'Even with mobilisation the position was thoroughly unsatisfactory. It would be possible after a few weeks, to send only a small force abroad and this with no modern armaments such as up to date tanks, anti-tank guns etc. There was no trained regular anti-aircraft personnel and only a limited amount of anti-aircraft ammunition, although supplies had now begun to arrive . . .'[28] Colonel Pownall's diary entries, which gain interest from his intimate contacts with the COS and the War Office, echo the CIGS's sense of impotence and anxiety lest Britain's unready forces should become entangled in war through supporting the French. On Sunday 8 March Pownall noted:

> We are certainly in no position (even if we wanted to) to use force—nor are the French though they will squeal and sulk and ask for help. It is the inevitable result of trying to keep down a virile population of 70 million. The kettle has been seething for years, now it has boiled over. The French are to blame for trying to keep the lid down . . . and we are to blame for condoning, even seconding, the French.

In his next entry Pownall remarked: 'I cannot see this country *going to war* because somebody has re-occupied *his own* territory, however indecent the manner of its doing. How these Leagues and Covenants and Pacts bring trouble in their train . . .'[29] For once Liddell Hart was unwittingly in accord with his arch critic, Pownall, for in a 'Note on the Re-occupation' he wrote: 'Leaving aside the breach of faith, the right thing has been done in the wrong way. But the breach of faith is wrong in itself.' Curiously he did not analyse the strategic significance of the reoccupation but concluded his memorandum by noting that the demilitarized zone had been forced on the French (by British pressure) as well as on the Germans.[30]

Although it has been argued[31] that Britain, France, and Belgium salvaged something from the débâcle of the Rhineland crisis by holding staff talks in London in mid-April 1936, it is abundantly clear that the British military advisers fully shared the Cabinet's view that the talks must be low level and strictly limited to an exchange of information. In March the COS urged the extreme difficulty, so long as the Locarno Treaty remained in force, of holding talks with France and Belgium without including Germany. Such talks, the Joint Planning Committe added, would only serve to arouse German suspicions while revealing Britain's weaknesses. In the privacy of his diary Pownall recorded that he regarded the talks as 'more of a political gesture to please the French than as of any real practical value'. He feared that Germany would conclude that matters of real importance were being discussed and this would make it difficult for Britain to have talks with her later about mutual assurances and pacts to replace Locarno. In the event Pownall was agreeably surprised by the amiable French and Belgian reception of the British Service Attachés' severely restricted brief. The latter were only allowed to say 'what was in the cupboard (bare enough)' and to ask what facilities France and Belgium could put at Britain's disposal if they were asked. Instead of pressing for joint planning as the British had feared, they 'cheerfully accepted the position'.[32]

Private sources reveal, however, that the French and Belgian response was conditioned by the hope that these first exploratory talks would soon be followed by more substantial discussions. The French military representative, General Schweisguth, advised the British that his country would look after her own frontier and while he would be happy to see British troops in France he would prefer to see them lend assistance to the Belgians. He spelt this out even more plainly in a private conversation with General Dill after the formal proceedings were over. The Secretary of State for Air, Lord Swinton, told the Cabinet that the French had been 'much alarmed' at the poor state of Britain's forces and especially her undue concentration of strength in the Mediterranean. In mid-May Sir Ronald Adam (DDMO) and Lieutenant-Colonel Bernard Paget* (GSO1, WO) informed Liddell Hart that the Belgians were making it clear that they would not feel happy until British troops were there. Both officers believed that there would be time for the Field Force to arrive since they doubted if Germany was ready to take the offensive in the West, whereas if France attacked first Britain was unlikely to come in, at any rate at first. However, Paget confirmed Liddell Hart's suspicion that neither the French Government, nor the Army, nor the people favoured taking the initiative: they would not move unless attacked.[33] In June 1936 the COS were informed that the Belgian Prime Minister, M. Van Zeeland, had requested that British and Belgian Service Attachés should hold conversations (without the French) to discuss actual plans. Eden was opposed so long as Britain was negotiating with Germany, since it would give

Germany an excuse to break off the talks, but he was in favour if the talks failed. In those circumstances, he felt, neither France nor Germany was likely to object, and in addition an agreement with Belgium should suit the British public since it would be a limited commitment to defend a vital interest and would not involve Britain elsewhere—as an agreement including France might.[34]

Although the Rhineland crisis and the subsequent staff talks left Britain's commitment to the security of Western Europe apparently unimpaired, these events surely marked 'a long step in the approach to that policy of political and military "limited liability" which reached its peak in 1938' The Chiefs of Staff's reluctance even to contemplate practical military arrangements with France and Belgium, the Government's failure to follow up the April Staff talks, and the failure to achieve a general political agreement with Germany to replace Locarno, all suggest that 'even if a "continental" interest was being reaffirmed, the means to protect it were at the same time being denied'. In London suspicion towards France was at least as much in evidence as fear of Germany.[35]

In the summer and autumn of 1936 the basis of Britain's military commitment to Europe was further eroded by the gradual movement of Belgian policy towards strict neutrality, itself influenced by the Belgian anxiety arising from Britain's increasing strategic detachment from the Continent. Before we examine this development, however, it is important to discover to what extent the War Office and the General Staff had sketched out what role the Field Force would play if it was dispatched to the Continent.

In November 1935 the War Office and Air Ministry carried out an elaborate paper exercise in which eight syndicates represented the armies and air forces of Britain, Belgium, France, and Germany. Although the exercises were set conveniently far ahead in 1947, at least one bore a close resemblance to the way events actually unrolled in 1940. As Burnett-Stuart relates in his memoirs, he was selected to command the German armies with Air Vice Marshal Sir Philip Joubert de la Ferté* commanding his air forces. He felt that, given his well-known opposition to the continental role for the Army, he owed this honour at least in part to the War Office authorities' wish to see him on the defeated side. Burnett-Stuart based his plan on the fact that he had no confidence in the Maginot Line or in the morale of a once offensively minded nation which had put its faith in a fixed defensive barrier. His staff drew up an elaborate plan in which the German forces broke through between Maubeuge and Verdun, avoiding Holland and Belgium altogether, and completely left the British Expeditionary Force out of the picture. The Directing Staff was displeased by this solution and instructed the 'German Government' to include Belgium in the attack. In his revised plan Burnett-Stuart added a broad sweep through Holland as well as Belgium but impishly decided to halt the advance only as far westward as Brussels. This would provide sufficient space for the German ground forces, closely supported by their air force, to attack the French defences between Maubeuge and Verdun with the aim of turning the defences of the Vosges salient. A break through on this front, followed by a direct advance on Paris, offered the best means of bringing the French armies to battle and of defeating them before British military intervention could become effective. Once again the plan did not envisage collision with the BEF. As the exercise came to an abrupt end and no conference was ever held on it, Burnett-Stuart reasonably concluded that the umpires were not best pleased by his ingenious solution. In September 1936 Liddell Hart sent a copy of Burnett-Stuart's memorandum on the exercise to Barrington-Ward (Deputy Editor of *The Times*) with a covering letter in which he (Liddell Hart) drew the lesson that under its present conditions of mobilization and transport the BEF 'apparently proved unworkable' in the task of checking a German advance through Belgium and Luxembourg which avoided the routes west of the Meuse taken by Kluck in 1914.[36] In other words this war game and its aftermath strengthened the advocates of limited liability in their views that the Field Force could not make an effective contribution to the defence of Belgium.

At the end of April 1936 the Joint Planning Sub-Committee prepared an 'Appreciation of the Situation in Event of Unprovoked Aggression by Germany'. It assumed that Germany would act alone and on land would have 3 armoured and 29 infantry divisions. It thought the French would probably advance towards the Rhine, but Germany was too weak to risk a land offensive in the west. She might attempt to knock-out Britain from the air but it was doubtful if she would succeed. Britain's chief instruments should be economic blockade and air attacks on Germany from the Continent. If political considerations allowed, the Field Force would be dispatched 14 days after mobilization. It would consist of two divisions, a Corps headquarters, and certain Corps troops. So long as the present situation existed in Egypt there would be no tank units or Air Defence Brigade and no modern equipment such as anti-tank guns and mortars.[37]

In the Army's outline plan it was stressed that it was impossible to make commitments regarding reinforcements beyond the original contingent of two divisions.[38] Shortage of ammunition might be a decisive limiting factor. Within these severe limitations three possible roles were suggested: (*a*) to occupy a sector between the French and Belgian armies; (*b*) to take up position on the Belgian left wing; and (*c*) to remain in reserve behind the Belgian left flank. Option (*a*) was virtually ruled out because it would entail operating far from the sea and losing freedom of action—an unrealistic hope that remained prominent in General Staff appreciations. Role (*b*) would be better as the defence of Belgium was an essential part of British policy, though freedom of action would still be curtailed. Role (*c*) was consequently considered best of all.

Despite the grave risk of German bombing the Joint Planning Committee thought it desirable that the BEF should disembark north of the Seine. Boulogne and Calais were selected for personnel; Dunkirk for transport, vehicles, and stores; and Havre and Rouen were base ports from the first because the Channel ports would be inadequate if the BEF was later to be increased. Alternative arrangements should be made to use St Nazaire and La Rochelle. If the Channel ports were used, the assembly area would be St Omer–Hazebrouck and if the Biscay ports, Amiens–Beauvais. The concentration area for roles (*b*) or (*c*) would be Malines–Brussels–Termonde, but in the unlikely event of an initial German land offensive the alternative would be Ghent–Brussels–Termonde. In May 1936 the CAS reaffirmed that the Low Countries were still vital to Britain, though because of the risk of air interference it might be necessary to dispatch the BEF from Bristol and Liverpool to the more westerly French ports.[39] It needs to be emphasized that these were purely outline paper plans and were not discussed with either of Britain's likely allies.

Even before the Rhineland crisis the Belgian Government was reappraising its position with a view to reducing its obligations under Locarno without prejudicing the chances of British and French support in the event of trouble.[40] The end of the Franco-Belgian defence agreement in February 1936 was greeted with relief in Brussels, since there was understandable fear that Belgium would become involved in a war that did not concern her, through France's eastern European commitments. In the succeeding months domestic rivalry between Flemings and Walloons pushed Belgian foreign policy towards a return to strict neutrality.[41] By the mid-1930s Belgium's strategic position was, to say the least, unenviable; it looked certain that her country would become the battlefield in a Franco-German war and she was bound to lose whatever the outcome. Britain's manifest military weakness and marked unwillingness to undertake any definite continental military commitment further dismayed the Belgians, particularly the significant group who preferred British military aid to French as being more disinterested. In July 1936 M. Spaak, the Belgian Foreign Minister, made clear his Government's new position: Belgian integrity should be guaranteed by all her neighbours but she herself would not be a guarantor in any treaty. Neutrality would bestow internal unity and enhance her ability to defend her frontiers against any aggressor. At a London meeting of the Locarno Powers on 23 July Britain declared that she had no objection to this new policy but felt sure that France would have, since France's military strategy depended on extending the Maginot defences along Belgium's eastern frontier, co-ordinating strategy with her, and fighting an advanced battle on Belgian soil.[42] Although the Belgians hoped to have the best of both worlds by continuing informal staff talks with the British, Eden politely declined. The COS remained adamantly opposed to staff talks with either France or Belgium on the grounds that news of them would be leaked and Britain would find herself militarily committed.[43] It would be a repetition of the tragedy of 1914 all over again.

A new phase in Anglo-Belgian relations was initiated in

October 1936 when King Leopold's rather blunt announcement of his country's return to neutrality, originally intended only for the ears of his Cabinet ministers, was made public. The French reaction was, as might be expected, one of fury, but Eden was also irritated and the Air Ministry was annoyed. Curiously the COS, whom the Foreign Office castigated as 'exceptionally stupid', maintained their opinion that Belgium's strict neutrality was in Britain's interest. In discussing the position of Belgium on 9 December 1936 the CIGS, Deverell, made the following revealing statement:

> The Army was not in a position to intervene on the Continent at the present time, particularly having regard to our small force of five divisions and the time taken to get them across. By the time we were in a position to intervene, the Germans would have overrun Belgium. It was obvious that the less territory there was to fight in and the less room for manoeuvre for the Germans, the better it would be for us.

Admiral Chatfield, summing up as Chairman of the COS, remarked that their overriding consideration had always been to avoid war while they were rearming. The suggestion that hostilities might be expected any time after the spring of 1937 had come as a great shock to them.[44] The COS, and Chatfield in particular, felt that the Foreign Office bore a heavy responsibility for the worsening international situation and, more specifically, that Eden's support for staff talks would have the effect of alienating Germany and pushing Britain towards an undesirable alliance with France. The Foreign Office predictably reacted by accusing the COS of exceeding their brief by interfering in political matters, but the CID tended on the whole to uphold the rights of the military experts. Chatfield summed up the COS's attitude when he inquired of the newly appointed First Lord of the Admiralty, Sir Samuel Hoare: 'Is our military unreadiness going to dominate our Foreign Policy, as we feel it should, for the next few years, or is our Foreign Policy going to carry us into a war when we are not ready for it . . . A very definite answer is needed to those two questions for the guidance of the Defence Departments.'[45]

Throughout the second half of 1936 Duff Cooper kept up what, from the military viewpoint, must appear as an heroic fight in the CID and the Cabinet for the rearmament of the Regular Army and a clear policy for the Territorial Army. That he achieved so little is doubtless in part due to the fact that the department he headed and the policy he advocated occupied very low positions in the Government's priorities. But the minister also had his personal limitations. He himself admitted in his memoirs that he had a hasty temper. Also his courageous, if injudicious, speech at the Anglo-French Society's annual dinner in the summer of 1936 when he insisted that the two countries must stand together and would defeat Germany if she dared to attack, caused Baldwin's Government considerable embarrassment. Nevertheless, Duff Cooper's chief failing was lack of energy and drive in dealing with the notorious inertia of the War Office. Within the department, as a colleague, Lord Percy, remarked, 'long tradition had built up its civilian finance officers in time of peace into a crippling *imperium in imperio,* intent upon checking every initiative of the professional soldiers'. Duff Cooper, though radical in his approach, seemed incapable of imposing his will. Pownall bears out this impression when, writing of the Army's need to accelerate its rearmament programme, he noted: 'The War Office need ginger I'm sure. Duff Cooper doesn't seem to interest himself in it much . . .' In June 1936 Pownall found it deplorable that a departmental committee had had to tell Duff Cooper how to organize production. 'They [the War Office] need an administrator like Swinton, not a literary politician.'[46]

As discussions about the priority of the Army's role dragged on inconclusively through 1936, Chamberlain, with the immense authority of the Treasury behind him, grew ever more impatient at the Government's failure to reach a definite decision. His own mind was made up. Though temperamentally averse to any continental commitment of land forces, he was prepared to accept the necessity of a Field Force for overseas service composed of the four Regular divisions and a mobile division. This would have to be maintained, if necessary, by drafts though the Chancellor showed no awareness of the difficulties. The Territorial Army, he believed, should be used for anti-aircraft defence at home. By contrast, the attitude of the War Office and the professional service advisers was, to say at least, ambivalent. On the one hand they upheld the continental commitment in principle and in incautious moments even suggested that the dispatch of the Field Force and the Territorial Army divisions would form only the prelude to the raising of a mass army on the lines of 1914–18. On the other hand, the COS and the JPC not merely accepted the Government's policy of 'appeasing' Germany but repeatedly urged it to do so. Both attitudes were evident in a strategical review by the JPC presented to the COS on 3 July 1936. Although the security of the Low Countries was essential to Britain, they suggested, 'Our military backwardness and the very unreliable military condition of France have placed us in a very weak condition. Collective security rests ultimately on the military strength that can *and will* be put into the field.' Britain should not expect altruistic support from other powers; they would fight only when their vital interests were involved. Not only, they concluded, must Britain strictly limit and define the issues on which she would go to war:

From a military standpoint, owing to the extreme weakness of France, the possibility of an understanding between Germany and Japan, and even in certain circumstances Italy, and because of the immensity of the risks to which a direct attack upon Great Britain would expose the Empire, the present situation dictates a policy directed towards an understanding with Germany and a consequent postponement of the danger of German aggression against any vital interest of ours.[47]

When, in the autumn of 1936, the JPC drew up an appreciation of the situation in the event of war with Germany three years on, they stressed that if the enemy attempted first to knock out Britain by air attack the land forces' duties would be to defend the country and maintain confidence, law, and order among the civil population before attempting to fulfil any other role. They predicted gloomily in a covering note that by 1939 Germany might well succeed in demoralizing the people and/or disorganizing food supplies by air attack. If, however, Germany struck first at Britain's probable allies the Field Force must be dispatched to northern France with minimum delay. The most likely role of the Field Force would then be to co-operate with the French and Belgian armies in a counter-offensive during the second phase, i.e. after Britain's allies had checked the original German onslaught. Perhaps rather complacently, the Joint Planners considered that British intervention on land would help bring the divergent strategic interests of France and Belgium into accord and co-ordinate the operations of their armies. 'We only, of the three Allies, might be able in the course of time to bring into the field mobile mechanised forces on a scale which would make a counter-offensive possible.'[48]

Despite the JPC's apparently confident assumptions about the aid and comfort which the Field Force would bring to continental allies, and despite the fervent support which Hankey, Vansittart, and the General Staff continued to give to the principle of the continental commitment,[49] it was apparent even before the Army's role came under renewed political attack in December 1936 that the General Staff was exceedingly vague on what exactly the Field Force would do and to what extent it would be expanded.

This uncertainty of principle and the obstinate imperviousness to criticism is evident in the note of a long discussion which Liddell Hart had with Deverell (the CIGS) and General Haining (the DMO and I) on 12 November 1936. Haining argued that Britain must be prepared in another war to go all-out with all the resources of the nation. The Army could not be confined to a limited role, leaving the main effort to the other Services which would not be able, as the Abyssinian war had demonstrated, to force a decision by themselves. There would be five million men left over when all industrial needs and those of the other Services had been met. It was unthinkable, said Haining, and Deverell agreed, that they should not be used by the Army. Haining then argued that the French would not be satisfied unless Britain sent an army: it was essential to sustain their morale. Liddell Hart queried this, suggesting that the Field Force, arriving late, would be more of a complication than an asset whereas air assistance would be ready immediately. The soldiers proved to be on safer ground in arguing that Liddell Hart (in his recent articles and in a letter in *The Times*) exaggerated the superiority of the defence by relying too much on the experience of the last war. Liddell Hart also refused to accept Haining's contention that Britain could no longer opt for a war of limited liability, such as she had practised in the past, because 'the heart of England had never been in danger in the event of defeat, as it was today'. Liddell Hart was depressed by this evidence that 'the General Staff want a field force that can be sent across the Channel, as the preliminary to the creation of a large national army', though he wrongly assumed that the other Services would not put up stout opposition to the Army's wishes. He was surely correct however in concluding that 'The force itself has no structural plan other than a vaguely general modernising of the five Divisions we happen to have. There is no sign that they have tried to *think out* the problem of its form, use and effect—in all its implications.'[50]

In December 1936 Duff Cooper revived the debate on the role of the Army by asking approval for the modernization of the 12 divisions of the Territorial Army as reinforcements for the five Regular divisions comprising the Field Force. When this was discussed by the Cabinet on 16 December, after an exchange of critical memoranda between the War Minister and the Chancellor,[51] Duff Cooper pointed out that a lack of a decision on the duties of the Territorial Army was also holding up the supply of new equipment for the Regular Army. He was supported by Inskip, the Minister for the Co-ordination of Defence, who argued that the Territorial Army was not in a fit state at present to provide reinforcements and that, if it was to be re-equipped over the next three years, the plans at least must be confirmed at once. Because firms did not know how to plan their programmes it would be extravagant and costly to wait until after the Regular Army had been re-equipped. Vickers-Armstrong, for example, were engaging apprentices for five years and were prepared to take on more men if orders justified it. Moreover, the Director General of Munitions Production at the War Office could not go ahead with his programme unless he knew whether he had to provide for only five divisions or for the Territorial Army as well. It was not, he stressed, a question now of committing either the Field Force or the Territorial Army to a continental role but only of ensuring that they were ready for war if required.

The Chancellor not only challenged Duff Cooper's proposal on financial grounds but also disputed that a decision of principle had been taken to modernize the Territorial Army. He then made an extraordinary remark: 'The fact that successive Chiefs of Staff and Secretaries of State for War had taken the view that, in the event of an attack by Germany on France, we should be prepared to send a land force to Belgium or France did not weigh very much with him as the War Office was *the interested Department* [emphasis added].' Chamberlain raised the larger question of whether by equipping twelve Territorial divisions as well as the Regulars Britain would be making the best possible use of her resources. He urged the Government to reconsider the wisdom of sending the Territorial Army abroad and the possible alternative of using the Air Force, even if that would entail increased expenditure. 'Our aim should be to deter war and that might be better done by increasing the Air Force.' When Stanhope (First Commissioner of Works) supported Duff Cooper by suggesting that continental powers would not regard air forces as a sufficient deterrent to war the Chancellor made his strategic attitude even clearer. He was not, he said, approaching the matter from a financial standpoint.

> The doubt he felt was as to whether we were right in approaching any war from the point of view of the last war. To think we could send an Expeditionary Force at the outset might involve a rude awakening . . . He himself doubted whether we were right in equipping the Territorial Force *for the trenches* [emphasis added]. He thought the question had not been considered impartially. It was always assumed that we must make a contribution to a land war. As one of his colleagues had said, the French might not be satisfied, but it was not for France to dictate to us the distribution of our Forces. He did not want to say that no Army should go to the Continent, but he had tried to make a *prima facie* case to show that the idea of sending 5 Regular divisions to France at the outset of war and 12 [Territorial] divisions later required re-examination.[52]

Although Duff Cooper reminded his colleagues that the Chiefs of Staff had reported on this again and again and were unlikely to change their views, Baldwin tamely accepted a suggestion that it be referred back to them, apparently overlooking the Chancellor's thrust that they were 'an interested party'. On the day after the Cabinet meeting Hankey wrote angrily to Inskip that 'If someone is to put this view to the COS it will have to be Neville Chamberlain himself because he [Hankey] knows of no one else who shares it with sufficient conviction to put it forward.'[53]

Duff Cooper's confidence that the Chiefs of Staff would adhere to their previous line of consistent support for a continental commitment of the Army proved justified. However, the minutes of their full discussions of the issue on 12 and 19 January 1937 reveal that the Chancellor's repeated challenges had touched some sensitive areas. In a memorandum the CIGS rehearsed the basic argument for preparedness: the earlier British forces could intervene the more valuable they would be. The first aim must be to survive the opening stages. Public opinion would not tolerate the dispatch of an ill-equipped British force to confront a more powerful and better equipped enemy. When Deverell insisted that all 12 TA divisions must be fully equipped before the war began, the CAS (Ellington) asked him why it had to be twelve divisions; he feared that the land commitment would be expanded at the expense of the other Services. Deverell rather lamely replied that 12 divisions was a small number—less than a quarter of the number maintained in the First World War. Britain would not have time to build up an enormous army comparable to that of the last war because the dictator states could never last out a long war ('Their population would not have the stamina to do it'). Both his colleagues lacked the CIGS's faith in a short war, and the CNS later remarked tartly that they must have some better reason for recommending 12 TA divisions other than the bald statement that there had always been that number.

Although the CIGS continued to insist that the Regular divisions and the whole of the Territorial Army must be modernized, Inskip, who took the chair at the COS meeting on 19 January, pointed out that the Chancellor had misrepresented the situation in that there was no question of beginning the re-equipment of the Territorial Army before 1939. All that could be done at present was to think about their equipment. Hankey, whose tireless support of the Army was still of vital importance, added that no one had ever suggested that all 17 divisions should go to the Continent at the outset of war: the first step was to ensure that the whole of the first (Regular) contingent could arrive within a fortnight. The CIGS again took the somewhat contradictorary position of maintaining that a land commitment was essential to bolster up French morale, while also insisting that he did not ask for a precise mandate since that would result 'in our becoming tied to the heels of the French'. The vital point on which the COS at least managed to maintain an appearance of unanimity was that air power alone could not stop the German Army, and that (*pace* the Chancellor) air and land forces were complementary rather than rivals or alternatives.[54]

In their report of 28 January 1937, the COS insisted that, though it might suit Britain, her continental contribution could certainly not be limited to air and naval forces:

We assume that any idea of leaving to our Continental allies the exclusive burden of providing these land forces, and thereby limiting our contribution to air forces, however greatly expanded, is out of the question for political reasons . . . It is therefore impossible to discount altogether the contingency of having to send military forces to the Continent at some stage of the war and perhaps at its very outset.

As for the Territorial Army, the COS argued that the Field Force, if sent, must be supported and the TA was the only possible reserve. Its present strength, however, was dictated by administrative rather than strategic reasons. It would need many more men and four months intensive training before it could take the field and, most important, it must ultimately have the same equipment as the Regulars. The report concluded by stressing the COS's concern at the serious effect that the Government's indecision about the role of the Army was having.[55]

The COS's unequivocal and unanimous report had depressingly little impact. In February 1937 Inskip concluded that the TA constituted the only possible reserve for the Field Force and that Parliament and the country expected it to fulfil this role, but in his view it did not follow that the TA should be maintained in the same state of readiness as the Regulars. The country was unwilling to prepare an army on the 1914–18 scale. He proposed as a compromise solution that the TA should be given enough modern equipment to train, spread over all twelve divisions, but that in an emergency equipment should be drawn from the force as a whole to enable one or more TA divisions to be dispatched overseas after four months. This was of course a severe curtailment of the scheme for three TA contingents each of four divisions which Duff Cooper had proposed and the COS had supported.[56]

This difference of outlook was again highlighted when the War Office estimates were presented to the Cabinet on 5 May 1937. Duff Cooper reckoned that the Regular Army and two anti-aircraft divisions of the TA could be fully re-equipped and provided with war reserves by April 1940 for approximately £208 million. The cost of providing enough new equipment for all 12 TA divisions to train in peacetime was put at over £9 million with the same date for completion. These proposals were approved by the Cabinet, but two additional proposals by Duff Cooper, who asserted that the notion of equipping the TA only for training purposes was not a military policy, were vehemently and successfully opposed by Chamberlain. These proposals were that full equipment and reserves should be provided for a Territorial contingent of four divisions at a cost of about £43½ million by April 1941; and, secondly, that investigation should be made at once into the industrial capacity needed to prepare the remaining eight TA divisions for service overseas six and seven months after the outbreak of war. There is no need to rehearse the Chancellor's contrary arguments yet again. He told his Cabinet colleagues that he definitely did challenge the policy of the professional military advisers. He argued that the other two Services must enjoy priority in rearmament. The Government should not prepare, and in the event would not be allowed by the country, to fight another continental land war on the scale of 1914–18. If Britain had to fight she would have allies who were obliged to maintain large armies. Her liability as regards a land contribution must be strictly limited. A final decision was deferred once again by referring the issue to yet another ministerial DP(P) Committee.[57]

One other important consideration may be mentioned. Despite the unanimity of their reports, the COS Committee had from its origins been internally at odds—sometimes with acute friction—over various issues, particularly those concerning the employment of air power in conjunction with or as an alternative to the two older Services. It is evident that, despite what the CAS was reluctantly approving in the COS, opinion in the Air Ministry grew increasingly sceptical about and even hostile to the Army's view of its continental commitment.[58] Indeed, despite the COS's apparently unanimous report in January 1937: 'The R.A.F. would never again lend so much support to the War Office. Ellington's successor, Air Chief Marshal Sir Cyril Newall, took just the opposite view, frequently demonstrating a doctrinaire disbelief in the Field Force's strategic utility while pressing the Air Ministry's case for the bomber as the decisive weapon of war.'[59]

Chamberlain's awareness of this deep rift in the superficially united resistance to his determined efforts to limit the Army's continental liability is clear in a letter to his sisters of 6 February 1937: 'The amusing thing is that the 3 Chiefs of Staff acting together reported in favour of having 12 Territorial Divisions ready in 4 months but after the Cabinet had taken its decision I heard from the First Lord and the S/S Air, independently, that their Chief of Staff really agreed with my view. Of course I always felt that when it came to the point dog would eat dog . . .'[60]

Duff Cooper kept up his valiant but unavailing fight to secure a definite decision on the place of the Regular and Territorial armies in strategic, and hence in rearmament, priorities, but with Baldwin's retirement in the spring of 1937 his days at the War Office were evidently numbered. Chamberlain was to write (to his sisters), soon after he had succeeded Baldwin and had rather unexpectedly promoted Duff Cooper to the Admiralty, that the War Minister had been lazy and had handled the Army's case clumsily 'and with little power of adaptation' in the Cabinet. On the contrary, however, the Cabinet documents show that Duff Cooper argued the Army's case energetically and clearly on every possible occasion, and that Chamberlain's view prevailed partly because it was formulated with great pertinacity and ministerial authority, but also because it was more acceptable to the majority of the Cabinet. 'The tide of finance and of strategic thinking was moving against him' (Duff Cooper). What is surprising is that Duff Cooper apparently failed to understand that Chamberlain's mind had long been made up on the role of the Army and that he was moving steadily towards attaining his objective.[61]

Duff Cooper's failure to appreciate that he had already overstayed his time at the War Office as far as the former Chancellor—and now Prime Minister—was concerned is clear from a conversation he had with Liddell Hart in May 1937. According to Liddell Hart, Duff Cooper 'had argued with Neville. But N influenced by mine [Liddell Hart] and Jock Stuart's arguments about the B.E.F. felt somebody else was better to implement his policy. Unfair [to ask] D.C. D.C. demurred and said he hoped to carry on, and could carry out [the policy], but Neville adamant.'[62]

Thus the period covered in this chapter, July 1935–May

1937, saw a seemingly paradoxical development in British strategic thinking. On the one hand, Germany was rearming at a dangerous speed and displaying an aggressive attitude which marked her out as Britain's most dangerous potential enemy in the near future. Her reoccupation of the demilitarized zone of the Rhineland and the rapid growth of the Luftwaffe posed obvious threats to the security of Britain and her interests in Western Europe. On the other hand, the period was one of growing reluctance on the part of certain influential ministers, endorsed by the Cabinet as a whole, to uphold and implement the policy advocated by the DRC and COS: to render the Regular Army and at least part of the Territorial Army capable of intervening promptly in a continental war. Such a military commitment was to be even more drastically questioned after May 1937 by the Government of Neville Chamberlain.

The explanation of this apparent paradox lies in the Government's acceptance of the Treasury argument that finance was the fourth branch of the armed services. In other words economic stability was one of the cornerstones of the nation's defence structure and an integral part of the defensive strategy. As a corollary it was widely believed that this economic and social stability would serve to deter potential enemies. As Inskip put it: 'Nothing operates more strongly to deter a potential aggressor from attacking this country than our stability, and the power which this nation has so often shown of overcoming its difficulties without violent change and without damage to its inherent strength.'[63]

By maintaining the stability of the pound and a strong position as regards international credit, Britain could draw upon these assets in the event of war to purchase arms abroad until such times as her industrial capacity could be converted to arms production. In the short term these overriding financial and economic considerations demanded a strategy of restricting Britain's military preparations to measures designed to prevent her succumbing to a sudden knock-out blow, whether from air attack or from the severing of her sea lanes of communication. In this climate of opinion the prospects for the Army and its Expeditionary Force were extremely bleak.[64]

CHAPTER 9

Limited liability or no liability at all? May 1937–September 1938

When Neville Chamberlain became Prime Minister in May 1937 he selected Leslie Hore-Belisha to succeed Duff Cooper at the War Office. At forty-four, Hore-Belisha was one of the youngest men ever to hold that appointment. He was also one of the few members of the Cabinet to have served in the forces in the First World War. This was an asset in helping him to understand and sympathize with the Army's everyday problems, but it is doubtful if his military record (he reached the rank of major in the Royal Army Service Corps) enhanced his status in the eyes of the Regular Army hierarchy. He was also warned that being a Jew was a disadvantage, though it seems more likely that this was later used as just another stick to beat him with by generals and politicians who disliked his policies and, perhaps even more, his flamboyant methods.[1] More to the point in 1937, however, was that he had acquired a reputation as a man of action. He had served succesfully as Financial Secretary to the Treasury from 1932 to 1934 and had become very much a 'Chamberlain man'. Promoted Minister of Transport in 1934, he had enlisted the help of Fleet Street, where he himself had considerable experience as a journalist for the Beaverbrook Press, to reduce the rate of road accidents. Indeed to the general public he is best remembered as the originator of 'Belisha beacons' at pedestrian crossings. Thus he seemed just the right kind of bustling, publicity-conscious politician on the rise to shake the War Office out of its notorious inertia and conservatism. Although Chamberlain had evidently chosen him as a more suitable instrument than the obdurate Duff Cooper to implement the Premier's 'limited liability' policy for the Army, Hore-Belisha, like his great Liberal predecessors at the War Office Cardwell and Haldane, began with no clear strategic vision of his own. This was by no means a handicap in the eyes of senior officers whose initial reactions to the 'new broom' were generally favourable. Thus General Ironside, newly appointed to Eastern Command, noted in his diary on 29 May: 'We are at our lowest ebb in the Army and the Jew may resuscitate us. I hope that he hasn't been ordered to cut us down, and yet surely we can be cut down in our overhead expenses . . .' And on the following day Ironside added: 'I lay awake in the morning and thought of Hore-Belisha. He will probably be our saving. He is ambitious and will not be lazy like some of the others were. He starts in when things are at their worst and will have to show results.'[2]

Within weeks of his arrival, Hore-Belisha had embarked on an intensive study of the whole range of problems confronting the Army. It was typical of his unorthodox approach that he should select as his chief (though unofficial) military adviser Liddell Hart, at that time Defence Correspondent of *The Times*, to whom he had been introduced by Duff Cooper. The resultant 'partnership' which lasted just a year, although it achieved a great number of beneficial reforms, also aroused bitter controversy that harmed the careers of both partners. Liddell Hart has described the relationship from his side very fully and vividly in the second volume of his *Memoirs*, but Hore-Belisha's whole period at the War Office, though well-described by the late R. J. Minney in 1960, badly needs a thorough reappraisal in the light of the vast amount of material which has since become available.[3]

Liddell Hart, as we have seen, had been since the early 1930s an eloquent advocate of limited liability as regards the commitment of the British Army to the Continent. This is not the place for a full discussion of whether he simply expressed a general trend of strategic thinking among soldiers and politicians in important positions or actually influenced the development of policy.[4] Certainly much of the strength of his position derived from the fact that he represented (in by far the most important newspaper) a strategic outlook already deeply held, but by becoming the real strategic brain behind the War Minister at a crucial period in 1937 and 1938 he did in fact exert a positive influence on the important issue of the order of priorities for the Army.

An exhaustive reading of Liddell Hart's articles and books in the 1930s leaves a strong impression that he was temperamentally opposed to the commitment of *any* British ground forces in Europe for fear of repeating the holocaust of the First World War—he admitted in his *Memoirs* that he was inclined to a policy of isolation—but in most of his memoranda for Hore-Belisha he adopted a more moderate position. This was to ask what type of land forces (in addition to air support which he emphatically favoured) would be most useful to potential European allies. He argued reasonably that under modern conditions of war ordinary infantry divisions would have little effect in offensive operations, whereas in defence the French did not need them. He repeatedly made the valid criticism that the War Office and General Staff appeared to be bent on providing a Field Force almost identical with that of 1914 but in drastically changed conditions.

His persistent fear that a small British Field Force would repeat the folly of the First World War by becoming involved in a French *offensive* was well expressed in a note of 1937:

> If an ally is inclined to take what one has good reason from experience to regard as a suicidal course, is it *necessary* to join in it—and make it a double suicide.? Is it not wiser to express disapproval, and to insist on the objections, and to influence him to a wiser course?
>
> If you send to France a complete force like that of 1914 you will be drawn along the same course. Even if the French are wise enough, despite our encouragement, to stay on the defensive if the Germans attack, we shall get drawn into an offensive later—with the fancied idea of winning the war.
>
> But if we only send specialists or specialist units, for example mechanised divisions, we *can limit* our effort [emphasis in original].[5]

What was needed, he reiterated, was two or more mobile divisions which would increase by 66 per cent the forces of this kind in France. 'They would combine high mobility and concentrated fire-power with economy of men.' Such an armoured force would be easier to transport across the sea and to maintain in the war theatre in face of modern air attack. As for Imperial defence he doubted whether a single armoured mobile division would suffice. He believed that more than two TA divisions should be devoted to anti-aircraft ground defence, while the 12 divisions theoretically earmarked for European warfare possessed neither the armament nor equipment for that role. By a drastic reorganization of the Regular and Territorial armies, he believed that an Imperial Strategic Reserve could be created composed of four Regular and two Territorial armoured mobile divisions, and eight Regular and eight (or more) Territorial infantry divisions of a handier type. Simultaneously the scale of anti-aircraft defence both at home and overseas could be doubled.[6]

Hore-Belisha at first carried on Duff Cooper's struggle to secure the rearmament of the first four Territorial divisions as a reinforcement for the Field Force, but Sir John Simon, the new Chancellor of the Exchequer, entirely endorsed Chamberlain's views on the role of the Army. On 13 July Hore-Belisha recorded a decisive rebuff by the Cabinet:

> My proposal for the provision of war equipment, war reserves and maintenance for four Territorial divisions was turned down today. . . . At some time a decision will have to be made that some of the T.A. divisions will have to be fully equipped, and there are many reasons why it would be advantageous to make a decision now. . . . I argued with Simon, but he was quite firm that at present there should be no increase in the cost of the Army's programme.

This was far from being just a temporary setback, for Simon persuaded the Cabinet that an absolute ceiling had to be imposed on defence expenditure. Whereas the White Paper issued on 16 February 1937 had mentioned £1,500 m as the *minimum* sum to be made available for rearmament for the period 1937–42, Simon now asserted that it must be regarded as the *maximum*. This would necessitate a radical reappraisal of priorities and the imposition of strict rationing. Hore-Belisha at once realized that the European role of the Army would be likely to suffer, but Chamberlain's mind was already made up on this issue and he attached little weight to the opinions of the Chiefs of Staff.[7] The effect of this prolonged indecision about the Army's role on the commanders responsible for its training will be described later, but the uncertainty was clearly demoralizing. As Ironside complained in August 1937: 'The nation does not believe an Army is necessary and the Government, so democratic is it, will not make up the nation's mind for it.'[8]

The financial review set in motion by Simon in July was to culminate in December 1937 in a Cabinet decision which drastically altered the order of the Army's priorities. Before discussing that decision, however, it is essential to say something further about both the financial and strategic debates that preceded it.

It was for long fashionable to make the Treasury the scapegoat for Britain's military unpreparedness at the outbreak of the Second World War, but recent scholarly reappraisals have challenged at least the more simplistic criticisms. Several points have been argued in defence of the Treasury's drastic intervention in the rearmament process in 1937.[9] The balance of payments situation really was worrying in the mid-1930s so that the orthodox Treasury view of the need to balance budgets was not merely alarmist. The Treasury understood Government policy to be to secure peace rather than to make war: it was hoped that a normal state of balanced budgets could be achieved again after 1941. From 1935 onwards the Treasury was prepared to abandon financial orthodoxy and permit borrowing in the light of Germany's increased expediture on rearmament but it was not in favour of that expedient in principle. Even the modest Defence Loan of £400 million in February 1937 to be spent over five years was subjected to much adverse press comment. Unwillingness to risk a repetition of the 1931 financial crisis by over-rapid rearmament was one of the Treasury's chief nightmares; another was the fear of making the major financial and industrial effort too soon and being exhausted before war began. The Treasury could not know in advance that war would begin in 1939, or how long it would last.

Quite apart from the possibility that she might have to face more than one enemy, Britain was at a disadvantage in several respects in rearming in competition with Germany. Germany began her effort two years earlier (in 1933) and between then and 1938 spent approximately three times as much on rearmament as Britain. In some vital areas such as the production of steel and machine tools she possessed a stronger industrial base; and the Government believed that British business would not accept the German method of very high taxation (a 40 per cent tax on profits) or the public the high rate of German income tax. Nevertheless German financiers were probably as alarmed as the British at the consequences if her high rate of spending on armaments were to be prolonged beyond 1939.

While it is possible to present a strong defence of the Treasury's advice, however, on the basis of its own assumptions about the economy and the financial situation, the predominantly Conservative Government is open to criticism for continuing to put financial stability before defence until almost the eve of the war. The Government was extremely reluctant to antagonize business interests by interfering in such matters as labour or the level of profits, or by imposing controls. It maintained the pretence that business was co-operating voluntarily in the rearmament programme long after it became apparent that certain key sectors, like the machine-tool industry, were not doing so. Symptomatic of this deference to the business community was the Government's resistance to repeated requests from ministers directly concerned with rearmament to establish a Ministry of Supply. In January 1939 Inskip was dismissed as Minister for the Co-ordination of Defence when he persisted in presenting this issue to the Cabinet. A bill to create a Ministry of Supply was not introduced until May 1939 and even then it was to wield very limited powers. Further evidence of the Government's delay in giving rearmament priority over 'business as usual' lies in its failure to make any serious attempt to consult and gain the co-operation of the TUC leaders until the spring of 1938. Lastly, it seems likely that the Treasury was mistaken in rejecting Keynes's argument that, given the high level of unemployment, Britain still had considerable scope for borrowing without running the risk of serious inflation.

Whether or not Chamberlain and the Treasury were right to place so much emphasis on financial and economic stability as 'the fourth arm' of defence is therefore debatable. As Dr Keith Middlemas has pointed out, for example, defence costs had cut only very slightly into the 'civilian' budget in 1937, and Britain was in no sense on a war economy. Indeed, despite the fears of interested ministers and the Governor of the Bank of England, the rearmament programme actually had a beneficial effect on the level of economic activity up to 1939 and neither the social services nor the export trade suffered. Earlier and more intensive rearmament might even have brought an economic gain in the reduction of unemployment. In the short term Chamberlain's concern to maintain foreign and domestic confidence was understandable but the notion that financial stability would be an asset in a long war was a strange delusion. In fact in order to survive in a total war Britain quickly became financially and economically dependent on the United States.

A major charge, however, is that because Chamberlain was Prime Minister the Treasury view gained excessive influence and in 1937–9 was heeded largely at the exclusion of Service advice: 'The imbalance became worse because of a circular process: the more the Treasury emphasised the need to fortify the economy for a long war, the more the Chiefs of Staff themselves tended to think in terms of a war of attrition waged primarily by blockade and air defence; and the more hostile the Cabinet became to a policy of military co-operation with France.'[10]

Students of British defence policy in the 1930s must be impressed by the definiteness of the Treasury's views on strategic issues and the persistence its officials displayed in pressing for their acceptance by the Government. It is perhaps hardly a cause for surprise that Treasury officials should hold personal views on strategic issues; they were after all highly educated men closely in touch with political and military thinking, and Sir Edward Bridges* in particular had fought on the Western Front for most of the First World War. As Dr Peden remarks furthermore: 'It is not to be supposed that the Treasury officials were unaware of the need to build up the British arms industry, or that they put cost-accounting before national security.' Sir Warren Fisher was also justified in doubting the ability of the COS to formulate a co-ordinated defence policy, as distinct from totting up their individual needs and costs. Some higher political authority had to step in and decide on the priorities of a national defence policy, but this was surely the responsibility of the CID initially or, failing that body, ultimately of the Cabinet. In fact the inherent strength of the Treasury's position as the controller of the purse strings and the fortuitous advantage of its close association with the single most important minister between 1931 and 1939, Neville Chamberlain, together gave it an influence on strategic issues which was not justified by professional expertise.

This is not to suggest that the Treasury's views on military matters were always mistaken; for instance Fisher and Bridges were right to urge Hore-Belisha in July 1937 to economize by reducing the number of troops in India. It was, however, in backing Chamberlain's views on the primacy of air power that the Treasury's strategic influence was most clearly displayed. On this vital matter its view faithfully mirrored the Air Staff's until 1937. The Treasury accepted the Trenchard doctrine of deterring Germany by building up an offensive bomber force rather than by relying on air and ground defence. In this context a Field Force was justified to secure the Low Countries both for the defence of Britain and as an advanced bomber base against Germany. By July 1937 the Air Ministry had submitted proposals for a radar chain at the very modest cost of £1 million and the Treasury promptly switched its support to a preference for fighters and a defensive posture, a switch which, predictably, irritated the Air Staff. This change of emphasis to defence appears to have ended the Treasury's support for advanced air bases on the Continent, but it is doubtful if the issue was ever assessed for a strategic viewpoint. Although Treasury officials, including Bridges and Hopkins,* continued to see the need for a Regular Field Force throughout 1937, and even the ultimate need of an Army of 17 divisions, nevertheless in the short term the Treasury agreed with the Prime Minister that air strength should have an absolute priority.[11]

In conclusion, while several arguments can be advanced in support of the Treasury's role in the formulation of strategic policy certain basic criticisms remain. The Treasury's views on strategy were essentially defensive and anti-European: 'Priority for home defence meant withdrawing promised resources from France. Imposition of a fixed budget for the Services meant that each would compete for scarce resources at the eventual expense of the duty their armaments were supposed to perform.' Though the failure of the Chiefs of Staff to agree on a co-ordinated defence policy undoubtedly exacerbated the problem, it was essentially a shift of influence within the Cabinet which permitted the Treasury to play a much greater part in the formulation of strategy than had been possible before 1937.[12]

At the end of October 1937 Simon informed the Cabinet that the Treasury had been unable to give 'a figure the nation could afford', so the unenviable task of trying to bridge the impossible gap between the Service estimates and the Treasury totals was handed to Sir Thomas Inskip and a small committee in which Treasury officials predominated. In theory Inskip was supposed to produce an authoritative review of strategic priorities but, given his own lack of military expertise and the declining influence of the Chiefs of Staff, it was only to be expected, as Pownall was to note bitterly when the results were known, that the role would be altered to fit the purse—'the tail wagging the dog'.[13] This, however, is to anticipate the outcome of the simultaneous, though largely independent, strategic reappraisal which Hore-Belisha was conducting at the War Office with the close assistance of Liddell Hart.

In March 1937 Chamberlain wrote to congratulate Liddell Hart on his latest book *Europe in Arms* and commented: 'I am quite sure we shall never again send to the Continent an Army on the scale of that which we put into the field in the Great War.' On 29 October Chamberlain recommended the book to Hore-Belisha, advising him especially to read the chapter on the 'Role of the British Army'. Hore-Belisha replied: 'I immediately read the "Role of the British Army" in LH's book. I am impressed by his general theories.'[14]

By this time Hore-Belisha must have been well acquainted with Liddell Hart's ideas because through the late summer and early autumn they were in regular contact as Liddell Hart's memorandum on the reorganization of the Army was batted to and fro between the minister and his professional advisers. In mid-September a three-day War Office exercise without troops in Bedfordshire, the largest of its kind since the war, confirmed Liddell Hart's worst fears that the General Staff was still contemplating an offensive role on the Continent. The exercise, divised by General Alan Brooke, then Director of Military Training, required the 'Anglian' Force (really the Field Force of four infantry divisions and one mobile division) to attack through a corridor barely forty miles wide which represented the Aachen Gap between Belgium and the Ruhr. Liddell Hart was even more dismayed to discover in conversation that Brooke favoured the idea of leaving the tank brigade out of the mobile division, which would make the resemblance to the old horsed cavalry division even closer. Commenting on the exercise in *The Times* on 24 September, Liddell Hart referred to it as 'a somewhat fantastic conception' since the Field Force was unlikely to reach the Continent in time. Moreover, the exercise demonstrated the futility of the offensive by a force of this traditional kind used in the traditional way. In his *Memoirs* Liddell Hart was later to write that this exercise deepened his doubts about the British Army's capacity to develop new offensive techniques and caused him to concentrate on devising defensive or counter-offensive methods better suited to Britain's situation.[15]

Meanwhile, during the Bedford exercise in mid-September 1937, Hore-Belisha had paid a fateful visit to the French military manœuvres. He was impressed by the efficiency of the French Army and also by the still incomplete Maginot Line which, he was told, required only 100,000 troops to hold it, thus making possible a large reserve for the Field Army. 'When the French realise that we cannot commit ourselves to send an Expeditionary Force,' he noted in his diary, 'They should be all the more inclined to accelerate the extension of the Maginot Line to the sea.' The General Staff did not, however, share Hore-Belisha's optimistic view of the French Army or his belief that the Maginot Line could hold up a German offensive indefinitely. Indeed Deverell had attended the German manœuvres while Hore-Belisha was in France and returned 'infatuated', declaring that 'the attack will always conquer'. In January 1938 the French Military Attaché in London, General Lelong (who of course as Ismay minuted 'had an axe to grind'), confirmed that the Maginot Line could delay a German advance but could not hold it up for ever, unless the French Army were reinforced by the British. Meanwhile, however, Hore-Belisha had reported to the Prime Minister on 23 November:

> My view, after the fullest survey, including a visit to France, is that our Army should be organised to defend this country and the Empire, that to organise it with a military prepossession in favour of a Continental commitment is wrong. The C.I.G.S., although he may overtly accept this view, does not accept it in fact or in practice, and he has told me that he is unable to advise any modification in our organisation.[16]

As the autumn of 1937 wore on the General Staff, and the CIGS in particular, grew increasingly exasperated by the suspicion—entirely justified—that on the vital issue of the role of the Army they were dealing nominally with the War Minister but in reality with Liddell Hart. Not only did his views on limited liability differ sharply from theirs but he was also free to criticize their doctrine—on which of course he had inside information—in *The Times*. Inskip and Hankey as well as Gort and Deverell reacted critically to three articles he published on 25, 26, and 27 October under the heading 'Defence or Attack?' In the second article he invoked the 'lessons of six centuries' against the folly of a continental commitment and warned that the Army seemed bent on repeating the sequence of 1914—'commitment, entanglement, illimitable expansion, futile sacrifice and national exhaustion'; while in the third—though blurring his conclusion—he stressed that 'Modern weapon development has been predominantly defensive' so that the attacker had little chance of success in the next war. But it was the first article which provoked most controversy at the War Office, for he named and quoted Deverell as believing that 'the attack will always get the better of defence' and that 'Our army must be trained for the offensive.' The file on this controversy in the Cabinet Papers shows how seriously Liddell Hart's views were taken. Deverell defended himself, justifiably surely, by stating that Field Service Regulations did not support the charge that the Army was being trained solely on the principle of *offensive à outrance;* Britain was *not* committed to send a huge army to the Continent; it was *not* the Army Council's view that the offensive must be taken at the outset of a continental war whatever the circumstances; and, finally, there was no reason whatever to believe that France would adopt the offensive at the outset for that would be to throw away the asset of the Maginot Line.[17]

Although Deverell figures as a reactionary Colonel Blimp in the Liddell Hart *Memoirs,* it is difficult not to sympathize with this simple, straightforward, but intellectually limited soldier who was patently out of his depth in these political machinations which he sensed would end by virtually destroying the Field Force. Thus when Hore-Belisha asked him, in mid-November, what changes he would advise if the Cabinet decided there should be no Expeditionary Force, he allegedly declared that 'he would not alter present arrangements one iota'. On 18 November the CIGS entertained Liddell Hart alone at his flat and maintained that he had been misquoted in the 'Defence or

Attack?' article. Liddell Hart persisted in his view that the Field Force was being trained for continental war and asked where else such a force could be employed. Deverell replied vaguely 'places like Libya'. According to Liddell Hart, he then became 'confused and heated', declaring that it would be impossible to send the Regular Army out of England at all in the early part of another war. Liddell Hart also noted that Deverell had been much impressed by what he had seen of the German Army and was rather contemptuous of the French. According to Deverell, Hore-Belisha, lacking knowledge, had been too easily impressed by the French.[18]

This controversy was symptomatic of the rigidly conservative and unco-operative attitude which Hore-Belisha and Liddell Hart felt their plans for reform were receiving from the Army Council and the General Staff. Supported by the Prime Minister, by Lord Weir, and by some senior soldiers including the Military Secretary, Lord Gort, Hore-Belisha decided to make a clean sweep. On 2 December the CIGS and other military members of the Army Council were summarily dismissed. There had been no military purge like this since the Esher Committee had removed the last Commander-in-Chief, Lord Roberts, and his military colleagues in February 1904. As Ironside noted, 'The method of telling Deverell was not of the kindest, just a note to say that he had been suspended at once.' Gort only learnt that he had been selected as the new CIGS when his new deputy (DCIGS) Sir Ronald Adam arrived from the Staff College. Hore-Belisha's bold and courageous move was widely approved not only in the Press, but also in the Army.[19]

This is an appropriate point, at the zenith of the Hore-Belisha–Liddell Hart partnership, to make some observations on the latter's approach to the issue of the role of the Army. His numerous draft memoranda for the War Minister were based on political and military assumptions which were never exposed to critical analysis. His overriding concern was to avoid a repetition of the attrition warfare of 1914–18; he believed that the French would open the war with an offensive and if the Field Force arrived in time it would be drawn into it. In the later 1930s he argued with increasing conviction that the initial offensive had little chance of success in modern conditions: it would be better for the French and British (if they took part) to prepare for an initial defence with the eventual hope of counter-attack. He dealt with the composition of the Field Force throughout from an operational viewpoint, stressing repeatedly that two or more mobile armoured divisions would be more useful to France than a larger number of slow, vulnerable, and under-equipped infantry divisions. Within his own assumptions these proposals made sound sense, and it has often been remarked that two British armoured divisions might have made a vital difference in May 1940. Certain other vital considerations were neglected, however. He never grappled with the intractable financial situation but simply assumed that if his reorganization of the Army was carried out *in toto* the necessary savings could be made. This was greatly to underestimate the War Office's problem, since in 1937–8 it was required to make considerable reductions in expenditure on figures previously approved by the Cabinet. Similarly Liddell Hart's plans for the creation of mobile divisions bore no relation to reality in terms of production: the target date for the completion of the existing mobile division was 1940 and it did not follow at all that money saved by reduction of infantry units could promptly be transferred to the production of tanks. The only way for such a transformation to have been achieved, given the financial, political, and strategic assumptions current in 1937, was for the Army's continental role to have been given immediate top priority, not merely at the expense of the Army's other responsibilities but also of those of the other two Services. This would have required, first and foremost, an unequivocal *military* commitment to Britain's continental allies. In fact, paradoxically, the whole thrust of Liddell Hart's military doctrine was to deny the validity of the role the acceptance of which alone could have offered prospects of achieving the kind of Army he desired. One can only sadly agree with Dr Middlemas's conclusion that neither Liddell Hart nor Hore-Belisha 'in their inconoclastic fervour against the old structure, realised how little Chamberlain and the Treasury would be prepared to give in order to create the new model Army they desired'.[20] In conclusion, though he can hardly have been unaware of it, Liddell Hart showed no consideration for French and Belgian *morale* and the fact that, however small and ill-equipped the British Field Force, her potential allies would welcome its definite military commitment both as an earnest of present political support and as a promise of more substantial military reinforcements in the long term. In 1937 Liddell Hart's strategic outlook, like the Government's, was essentially isolationist and imperialist.[21]

While Hore-Belisha's policy was hardening against the Army's continental commitment in the second half of 1937, the Army lost the backing of one of its staunchest and most influential supporters, Sir Maurice Hankey. When specifically requested by the Cabinet to give his advice on strategic priorities in October 1937, Hankey placed the RAF first in the role of defence and deterrence of a German air attack, the Navy second, and the Army third with a low priority on an Expeditionary Force for the Continent and a recommendation that the Territorial Army should no longer be regarded as a reserve for that force. He had reached this conclusion on the role of the Army reluctantly, partly because 'France no longer looks to us . . . to supply an Expeditionary Force on the scale hitherto proposed'. The completion of the Maginot Line, he felt, had provided France with great powers of resistance to attack by Germany. Henceforth the primary duty of the Expeditionary Force should be to provide for the military requirements of the Empire. Hankey's biographer also claims that he was the first person in authority to propose that the RAF should henceforth give priority in production to fighters over bombers.[22] Another interpretation of Hankey's change of view, probably complementary rather than contradictory, is that he endorsed the Admiralty proposal put forward by Tom Phillips (the Admiralty's representative on the JPC), and endorsed by Chatfield on 10 November 1937, that the Field Force's role in support of European allies should be put lower in priority than its responsibilities in Imperial defence. Whether or not the Admiralty's recommendation, backed by Hankey, was of greater significance than the views of the Treasury, the War Office, and the Air Ministry it is impossible to be sure. What is certain is that by the time Inskip's momentous reappraisal of defence priorities came before the Cabinet on 22 December 1937 the Army's European role had virtually no supporters.[23]

Inskip proposed to a generally sympathetic audience that the rearmament programme should henceforth be based on a new order of priorities: first, the security of the United Kingdom (particularly from air attack); second, the protection of imperial communications; third, the defence of British imperial possessions; and fourth, 'co-operation in the defence of the territories of any allies Britain might have in war'. He added that the fourth priority could only be met after the first three had been satisfied and, given the needs of imperial garrisons and the poor state of defence preparedness, it was unlikely that Britain would be able to do much to assist allies. Accordingly, the Army's role in providing anti-aircraft defences was to be its first task, followed by reinforcement of imperial garrisons, the dispatch of the Field Force to 'an Eastern theatre', and, last of all, the continental commitment. Correspondingly the role of the TA was also changed: its main responsibilities were to be anti-aircraft defence and the maintenance of order and essential services at home in time of war. Units of the TA should be made available to support the Regular Army in its Imperial defence duties as soon after the outbreak of war as their training and equipment permitted. Inskip explained that although the Regular Army would still need to be re-equipped with modern armaments it should be possible to effect substantial reductions in the scale of reserves. Specifically, there would be less need for tanks, especially the heavier types. Although it was impossible to foretell where the Field Force might have to fight, in the kind of Imperial campaign envisaged it seemed reasonable to assume that operations would be on a smaller scale and of less intensity than on the Continent. The Minister for the Co-ordination of Defence concluded with a warning that his colleagues must be fully aware of the risk being taken in virtually scrapping the Army's continental commitment: 'If France were again to be in danger of being overrun by land armies, a situation might arise when, as in the last war, we had to improvise an army to assist her. Should this happen, the Government of the day would most certainly be criticised for having neglected to provide against so obvious a contingency.'

Inskip's proposals were supported by the Prime Minister, the Chancellor of the Exchequer, and the Secretary of State for War. Other ministers were evidently favourably impressed by the argument that the reordering of priorities could result in a considerable saving on the Army Estimates. While no one questioned Inskip's basic assumption that defence priorities must be revised in the light of the financial and economic situation, one or two ministers, including Halifax, expressed doubts about the actual strategic programme proposed. Eden, especially, felt that too much emphasis was being placed on the defensive; he was worried about the country's inability to assist her allies on land. He was not entirely satisfied by Hore-Belisha's reiterated confidence in the Maginot Line: if Germany attacked France and threatened the Channel ports Britain might still have to intervene. Furthermore, he queried the assumption that Belgium could be left to look after herself. If Germany invaded Belgium or Holland—and the Chiefs of Staff had always thought that would be the most likely route—then Britain would still need to dispatch the Field Force. He did not, however, press his dissent so far as to challenge Inskip's priorities but merely suggested that France ought to be fully informed of the new position. Inskip's proposals were consequently accepted by the Cabinet. As far as the Army was concerned this marked the culminating point of Neville Chamberlain's long campaign. 'What was generally termed a policy of "limited liability" in Continental warfare had now shrunk to one of no liability at all.'[24]

What had happened to the Chiefs of Staff's arguments of the mid-1930s about the vital need to hold Belgium as a protective *glaçis* against air attack, and about the political importance of British troops fighting by the side of the French? The reasons for the abandonment of the first of these points, as Michael Howard notes, remain rather obscure. On the second point, however, he is surely mistaken in suggesting that they had 'totally reversed their position'.[25] The Chiefs of Staff had never favoured politically or militarily binding commitments to the Continent in peacetime, as distinct from upholding such a strategy in principle and preparing the forces to implement it should such a step seem desirable on the outbreak of war. What this study has suggested is that the apparent unanimity of the Chiefs of Staff's collective reports and memoranda was always superficial and often concealed sharply divergent opinions or at least differing priorities. By 1937 both the RAF's and the Royal Navy's interests in a continental commitment had declined for different reasons, while the Army, though still clearly most affected by and interested in such a possible venture, was ever more keenly aware that in its present state of unpreparedness the outcome was likely to be disastrous. The case for a continental commitment had also been temporarily obscured by the eclipse of its chief supporters in the Cabinet and Foreign Office respectively, Duff Cooper and Vansittart, and by the defection of Hankey. Above all the Army's stand on this issue had been fatally undermined in 1937 by the conversion of its own minister, Hore-Belisha, under the political influence of Chamberlain and the strategic tutelage of Liddell Hart.

One senior soldier who never changed his view that a Field Force capable of fighting in Europe was a necessity was Pownall. He had spent eighteen months away from Whitehall as Commandant of the School of Artillery at Larkhill, but in January 1938 he returned to the War Office to fill the important post of Director of Military Operations and Intelligence. He was in no doubt that the Cabinet had erred in allowing Inskip to alter the Army's role on grounds of lack of money with the effect of putting support for an ally last. He bluntly told Hore-Belisha at their first meeting that it was his firm belief that if there was a war British troops would go to France sooner or later and he believed sooner. If this was not recognized or was glossed over in peacetime, then the troops would go untrained and ill-equipped—with dire results. In his diary he noted that 'All one can do now is to accept it [the policy of limited liability] and try to get the business on its legs; but secondly to watch for the time when it can be reversed.'[26]

The Chiefs of Staff and the leading soldiers seemed to grasp better than the politicians that limited liability was essentially an artificial policy. The range of strategic and political options open to Britain was much narrower than the Government was prepared to admit. Any commitment to France or the Low Countries would inexorably draw her into a continental campaign. Once she committed herself to an alliance in war conditions she would in practice lose the power to limit her liability. Ironside saw this clearly, even though his own view was ambivalent, when he noted on 29 December 1937:

> The Cabinet, in a muddled kind of way, are terrified of making an Expeditionary Force. They reason that if they have such a Force they may be forced to send it to Europe once more. They dread a Continental commitment such as we had, and honoured, in 1914. I don't blame

them, for France will scream louder than ever for help in the next crisis. Once we are landed our commitment is limitless.

But on 5 February he told a conference of senior commanders that 'our wretched little corps of two divisions and a mobile division was unthinkable as a contribution to an Army in France . . . let us make Imperial plans only. After all the politicians will be hard put to it to refuse to help France and Belgium when the 1914 show begins again.'[27]

That soldiers like Pownall and Ironside should perceive the Government's decision on the role of the Army as a Canute-like effort to resist the tide is not odd since they and their men would be directly involved in event of war. What is noteworthy is that even the Treasury thought the Government had gone too far in virtually denying a possible European role to the Field Force, though it did believe that the Territorial divisions should not be regarded as the reserve except for supplying drafts. What the Treasury objected to specifically was the definiteness of assigning the Field Force to 'an Eastern theatre' (i.e. Egypt), preferring and urging successfully that it should be designated as 'for general purposes'. The Treasury was, however, in line with Government policy in believing that the highest priority must be given to defence against air attack and that the Army, at least in the first phase of the war, must be largely absorbed by this role.[28]

The potential and imagined horror of aerial bombardment had become something of an obsession in Britain in the 1920s long before the dramatic growth of the Luftwaffe under Hitler.[29] The possibilities of air and ground defence against such assaults had never been entirely overlooked; indeed air defence was quite successful over London in 1918. But in general there was a tendency, not without technical justification, to believe in Baldwin's chilling affirmation in the House of Commons on 10 November 1932 that 'the bomber will always get through'. The Air Staff's answer was that RAF bombers must get through first in greater numbers and bomb the enemy into submission while the British public stoically endured its ordeal. A more reassuring way of advancing the same doctrine was to declare that a superior bomber force would deter potential enemies and thereby avert war altogether. Indeed the term 'deterrent' was frequently employed by Chamberlain and others in the 1930s but without making the imaginative effort to put themselves in the enemy's shoes. By 1937, however, the advocates of the feasibility of defence against air attack had two new and decisive arguments in the invention of radar and the development of faster and better armed fighters in the Hurricane and Spitfire (operational in 1937 and 1938 respectively). Given these assets it seemed more worthwhile, indeed imperative, to pay more attention to auxiliary defences in the form of anti-aircraft artillery, searchlights, and civil defence. To their credit, as has already been noted, Inskip and the Treasury urged on a reluctant Air Staff in 1937 that henceforth fighters should be given priority over bombers in production, and air defence generally given the highest priority.

Although the Cabinet decision on 22 December 1937 showed that this notion was broadly accepted, the precise allocation of inadequate industrial resources for the various roles of the Army remained unclear. Hore-Belisha therefore asked at a CID meeting on 17 March 1938 whether the priority of home defence was so absolute that the extension of the country's air defences (ADGB) must be pressed forward without any regard whatsoever to every other military commitment. The War Minister suggested that his colleagues might not be aware that at present the Field Force had no proper guns at all. Lord Gort (now CIGS) confirmed this depressing statement: British field guns, for example, were a 1905 18 pdr., pattern with ranges of 6–9,000 yards whereas foreign field guns had a range of 12–15,000 yards. The chairman (Chamberlain) refused to make any concessions, and the discussion concluded with Inskip's statement that 'the air defences of Great Britain must have first priority of all'. The Field Force would only get the benefit of any additional production capacity which might be created.[30]

Quite apart from problems of guns and equipment, from 1936 onwards—as the fear of a German knock-out blow from the air intensified—expanding schemes of air defence made demands on manpower which were virtually impossible to meet under a system of voluntary enlistment. In February 1937 a committee under the chairmanship of Sir Hugh Dowding* (GOC.-in-C. Fighter Command since 1935) reported to the CID on what became known as the 'ideal' air defence scheme for Great Britain—though 'adequate' or even 'minimum' would have been more accurate terms. The previous scheme of defence ran from Portsmouth to the Tees, but because of the ever-increasing range of aircraft the Dowding Committee recommended that the defences should be extended to cover Glasgow and Edinburgh. As far as the Army's responsibilities were concerned (i.e. excluding aircraft), this would mean increasing anti-aircraft batteries from 76 to 158 and searchlight companies from 108 to 196. The then CIGS, Deverell, calculated that an additional 50,000 men would be required. Although Hore-Belisha made a tremendous effort to improve recruiting in his first year in office (particularly for the TA), the results were not encouraging. Early in 1938, for example, he had to report that the first two TA anti-aircraft divisions were still 20,000 short of their establishment of 48,000. Equally seriously, as noted above, he became anxious that the attempt to fulfil the ADGB programme was seriously delaying rearmament in other directions. Thus Ironside was only exaggerating slightly when he noted, on 3 February 1938: 'The Air Defence of Great Britain is absorbing all the money which was intended for the Field Force. The Air Ministry dictates what it wants and the Army estimates bear the cost.'[31]

Ironside's later diary entries seem to waver between regret for the virtual scrapping of the Field Force and approval that anti-aircraft defence had been given priority over other possible Army roles despite the obdurate resistance of Deverell and the General Staff. Thus he reflected on 29 May that the situation was becoming ever clearer: 'The decision to form six A.A. divisions seals the fate of the Territorial Army as an Army able to go into the field. All our guns and money and energy will be expended in making these divisions . . . We ought to have done it before.' He added: 'Never again shall we even contemplate a Force for a foreign country. Our contribution is to be the Navy and the R.A.F.' On 29 August he deplored Deverell's delay in placing orders for the 3.7-inch anti-aircraft guns, a delay due to his obsession with maintaining the Expeditionary Force. Meanwhile the Germans had gained the advantage in the air. 'You must make your fortress secure', Ironside concluded, 'before you think of issuing from it. What an eye-opener we shall get.'[32] Here, as we shall see, he was expressing a widespread view on how Britain would be affected by the first phase of the coming war: that the prior need was to survive an immediate all-out air attack before there could be any thought of sending a Field Force overseas.

From the other side of the hill, the Liddell Hart papers contain substantial evidence that the General Staff continued to resist throughout 1937–8 the extinction of the Field Force by excessive concentration on the needs of ADGB. Thus in May 1938 General Hobart complained to Liddell Hart that Generals Gort and Kirke (Director-General of the TA) wished to build up the Field Force and regarded ADGB as 'something foreign to the Army'. Kirke wanted to re-equip 12 TA divisions but was not clear where they could be used, except in France. In a longer memorandum of 30 July 1938 Liddell Hart recounted how he and Hore-Belisha had forced the General Staff to accept the urgency of ADGB, though Gort, Brooke, and others remained obstructive.[33] Gort in fact had plainly expressed his unease in the COS Committee that the importance of ADGB was being over-stressed in relation to other vital commitments, such as the defence of Egypt against an Italian attack.[34] Another influential soldier who developed doubts about the wisdom of placing so much emphasis on ADGB was Colonel Hastings Ismay, who replaced Pownall as Hankey's Deputy on the CID in mid-1936 and in 1938 succeeded Hankey as its Secretary. Soon after rejoining the CID Secretariat, Ismay had prepared a memorandum which Hankey passed on to Inskip and in which he argued that the needs of the Expeditionary Force should be downgraded in comparison with those of air defence. By December 1937 he had come to doubt the wisdom of this view because, he told Hankey, France expected Britain to come in with an Army, and if she were in trouble on the outbreak of war Britain would be hard put to stay out or to think in terms of limited liability; moreover, a Field Force would have to be ready for a major war anywhere, such as one to defend Egypt against Italy.[35]

One additional aspect of ADGB needs to be mentioned: the prevalent alarmist views that in the event of a massive German air attack a primary duty of the Territorial Army, and perhaps part of the Regular Army, would be to preserve order in conditions of civilian panic. At a meeting of the DP(P) Ministerial Committee in April 1937, for example, Sir John Simon (then still Home Secretary) suggested that if Germany wanted to create alarm and panic in Britain she might first induce the Government to send the Field Force to France and then turn the whole of her air force on the undefended population. On that occasion Lord Swinton reacted to this extreme pessimism by replying that if we had to retain five divisions of the Field Force at home to prevent civilian panic the prospect was indeed a parlous one. A reference in the Ironside diary shows that this fear was not easily dissipated, and indeed it persisted into the Second World War: 'The Cabinet had decided behind closed doors that the Territorial Army is required to keep the peace in England and restore law and order in air raids. They daren't give this out because it would be unpopular and would result in the Terriers fading away.'[36] Thus in 1937 and 1938, well before the Munich crisis exposed Britain's extreme vulnerability to air attack, the needs of air defence had come to occupy a dominant place in the Army's already reduced share in the rearmament programme. Despite the efforts of a few soldiers, such as Gort, Brooke, and Pownall to keep the issue open, the possibility of raising a Field Force for the Continent seemed to be fading out of sight.

Although Italy was never rated so formidable a potential enemy as Japan, let alone Germany, her possible hostility had to be taken seriously from 1935 onwards. This added a further dimension to the already complex strategic calculation of the planning experts and worried them to an extent that has only recently been fully brought out.[37] It also created an intractable political and diplomatic dilemma as to which, if any, of Britain's three potential enemies she should try to conciliate first.

By the Anglo-Egyptian Treaty of Alliance signed in 1936 Britain was granted extensive basing privileges in Egypt but agreed gradually to remove her troops from Cairo and Alexandria and to concentrate them in the Canal zone. The Egyptian Army was to be modernized under the supervision of a British military mission. The treaty restricted the British garrison to 10,000 troops and 400 pilots but these figures could be (and in fact were) raised at Egypt's request.

Throughout 1937 the House of Commons and the British press tended to exaggerate the dangers inherent in the build up of Italian forces in the Mediterranean and Africa. As far as the British Army was concerned, the most ominous development was the creation of a North African High Command, an increase in the Libyan garrison to at least 40,000 troops, and the opening of a coastal road which pointed menacingly towards the Suez Canal. The Chiefs of Staff, however, persistently refused to be stampeded by alarmists on the spot, notably Sir Miles Lampson, who was backed by Vansittart in London. Official British policy remained to concentrate scarce resources so as to secure the home base against German attack. The COS received extremely strong support from Hankey who returned from a visit to Italy in August firmly convinced that it was in Britain's best interests to appease Mussolini, whose regime he had admired. Quite apart from his emotional approval of Fascism, Hankey was concerned lest war should break out in the Mediterranean while Britain was so ill-prepared to deal with Germany.

Not that British students of strategy overrated Italy's actual military power. On the contrary, it was precisely because her strategic position *vis-à-vis* Britain and France would become progressively weaker as they rearmed, and because she was economically incapable of waging a protracted war, that it was feared that Mussolini might commit a 'mad dog' act rather than lose face. A lightning *coup* against Egypt, including the seizure of the Suez Canal, seemed to offer the best hope of a quick and dramatic success. Since Britain was superior at sea, the most promising form of attack appeared to be an overland offensive from Libya supported by massive air raids. It was estimated that Italy could spare 650 aircraft to attack a virtually defenceless Egypt. On land, by 1937 Italy had built up regular units amounting to two mechanized army corps. This was numerically impressive compared with the British garrison in Egypt but it was doubtful if logistical problems would permit an attack across the desert in the near future. Nevertheless, the pressure to reinforce Egypt mounted as much for reasons of imperial prestige as for actual security. In conclusion, the British failure in the Mediterranean stemmed not from poor intelligence of Italy's military power but from a lack of will caused by the preoccupation with the German and Japanese threats.[38]

From a wider strategic viewpoint the importance of holding

Egypt and Palestine increased after 1935 as Italy's hostility, if Britain became involved in a global war against Germany and perhaps also Japan, became more likely. First, in such a widespread conflict Egypt might have to provide the base not only for the defence of the Canal but for operations in the Mediterranean and Middle East generally. Secondly, it was generally assumed until the summer of 1939 that, in the worst case of simultaneous war against all three potential enemies, the Royal Navy would probably have to abandon the Mediterranean, at least temporarily, in order to meet the higher priorities at home and in the Far East. In these circumstances, defence of Egypt and its bulwark, Palestine, would devolve largely upon the RAF and upon Army garrisons which could only be reinforced via the Cape and India, except perhaps for one fast convoy carrying fighter aircraft through the Mediterranean after the outbreak of war. With this latter problem in mind, the COS Mediterranean and Middle East Appreciation of February 1938 stressed that the provision of reinforcements for Egypt must have first priority within that potential war theatre and also that there was an urgent necessity to build up stocks of equipment and warlike stores in peacetime.

The broad strategy envisaged for the security of Egypt was an initial defensive based on Mersa Matruh with a mobile force and aircraft operating in the Western Desert. Behind this cover reinforcements would be assembled both to strengthen the defence and to go over to an attack into Libya. What was envisaged was the deployment of a mobile division and two infantry divisions with perhaps a third division in reserve— in other words the whole of the Field Force might be involved.

At the beginning of 1938 the British garrison in Egypt—by then concentrating in the Canal zone—consisted of two infantry brigades, a mechanized cavalry brigade, two artillery brigades and a tank battalion. The Libyan frontier was manned entirely by Egyptian troops which were likely to prove less of a barrier to the Italian forces than the 200 miles of waterless desert behind them. Reinforcements were urgently needed in both Egypt and Palestine. On 23 March—despite the recent European crisis over the Anschluss—the Cabinet agreed that an additional infantry brigade should be dispatched as a general reserve. Thus by the spring of 1938 Egypt was increasingly regarded as a base for defensive and offensive operations over a wide area which in effect would make it second in strategic importance only to the United Kingdom.[39]

The security of Palestine was hardly less vital than that of Egypt for Britain's Middle Eastern and Imperial strategy. It provided a buffer zone for the defence of Egypt and the Suez Canal. It was an essential staging post for Britain's air and overland routes to Iraq, India, and the Far East. It would lie at the western end of the route for reinforcements from India via the Persian Gulf should the Mediterranean and Red Sea routes be closed by a hostile Italy. And Haifa was the Mediterranean terminus of the pipeline for vital oil supplies from Persia and Iraq, and also provided a base for light naval forces. From April 1936 to the eve of the Second World War all these assets were thrown into jeopardy by the persistent if sporadic rebellion of the Palestinian Arabs. This local nationalist rebellion, wrongly believed at the time to be fomented and encouraged by Axis propaganda, constituted a difficult policing operation for a War Office already desperately short of troops.[40]

After a year or so of comparative quiet, full-scale rebellion broke out again in Palestine in the summer of 1938 and continued well into the autumn, thus putting an additional strain on Britain's military capabilities just at the time of the developing crisis over Czechoslovakia. In July two battalions were dispatched from Egypt at the urgent request of the Colonial Office, but this was insufficient and in August a full division was requested from Britain. The War Office refused, since this would seriously interfere with the possible dispatch of the first contingent of the Field Force to France, but it undertook to gather units to the equivalent of a division from India. Pownall's diary entry for 29 August vividly describes the problem as seen by the General Staff:

> With Europe in the state it is in and with the general, though as yet unacknowledged, swing to the Western Commitment how can we be expected to despatch the half of our meagre land forces to carry out a role of internal security—and internal security in the sense of preventing Arabs and Jews slitting each others throats? If as seems likely Germany (and perhaps Italy) are at the back of this trouble to a large extent then surely it is playing into Germany's hands to despatch forces there . . .

> But sending troops to Palestine is like pouring water onto the desert sands—they are immediately absorbed, the thirsty sand cries for more and one never gets a drop back. At the end of September they'll have 11 battalions and a cavalry regiment—12 units— two of our 'colonial' divisions in effect. They really cannot expect us to lock up *20* battalions on this futile business. God, what a mess we have made of the whole of this Palestine affair!

Only at the end of September did Pownall record that Palestine had quietened down sufficiently for two battalions and a cavalry regiment to be returned to Egypt and thus allow the commander there (General 'Copper' Gordon-Finlayson) to occupy Mersa Matruh with British troops.[41] British fears for the security of Egypt during the simultaneous Palestine and Czechoslovakia crises may seem exaggerated unless it is recalled that, at British insistence, the Anglo-French Staff talks of 1938 had excluded any discussion of joint action in a war with Italy. Consequently, although France had as many as 14 divisions behind the Mareth Line in Tunisia—quite enough to cause the Italians to think again before invading Egypt—Britain had no knowledge whatever of French plans or dispositions in the Mediterranean.[42]

In the opening weeks of 1938 Hore-Belisha, closely assisted by Liddell Hart, struggled to implement the Cabinet decision of 22 December by formulating a detailed programme on the 'Role of the Army' which would be acceptable first to the General Staff and subsequently to the Cabinet. The War Minister quickly discovered that the removal of Deverell and his senior colleagues had not had the desired effect of making the General Staff more progressive and co-operative. After Liddell Hart had rejected several drafts by the new DMO, Pownall, as unsatisfactory he concluded that the new team was shirking the issue of reorganizing the Field Force for its imperial role. They envisaged the same scale and type of force as Deverell had done with merely the difference that 'instead of being plunked into France it was to be plunked into Egypt'. This criticism was fair enough on purely military grounds but did not take into account that as a result of the Army's change of priorities the War Office was now being pressed to make such large reductions in expenditure that it was becoming virtually impossible to meet *any* of the prescribed roles at all adequately. The War Office was asked to cut the aggregate of £347 million previously allocated for the period 1937–41 by £82 million over the next two years, but Hore-Belisha calculated that the maximum he could manage was £70 million. These reductions entailed drastic cuts in the programmes of ADGB and the Field Force and abandoning the plan to provide war equipment and reserves for the TA. As Pownall noted with understandable bitterness: 'not only do we come third in priority over money but in the money we *are* allotted the other Services have a very shrill voice; they want the things which help *them*. Any more money from the Field Force, however, will simply reduce that organisation to a farce; it is near enough to that already.'[43]

The Cabinet considered Hore-Belisha's memorandum on the role of the Army on 16 February. Although the Army's primary duty was now anti-aircraft defence at home the discussion revealed that it was nowhere near fulfilling the ideal scheme requiring 1,264 anti-aircraft guns, 4,684 searchlights, and 93,000 troops. At least two additional Territorial divisions needed to be converted to this role but costs made it impossible. Yet Hore-Belisha resisted Halifax's suggestion that some of the redundant Territorial divisions might be scrapped on the grounds that 'public sentiment' would react unfavourably. He pointed out that the abandonment of the continental hypothesis had resulted in a possible saving of only £14 million. In its present state of lower preparedness and reduced equipment a Field Force of only two Regular divisions and a mobile division could be sent overseas after about three weeks and reinforced by a maximum of two further divisions after forty days. Hore-Belisha stressed that these divisions were equipped for an eastern theatre so that their equipment and war reserves would not be on a continental scale. It was also planned to reduce the size of existing divisions and to increase their fire power and mobility. At Simon's insistence the Field Force's role was rephrased as 'for general purposes', and it was also agreed that France should be informed of this definite adoption of a role of limited liability so that she should be under no illusions about the likelihood or amount of possible British support on land.[44]

The climax of the Government's steady progress towards a strategy based on the ability to survive a knock-out blow from the air, a capacity for prolonged resistance through economic stability, and reliance on a policy of limited liability towards any possible European ally was reached at the beginning of March 1938. The Prime Minister set forth these arguments in detail when Parliament debated the White Paper on defence on 7 March and concluded that the Government's rearmament programme was contributing to peace: 'The sight of this enormous, this almost terrifying, power which Britain is building up has a sobering effect, a steadying effect, on the opinion of the world.' Apart from doubts voiced by Harold Nicolson (National Labour) about the continuing uncertainty over Army policy and the feasibility of limiting liability in event of war, the general opinion expressed in the debate was favourable on this issue. There was a similiar reaction three days later when Hore-Belisha presented the Army Estimates for the first time. In both debates Sir Archibald Sinclair (leader of the Liberal Party) denounced the concept of a continental commitment and warmly supported the Government's policy. In the latter debate even Leopold Amery, though a keen advocate of conscription, stressed the prior importance of withstanding an air attack and the superior value of air support to a continental ally. Major-General Sir Alfred Knox pointed out that huge armies were not being created on the Continent for fun, but this discordant voice evoked little sympathetic response concerning a policy now strongly endorsed by both the Cabinet and Parliament.[45]

On the political side limited liability could hardly go further than in the spring of 1938. While Parliament generally greeted this policy with relief, the Army's commanders were approaching the nadir of depression. Ironside, for example, thought the White Paper 'truly the most appalling reading. How we can have come to this state is beyond belief.' Even the first two divisions of the Field Force were deficient in many essential items of equipment. From Ironside's long catalogue of general deficiencies, those in armoured fighting vehicles will serve to illustrate the position: obsolete medium tanks; no cruiser tanks or infantry tanks; obsolete armoured cars; no light tanks except for one unit in Egypt. The German Military Attaché attending British manœuvres simply refused to believe that the cupboard could be so bare. When, a few weeks later, Gort told a Commanders' Conference that he thought the Cabinet was slowly coming round to the view that the BEF would have to be sent to France in case of war with Germany, his statement was received in complete silence.[46] Meanwhile, on the day after Hore-Belisha's new Army policy had been approved by the House of Commons, German troops marched into Austria.

The Anschluss might have been expected to cause a drastic reappraisal of the 'limited liability' policy since it was immediately apparent that Hitler's next objective was likely to be Czechoslovakia. France was committed by treaty to that country's defence and her involvement in war with Germany was likely to entail an urgent demand for British military support. General Pownall, who was well-placed to know, wrongly believed that the Government was reconsidering the need for a continental role for the Army; and even Liddell Hart, the chief advocate of limited liability, at once perceived that British security was interlinked with that of France. 'Whether we like it or not,' he told Hore-Belisha, 'her risks are our risks', but he still thought that this commitment could be fulfilled solely by air support in the first few crucial days of the war. In fact, the Government undertook no reappraisal of its military policy. Assured by the Chiefs of Staff that Britain could do nothing to save Czechoslovakia should Hitler have designs upon it, the Government determined to settle German claims by peaceful means while dissuading France from taking any action which might encourage the Czechs to resist. The Anschluss did, however, underline the necessity for staff talks with the French which had already been agreed upon in principle.[47]

The Government was by no means approaching France in a spirit of friendly co-operation with a view to concerting a firm military agreement. On the contrary, the move was at best prompted by an honest desire, particularly on Hore-Belisha's part, to leave Britain's likely ally in no doubt as to how little Britain could offer her in the event of war. Moreover, Halifax's contempt for, and dislike of, the French, now became a major factor in policy-making. The soldiers' antipathy, at least as great and probably greater than the politicians', was due chiefly to their belief that France wanted to inveigle Britain into a military alliance against Germany. The pre-1914 Anglo-French staff conversations cast a long shadow. Thus Deverell had informed ministers in April 1937 that 'the French had become embarrassing in their endeavours to acquaint us with their plans, although we had . . . communicated nothing to them'. The COS felt that the decision on the role of the Army obviated the need for staff talks since there was almost nothing to discuss. Pownall deplored Vansittart's pro-French and anti-German sentiments, and feared that Hore-Belisha, being pro-French and, as a Jew, anti-German, was 'quite open to be gulled' by the former who wanted to get us 'nicely committed and tied by the leg—not merely militarily but politically as well'. Ironside was simularly alarmed by Churchill's advocacy of an immediate and close military alliance with France.[48]

When Eden reopened the question of staff talks with France and Belgium at the beginning of 1938 the COS firmly advised against it and made it clear that their attitude was determined partly by an anxiety to do nothing likely to harm the prospects of a détente with Germany. The Cabinet decided that there ought to be an exchange of confidential information on air matters, initially at the low level of air attachés but perhaps to be followed up later by the visit of RAF officers to France. Early in April 1938 the Prime Minister and some of his colleagues took a different line, arguing that it would be best for both Britain and France to know precisely what each expected from the other, but within days ministerial opinion had veered towards the extreme caution and reluctance to indulge in any talks which had consistently marked the COS attitude. The COS were clearly reluctant to divulge to the French the derisory amount of land support which Britain might be able to provide not only in 1938 but for several years to come. By April 1939 a maximum of only four divisions with considerable deficiencies would be available and by April 1940 the mobile division would be the only addition. Such underequipped forces would only be capable of holding a defensive sector and, worse still, it was doubtful if they could receive any reinforcements for a year or more after war broke out. What if the British contingent proved inadequate or was wiped out? Were the French to be told categorically that four divisions was the maximum they could expect in 1939?[49]

The CID meeting on 11 April 1938 to discuss the scope of possible Anglo-French staff talks was so revealing of ministerial attitudes that it deserves to be quoted at some length. After

Chamberlain and Halifax had expressed the optimistic view that Italy need not be included among potential enemies, the Home Secretary, Sir Samuel Hoare, sketched the kind of war which seemed to him most probable:

In a war against Germany our own home defence would be the crucial problem. The French would take up a defensive position behind their Maginot Line. Their Air Force was of low efficiency. The problem before us was to win 'the war over London'. In order to do so we might have to station certain squadrons of our Advanced Air Striking Force in France. He . . . viewed the prospect of the despatch of a field force with the gravest misgivings. We should need, at any rate in the initial stages all our available troops to assist in the defence of this country.

The Prime Minister and Lord Halifax expressed strong agreement, the former remarking that it was difficult to see into what strategic plan the small Field Force would fit. The most probable eventuality seemed to be a German air attack against the United Kingdom while the French Army remained behind the Maginot Line with the German Army facing them. In such circumstances Britain could hardly contemplate sending the Field Force to help defend that line. Halifax added:

We should aim at getting the French to think along more realistic lines as to how a Continental war might develop, i.e., not the 1914–18 conception of trench warfare, but of war in the air. He [Lord Halifax] was as anxious as anyone that the field force should not be sent, and he was strongly opposed to any corollary involving the subsequent despatch of a national army, but he hoped that we should not categorically say that in no circumstances would a field force be sent to the Continent.

Hore-Belisha pointed out that, since it was really a matter of telling the French what Britain *could not* do, there was no need for extensive staff talks. When they realized just how little Britain could do for them they might actually expedite the completion of the Maginot Line. Lord Gort agreed and suggested that the land commitment might involve only about 5,000 men to provide base and lines-of-communication troops for the advanced air striking force. Such a small force would not raise difficult administrative problems for the French.

A basic assumption of the 'limited liability' advocates, such as Liddell Hart, had always been that Britain would compensate for the small size of her land contribution by offering substantial air support to her allies. Now Lord Swinton gave the lie even to this self-deception by stating that

The primary object of our Air Striking Force was the defence of the United Kingdom. The use of French advanced air bases was required solely to further our own counter-offensive schemes, and it was of great importance that any squadrons based in France should not be drawn into any French plan which might divorce these squadrons from their primary role. At the same time any action which our Air Striking Force might take to reduce the weight of German air attack on England would indirectly contribute to the defence of France.

The CAS, Sir Cyril Newall, supported his minister and stated that though the French would be anxious for Britain to give air support to their army he hoped that the British Government would not give way. It was even to be suggested that if the main German air attack was concentrated against Britain we should hope for help from the French air force.

The only dissentient note was struck by Duff Cooper who said, with masterly understatement, that

If one of our objectives was to reassure the French, it seemed doubtful if the scope of the conversations now contemplated would have that effect . . . In his own view, we should not be able to escape, in the event of war against Germany, sending a field force to the Continent. It was impossible to contemplate France with her back to the wall and three million young men in this country in plain clothes.

The Prime Minister concluded, disingenuously, that the object was not so much to reassure the French as to place the British in the best position possible to discharge their treaty obligations. Whether this would be achieved by such a defensive, fortress mentality was doubtful. 'Chamberlain's policy virtually guaranteed that Britain would not have any allies in case of war.' At the end of April, after much hesitation, the Cabinet decided that staff talks should be held with France and Belgium on matters concerning all three Services, but also that Germany should be advised by the Foreign Secretary not to take an exaggerated view of their significance.[50]

Ministerial meetings at the end of April brought staff talks a stage nearer. M. Daladier accepted the small and conditional land contribution with surprising calm, remarking that even two divisions would have a great moral effect and might influence Belgium's decision whether or not to remain neutral. His only condition was that the two divisions should be motorized.

Gamelin told Hore-Belisha that he thought it likely the Germans would come through Belgium again and hoped Britain could send some mechanized units to stiffen the resistance. He was informed that it was doubtful if Britain could do this at the start of a war. Daladier did, however, justifiably object to confining the initial staff talks to air matters. He pointed out—what the British Government was so reluctant to accept—that it made no sense to cut up defence into sections or to discuss single services in isolation. Further discussions in Cabinet and consultations with the Chiefs of Staff were necessary before the staff talks began. Rigid limitations were laid down. As regards the Army talks, arrangements must be confined to the embarkation and installation of up to two divisions within fifteen days of the outbreak of war but there must be no prior undertaking that any troops would actually be sent. Secondly, it was not proposed to equip these divisions specifically for a war on the Continent because the British public was nervous about such a commitment and the Government wished to avoid being dragged in against its will. Thus it was made absolutely clear to the French that they must not count on any British land contribution in drawing up their own plans. The staff talks were to take place at the level of service attachés and any French pressure to raise the level was to be rejected. Parallel talks were to take place with the Belgians but triangular Anglo-French-Belgian talks were to be avoided.[51]

The ensuing talks, held between May and November, were successful within the rigid confines set by Britain. As regards the Army, plans for the dispatch of two divisions and the advanced air striking force—and their movement to the assembly area—were discussed in detail, but there was no discussion of concentration areas, much less of this contingent's actual role since this would risk committing the British to a specific part in the French plan. It can hardly be doubted that, though they put on a brave face, the French were disappointed by the talks. Although immediate intervention by the RAF was suggested—500 or 600 planes were optimistically mentioned—the French tended to evaluate British support primarily in terms of how many divisions they would promise to dispatch. As Duff Cooper correctly perceived, the offer of a maximum of two divisions, even then hedged about with political conditions, hardly encouraged them to pursue a firm line towards Germany: but then the British Government had no wish that they should. It was hardly unexpected if, many months before the Munich crisis, France was beginning to discount the value of an alliance with Britain and adjusting its foreign policy accordingly.[52]

The British Government's policy towards the problem of Czechoslovakia was determined in March 1938. No one in the Cabinet challenged the utterly pessimistic report of the COS who concluded that

> No pressure that we and out possible Allies can bring to bear, either by sea, or land or in the air, could prevent Germany from invading and overrunning Bohemia and from inflicting a decisive defeat on the Czechoslovakian Army. We should then be faced with the necessity of undertaking a war against Germany for the purpose of restoring Czechoslovakia's lost integrity and this object would only be achieved by the defeat of Germany and as the outcome of a prolonged struggle.

Moreover, the COS also believed that Italy and Japan would seize the opportunity to join in so that war would become unlimited and world-wide. Whereas France, though prepared to put pressure on the Czechs to make concessions to Hitler, felt that if reasonable terms were rejected they must at some point make a stand, Chamberlain and Halifax believed that, owing to the allies' military unpreparedness, resort to force must be avoided at all costs. In short, diplomacy must be substituted for military strength. This policy, fully supported by the COS, remained unchanged from the false alarm over Czechoslovakia in May until the Munich crisis.[53]

It remains puzzling that the military experts took counsel of their fears to the extent that they did, for in 1937, 1938, and even 1939 it was not difficult to discover that Germany, though rearming rapidly and ominously, was far from ready for a general war against at least two major powers. Thus Ironside, witnessing 'the popping and banging' at the German manœuvres in September 1937, noted: 'It showed what a force Germany had created in such a short time, even though at the moment it is in many ways an experimental one. They still require a long time to perfect this great instrument of theirs.' And the next day (27 September) he added: 'There is no danger now but there will be in, say, five years. We want to get a move on pretty quickly to be sure.' Yet, exactly a year later, though deploring the sacrifice of a small state to the wolves, he wrote: '*We cannot expose ourselves now to a German attack. We simply commit suicide if we do*. At no time could we stand up against German air bombing.' Churchill has often been criticized for exaggerating the strength of the French Army, though it seems rather that he correctly believed it to be unassailable during 1938 but that from that year on Germany would have an increasing advantage. The testing time would come in 1940.[54] An even better-informed soldier, General Pownall, thought Chamberlain was doing the right thing in his foreign policy to gain time. In contrast to Eden and Vansittart with their pro-League of Nations and pro-French leanings, Pownall felt: 'We are much safer—or at any rate we shall get a much longer breathing space that the Services need so badly—with a realist like Chamberlain and a decent man like Halifax who has had experience of tempering ideals with realities.'[55] These quotations demolish any question of a neat contrast between courageous generals and timorous, appeasing politicians.

It is somewhat ironic, given Liddell Hart's persistent belief that the General Staff was prepared to risk the Field Force being swept up into a French offensive, that the British generals had no faith in the French Army's capacity or will to attack the much weaker German forces in the West in support of Czechoslovakia. Ironside, again when attending the German manœuvres, asked himself whether the French Army could carry out an offensive in support of an ally so far away. He doubted it: 'An offensive against Germany from the West must penetrate very deeply and would be a question of an enormous invading force. It would mean something that France couldn't, in my opinion, sustain for a minute.' In July 1938 the Chiefs of Staff agreed that Germany would be very apprehensive about becoming involved in a two-front war and she could not be sure whether or not France would fight. Admiral Chatfield, however, rightly thought it improbable that France would launch an attack over her frontier. During the Munich crisis Gamelin confirmed that he merely planned an advance to the Siegfried Line followed by withdrawal behind the Maginot Line. That, as Pownall noted, wouldn't have helped the Czechs much.[56]

This accurate perception of the French Army's essentially defensive outlook, together with the hardening but illusory belief that war would begin with an all-out German air offensive against Britain, had important repercussions on the role of the Army. In short, quite apart from political reservations, it seemed doubtful for military reasons that the Field Force would be dispatched at the outset of war; it would more likely go to France, after the initial German offensive had been checked, in time to take part in a counter-offensive. This assumption was reinforced, in the eyes of the COS, in an appreciation of 25 July 1938, by the calculation that it would take about three weeks for the first two divisions of the Field Force to be concentrated in north-eastern France and that they would probably arrive too late anyway to take part in the opening battle. Though they did not mention any specific period, the COS clearly had a long delay in mind before the counter-offensive was launched, since they reported: 'In the course of time it might be Great Britain, rather than France, who would be able to bring into the field forces on a scale which would make a counter-offensive possible.' This was underlined by the conclusion, in bold print, that Germany was fully prepared and had the initiative. Britain must be prepared to withstand a major offensive, weaken Germany by economic pressure, and develop her resources and the Empire's for an eventual counter-offensive.[57]

It is not our purpose here to provide yet another detailed account of the Munich crisis of September 1938. The crisis had remarkably little effect on British strategy in general or the role of the Army in particular. In March 1938 the Government, fully supported by the COS, had made it clear that the political problems of central and eastern Europe were no concern of Britain's in military terms, though the Government was never openly prepared to give Hitler a free hand in that area. At no point was the Government prepared to risk being drawn into war on the issue of the Sudetenland. An overwhelming sense of Britain's military weakness doubtless played its part in shaping this attitude but some members of the Government, including the Prime Minister, actually looked with favour on Germany's Sudeten claims and—until March 1939—only deplored Hitler's methods. In other words even had Britain's rearmament programme been considerably more advanced, it is far from certain that Beneš would have been advised to resist Hitler's demands or would have received military support if he had.[58]

The view that Chamberlain was more concerned to achieve a lasting agreement with Hitler by 'appeasing' his supposedly specific and limited claims, rather than to buy time through a more or less cynical deal, is supported by the amazingly little attention given to strategic factors throughout the crisis on the Anglo-French side. The Chiefs of Staff examined the question largely from the British point of view. On 23 September, after assuming that the Field Force would not initially be dispatched to France, they advised that Britain must refrain from provocation action such as bombing Germany. The Services and the auxiliary defence forces must first be put on a war footing, otherwise the country would be in the position of a man who attacks a tiger before loading his gun. As for the Field Force, the COS pointed out that all the anti-aircraft units would be needed for ADGB and there would be many calls on the Regular and Territorial divisions for assistance to the civil power. On a wider view, taking account of possible intervention by Italy and Japan, the first commitment of the land forces after securing the home base should be Egypt and the Middle East. They recognized that it might, ultimately, be necessary to send the Field Force to France and the intermediate contingent should be preserved for that purpose. The COS repeated their pessimistic view that 'no pressure Great Britain and France can bring to bear, either by sea, on land or in the air, could prevent Germany overrunning Bohemia and from inflicting a decisive defeat on Czechoslovakia'.[59]

Only Oliver Stanley, with some support from Inskip, raised in Cabinet what might have been regarded as a vital issue: what would be the strategic picture in 1939 if Germany secured her territorial objectives in Czechoslovakia and then threatened expansion in other areas? The Joint Planning Committee prepared a draft paper by 13 September but it was not approved by the COS until 24 September and its conclusions 'failed to penetrate in the crisis atmosphere of the last few days before Munich'. At no point during the crisis did either the Cabinet or COS try to draw up a balance-sheet on an issue which was to be much discussed afterwards: whether it was better to fight Germany in 1938 in order to gain the considerable asset of the Czech Army (35 well-equipped divisions) and Air Force and to try to deny these forces, together with Czechoslovakia's Skoda armaments complex, to Germany. Instead the Government appears only to have taken account of Britain's own pathetic unpreparedness which, not surprisingly, was expected to improve with a year's respite. Colonel Ismay (Hankey's successor as Secretary to the CID) sent a Service appreciation to Inskip and Sir Horace Wilson on September 20 on the relative military advantages of immediate war or war six months later. His report stressed Germany's great lead over the allies in air striking power. By improving active and passive defences against air attack Britain could substantially reduce Germany's only chance of a rapid decision and might thereby deter her from making the attempt. The clear conslusion from a military viewpoint was that time was on Britain's side; if war with Germany was inevitable it would be better to face it in six months' or a year's time. This was certainly the kind of advice the Government wished to receive from its military advisers but precisely what influence it had it is difficult to say.[60]

The suggestion that the Government was prepared to ignore or discount unpalatable advice is borne out by its treatment of the intelligence reports from the British Military Attaché in Prague, Brigadier Stronge.* He had been impressed by the high state of morale and efficiency displayed by the Czech Army when mobilized in May 1938, and he reported that, with allied support, the Czechs were capable of holding out for two or three months. Daladier and Gamelin expressed the same view as late as 26 September and it has received support from subsequent investigations. For example, Professor David Vital writes, 'The defence of Czechoslovakia was far from being a desperate undertaking. It was certainly not hopeless.' Milan Hauner's excellent recent article inclines to a similar conclusion. The Government preferred, however, to heed the pessimistic assessments of its Berlin Military Attaché, Colonel Mason-MacFarlane,* who paid only a fleeting visit to Czechoslovakia and knew practically nothing about her Army or defences.[61] As for the French, nothing was done to secure a common front with them before the final meeting at Munich. There was no exchange of military plans, while at the Conference itself Chamberlain and Daladier 'arrived, behaved, and left as if they had no more in common than total strangers'.[62] Rather strangely perhaps, Stronge's relatively optimistic assessment of Czech defensive capability received contemporary support from Liddell Hart who wrote an appreciation of the situation for Churchill, Dalton, and other Government critics dated 28 September 1938. Liddell Hart thought the Czechs could confine the German advance to the frontier districts given three important conditions: (*a*) that they could parry the German thrust from Austria; (*b*) that Russia sent large-scale air reinforcements; and (*c*) that Poland and Hungary remained neutral. The French Army, he added, could help by detaining large German forces in the West, and unless France were to be neutralized he doubted whether Germany was capable of conquering Czechoslovakia as a whole.[63]

Although, as has been suggested above, Chamberlain was not primarily, if at all, motivated by strategic factors—in the technical sense as distinct from simply averting war—when he took the initiative to solve the Sudeten problem, two strategic aspects deserve special mention. First, one of the great unsolved mysteries of the period is whether Russia would have made good her repeated promises to intervene in support of her treaty with Czechoslovakia, provided France first fulfilled her obligation. Moreover, it is not known where or in what strength Russian forces would have been deployed. If Russia was merely bluffing, she ran great risks of having her bluff called. As late in the crisis as 23 September she threatened Poland that if the latter attacked Czechoslovakia the Russo-Polish non-aggression pact would be destroyed. Moreover, soon after Munich Beneš related that Russia had promised *unilateral* assistance in event of German invasion of Czechoslovakia. All this counted for nought. The COS believed Russia was in no condition to mount offensive operations and would not fight unless actually invaded. Despite the efforts of Churchill and Vansittart, Russia was completely excluded from the settlement of the Sudeten issue and her potential value as an apparently fervent supporter of collective security was not even debated in the Cabinet. The cold-shouldering of Russia as an interested party in the affairs of Central Europe was one of the Anglo-French mistakes at Munich whose cost was not perceived until later.[64]

The second and much stranger strategic aspect of the Munich crisis to be mentioned was the extent to which the almost universal obsession with an immediate all-out German air attack deluded the public, experts, and Government alike.

Hore-Belisha, Ismay, Warren Fisher, and most of the Cabinet ministers believed in September 1938 that war would begin with a massive German air attack on Britain, and that the Field Force would not go to France but would be involved in assisting with ADGB and in keeping order.[65] No one, it seems, seriously questioned whether Germany even had the intention, let alone the capability, of beginning a major war in this fashion. Had the Government's professional advisers been less obsessed with Britain's weaknesses, above all with the vulnerability of London to air attack, they might at least have questioned whether their worst-case assumptions were justified.

After the needs of the ground forces operating against Czechoslovakia for air support had been met as well as those of Germany's extremely weak forces opposing France (only 8 or 9 divisions against about 60), it was hardly likely that she would have sufficient bomber forces left to attack Paris, let alone south-eastern England where her bombers would have been operating at maximum range and well beyond fighter cover. Recent research has confirmed that Germany had not made serious plans to bomb London before the Munich crisis and that she would in any case have been incapable of doing so with any hope of success. Indeed, while the RAF's earlier emphasis on strategic bombing in no way deterred Hitler from aggressive diplomacy backed by force, it did work to the extent that in 1938 Germany too was frightened of long-range bombing. After a careful examination of the Luftwaffe's numbers, training, maintenance, and supply problems; and limitations imposed by range, direction-finding, and targeting, a recent study concludes that in 1938 Germany could not have launched a significant bombing offensive against Britain. The Luftwaffe was unprepared for such a task in nearly every respect; indeed it would have had difficulty in fulfilling its operational commitments to support German ground forces against Czechoslovakia and in the west.[66]

There is no need to rehearse all the criticisms that various historians have made of British policy towards Germany in 1938. Although, in a narrow interpretation, strategy and policy went hand in hand in that the COS provided military reasons to underpin Government policy, on a broader view there was a clear divergence between policy, whereby Britain intervened positively to secure a diplomatic settlement in Central Europe, and strategy where the emphasis lay increasingly on defensive isolationism and Imperial commitments. As this and previous chapters have shown Britain never completely and categorically denied her strategic interests in north-west Europe (how could she, given the facts of geography?), but in 1937 and 1938 she went about as far as any power in her vulnerable situation could to shuffle off military responsibilities to potential allies. As Dr Middlemas neatly sums up: 'Incapacity to engage in continental war became an overriding reason for avoiding one at any cost; but the existence of an umbilical cord across the Channel worked to the ultimate detriment of plans for an Anglo-German détente.' Chamberlain's personal foray into diplomacy came too late to take possible advantage of Hitler's apparent friendliness towards Britain, and by sacrificing Czechoslovakia he increased the mistrust of France and Belgium, who not unreasonably felt they were being abandoned to their fate. When every allowance is made for Britain's military and political unpreparedness for war, the fact remains that a weak hand was played with crass ineptitude. Defence priorities were excessively influenced by economic considerations with a long war in view, and by the Cabinet's sense of what 'public opinion' would tolerate. The professional military advisers dutifully answered the specific questions put to them but there was no fundamental reappraisal of vital national interests. On a more tactical level Chamberlain not only committed the cardinal error of displaying Britain's military weakness in advance but also made it clear that he planned to pursue a foreign policy commensurate with that weakness. Moreover, and this is truly astonishing, there was no attempt to evaluate Germany's weaknesses, much less to exploit them or to bluff with the not inconsiderable assets in Britain's favour. On the contrary, Chamberlain and his Government made the fatal assumption, against a great deal of evidence, that Hitler shared their own profound commitment to preserving peace and that he would keep his word.[67]

As far as the role of the Army was concerned, Chamberlain's policy underlines this dichotomy between policy and strategy: while diplomatically Britain was intervening forcefully and unilaterally in Central European problems, strategically her isolation from the Continent was made increasingly clear to potential friends and enemies alike. In other words Chamberlain aimed to bring about a political settlement while ensuring that there would never be the slightest risk of a resort to war on Britain's part. Indeed we can go further and point out that south-eastern England's vulnerability to air attack, already suspected but sensationally confirmed by the deployment of anti-aircraft defences during the Munich crisis, made it even less likely than before that the Government would risk sending any part of the Field Force to France.[68]

Although the Government's official military advisers, like Ismay and Pownall, correctly from their limited viewpoint, could judge the outcome of Munich a success in terms of time gained for rearmament, particularly in home defence measures, some critics at once perceived that, in addition to the moral dishonour, the undermining of Czechoslovakia's national integrity was a strategic disaster of the first order. No one faced this unpleasant fact more boldly that Churchill when he told the House of Commons that: 'We have suffered a total and unmitigated defeat, and . . . France has suffered even more than we have.' Duff Cooper felt the same and was the only minister to resign. Liddell Hart, now one of Churchill's supporters, likewise felt that the writing off of Czechoslovakia's forces necessitated a complete reappraisal of the strategic situation. Belatedly he began to face the likelihood that Britain would have to send an army to France whether she possessed armoured divisions or not.[69]

Although there was some truth in Liddell Hart's notion that the Munich settlement had radically altered the strategic balance in Central Europe, it could also be argued that these events only served to confirm and underline what less theoretically minded soldiers such as Gort and Pownall had been saying for years. They understood that France's security against a potentially stronger Germany depended on her ability to create—or at least threaten to create—a second front through her Central and East European alliances in which the role of Czechoslovakia was crucial. But the corollary, which received more lip service than real support, was that Britain's security was ultimately bound up with that of France. However unpleasant the contemplation of this common predicament might be, it could not be glossed over or wished away as Chamberlain and his supporters attempted to do in 1938. Pownall got to the heart of the matter earlier in the year when he noted: '*My* view is that support of France is home defence—if France crumbles we fall.'[70] British statesmen and their Service advisers alike had tended to lose sight of this political and strategic fact of life in 1937 and 1938, but in the months following the Munich settlement they would be forced to consider it again.

CHAPTER 10

Return to reality, October 1938–April 1939

During the six months following the Munich settlement there was an astonishing transformation in the British Government's attitude to the continental commitment and, in consequence, dramatic changes in the Army's priorities, size, and strategic plans. Paradoxically, however, the immediate impact of Munich was slight. The transformation was gradual and cumulative, and owed at least as much to external events and pressures as to a dispassionate strategic reappraisal.

Contrary to what has often been stated, there was no marked increase in the scale of the rearmament programme in the remaining weeks of 1938, but merely a slight acceleration of existing programmes, in particular of air defence measures designed to avoid a knock-out blow from the air. Financial stringency was scarcely eased at all, and on 26 October the Cabinet decided to postpone indefinitely the crucial question of creating a Ministry of Supply. Earlier, on 3 October, the Prime Minister informed the Cabinet that the position was now more hopeful in that the contacts he had established with the dictator powers opened up the possibility of an agreement which would stop the armaments race. Britain could not take the risk of stopping rearmament unilaterally, but she should certainly not embark on a great increase in her rearmament programme. In particular Chamberlain repeated his pledge that the Government would not introduce conscription in peacetime. 'It must be remembered', he told the House of Commons on 1 November, 'that we are not today in the same position as we were in 1914, in this respect: that we are not now contemplating the equipment of an army on a continental scale.' All that was deemed necessary was a Ministry of National Service (under Sir John Anderson) to compile a register of manpower resources. Similarly Chamberlain made it clear in Parliament that there would be no new willingness to accept continental military commitments or to seek military alliances: in short, the quest for a general agreement with Germany and Italy would continue. As Ironside recorded in his diary on 2 November: 'A most unsatisfactory statement by the Prime Minister as regards his Foreign Policy and Defence. He made it clear that our rearmament was not against Germany. No compulsion and no Ministry of Supply.'[1]

The Prime Minister's decision to continue 'business as usual' was made in spite of Inskip's warning, on 21 October, that the forecast of supply for the Regular Army and, far more, for the Territorials was disturbing. By 1 August 1939 the re-equipment of the Regular Army should be virtually complete except for armoured fighting vehicles, anti-aircraft guns, and chemical warfare companies. But its scale of equipment and reserves would still be calculated on the basis of an Eastern theatre, a basis inadequate for the Continent. The present scale of equipment for the Territorial divisions would not even allow them to train effectively on embodiment. No fully equipped Territorial formation could take the field until at least eight months after war began. A number of firms working on Army contracts would become idle early in 1939 unless increased orders were placed soon.[2]

It is now clear that from a purely military viewpoint France should have been prepared to risk war by supporting Czechoslovakia in 1938. This was her last opportunity to fight Germany on favourable or at least even terms. Failure to do so tilted the strategic balance decisively against her; for Germany was rearming faster and more purposefully. French morale deteriorated and, not least important, France lost the support of some 34 Czech divisions much of whose equipment, including tanks, would soon be taken over by Germany. France's inertia can be explained on several levels but two related considerations seem particularly significant. As will be more fully explored later, she was preoccupied to an astonishing degree in 1938–9 with Italian and Spanish threats to her interests in the Mediterranean region.

The French General Staff had no plans to aid Czechoslovakia by an offensive across the Rhine. In any case France's policy at Munich, like Britain's, was not primarily determined by military weakness but more by the desire to avoid war altogether by a European détente. If agreement could be reached with Germany, she in turn might counsel moderation in Rome. The shock of Munich did not change this policy; on the contrary, 'Relief at a hairbreadth escape from war . . . brought a determination to work all the harder for a Franco-German settlement.' France clung steadfastly to the hope of a genuine *rapprochement* with Germany until March 1939.[3]

In one more important respect the Munich settlement had an immediate effect on Anglo-French relations. Though France still did not openly challenge Britain's diplomatic leadership, she did now question the extent of the former's continental commitment. Whereas the French had hitherto rather surprisingly appeared satisfied with her conditional offer of a token force of two divisions, from the autumn of 1938 they began to press ever more insistently for the definite promise of a sizeable army. Within days of the Munich settlement General Dentz, Gamelin's deputy, warned the British Military Attaché: 'Take care of French public opinion: France does not intend to allow England to fight her battles with French soldiers.' As another staff officer put it bluntly a few days later, what the French were expecting was *'l'effort du sang'*—in short, conscription. So far from accepting this obligation to her likely ally, the British were if anything even less friendly than before Munich. Until January 1939 'Britain failed to show enough imaginative sympathy to make even a slight gesture to secure the future of her only assured European ally.' Thus Britain bears a heavy share of responsibility for undermining the will of France to resist. Lord Halifax characteristically suggested that France's failure to take adequate steps to remedy her weakness in the air would provide Chamberlain with a convenient counter to French pressure for a larger British contribution on land. In effect Britain was relying on the French to hold the Western Front *and* provide air reinforcements while she concentrated on making her island an impregnable fortress. This was altogether too much to expect of French altruism, particularly as Britain continued to refuse to hold meaningful staff talks or to commit unequivocally even the Regular divisions of the Field Force.[4]

While the War Office and the General Staff were as indifferent to French needs and anxieties as Chamberlain and Halifax, they tended to draw a less complacent lesson from Munich. Hore-Belisha's view was simply that if the Government did not intend to send the Army to Europe in any circumstances it should say so; he now believed that history would repeat itself and it *would* go. He was appalled at the thought of what would have happened to the Field Force had it been dispatched to France during the Munich crisis. Quite apart from lack of tanks, guns, and ammunition reserves, the troops would have had no winter clothing. This was a state of neglect almost comparable with the condition in which the army had been sent to the Crimea. Pownall felt that the crisis had proved the correctness of the General Staff's view: 'The first and main lesson', he wrote on 3 October, 'is that we must *expect* to have to send troops to help the French.' The General Staff resurrected the programme refused two years previously (including four Territorial divisions to be ready for embarkation after four months) which would cost about £198 million. When these proposals came before a Cabinet subcommittee at the end of October most ministers, according to Pownall, 'hated the idea [i.e. of greatly increased expenditure on the Army to equip it for a European role] and shirked the plain issue':

> Only Inskip showed the least sympathy and he quite a lot. Simon was studiously polite, and indeed appreciative of the motives which underlie its submission—but he didn't like the cost, one could hardly expect him to. Stanhope, who had not read it I think, made some very stupid remarks which were fully answered if he had taken the trouble to read the paper. Ernest Brown was violent but confused. Sam Hoare thoroughly beastly. He started off by grumbling at the cost and said he wished he could see more results from the money spent by the Army—where was it all going to? He added peevishly that he thought that this question had been settled—why was it coming up again?

Early in November Pownall noted that the War Office's gambit would henceforth be that the Army's role was not in dispute; it was merely a matter of changing the European commitment from last priority to first so as to loosen the iron grip of the Treasury. Hankey, now out of office but still in a position to influence decisions, had been briefed by Weygand on France's military weaknesses and reluctantly concluded that the Army must after all be prepared for continental war. As a consequence of Chamberlain's niggardliness, Hankey wrote gloomily that the Field Force would be initially even weaker than in 1914. The Army's case now appeared stronger even to some advocates of limited liability. For example, though his published views continued to be ambiguous, Liddell Hart privately accepted that the Munich capitulation had weakened Britain's chances of avoiding involvement with land forces in support of France.[5] Yet he added his authority to a series of letters in *The Times,* along with General Burnett-Stuart and Sir Auckland Geddes, which caused dismay in France by upholding the 'limited liability' policy despite the radically altered strategic balance. The French feared, with some justice, that these letters represented a wide sector of British public opinion. The Foreign Office became alarmed lest France lose heart and make the best terms she could get with Germany.[6]

In this atmosphere it was hardly surprising that the visit of Chamberlain and Halifax to Paris from 23 to 25 November turned out to be no more than a hollow gesture. Before departing the two ministers had made it clear to their colleagues that they had no intention of yielding to French pressure for increased military support. On land there was no question of adding to the conditional commitment of two divisions at the outset, though more might be done in the event of a long war. If the French thought they could rely on any British air contribution to the defence of Paris they were wrong: the RAF was being built up for home defence. Halifax said he was opposed to staff conversations on British support to France, but they might be acceptable if they also covered French assistance to Britain. Neither the CID nor the COS were consulted as to whether these views were valid in the post-Munich situation.[7]

Contrary to his expectations, the Parisians received Chamberlain with considerable coolness rather than gratitude for saving them from war. There was some booing and cries of '*à bas Munich*'. At the conference on 24 November Daladier made the predicted demand for an increased land contribution from Britain in the form of motorized divisions. As for the first contingent of two divisions, three weeks was far too slow for their mobilization and dispatch to France—they should arrive in eight days. Chamberlain refused to budge from the figure of two divisions at the outset of war, and counter-attacked by saying that Daladier was grossly inflating the estimates for future aircraft production. The French Premier repeated his willingness to announce publicly that if Britain were attacked France would feel bound to go to her help. In return Chamberlain agreed to further staff talks while remaining non-committal about their scope.[8]

The failure of the French to force the issue on their need for a large and fully equipped British Army disappointed the British General Staff on whose behalf Pownall had carried out some covert lobbying via the Military Attaché in Paris. On his return, according to Pownall, the Prime Minister remarked to Hore-Belisha that as the British Army was so small it was hardly worth worrying about whether it was ready or not. This was a maddening attitude on the part of 'The Coroner', Pownall reflected, 'for we *know* we shall be sent if there is a war in Western Europe—the only point therefore is whether our men shall be properly equipped for it—or ill-equipped and slaughtered'. He also considered that by heroic efforts it might be possible to get the first two divisions to France in sixteen days but Daladier's target was out of the question because it would take several days to collect the transport ships and—in contrast to 1914—the threat of air attacks would rule out the use of the French Channel ports.[9]

Despite their apparent failure to promote Anglo-French military co-operation, the Paris meetings exerted an important indirect effect on the role of the British Army. If Chamberlain returned as deaf as before to French pleas for tangible evidence of British good faith, the same was not true of Halifax. He was experiencing a conversion. As early as 1 November he admitted to the British Ambassador in Paris that there was a risk that France might in certain circumstances become so defeatist as to give up the struggle even to defend her own frontiers. He, and even more his private secretary, Oliver Harvey, were fully exposed to manifestations of French defeatism in Paris and he returned much more doubtful as to whether Britain could simply continue to rely on France as her shield. Indeed, the Foreign Office began to take seriously the nightmare possibility that Daladier and Bonnet, both weak men, might seek a *rapprochement* with Germany at Britain's expense.[10] If Britain was prepared to do so little for France it was sobering to ask whether France was likely to make a major sacrifice in the event of a German attack on Britain only. Limited liability might not after all be a British prerogative.

In December 1938, exactly a year after he had played a leading role in securing the Cabinet's approval of the 'limited liability' policy for the Army, Hore-Belisha was preparing a memorandum whose effect would be to reverse that decision. Wisely, though to the annoyance of his professional military advisers, Hore-Belisha insisted that the strategic arguments for increased spending on the Army be omitted. It was not that these arguments were unsound but ministers hated being faced with them. 'They are tired of them no doubt', wrote Pownall, 'and would much prefer to shirk them too since they lead to uncomfortable conclusions.' Gort, Pownall, and the Permanent Under-Secretary, Sir Herbert Creedy, all spoke bluntly to Hore-Belisha to the effect that if war broke out in Western Europe the Army would have to go despite its unprepardness and 'there would be a first class scandal'. The General Staff were determined to ensure that, if the Army was not to be prepared for continental operations, responsibility should clearly lie with ministers. As Pownall put it: 'we wanted to make sure that if anyone was to hang on lamp posts it should not be the War Office'.[11]

In his memorandum of 13 December, Hore-Belisha rather disingenuously claimed that he was not attempting to change the priority of the Army's roles but merely to make it capable of fulfilling the roles already approved. For this he requested an additional expenditure of £81 million. His main proposals were to split the mobile division into two smaller divisions; provide the first two divisions with extra stores, reserves, and units to enable them to adopt counter-offensive as distinct from purely defensive measures; provide full-scale reserves and ammunition for the next two divisions; and provide war equipment and reserves for the first four TA divisions and training equipment for the remainder. He also proposed to organize two 'colonial divisions' from units supernumerary to the Field Force, including one from the 18 battalions at present in Palestine. He invoked the lesson of 1914 to support his case that there must be fully equipped contingents ready to reinforce the first two divisions. At present, for example, the second contingent had only half-scale ammunition. It was an intolerable situation, he argued, when vehicles and ammunition were being 'borrowed' from the Field Force for the battalions in Palestine. Finally, it was imperative to equip the infantry divisions of the TA beyond the bare minimum for training purposes.[12]

When the memorandum came before the CID on 15 December the War Minister received scant support from his colleagues. Hoare was chief spokesman for the opposition to even these modest proposals: it was wrong to distinguish between ADGB and the Army's other possible duties. 'The air defence of Great Britain was, in fact, the principal role of the Army.' Halifax agreed that this was the most urgent need, but added significantly that when he was in Paris (on 24 November) the French had pressed very strongly for a British land contribution. This pressure had been withstood and the French had been told that, as Britain did not possess an Army equipped for war, further discussion of possible assistance to them would be academic. However, he added euphemistically, 'France would cease to be enthusiastic about relations with Great Britain if they were left with the impression that they would have to bear the brunt of the fighting and slaughter on land.' Hoare riposted revealingly that 'whatever the French might think their interests were so bound up with ours that they could not afford to stand aloof'. Halifax countered with the frightening suggestion that Germany might persuade France to stand aside while she attacked Britain. Incredibly, ministers once again evaded a decision by referring the issue back to the Chiefs of Staff.[13]

The minutes of the COS meeting on 21 December reveal that there was still profound disagreement on the role of the Army. Gort cited Lord Kitchener to support the view that no great country can wage a 'little war': war with Germany, he insisted, would be a life-and-death struggle. His strongest argument was that it was doubtful if Britain could survive should Germany establish air and submarine bases in the Low Countries and the Channel ports. If Britain made a definite commitment to France to send the Field Force as soon as possible France might contribute decisively to the defence of Belgium. He also emphasized that it made no sense to limit our contribution to two divisions equipped for defensive operations only and with no reinforcements to follow. The Army's case received valuable support from Chatfield's successor as C.N.S., Sir Roger Backhouse,* who, though opposed to unlimited Army expansion, endorsed Gort's opinion that it was essential to reassure the French. The C.N.S. thought the allies' aim should be to try and stop the Germans at about the same place as in 1914. 'If Dunkirk and Calais were taken, the effect would be serious, but it would be still more so if German penetration reached Havre and Rouen.' The CAS (and Chairman), Sir Cyril Newall, remained unimpressed by any of his colleagues' arguments and adhered obstinately to the 'limited liability' view. He did not believe the allies could hold the Low Countries, but he did not regard German occupation of the Channel ports as necessarily fatal. He was opposed to equipping any of the Territorial divisions for war because that would open the door to unlimited expansion of land warfare. General Ismay mildly supported the Army's case, and made the shrewd point that the Field Force and reserves needed to be much better equipped even for an Imperial war. On this note, the meeting ended inconclusively.[14]

Before the Chiefs of Staff met again in mid-January 1939 a steady flow of reports from Britain's Ambassador, Sir Eric Phipps, and the Military Attaché in Paris made it absolutely clear that French public opinion as well as her military and political leaders demanded that Britain should demonstrate her willingness to make *un effort du sang*. As Phipps summed up their case:

> To the argument that no country can afford to maintain simultaneously a great fleet, a great air force and a great army, they reply, 'a professional army, no; but a conscript army is much cheaper; and for the price of her present professional army Great Britain could maintain a national army of far larger proportions'. They do not expect a military effort on the scale of their own. They do not even demand the immediate despatch to France of an expeditionary force in the event of war, although they consider that this would have a great effect, both material and moral. But they do demand that at the end of a limited period, say three months, Great Britain should be in a position to despatch to this country an army of a size to do something to redress the balance between France and Germany.

Colonel William Fraser,* the Military Attaché, added that in the event of war against Germany and Italy, France would be greatly outnumbered and the outcome could only be a matter of time. 'From this it becomes apparent that all French strategy must depend finally not only on friendship with Great Britain, but also on a knowledge of what Great Britain is prepared to do to help her on land. For, in the opinion of the French, it is she who provides the only source from which the thirty-four Czech divisions lost in Central Europe can be replaced.' On 16 January 1939 Phipps sent Halifax a pamphlet entitled 'La Conscription Anglaise peut seule empêcher l'Allemagne d'écraser l'Europe' with the comment 'another example of the tendency which I have repeatedly drawn attention to in recent despatches, to suggest that . . . the armament effort which is being made by Great Britain on the sea and in the air is not sufficient unless supplemented by an important increase in the Army'. Failure to do so, he added, would be grist to the mill of the minority who were urging that it might be well to compound with Germany.

In any case, British strategic arguments in favour of limited liability, whether valid or not, were fast becoming irrelevant. It was now a question of morale and of reassuring French public opinion:

> If the French thought of British assistance in terms of the number of soldiers in Europe . . . then it was of no use pointing to the size of the British Navy or Air Force, or talking of Britain's financial stability as the fourth arm of her defence. Rightly or wrongly, French public opinion wanted large numbers of British troops in Europe, and rational military arguments could not prevail over desires that had deep psychological and historical roots.[15]

In the light of these pressures from France which gave added impetus to the doctrine consistently advocated by the General Staff, Michael Howard's verdict that early in 1939 the Chiefs of Staff 'carried out a remarkable volte-face' seems exaggerated. It would be more accurate to say that the COS had never in fact been so internally at one as their reports suggested, and that the CNS's support was now decisive in getting the Army's view adopted. Pownall, who was alert to every shift of opinion in the COS had no doubt that Backhouse's support was vital. On 9 January Admiral Backhouse wrote to Ismay, 'You soldiers . . . have got to tell us what minimum size Expeditionary Force could have any effect', and Ismay suggested four infantry divisions and two mobile divisions for a start. It seemed likely that

Germany would again wheel through Belgium and the French were unlikely to intervene in that country unless Britain contributed a Field Force. Backhouse then sent Ismay a paper on the role of the Army but significantly omitted to show it to the CAS. 'I cannot help feeling', Backhouse remarked in his covering letter, 'that it is not only a matter of letting down France but, ultimately (unless Germany breaks up), of finding ourselves in a most dangerous position. It may be that too much is being undertaken in the way of Empire responsibilities by this Island, but the fact remains that it is our future security that we are primarily concerned with in this matter.'[16]

When the Chiefs of Staff reconvened on 18 January 1939, Backhouse reiterated these points and appeared almost to speak as the Army's advocate. While agreeing that conscription was out of the question, he sided with Gort against Newall in believing that in practice it would be impossible to wage a war of limited liability against Germany: 'we should be compelled to increase our strength much the same way as we were in the last war'. What most struck him as indefensible was to retain a Territorial Army which was not equipped for war. The CAS acquiesced and, as chairman, concluded that they were agreed that the equipment asked for by the Secretary of State for War should be provided to enable the Army to carry out the role allocated to it.[17]

In their report of 25 January 1939, the COS took care to stress that they not advocating a mass army on the scale of the First World War or more specific commitments. Nor in general did they dispute the low priority assigned to the Army in the rearmament programme as a whole. Nevertheless their report amounted to a complete endorsement of Hore-Belisha's proposals. In terms of production they had no doubts that a much larger Army could be raised, since only about 30 per cent of industry was currently employed on armaments work. Strategically it was a perilous situation to have only the first contingent prepared for a second-class theatre of operations with no hope of remedying the position in the early months of the war. The COS report repeatedly stressed that the Field Force, or part of it, might be needed for Imperial duties and this constituted another argument for greater preparedness: not only might Britain lose the war through inability to check a continental enemy; she might also forfeit a good opportunity for offensive action overseas. In sum the report urged that the existing land forces—five Regular divisions, one mobile division, 13 Territorial infantry divisions, and five anti-aircraft divisions—should all be made more efficient, and at least the first four Territorial divisions fully equipped as a reserve for the Field Force ready to be dispatched after four months at war. Finally, Admiral Backhouse had carried his point about the vital importance of the security of the Channel ports. Prevention of their occupation by the Germans ought, the report urged, to be included under the first rather than the last of the Army's priorities, namely as part of home defence: 'the corner-stone of our Imperial Defence Policy is to maintain the security of the United Kingdom'. Despite their avowed acceptance of the Government's defence policy the COS's report signified the impending abandonment of limited liability.[18]

Hore-Belisha took the issue a stage further at a CID meeting next day when he urged that a Ministry of Supply be created before war began. The policy of limited liability inhibited proper use of Britain's industrial capacity in peace and to wait until the outbreak of war might be too late. From the chair Inskip implied there was no hurry, but Halifax strongly supported Hore-Belisha. 'For a long time he had tried to think that a war of limited liability was possible but he was now convinced that we must abandon such a conception.' Serious preparations now would help to hold the French steady.

A few days later Hore-Belisha recorded that the CID had approved his proposals for complete equipment and reserves for the Field Force; war equipment and reserves for four Territorial divisions, and full training equipment for the remainder.[19]

The move away from limited liability towards a definite continental commitment accompanied by high-level staff talks received impetus towards the end of January 1939 from what proved to be an unfounded rumour of an imminent German attack on Holland. The COS reported unequivocally that, in spite of Britain's military unpreparedness, the strategic importance to the British Empire of Holland and her colonies was so great that a German attack on her must be regarded as an attack on Britain's interests. Even though France and Belgium were Britain's allies they admitted that nothing could be done to save Holland, but the Field Force should nevertheless be dispatched to France in the hope that it might encourage her to support Belgium. In sum, however depressing the military prospects, Britain would have no choice but to intervene. Failure to do so would have such moral and strategic repercussions as would seriously undermine the British position in the eyes of the Dominions and the world in general. On 27 January the Foreign Policy Committee confirmed that if Germany attacked Holland and she resisted Britain should regard it as a *casus belli*. The Foreign Secretary was authorized to approach France and Belgium regarding staff talks and to propose informal talks with the Dutch. Britain should assure France that she would go to war if Germany invaded either Holland or Switzerland provided France would give mutual pledges in return. At the same meeting the Committee made the momentous recommendation that joint staff planning should be arranged with France and Belgium even though this would constitute a far more binding obligation than hitherto contemplated. Equally momentous was the decision to include Italy in combination with Germany (even at the risk of upsetting the Italians), and to broaden the scope of staff conversations to include all likely fields of operations. Finally, it was accepted that henceforth there would have to be regular periodic liaison with the French and Belgian staffs. On 1 February the Cabinet agreed that though these proposals were almost tantamount to an alliance they must be accepted. Thus the illusory German threat to Holland achieved a change of emphasis which the actual threats to Austria and Czechoslovakia had failed to accomplish.[20]

In February 1939 the Prime Minister yielded to the arguments of his colleagues and professional military advisers in favour of accepting most of Hore-Belisha's proposals for increased expenditure on the Army, and the corollary of a more definite military commitment to France. But he did so with marked reluctance and after a protracted rearguard action. Thus on 2 February he remarked in Cabinet that though Hore-Belisha's proposals might be 'modest', speaking as a former Chancellor the financial position looked to him extremely dangerous. He did not like the COS's suggestion that unless Britain promised to help the French on land they might not help if Britain were attacked by Germany; the country should rather concentrate on making the best of her combined resources. He still cherished the delusion that in closer staff conversations the French might come to accept our position. He was strongly supported by the Chancellor, Simon, who pointed out that if Hore-Belisha's proposals costing £82 million were accepted the Army Estimates for 1939–40 would be doubled. He feared that the financial situation was threatening to get out of hand. The Army's claims were no doubt urgent but were they more so than many others such as agriculture, shipping, air raid shelters, and air defence precautions? Hoare supported his view that air defence should retain its absolute priority. Opposing his colleagues, Halifax stressed the sensitivity of French feeling on this issue. Surely, he suggested, Britain could risk borrowing money in these exceptional circumstances: either war would come soon or the Nazi regime would collapse. He allegedly said he would sooner be bankrupt in peace than beaten in a war against Germany. Oliver Stanley went futher: this was probably the crucial year and the tense situation could not last. It was unrealistic to allocate defence expenditure up to March 1942 and to say that the country could not afford particular preparations now. This meeting ended inconclusively and the War Office was left to haggle for money with the Treasury.[21]

After futher discussions in yet another *ad hoc* ministerial subcommittee, the Cabinet approved the greater part of Hore-Belisha's programme on 22 February. The four infantry divisions of the Field Force and the mobile division were to be provided with full equipment and reserves on a continental scale, and war equipment and reserves would also be provided for four Territorial divisions at a total additional cost of about £48 million. Even at this late stage, however, financial restrictions amounting to penny pinching were prominent. By postponing the estimated dates of embarkation for the second contingent of the Field Force (from 40 to 60 days) and the four Territorial divisions (from four to six months) after the outbreak of war, the Prime Minister hoped to save about £5 million. Though he mentioned that 'public opinion would become restive if the present position became widely known', these measures suggest that Chamberlain was still not properly aware of the urgency of the situation. The records leave a strong impression that financial economy still counted for more than military preparedness. The meeting concluded that in the following staff conversations the French could be allowed to assume that the Regular Field Force would be dispatched to the Continent in the event of war, but there was to be no suggestion of any commitment of Territorial units, though in fact it was hoped that some might be ready within the first year of war.[22] However half-hearted, these decisions show that by the end of February the Cabinet had at last become reconciled to seeing the Field Force prepared for continental war. Taken together with the Prime Minister's declaration on 6 February that 'any threat to the vital interests of France from whatever quarter it came' would evoke 'the immediate co-operation of this country', it seemed as though the Government was preparing to jettison the last restraints of limited liability.[23]

Nevertheless there is more than a suspicion that this new phase in rearmament was dictated as much by the supposed wishes of 'public opinion' (British and French) as by strategic considerations. Certainly Hore-Belisha, who had completely reversed his views on the continental role of the Army since March 1938, was aware of a definite shift in parliamentary opinion. As he told his Cabinet colleagues on 22 February, 'Up to this year there had been no Parliamentary pressure regarding the Field Force, but pressure was now becoming evident. It was argued that our solidarity with France involved the growing importance of assistance on land.' Archibald Sinclair, the leader of the Liberal Party, provided a striking illustration of this rapid shift in opinion: in March 1938 he had vigorously opposed committing any British troops to the Continent but now, a year later, he admitted it was a necessity which Britain could not refuse to contemplate. A Conservative minority including Amery and Boothby pressed openly for conscription, while a wider group favoured the introduction of some milder form of compulsory national service training. In mid-March Hore-Belisha told the short-lived Strategical Appreciation Sub-Committee that the Opposition reaction to his recent speech on the Estimates was that Britain's undertaking to assist France on the Continent did not go far enough.[24]

It was further indicative of the changing climate of opinion that in January 1939 Liddell Hart, one of the arch-advocates of limited liability, advised Eden that as a result of Munich British land reinforcements were now necessary for France. This conversion was unfortunately muffled because, as a consequence of the growing rift between his own and *The Times*'s editorial views on the strategic situation, some of his most important contributions were held over for several months and then published against a changed political background. In particular his two articles written in the autumn of 1938 entitled 'An Army across the Channel?', but not published until 7 and 8 February 1939, still stressed 'limited liability' arguments. Not surprisingly in the changing climate of opinion, they met with generally hostile receptions in Parliament, the Press, and private correspondence. For example Major-General Sir Edward Spears wrote that he had read the first article 'with interest and at the same time with great concern . . . I don't know what is coming, but I beg you not to lose sight of the fact that from the very comprehensive examination of French opinion which I carried out, it was quite clear that France will not consent to do all the fighting whilst we . . . only prepare for the kind of warfare which will not involve similarity of sacrifice.'[25] As we have seen, some ministers, including Halifax and Hore-Belisha, accepted the argument expressed by Spears comparatively quickly at the beginning of 1939 whereas others,—notably Hoare, Simon, and Chamberlain —were belated and extremely reluctant converts. Events and public pressure would drive the Chamberlain group further in March and April than they would have believed possible even in February. Ministers who had appealed somewhat rhetorically for years to the alleged wishes of 'public opinion' as a pretext for opposing military expenditure, were now hoist by their own petard as 'public opinion' was clearly seen to favour increased military support to France and resistance to any further act of German aggression.

In presenting his second Army Estimates on 8 March 1939 Hore-Belisha found himself defending a role for the Field Force virtually identical with that so courageously but vainly championed by his predecessor Duff Cooper. While paying due attention to the threat of air attack and the need to strengthen Imperial defences, beginning with the creation of a Middle East strategic reserve in Palestine, the War Minister admitted that the position regarding a continental commitment had changed drastically since the previous year. Although, he stressed, there was no binding political commitment to France, if Britain did become involved in war her effort would not be half-hearted or based upon any theory of limited liability. In describing the potential Expeditionary Force, Hore-Belisha indulged in a characteristic piece of showmanship. Whereas, he said, the BEF created by Haldane before 1914 had only six Regular infantry divisions and one cavalry division, the force which he was organizing would have four Regular infantry and two Regular armoured divisions augmented by thirteen Territorial divisions of varying type, making a grand total of nineteen divisions. This was, to say the least, optimistic. Such a force might eventually come into being but, as we have seen, the Territorial divisions had been so starved of modern equipment —not to speak of manpower deficiencies—that it would take many months before even the first contingent would be ready for war. Pownall's reaction to Hore-Belisha's forecast was that 'he has again mortgaged the future, a dangerous trick he is always playing'. The diarist, on reflection, applauded him for what he took to be a deliberate gambit to increase the Army's financial allocation, 'for he's as artful as a fox and is now thoroughly interested in the game of squeezing millions out of the Treasury'. The War Minister in fact gained considerable political capital and kudos from his impressive reference to nineteen divisions, several of which scarcely existed other than on paper.[26]

On a wider view, however, Hore-Belisha's speech offered little to reassure the French since he carefully avoided the controversial issue of conscription. There was no evidence that Britain's initial commitment would exceed the derisory two divisions already mentioned in Anglo-French staff talks, yet it was the initial deployment which now increasingly worried the French because of their policy of extended frontier defence. It was also unfortunate that in attacking the now obsolescent 'limited liability' doctrine, Conservative spokesmen in the House of Commons emphasized the value of numbers rather than mobility and firepower. Their criticism was for the most part channeled into demands for conscription but there was also a tendency to criticize mechanization. Lord Apsley, a veteran champion of national service, made fun of the Royal Tank Corps, charging around familiar country with 'two pounders banging, machine guns clattering and lots of noise and smoke' reminiscent of the Kaiser's theatrical cavalry charges before 1914. He repeated the old joke that this was magnificent but not war. The well-founded arguments of Liddell Hart and others that sheer numbers of infantry was a poor criterion of strength in modern mobile warfare were swamped as the campaign for conscription to produce a large army gathered momentum.[27]

In March 1938, as Hore-Belisha later admitted, Hitler's anschluss of Austria had undermined the assumptions of his policy for the Army on the day following the presentation of the annual estimates. Though in 1939 Hitler allowed a few more days to elapse before occupying Prague and the rump of Czechoslovakia on 15 March, the repercussions on British (and French) policy were this time far greater. Chamberlain reacted 'like a lover spurned'. It used to be thought that this brutal shattering of the last illusions resting on the Munich settlement and belief in Hitler's reliability and limited territorial ambitions signified the abrupt end of 'appeasement'. There is wide agreement among scholars that though Prague did indeed lead to a new emphasis on armed strength and firmness by Britain and France, it did not end their conciliatory quest for a European détente. Neither democratic Government was as yet prepared to face the prospect of war wholeheartedly with the consequence that their demonstration of firmness failed. Only a grand alliance, if even that, could have effectively deterred Germany in the summer of 1939, but neither Chamberlain nor Halifax was prepared to seek an alliance with the essential East European partner, Russia, until it was too late.[28]

If Prague did not fundamentally alter Britain's grand strategy of appeasement, the same is far from true of her military policy in general and that of the Army in particular. Here the transformation in late March and April 1939 was truly astonishing. Where ministers had previously hesitated to acknowledge a definite military commitment on the south side of the Channel (let alone the Rhine), they now almost casually shifted Britain's frontier (as Daladier said) to the Vistula.[29] Where they had for years begrudged money and resources to equip twelve divisions for war, by two successive strokes of the pen they laid the foundations for a national conscript army of infantry divisions approaching the scale of the First World War. Ironically the soldiers, who had so long pressed in vain for a small but well-prepared Army, were virtually ignored in the making of these momentous changes.

The first of these dramatic decisions was announced to both Houses of Parliament on 29 March. On the previous day Halifax had impressed on Hore-Belisha that it was imperative that some forthright action be taken as immediate evidence of Britain's determination to resist aggression. The War Minister now favoured conscription but Chamberlain had recently again pledged that he would not introduce it in peacetime. Moreover, the trade unions were adamantly opposed. On the spur of the moment and without first consulting the Army Council, Hore-Belisha suggested doubling the Territorial Army so as to take full advantage of the recent flood of volunteers. Chamberlain jumped at the idea and accepted, at Hore-Belisha's insistence, that it should be announced within twenty-four hours. The plan was to increase the peace establishment of the TA from 130,000 to war strength (170,000) and then double it (340,000). This would be achieved by allowing all units to over-recruit beyond their establishment to provide the cadres for duplicate units. The Treasury vainly opposed the measure because it doubted whether national savings were sufficient to finance the new Army programme without inflation; and it was also deeply worried about the accelerating deterioration of the nation's international credit position. The proposal was also 'a new step towards a commitment to fight the next war, like the last, in the trenches of France'. With masterly understatement Hore-Belisha warned Chamberlain that it would not be all plain sailing. The existing drill-halls were nowhere near adequate in number or capacity. There was a great shortage of equipment and uniforms and, perhaps most seriously, of instructors, many of whom had to be taken from regular units.[30]

As General Ismay, then Secretary of the CID, later noted in his *Memoirs* this decision was all the more extraordinary when one recalls the endless arguments about the size and the role of the Army and the years in which it had lived from hand to mouth without any consistent policy. Sir John Slessor recalled 'the expression of almost incredulous bewilderment on the usually cheerful countenance of the DCIGS' (Sir Ronald Adam) who had only just heard of it as a *fait accompli*. Slessor adds scathingly that there was no prior military discussion: 'No—it was a political decision—just like that; well-meaning no doubt but actually quite meaningless; there was not the remotest chance of actually getting an effective Field Force of thirty-two divisions for years and its only immediate effect was that with which we had long been familiar in the R.A.F.—a weakening of the existing force by the inevitable dilution involved'. An immediate consequence was that the General Staff put up 'a colossal demand' for no less than 1,440 first-line aircraft to co-operate with this New Model Army. By contrast the often acerbic Pownall took the decision comparatively calmly: it would pose vast problems of instructors, accommodation, and equipment but would have a less disruptive effect on the training of the Regular Army than the sudden introduction of national service. Nevertheless there is no evidence that the measure impressed anybody.[31]

Almost simultaneously with the decision to double the Territorial Army Chamberlain, on 31 March, gave a definite guarantee to Poland that if she were to be attacked by Germany, Britain would go to war and, on 7 April, after Italy had invaded Albania, he gave further guarantees to Roumania and Greece. The motives behind the guarantee given to Poland have been the subject of considerable historical controversy. Simon Newman has argued persuasively that the critical decisions leading to the unilateral guarantee (subsequently made reciprocal by Colonel Beck) were taken in an atmosphere of 'panic, humiliation and moral hysteria'. Halifax and the Foreign Office had little faith in Poland's military capacity, but felt an urgent need to demonstrate to the world that Britain would resist any further act of German aggression. More specifically, Halifax and Chamberlain feared that the Poles were about to do a deal with Germany which would demolish the hope of a second front in the east. Thus Halifax and Chamberlain were not dissuaded either by the knowledge that Britain could not effectively aid Poland or by the thought that their guarantee would make war more probable. Rather they calculated that Germany was likely to attack Poland first which would absorb some of her divisions and give Britain and France a long breathing space in which to intensify their rearmament. It is hard to be sure, however, that Chamberlain did not hope that the guarantee would deter

Hitler from attacking Poland. Whatever his hopes may have been, we now know that on 3 April Hitler ordered his armed forces to be ready for an attack on Poland at any time after 1 September.[32]

In this case it seems clear that professional military advice was deliberately suppressed until after the political decision had been made. The COS and their Joint Planning Sub-Committee worked continuously through 28 March to produce a preliminary report. They underlined the serious risk involved in surrendering 'the issue of war and peace with Germany to the actions of Governments [i.e. Poland and Roumania] over whom we have no control, and at a time when our defence programme is far from complete'. Their conclusion was as pessimistic (and with better reason) as their report on possible military support of Czechoslovakia a year previously:

> Neither Great Britain nor France could afford Poland and Roumania direct support by sea, on land or in the air to help them to resist a German invasion. Furthermore, in the present state of British and French armament production, neither Great Britain nor France could supply any armaments to Poland and Roumania. This emphasises the importance in this respect of assistance from the U.S.S.R.

It is evident that the Cabinet did not have the COS's report before them—with its unequivocal objections to the proposed guarantees to Poland and Roumania—when it met on the morning of 29 March. On the following day Chatfield (Minister for the Co-ordination of Defence) gave the Cabinet an inaccurate summary of the COS's views when the issue was now a guarantee of Poland alone, without Roumania. According to Chatfield the COS favoured fighting with Poland as an ally rather than seeing her defeated without a fight. Doubtless she would be overrun in two or three months, but it was still right to declare war if Poland was attacked by Germany and resisted. As Sidney Aster points out, Chatfield seriously misrepresented the COS's viewpoint in that they were critical of the guarantee; did not advise an automatic British declaration of war in event of a German attack on Poland; and, most important, had laid particular stress on bringing in the USSR as the only way to give practical aid to the Poles. Aster concludes that most members of the Cabinet did not see the report until 3 April (and then in a revised form) after the guarantee to Poland had been publicly announced. It would be wrong, however, to assume that had the COS's report been fully circulated it would have modified the Cabinet's policy, particularly as Sir Samuel Hoare and Walter Elliot had both vainly urged that the Soviet Union be brought into the new plan.[33] What the episode does suggest is that Chamberlain was prepared flagrantly to ignore unpalatable military advice, and also that the vital importance of the Soviet Union was not entirely overlooked at the time, as critics like Lloyd George and Liddell Hart would later allege. British military intelligence did not rate Russia highly, but her political unreliability was probably more influential. Pownall called it 'a continental commitment with a vengeance!' but added rather surprisingly 'I'm sure it's the right policy. The only way to stop Hitler is to show a firm front'. Group Captain Slessor, then the Air Representative on the Joint Planning Committee, realized at the time that Britain and France would be able to do nothing to save Poland. He therefore tried to warn the Polish Foreign Minister, Colonel Beck, via the CAS Newall, that the Poles would have to rely almost entirely on self-help. Whether his warning was passed on or not is not known, but the Poles maintained their opposition to the only power which might have been able to aid them—the Soviet Union—until the bitter end.[34]

In the course of April 1939 Chamberlain was pushed inexorably towards the introduction of compulsory service despite repeated declarations that he would never do so in peacetime. As we have already noted, French pressure on Britain to introduce conscription as proof of her intention to make a major contribution to continental land warfare had been mounting steadily since December 1938. On 27 March, for example, Sir Eric Phipps reported from Paris that the French regarded national service as the 'touchstone' of British policy towards Germany, and a Foreign Office official minuted 'All our telegrams from Paris tell the same story'. On 20 April Phipps reported that Daladier had made an urgent appeal for the introduction of conscription at once, even though it would only be a gesture. Only such a gesture, he said, could counter the effects of German propaganda in France. There was also a remarkable upsurge in the British Press and in Parliament in favour of conscription. Practical objections by military critics such as Liddell Hart made little impression. Indeed, in the euphoric atmosphere generated by public opinion it seemed that almost miraculous results would immediately flow from compulsory service. It would be good for Britain's youth; produce a powerful army almost overnight; and exert a priceless influence in Europe by reassuring the French and deterring the dictators. Unfortunately for the Government, one group of crucial importance remained unaffected by these sentiments: the TUC leaders remained flatly opposed to compulsory service.[35]

To mounting pressure from France was added an important domestic consideration. Obsessed by Britain's weakness in face of the expected German attempt to deal a knock-out blow from the air, the Government wished at least a portion of the anti-aircraft defences to be manned round the clock. Chamberlain suggested that the Territorials might keep their normal daily jobs and man their guns and searchlights at night for periods of three to six months, but the General Staff advised that this was absolutely impractical because it would disrupt training. Hore-Belisha decided that conscription was the only solution to this manpower problem—not only for AA defences, but for overseas garrisons and the Field Force. He became utterly exasperated by the Prime Minister's stalling and risked his political career by forcing the issue.[36]

Chamberlain was reluctantly obliged to bow to these combined diplomatic and domestic pressures on 20 April, but in introducing the Military Training Bill to Parliament a few days later he stressed that compulsory service would merely supplement not replace voluntary service. The plan was for Territorial units to take turns to provide permanent manning of the air defence *couverture* for the next four months. Meanwhile, from approximately 200,000 medically fit conscripts (more politely termed 'militiamen'), 80,000 would receive three-months initial training and then batches of 20,000 would take over the air defence duties for three-month periods i.e. each conscript would do three-months initial training followed by three 'in the line'. The remainder not required for air defence duties, after a similar period of training, would be attached to Regular Army or specially organized units. Once conscription was fully operational the War Office proposed to call up a certain number of reservists to complete under-strength Regular units, man extended AA defences, and act as instructors for the new Territorial units and conscripts. Unless war broke out conscripts would only be employed on duties at home.[37]

Contrary to Chamberlain's suspicions in his confrontations with Hore-Belisha, the General Staff was not pressing for conscription because—though they recognized that a political gesture might be valuable—they were only too well aware what enormous problems an additional expansion of the Army would bring. Their philosophical acceptance of the inevitable chaos that conscription entailed was graphically expressed by Pownall:

> It is a proper Granny's knitting that has been handed out to us to unravel—on top of the new role of the Army and the doubling of the T.A. What an unholy mess our politicians have made of the rebirth of the Army through shortsightedness, unwillingness to face facts and prejudice against the Army. There is but one alleviating feature. I have no doubt that these things, or something equivalent, would have been chucked at our heads to do immediately on the outbreak of war. It is better therefore that we should have them on us in advance, since every day, week and month is so much gained.[38]

Even seen as a political gesture the introduction of conscription had its limitations and drawbacks. As Lord Halifax and D. J. Colville, Secretary of State for Scotland, perceptively pointed out in Cabinet, because the legislation was hurried through, the emphasis of the scheme was heavily on home defence and therefore its potential value was diminished both as a reassurance to potential allies and as a deterrent to enemies. Those who favoured the deterrence theory could argue that Hitler would at once realize that in six or nine months' time Britain would possess a large Army which, together with the forces of her allies, would constitute too formidable an opposition to be worth the risk of a major war. But it could equally be the case that the six to nine months' interval before the new reservoir of trained manpower became available would actually provoke Hitler to pursue his aggressive plans in the period when the British Army would be experiencing the maximum degree of dislocation. Judging by events of the summer of 1939, Hitler was not in the least deterred and may indeed to some extent to have been 'provoked' by the combination of the Polish guarantee and the temporary weakening of the Army through the introduction of conscription. This is not to suggest, however, that

Britain 'caused' the Second World War by her guarantee to Poland. Seen in the short term, conscription was only in part intended to meet a military problem and in that respect it was, if anything, counter-productive. But psychologically the measure at least boosted British morale and gave a new feeling of purpose at home and in the Dominions. Together with other events and decisions that happened after Munich, it could be seen as a symbol that Britain was preparing to play a major part in a continental war.[39]

CHAPTER 11

Belated preparations for continental warfare, April–September 1939

Once the British Government had definitely accepted a continental military commitment in the spring of 1939, determined efforts were made to concert detailed arrangements with France. Simultaneously there was a hectic, and even desperate, endeavour to prepare the greatly expanded Army for its more onerous European role.

What proved to be an all-too-brief final phase of allied preparations for war with Germany began at the end of March 1939 when Anglo-French Staff talks were held on a higher level and with much wider scope. Almost up to the eve of this first conference the Chiefs of Staff continued to look on staff talks on anything potentially binding with suspicion and reluctance but they were overruled by the Foreign Office and the Cabinet. Then at the last stages, in February and early March, the French hung back, perhaps hoping that the swing in British public opinion would improve their bargaining position. Eventually the first session began on 29 March, amid the momentous diplomatic events following the German invasion of the rump of Czechoslovakia, and ended on 4 April, covering the formulation of a common policy for the conduct of war. The second stage, between 24 April and 3 May, dealt with the formulation of joint plans for all the likely war theatres. Thereafter liaison continued at various levels throughout the summer to settle outstanding questions ranging from the dispatch of the Field Force to the higher military and political command organizations.[1]

At an early point in the first meeting the French were bluntly informed of the limited and delayed support on land which they could expect from Britain in the immediate future. The first two divisions could not arrive in their assembly areas in France until 30 days after mobilization and the third division would not embark until about three months after mobilization. The time-table for the remaining forces—the fourth division, the mobile division, and (if conditions permitted) some Territorial divisions—filled the French representatives with dismay. Although they fully understood that conditions would be very different from those of 1914, they reasonably argued that the French people would not understand and would only remember that in 1914 Britain had sent an Expeditionary Force of six divisions much more rapidly than was now contemplated for a much smaller contingent. They were anxious about the first phase when the French Army would have to carry a heavy burden alone while the British divisions slowly assembled.

There was general agreement, however, that Allied strategy should initially be defensive. The first task would be to hold up a German offensive, and here the Maginot Line would be essential. Secondly, Britain and France should try to surround Germany with allies who would bring economic pressure to bear. In the third stage, they would go over to a counter-offensive, but it was not in the French interest to attack Germany directly. Assuming that the Low Countries remained neutral, the most profitable counter-offensive would be against Italy, in which case the British might replace some French divisions to release them for that role. When warned that Poland might become an ally, both delegations hastily prepared appreciations of the new situation. The British view was that neither ally could afford Poland (or Roumania) direct support against a German invasion. The French concluded that a Polish alliance would be of value only if it led to a long, solid, and durable second front in the east. Both appreciations emphasized the supreme importance of the Soviet Union as a source of military supplies for Poland.[2]

In the second phase of staff talks there was a more thorough appraisal of the strategic problems resulting from the allies' recent guarantees to Eastern European countries; and a completely new factor was introduced with the possible intervention of Japan as a third enemy. Both delegations confirmed their earlier pessimistic judgement that, if the Germans attacked 'It would . . . only be a matter of time before Poland was eliminated from the war.' The French took a more optimistic view of Russia's capability of operating outside her own territory, but the real problem was whether Poland or Roumania would invite the Red Army to intervene. At their final meeting on 3 May, the delegations considered the interesting question of what the allies could do if, as seemed increasingly possible, Germany stood on the defensive in the west and drove eastward against Poland. There was a far-fetched notion, more favoured by the French, that a joint attack on Italy would help to relieve Poland, but if Italy remained neutral even this very indirect approach would be ruled out. The leader of the French delegation, General Lelong, stressed that there was no question of a full-scale French attack on the Siegfried Line, and that Belgian and Dutch concern for their neutrality would probably rule out Belgium and Holland as an offensive springboard. Nor, he added, could there be any question of French forces being available for offensive operations elsewhere so long as the Germans were in a position to attack on the western front. The only prospect seemed to be to establish an eastern bloc comprising Poland, Roumania, Greece, and possibly Turkey. Group-Captain Slessor urged that air action in the West should be considered in order to ensure that Germany was faced with a two-front war, but the French had to refer this suggestion to Paris. The staff talks therefore ended indecisively on a matter of vital importance: the French were relying on an eastern front to take the pressure off themselves, whereas the British through military weakness were obliged to rely on the French to hold the western front for them. Neither delegation favoured creating a genuine western front by an immediate land offensive against Germany. Both delegations differed from their governments in that they recognized Soviet participation as essential to the creation of a real second front in the east.[3]

Because of the Anglio-French staffs' failure to reach agreement on any positive steps they could take to assist Poland if the Germans attacked eastward, the British tri-service delegation (at brigadier and equivalent level)[4] could not have departed with high hopes for the staff conversations due in Warsaw towards the end of May. Even so, the military realities and expectations in Poland came as a shock to them. The Poles were excessively optimistic about their own military capabilities but, at the same time, correctly assuming that the main blow would first fall exclusively on them, they expected the allies to launch major land and air offensives on the western front at the outset of the war. To make matters worse, the Poles had devised no plans for mutual military co-operation with Roumania, and were strongly opposed to the idea of Russian troops on their soil. Thus the problem was utterly intractable: Poland could certainly not survive long unaided but was bitterly opposed to co-operation with the only power which might give direct support. On the other hand, the Poles naturally (if naïvely) assumed that the allies would act in the spirit of their guarantee by attacking promptly and in force to create a second front. After further studies of the Polish situation in June and July, the COS concluded bluntly that the fate of Poland would depend upon the ultimate outcome of the war—that is, the eventual defeat of Germany. There was little we could do to relieve pressure on Poland, but even in regard to strategic bombing the COS were extremely cautious. They advised the Government to make it clear to the German people and to neutrals that air action taken by Britain would be directed only at objectives whose destruction would shorten the war. There was no intention of attacking the civil population as such and so Berlin, for example, would be excluded. This advice was tantamount to an obituary notice for Poland. In sum, the Government had given a pledge which it was unable or unwilling to implement militarily, while the same pledge had surrendered its political freedom to a country even further off than Czechoslovakia and, if anything, even less able to defend itself.[5]

It may seem strange that proposals to attack Italy should occur in discussions of how best to support Poland. This was, in fact, just one manifestation of the remarkable preoccupation of many British and, even more, French strategists with a policy of 'Italy first' which lasted through the spring and summer of 1939 almost to the outbreak of war. This strategic attitude was the product of several considerations not all openly avowed or fully thought out. Britain and France both had obvious reasons for wishing to secure their considerable interests in the Mediterranean at the outset in what might prove a long war; France mainly in order to devote her attention to Germany, Britain because she was constantly worried by the prospect of Japanese intervention when the strategic situation elsewhere was at its worst. Brief hopes in the spring of 1939 that the United States might take a more positive part in checking Japanese expansion in the Pacific encouraged British strategists, particularly in the Royal Navy, to contemplate a rapid knock-out blow against Italy. While it is also true that Service leaders in the Mediterranean theatre were mostly confident of their ability to defeat Italy, it is hard to resist the feeling that in Paris and London a more important (if unspoken) consideration was the pronounced fear of a direct military confrontation with Germany. In their staff discussions with the Poles the French made much of their plans to relieve Poland by an indirect attack on Italy. As if this were not circuitous enough, closer inspection reveals (and the British were aware) that the French had no intention of risking a direct air and land offensive against the mainland of Italy so long as there was the least danger of a German attack on their eastern front. What they really favoured, the attitude of Spanish Morocco permitting, was an offensive by their 14 divisions in Tunisia against Libya. In reality neither France nor Britain prepared detailed plans for a knock-out blow against Italy.[6]

It is unfortunate that British strategy towards Italy in 1939 was not thoroughly examined in the full context of British strategy as a whole at that time. Italy provided the most notable example of the chief military advisers' tendency to view each potential enemy in isolation in the light of the 'worst case' and so to exaggerate the difficulties of taking positive military action against any of them. Italy did indeed offer interesting possibilities because not only were all her armed services suffering from considerable weaknesses, but she also was terribly handicapped by lack of vital raw materials in the event of a long war. Whether or not, as the Joint Planning Committee advised, it would be impossible to knock her out quickly, was therefore irrelevant: it was all to the advantage of the western powers that a militarily crippled and battered Italian state be kept in the war at Germany's side. Even when, in July, the Chiefs of Staff did discuss Italy in the broad context of an allied strategy based essentially on putting economic pressure on Germany, they reached the conclusion that 'Italian neutrality, if it could by any means be assured, would be decidedly preferable to her active hostility'.[7]

Turning more particularly to the role of the British Army, we have seen in earlier chapters how some leading soldiers, notably Generals Ironside and Burnett-Stuart, welcomed the priority given to an Eastern theatre from the mid-1930s as being more within the competence of the small and underequipped Field Force. Sir John Kennedy later recalled that any suggestion that the Italians were a serious enemy was enough to enrage Lord Gort. With the important proviso *'so long as the Italians were the only enemy to be reckoned with'* (emphasis added), Kennedy recollected that the General Staff felt no alarm about the safety of Egypt: 'our only anxiety was that they [the Italians] might not advance far enough in the desert to come within striking distance'. In his diary for 1939 Ironside, who expected with some reason to command the Field Force in war, repeatedly maintained that the Mediterranean was the all-important theatre where Britain could win or lose the war, and the only place where a land offensive might be possible. Thus on 15 July he reflected that it was 'a snare and a delusion' to contemplate sending the Expeditionary Force to France. Why not send it to the crucial point, in the Middle East, where it could be more useful? He added that only by the capture of Egypt and the Suez Canal could Germany hope to win a short war. As late as 28 July he was urging (in a strategic paper) that Britain must try to inculcate an offensive plan: we should allot the minimum force to France and the maximum to an imperial strategy centred on the Suez Canal.[8] By the end of July, however, the majority of the Cabinet ministers (Hoare excepted) had come round to the Joint Planning Committee's view that it would be preferable for Britain if Italy remained neutral at the outset of a war against Germany. Indeed the JPC went even further and suggested that 'Italy could perhaps do us more harm at the outset than we her, for example by air attack on Malta and Egypt.'[9]

There is no need here to describe in detail the half-hearted efforts which Britain and France made in the summer of 1939 to secure allies in Eastern Europe. Now that a guarantee had been given to Poland she was the most obvious choice but the British Service delegation of middle-ranking officers in late

May brought back their disturbing news that the Polish military leaders were inclined to overrate their own strength and underestimate Germany's. On 4 July Ironside, who spoke Polish and knew the country, was instructed to fly to Warsaw at once to discover the Polish war plans, but it was typical of the desultory conduct of the quest for eastern allies that he did not leave until 17 July. Next day he sent an excessively reassuring telegram to the effect that the Poles would take no rash military action over the issue of Danzig; that their military effort was little short of prodigious; and that they were strong enough to resist. According to the editors of his diaries, however, he was more impressed by the Polish troops than their plans, correctly fearing that their main armies would not be able to withdraw quickly enough from the frontiers to avoid being encircled. On his return he was astonished to find that Hore-Belisha and Gort were going to discuss Poland at a CID meeting without having read his report or having even been properly briefed. Only at that meeting did most ministers become fully aware of the harsh reality that there was virtually no hope of confronting Hitler with a genuine two-front war.[10]

To be fair to the military advisers, they had appreciated more clearly than all but one or two politicians that since Germany's occupation of Czechoslovakia any chance of creating a second front in Eastern Europe depended on the co-operation of the Soviet Union. On 24 April the COS presented a full and well-balanced survey of 'The Military Value of Russia' in which they stressed the adverse effect of the purges on her capacity to conduct offensive operations. The only positive way Russia could assist Poland would be in air defence and attack, provided she were given advance bases there. She could not give much material assistance to any allies but her co-operation would be invaluable in denying sources of raw material to Germany.[11] Chamberlain and Halifax remained deeply opposed to a Russian alliance and when Ironside advised Chamberlain that, though it went against the grain, it was the only thing Britain could do, Chamberlain riposted, 'The only thing we cannot do.' Whether this meant that he thought such an alliance was ideologically unacceptable or unattainable is not clear. But the Anglo-French mission to Moscow in the late summer of 1939 was so belated, so low-level and lacking in authority to make definite contributions to an alliance that it was virtually doomed to failure unless the Russians felt they had no alternative. The German–Soviet Non-Aggression Pact signed on 23 August transformed the strategic situation in general and in particular sealed the fate of the Poles. The British Government and COS were already inclining to limit their air action severely to purely military targets so as to escape retaliation, and the loss of any possible air contribution from Russia only served to confirm that nothing could be done to save Poland. Her fate would depend on the ultimate defeat of Germany.[12]

In the summer of 1939 Anglo-French relations were closer and more friendly than at any time since the First World War. The definite commitment of the Regular Field Force to the Continent followed by the opening of full staff talks on 29 March had clearly helped to dispel the notion that Britain intended to leave all the hard fighting to her ally. Goodwill was further cemented by frequent visits and exchanges. Hore-Belisha and senior officers made regular visits to France to develop personal contacts and to look at the Maginot Line. Gamelin came to London early in June, nominally to see the Tattoo but really to meet Gort, Pownall, Chatfield, and other officers and tie up 'loose ends' after the staff talks. These included the nature and scale of British military missions at French headquarters; the air defence of the Field Force and its base ports; the concentration area for the Field Force; and the vexed question of operational control of the Advanced Air Striking Force. Gamelin's chief staff officer apologized for the incomplete state of the northern part of the Maginot Line, while Pownall proudly informed him that the first two divisions of the Field Force could now arrive 19 days after mobilization and the whole Regular Field Force in 34 days.[13]

Military sentiment was further fostered and co-operation enhanced by the attendance of Hore-Belisha, Churchill, Gort, Pownall, and other officers at the 14 July celebrations. Vital matters concerning the Field Force were amicably settled. A suitable assembly area for the British forces was agreed to be Le Mans. The French then proposed that the leading British Corps should concentrate in the St Pol area north of Amiens; but this was considered too far forward and so it was agreed that both Corps should concentrate in the Picquigny area on the

Somme north-west of Amiens. The British agreed that the Field Force should join the line on the French left if Belgium was neutral or between the French left and the Belgians if she came in. This arrangement, as Pownall noted, was commonsense even if it did look like repeating the line-up of 1914. It was also agreed that the British Commander-in-Chief should be subordinate to General Georges (Commander of the North-Eastern Front) but with adequate rights of appeal to the British Government similar to those of Sir John French in 1914. The British representatives, though satisfied by the outcome, felt acutely conscious throughout that they were in a weak bargaining position because of their small initial contribution on land. For the ceremonial march past on 14 July the British representatives took their place on the President's stand. The French troops looked as magnificent as ever, but the biggest cheer of the day greeted the British Guardsmen as they swung down the Champs Elysées. Churchill was heard to remark, 'Thank God we've got conscription or we couldn't look these people in the face.'[14]

The question of Allied Supreme Control was too important to be included in the staff talks. On 6 July Chamberlain proposed to Daladier that a Supreme War Council should be set up, meeting either in Britain or France, on which Britain and France would be represented by their Prime Ministers and other allies by their ambassadors. The Council would have no executive authority, leaving final decisions to Governments. Military advisers at the Supreme War Council would be subordinate to their own Chiefs of Staff, thus avoiding the difficulty of rival military authorities like those created at Versailles in November 1917. Britain also proposed the immediate creation of a permanent inter-allied joint staff in London but Gamelin disliked the idea and it was not implemented until after war began.[15]

Despite the rapid progress made between April and September, the Anglo-French alliance brought little reassurance to its friends and failed to deter Hitler. Although it would take the stresses of war to expose the deep political differences and misunderstandings, some flaws were apparent even in peacetime. In mid-July, for example, British military planners were disturbed to discover that, whereas their guidelines and proposals in the staff conversations had been fully approved by ministers, the French Service chiefs did not trust their politicians sufficiently to bring them into the picture at all. 'The attitude of the French General Staff', wrote Ismay, 'was to withhold from their politicians all strategical plans and policy against the possibility of leakage.' Other problems were not fully divulged, or not known at all by the other partner. Thus the British were not aware of the deep personal rift between the two senior French generals with whom they would have to co-operate, Gamelin and Georges, while the French probably did not know that Gort and Ironside were scarcely on speaking terms with Hore-Belisha. Moreover, it is doubtful if the French fully appreciated the complete lack of agreement among the Chiefs of Staff as to the role of air power in long-range bombing and co-operation with the other two Services.[16]

As well as its own weaknesses and deficiencies, the Army suffered throughout the inter-war period from its indifferent relations with the RAF, to which it inevitably seemed a suppliant with little bargaining power. When a continental military commitment was at last accepted in 1939, it served to bring to a head years of wrangling over the strength and composition of the Field Force's air-support squadrons and the means by which they were to be operationally controlled. These controversies revealed a long-standing deficiency in both the strength and quality of tactical air support for the Field Force but, despite the urgent need for closer inter-service co-operation, there was no marked improvement before war broke out.[17]

The extremely low priority of the Expeditionary Force during the operation of the Ten Year Rule makes it understandable that, as CIGS in 1926, Milne should have conceded that the Government could not be expected to provide sufficient funds to furnish the aircraft required for home defence and the Army. Because of this he had agreed that the air needs of an Expeditionary Force should be met from squadrons allocated to home defence if and when they were available. For his part Trenchard, the CAS, undertook to earmark ten home defence squadrons as the nucleus of an air contingent for the Expeditionary Force. Despite Trenchard's assurances, however, there is little evidence to show that these squadrons received any special training to prepare them for possible employment with the Army.[18]

Indeed, except for a brief period during the exercises of the Experimental Mechanized Force in 1927 and 1928, contacts between the two Services were minimal. In 1925, for example, an Army critic complained that out of seventeen stations in the RAF's Inland Area, all but two—Salisbury Plain and Farnborough—were completely out of touch with Army units. There were only four squadrons (48 aircraft) definitely allotted to co-operation with the Army and even in these pilots were not permanently assigned to inter-Service duties. Courses in co-operation were held in a few centres but they made little impression in the RAF where the great weight of official teaching emphasized the predominant role which independent air power would play in the next war. There was even a case of the War Office being taken to task by the Air Ministry for encouraging young pilots to carry out low-level attacks during joint-Service exercises.[19] In 1934 the CAS, Sir Edward Ellington, admitted that, although the Army kept in close touch with their co-operation squadrons, 'their contact with bomber and fighter units only took place at certain times during higher training exercises'. Air Vice Marshal A. J. Capel* later recalled that when he was Commandant of the School of Army Co-operation at Old Sarum between 1936 and 1938 there was very little if any instruction in close-support tactics. Nor did he recall any pressure being brought to bear by the Air Ministry or the War Office for the provision of such instruction.[20]

At that time the Spanish Civil War was providing abundant evidence of close-support tactics under battle conditions; for example, aircraft were successfully employed in combination with ground forces and in carrying out low-flying attacks on troop concentrations and lines of communication. Yet the Air Staff remained unconvinced that the Spanish experience offered valid lessons for Britain. Newall, the CAS, described such methods of air support on the battlefield as 'a gross misuse of air forces', and pointed out with some justification that most of the successful air attacks in Spain had been against inexperienced, untrained troops who lacked effective anti-aircraft defence.[21] Only a few months before the outbreak of the Second World War the Assistant Chief of Air Staff showed that official thinking remained unrevised when he asserted at an inter-Service meeting that close-support tactics required no specialized training. He claimed that, fundamentally, all bomber training was the same and that the nature of the objective had little effect on the methods employed.[22]

While the RAF was mainly to blame for this lack of co-operation, however, it must be stressed that the Army was far from guiltless. Very few soldiers, and not even some of the pioneers of mechanized warfare, fully grasped the potential importance of the integrated role to be played by aircraft in ground operations. It is significant that the War Office's 28-page booklet, 'Notes on Lessons of the Great War,' which was not published until 1934, contained only one anodyne sentence on the subject of close air support: 'The addition of low flying assault fighters as maintained by some foreign countries is also worthy of consideration.' Furthermore the War Office displayed little interest in trying out low-level air attacks on the rare occasions when the opportunity arose in the 1930s. In the large-scale Army manœuvres of 1935, for example, so much stress was placed on the avoidance of risks to pilots and ground forces that the possibilities of close air support in the attack were not given a realistic test.[23] The one area of the Empire where there was a considerable amount of warlike experience of direct air support of infantry was the North West Frontier of India, but the lessons do not seem to have filtered through to the Services at home. This was a pity because these operations raised important problems of general relevance such as the need for a more reliable means of direct contact between aircraft and front-line troops, and for closer liaison between the air and ground commanders.[24]

On the higher level of inter-Service policy the informal understanding reached by Milne and Trenchard endured without serious challenge until 1935 when the Army's air needs were reviewed in connection with the 'Western Plan' then in course of preparation. The War Office, now anxious to secure a definite allocation from the RAF, asked for seven bomber and five fighter squadrons to accompany the first contingent of the Field Force, and a further six bomber and four fighter squadrons for each of the three subsequent contingents. The Air Ministry considered this request excessive, particularly the bomber squadrons, and contended that the number of bombers allocated and how they would be controlled could only be decided in the circumstances prevailing when a crisis arose. It was eventually agreed that only two bomber squadrons could be considered as allocated to the field contingent, the provision of a further six being dependent on their availability when war began. Five fighter squadrons (later reduced to four but with the same number of aircraft) were allocated to the first contingent as requested. The allocation of bomber and fighter squadrons to subsequent contingents was to be resolved only after mobilization.[25]

Although negotiations continued between the two Services, the Air Ministry's preoccupation with an independent bombing policy and the War Office's uncertainty over the Field Force's role ruled out any definite agreement during the next three years. Thus at the beginning of 1939 the question of tactical control remained unsolved and the Army could only count on the support of a small air component consisting of two bomber reconnaissance squadrons, six Army Co-operation squadrons, four fighter squadrons, and two flights of communication aircraft. In March the Army Council requested the allocation of five additional Army Co-operation squadrons to meet the immediate needs of the much enlarged Field Force. Shortly afterwards, when the Government announced the 32-division programme, the CIGS, Lord Gort, made a direct challenge to Air Staff policy by demanding a small striking force of bombers as an integral part of the Field Force under military control and available for the day-to-day tasks associated with the bombing of close objectives.[26] On 12 June the War Office submitted a long memorandum to the Chiefs of Staff pointing out that several countries, including the Soviet Union and Germany, were committing reconnaissance and bomber aircraft to the close support of ground forces in an offensive role. The War Office stressed that it was not asking for an Army Air Arm analogous to the Fleet Air Arm, but it argued that the Army as the 'user' should exercise general control while the RAF should continue to be responsible for technical training, the administration of units, and the provision and maintenance of aircraft and other equipment. The memorandum called for an allocation to the Army of 1,440 first-line aircraft with special emphasis on close-support aircraft and short-range bombers.[27]

Not surprisingly, the Air Staff reacted sharply to the notion that any aircraft, other than the small Air Component definitely assigned to the Field Force, should be placed under military control and employed on tactical missions in close support of the Army. The CAS, Newall, warned that the dissipation of bomber squadrons into 'small packets' over a wide front would preclude the concentration of maximum effort at the decisive point. He was even further at odds with the Army view in arguing that fighter support should be used to strengthen the general defences of the Allied air front in France rather than for the close protection of the comparatively small Expeditionary Force.[28]

It is ironic that the Air Staff's chief critic of the War Office's memorandum should be the Director of Plans, Group-Captain (later Marshal of the Royal Air Force Sir John) Slessor, since in his *Air Power and Armies* (1936) he had displayed unusual interest in and understanding of the problems of air–ground co-operation. He raised three major objections to the War Office's requests: their aircraft figures were far too high to meet within a reasonable time and could only be achieved in the short term at the expense of home defence and the Metropolitan air forces; they had not been carefully thought out tactically and were far in excess of what other countries such as Germany considered necessary; and, finally, they betrayed a misconception of RAF bombing policy in support of ground operations. His fundamental point of disagreement was that in his view the bomber was not a battlefield weapon: it would be wasteful and inefficient to employ bombers in 'penny packets' under the orders of Army commanders on tasks which could be more suitably carried out by tanks and artillery. The bomber's task was to isolate the battlefield. Behind these arguments, however, there lurked echoes of the bitter inter-Service rivalry and mutual suspicion over 'substitution', as when Slessor remarked that 'when the soldier talks about co-operation between the Air Force and the Army he really means the subordination of the Air Force to the Army'. If the War Office proposals were accepted in full, he concluded, the RAF would become 'the manufacturers, garage proprietors and chauffeurs for the Army'.[29]

When the Joint War Office and Air Ministry Committee, set up to avoid an outright clash in the Chiefs of Staff Committee, eventually met on 30 June 1939 the two parties trod warily, skirting the fringes of the more explosive issues. The General Staff position was that they wished to inform the Air Ministry of the fullest requirements they could visualize. For their part the Air Staff recognized in principle the Army's need for air support but were anxious to avoid locking up air forces on a number of subsidiary tasks by a too rigid allocation. There was some progress on the question of Army co-operation aircraft but several major issues, such as the strength and command structure of the proposed bomber force, and the type of aircraft most suitable for the role of close support, were still undecided on the outbreak of war.[30]

The first contingent of the Expeditionary Force thus sailed for France with the very modest air support of the Air Component, consisting of two bomber reconnaissance squadrons, six Army co-operation squadrons, four fighter squadrons, and two flights of a headquarters communications squadron. It was preceded to France by the Advanced Air Striking Force of medium bombers whose commander was completely independent of the C.-in-C. of the Expeditionary Force (and of the French high command) and received orders direct from Bomber Command. The role of the AASF was not to collaborate with land forces but to bring bombers nearer to military targets in Germany. This peculiar command system provoked the wry comment from General Ismay that 'It almost seemed as though the Air Staff would prefer to have their forces under Beelzebub rather than anyone connected with the Army.' But as a senior soldier deeply versed in inter-Service politics he added impartially, 'When one recalls the views which were then held by the General Staff on the employment of air power, one can scarcely blame them.'[31]

It would take the greater part of the Second World War, and a great deal more controversy, before really effective battlefield co-operation was achieved between the RAF and the Army.

In the summer of 1939 the Army was in a profound state of disarray caused by the sudden changes which had been imposed upon its size, organization, and priorities and which had been introduced more in reaction to foreign and public pressure than in response to professional advice. The doubling of the Territorial Army by a proverbial stroke of the pen, the introduction of conscription, the expansion of anti-aircraft defences, and the definite commitment of the Field Force to France created conditions of near chaos which could not be remedied within a few months. Not the least consequence of these changes was the fact that, in spite of years of invoking the bitter lessons of the First World War, Britain in 1939 seemed to be once again bent on creating a mass infantry army that would be suitable only for a static war of attrition. As Pownall recorded in April when the Cabinet finally gave authority for the full equipping of the Army:

At last they have done it! But what a lamentable story of delays and uncertainties and indecisions lasting over three full years. If the story ever comes to be written it will be a terrible indictment of our Government. Better late than never, if you like, but late indeed it is, for it will take at least eighteen months, more likely two years, before this paper Army is an Army in the flesh.[32]

In a private letter of 2 June 1939, Laurence Carr,* the Director of Staff Duties at the War Office, graphically described the problems which the progressive expansion of the Army on paper had posed for the provision of arms and equipment:

We have led and still are leading an extremely busy life at the War Office, and from my point of view, namely the equipment of the Army other than A.D.G.B. it is a trying time. The main difficulty has been the gradual broadening of the basis of calculation. If only it had been possible to go large from the start all would have been well now. You will recall that in April 1938 we received a charter to prepare for a F.F. of 4 divs and a mobile div to be rearmed for a war in the Middle East, the rearmament to be spread over 5 years. The T.A. did not come in except for the necessity of providing them with a bare minimum training equipment. With this mill stone of 5 years in which to rearm the provision departments could not develop a very large increase in armament factories. As the basis of our readiness for war has been progressively increased the original lay out has proved quite inadequate. For heavy araments like Cruiser and 'I' Tanks and medium guns no new factory can start production in much under a year. In Oct 1938 our charter was changed to a continental war with a second Mobile Div and 4 T.A. divs added to the F.F. We worked out all requirements for this, and the provision departments had just got under weigh [*sic*] as to how the additional equipment might be produced. Then in February 1939 the Cabinet in order to save money reduced the rate of despatch of the above mentioned F.F. knowing that by so doing there would not be so many reserves to be held in peace. This meant another re-calculation.

At the end of March 1939 the P.M. suddenly announced the scheme of doubling the T.A. . . . and at the same time stated that the necessary equipment and war potential for the 32 divs regular and T.A. would be provided . . . This has meant a complete new conspectus involving a mass of work . . . You will realise the vast increase of all types of equipment (both unit and reserve) required to meet this charter . . . Even now working night shifts the factories can only make minor improvements on our output. So new factories have to be found, and we know that roughly speaking they will produce nothing for a year.[33]

In the light of the Government's belated acceptance of the continental commitment and the sudden increases in the Army's size, it is obvious that no amount of hard work and improvization could equip and train the Field Force for a major war in 1939, or even perhaps in 1940.

In July a review of the difficulties of the regular infantry divisions of the Field Force revealed that there were available only 72 out of 240 heavy anti-aircraft guns and only 30 per cent of the approved scale of ammunition; only 108 out of 226 light anti-aircraft guns and 144 out of 240 anti-tank guns. The shortage of anti-aircraft guns could only be remedied at the expense of ADGB, itself already short. Moreover, the field artillery units would not yet have received any of the new 25-pounder guns. Finally, at the risk of some delay in the embarkation of the Field Force, ADGB had been given priority for lorries and some other vehicles. In the final pre-war progress report from the War Office, tanks, small arms, cordite, gauges, and fuses were included in the list of items in short supply caused by inadequate production capacity. In August a War Office spokesman admitted that only 60 infantry tanks were available, against a total requirement of 1,646. As for training, there had been no large-scale Army manœuvres for several years and Ironside had been counting on the September exercises to get I Corps into good order. As he gloomily noted in his diary, the units he had observed lacked even rudimentary tactical skills. Thus in September the first four divisions of the Field Force sailed to France inadequately trained and short of every type of equipment, especially guns and tanks. The remainder of the growing citizen army at home was reduced to 'a token force of semi-trained troops' lacking the equipment for realistic training.[34]

It is often asserted that the BEF in 1939 was the only Army to go to war 'fully mechanized'. True, the Army no longer depended on horse transport, but a more accurate term would be 'motorized' and even then the situation was far from ideal. Montgomery, recently appointed to command the 3rd Division, recalled that on mobilization transport had to be supplemented by requisitioning from civilian firms: 'much of the transport of my division consisted of civilian vans and lorries from the towns of England; they were in bad repair and, when my division moved from the ports up to its concentration area near the French frontier, the countryside of France was strewn with broken down vehicles'. He also noted that the Field Force had an inadequate signals system, no administrative backing, and no organization for high command; all had to be improvized on mobilization. He was dissatisfied with his division's anti-tank weapons, and remarked that he never saw any tanks of the single Army Tank Brigade either during the winter or the operations in May 1940. 'It must be said to our shame', he recorded caustically in his *Memoirs*, 'that we sent our Army into that most modern war with weapons and equipment which were quite inadequate.'[35]

Justified though these criticisms undoubtedly were from the viewpoint of senior commanders and staff officers, it needs to be stressed that an extraordinary transformation was beginning to affect the Army's spirit, style of life, and working conditions in the months preceding the outbreak of war. Though Hore-Belisha benefited from the expert unofficial advice of Liddell Hart and received strong support from enlightened soldiers within the War Office, such as Sir Ronald Adam, he himself deserves most of the credit for introducing a wide variety of salutary reforms.

Like his great predecessor Haldane, Hore-Belisha began his ministry by firing a barrage of questions at members of the Army Council. In particular he asked why so few men were being attracted to the Army and why so many already in the Service were leaving it. Not content with their answers, he set out to see for himself. He talked to ordinary soldiers; inspected barracks; looked into the kitchens and sampled the food; and went aboard a troopship. He quickly reached the conclusion that the Army must be made a proper career and one that would provide a pension relatively early in life. The normal period of enlistment was seven years with the colours and five with the reserve: few privates were allowed to re-enlist to qualify for a pension and little effort was made to ensure that soldiers were equipped to secure a decent job on re-entering civil life. Hore-Belisha also cherished the grander ambition to enhance the soldier's standing in the community. 'The Army', as he neatly put it, 'is a part of the nation and not apart from the nation.'

Within a few months of taking up office, Hore-Belisha introduced a scheme to enable serving soldiers to extend their service to twenty-one years and a pension, and for reservists to rejoin the colours on the same terms. Despite the scepticism of some Army Council members there was an immediate improvement in recruiting. Simultaneously he set about removing or relaxing the petty restrictions which tended to degrade the soldier to a status below that of the civilian. An important concession, for example, was to permit married soldiers for whom no quarters were provided in barracks to sleep out. He also adjusted the absurd regulations regarding false teeth and slightly defective vision which were costing the Army the service of many otherwise perfectly fit recruits. Despite acute financial pressures for rearmament, large sums of money were invested in modern 'Belisha barracks' which were centrally heated, equipped with shower baths and well-sprung beds, and with recreation rooms containing wireless sets. Schools of cookery were established for the special training of Army cooks so that soldiers should enjoy a better cooked and more varied diet. There were also several improvements in dress. The awkward puttee was replaced by a more comfortable anklet far more suitable for drivers of tanks and lorries; a more attractive walking-out dress was devised and the battledress—subsequently adopted by several other armies—was introduced. The War Minister's genius for exploiting newspaper publicity for the Army's (and incidentally his own) benefit also gained him the services and support of several eminent public figures. Thus Sir Isadore Salmon MP, the Managing Director of J. Lyons and Co., was appointed Honorary Catering Adviser to the Army and Sir Frederick Marquis (later Earl of Woolton), the Managing Director of

Lewis and Co. of Liverpool, accepted a similar appointment dealing with clothing and textiles. Lord Nuffield donated one million shares in Morris Motors, yielding more than £100,000 interest per annum, towards improving recreational facilities for the Territorials and Reserve forces.

Lastly, Liddell Hart's influence was evident in the introduction of numerous measures designed for the improvement of military training, education, and junior leadership. A modernized and simplified system of infantry drill, more adaptable to battle conditions and less concerned with elaborate ceremonial movements, was adopted. More imaginative methods of basic training and fieldcraft, including practice in night operations, were introduced, particularly in Ironside's Eastern Command. Tactical schools were set up for junior commanders, and increased responsibility was given to NCOs by creating a new grade (Warrant Officer Class III) to command platoons. There was a notable improvement in the relations between officers and men and a new spirit of co-operation in urgent preparations to meet the impending war. Hore-Belisha, acutely sensing and reinforcing an awakening public interest in the Army, gave soldiering more dignity and purpose; under his regime the atmosphere of a 'People's Army' was replacing that of a leisurely and privileged gentleman's club.[36]

Montgomery's fleeting allusion to the lack of organization for high command refers in part to the scarcely credible fact that the Commander-in-Chief and Chief of Staff of the Expeditionary Force were not selected until after the declaration of war on 3 September. Nor did either of these appointments, or the most vital one of the CIGS, fall to the officers widely expected to fill them. The background to this astonishing omission on the part of the Government highlights the confusion and indecision concerning the Field Force and its leaders in the summer of 1939.

In the discussions that followed the acceptance of a continental role for the Field Force, the British Government paid considerable attention to the higher control of Anglo-French strategy but curiously little to a choice of commander for the force. Lord Gort's biographer attributes this omission, surely correctly, to the fact that 'the ruling cabal was utterly divorced, in interest and experience, from military affairs. The command would be of vital interest to the nation: yet, subject to the Cabinet's final endorsement, Chamberlain was content to leave the decision to the Secretary of State for War.'[37] The most obvious disadvantage resulting from this omission was that the staff officers and unit commanders could not train under their chief's direction and build up a team spirit before the war. Even more seriously, the last-minute selection resulted in some questionable appointments whose repercussions were apparent throughout the campaign in France.

In May 1939 Hore-Belisha consulted his *eminence grise*, Liddell Hart, about the relative abilities of Alexander, Maitland Wilson, Dill, Wavell, and Ironside as potential C.-in-C. Liddell Hart, characteristically, plumped for two dynamic outsiders in Hobart and Pile—who were both advocates of tank warfare—and also spoke highly of Adam, then DCIGS at the War Office (and really the mainstay of the General Staff since Gort was scarcely on speaking terms with Hore-Belisha). Hore-Belisha, however, announced that he intended to recall Ironside from Gibraltar with the title of Inspector-General of the Overseas Forces as the likely C.-in-C. of the Field Force if war came.

Ironside consequently returned to England with the conviction that he was to command the Field Force. A French staff officer had already told Gamelin on 8 June that Ironside would be easy to work with, and after a conversation with Gort on 1 July Ironside noted in his diary: 'The only thing I found out was that the main reason of my coming home was to command [the BEF] in case of war.' Hore-Belisha encouraged him in this belief, which was further strengthened by the fact that Sir John French had briefly had a similar post before being appointed to command the BEF in 1914. Another strong contender was Sir John Dill who was then GOC.-in-C. at Aldershot. Senior French officers, including Gamelin, who attended the Aldershot Tattoo in June certainly left with the impression that Dill was Commander-in-Chief designate and made it plain that he would be very acceptable to them. Yet, during this same French visit, General Lelong, their Military Attaché, mentioned to Brigadier Beaumont-Nesbitt,* formerly British Military Attaché in Paris and now back at the War Office, that Gort would be very acceptable to the French as commander of the Field Force whereas Ironside would not. Whether this opinion filtered through to Hore-Belisha and if so how much it influenced him is uncertain.[38]

The awkward situation that prevailed in the three months before the outbreak of war can be summarized as follows: the responsibilities of Ironside and Gort were not clearly distinguished and the former had good reason to believe that he would command the Field Force; Dill's experience and present command also gave him a strong lien on the appointment; Gort's relations with Hore-Belisha were so strained that he was eager to quit the War Office and knew the minister would be relieved to see him go.

Hore-Belisha's failure to reach a firm decision led to a tragicomic episode when war was declared on 3 September 1939. Ironside, reasonably assuming that he would be appointed, sent his chief staff officer, Lieutenant-Colonel Roderick Macleod, to Aldershot to organize his GHQ staff but then hung about vainly awaiting a call from the War Office. According to P. J. Grigg, the forceful Permanent Under-Secretary of State, Hore-Belisha was still set on making Ironside CIGS or C.-in-C. but Grigg urged that he should be given neither and that the best combination would be Gort as C.-in-C. and Dill as CIGS. Hore-Belisha, however, accepted only Grigg's first recommendation, and won over his fellow Service ministers and the new War Cabinet to Gort's appointment. According to Liddell Hart, 'Gort was eager to take the field as C-in-C of the B.E.F., so Hore-Belisha and the Cabinet met his wish', but there is no other evidence that the initiative came from Gort, though he was certainly delighted. Hore-Belisha's proposal of Ironside as CIGS met with some opposition from the War Cabinet on the grounds of his lack of judgement and discretion but Churchill's strong backing was decisive.

Ironside has described the dramatic scene at the War Office in which Hore-Belisha first persuaded him by an appeal to soldierly duty to accept the uncongenial post of CIGS, and then ushered in Gort from his private office with the words 'And here is our Commander-in-Chief.' Gort at once asked for Pownall (the Director of Military Operations) as his Chief of Staff, and got his way despite Ironside's objection that this would deprive the War Office of the two men chiefly responsible for military planning and liaison with the French, and so repeat the mistake of 1914.[39]

Of these appointments, Ironside's was the most questionable. He had had more experience of senior command in war than any other serving British general, but had no experience whatever of staff work at the War Office, and was by his own admission in his diaries unsuited to be CIGS. Whether he would have done better than Gort is impossible to say; he might conceivably been less complacent in accepting French strategic planning during the Phoney War, and he would surely have taken a stronger independent line during the early stages of the operations in May 1940. Dill was better suited in terms of physical fitness and ability to be CIGS than a Corps commander and he certainly proved better at the job than Ironside, whom he replaced in May 1940. Gort at least did well to quit the War Office, not only because of his exceedingly poor relationship with Hore-Belisha, but also because—in the admirably impartial summing up of his biographer—'he would have been far out of his depth as CIGS under Churchill's wartime Government'.[40] These last-minute appointments, upsetting as they were not only to most of the individuals concerned but also to the smooth functioning of the War Office, epitomize the Government's reluctance to face up to the prospect of continental war.

Perhaps the most creditable aspect of the War Office's pre-war planning lay in the detailed administrative arrangements for the movement of the BEF to France. That mobilization, transportation to its allotted French ports, and advance to its assembly areas all went according to plan, was primarily due to a year's painstaking staff work and liaison by Brigadier (later Major-General) L. A. Hawes* and a small team of officers at the War Office.[41]

When Hawes took up his appointment in mid-1938 he found nothing in the form of a worthwhile plan even for the scanty force than available. There was no accurate information about conditions in France, particularly about ports and railways. For example, the number of quays and docks available was useless without details of the depth of water and navigational hazards. Worse still, there were no up-to-date maps of France. There were so few administrative personnel available from the RAOC,

RASC, Royal Engineers, and Royal Signals that at the time of the Munich crisis it would have been practically impossible for the Army to mobilize: for one thing, the only mobilization tables to be had were for horse-drawn units. In fact, Hawes sums up, when war appeared imminent in late August 1938 the War Office 'was like an ant heap that had been stirred up with a stick'.

After gathering as much information from the French as possible by an exchange of questionnaires, Hawes and his subordinates paid several visits to the main ports which would be used by the BEF including Nantes, St Nazaire, Brest, and Havre, and he also arranged billeting for a vast GHQ in the concentration area.

The main points of the Army plan (W1) were:

1. Because of the risk of air attack the main ports of disembarkation were to be on the western coast. This meant a longer sea passage, but was thought to be safer than the use of the Channel ports both for shipping and for the landing of troops, equipment, supplies, and stores.
2. There were to be two main bases—a northern base at Rennes and a southern base at St Nazaire–Nantes. There was also to be a medical base at Dieppe.
3. The chief ports to be used were Cherbourg (for personnel, with motor transport drivers); Brest (all stores for the northern base, with motor transport and drivers); St Nazaire (ammunition and frozen meat for the southern base, with motor transport and drivers); and Nantes (other stores for the southern base and, again, motor transport and drivers).[42]

By July 1939 maps had arrived, the naval escort had been arranged, and planning was nearly complete. The last major peacetime achievement of the administrative planners was to mislead the Germans as to which ports would be used. Dummy reconnaissances persuaded the enemy to concentrate his submarines on the Havre–Rouen–Dieppe area and neglect Nantes–St Nazaire. Until 15 August arrangements existed for the dispatch of only two divisions but they were expanded to cover four just before the outbreak of war. The Directors of the War Office Departments were handed the detailed plans only at the last moment and the planners retired to the background.

In the event the movement of the regular contingent of the Expeditionary Force (four divisions) was carried out smoothly, on schedule, and (despite the dire warnings of a massacre from the air or from submarines), without a single loss of life. Advance parties sailed from Portsmouth on 4 September and the first main troop landings took place at Cherbourg on 10 September and at Nantes and St Nazaire two days later. By 27 September more than 160,000 soldiers and airmen with over 23,000 vehicles and a vast tonnage of equipment, stores, and supplies had arrived in France. On 3 October I Corps (1st and 2nd Divisions) commanded by Lieutenant-General Sir John Dill, began taking over part of the frontier defences on the sector between Maulde and Halluin allotted to the BEF. Nine days later II Corps (3rd and 4th Divisions) commanded by Lieutenant-General A. F. Brooke also began moving into the line.[43]

This prompt appearance in the front line, even though largely symbolic since the allies were not expecting a German attack before November at the earliest, was no mean achievement for an Army which only a year previously had been definitely cast for an extra-European role against inferior opposition. Nevertheless, for all the brave show, enthusiasm, and confidence the Expeditionary Force was still unready to withstand the might of the *Wehrmacht* and the *Luftwaffe*. Shattering though the débâcle in May 1940 was to be, it must be considered fortunate from the viewpoint of the British Army that the western front remained 'all quiet' in 1939.

CONCLUSION

The story unfolded in these pages has been unavoidably tinged with melancholy: years of neglect of the Army in peacetime and its relegation to imperial policing duties contributed to a predictable series of defeats and fiascos between 1939 and 1942 including Norway, France, Dakar, Crete, Greece, North Africa, Malaya, Burma, and Dieppe. It is therefore interesting to speculate what difference it would have made, particularly to the first nine months or so of the war in Europe, had Britain accepted—and firmly adhered to—a continental commitment as early as 1934 when the first DRC report strongly advocated such a policy. It is quite possible that such a positive political and military gesture would have prevented Belgium's return to neutrality and would have helped to consolidate a genuine Anglo-French–Belgian front against German aggression in the West. Since, as is now widely agreed, Hitler was reluctant to contemplate war with Britain and her Empire, he might well have been deterred by such a formidable combination bearing in mind that Germany was far from ready for a major war even in 1939.

Failing deferrence, however, a strong case can be made that an earlier British military commitment would have enabled the allies to check the German advance in 1940 and so would have provided time for that deliberate process of mobilization which both sides expected to favour the defenders. Much, of course, would have depended on the quality of the British contribution. A large conscript army was not essential; indeed, it would have been counter-productive because it would have diverted already inadequate industrial resources away from the Army's mobile offensive component, and would have interfered with the rearmament of the other two Services. But a small, well-equipped Regular contingent with a spearhead of two or three armoured divisions could quite conceivably have launched a decisive counter-offensive in May 1940. Such an élite force could only have been provided had the Army's European role been given a high priority by 1936 at the latest. In the event a long period of procrastination which culminated in the remarkable decision virtually to abandon the Army's European role in December 1937 militated against clear thinking and technical innovation. The unfortunate effects of this fatal indecision were most obvious in the development of armoured fighting vehicles. By the end of 1936 the great majority of existing tanks were light models only suitable for colonial warfare. The War Office had prepared a comprehensive requirements list for light mechanized cavalry tanks, medium models, and heavy infantry assault tanks, but throughout 1937 and 1938 little was done to produce new types, mainly because incentive was lacking so long as the policy of limited liability prevailed.

Close acquaintance with official documents can sometimes persuade the scholar that the line of policy followed was the only possible one. This temptation has been firmly rejected here. Despite the undeniably serious problems posed by the economic situation, the electorate's assumed hostility towards rearmament, and the rapid appearance of three potential enemies in widely separated theatres, British Governments in the middle and later 1930s allowed wishful thinking to blind them to strategic reality. The Chiefs of Staff and the Defence Requirements Committee were correct in their repeated affirmations that with the advent of air power Britain's vital strategic interests were, even more than in the past, inextricably bound up with the security of Western Europe. Furthermore, as they vainly reiterated against political scepticism or hostility, a small but modernized Expeditionary Force was essential for both strategic and moral reasons to safeguard these continental interests. It was ironic that intelligent senior Army officers, like Gort, Dill, and Pownall who saw the point so clearly, were conservative in their thinking about the kind of Expeditionary Force needed for a specialized European role, whereas Liddell Hart (and to a lesser extent Burnett-Stuart) were prophetically perceptive in pressing for a highly mobile, mechanized Army but opposed the European commitment which alone could have justified the creation of such an élite force.

This study endorses the argument advanced by Pownall at the time that the Government's reluctant move towards accepting a continental commitment in the months after Munich was not a revolution in strategy but merely a belated recognition of geographical and political realities. So late in the day was this commitment accepted, however, that time was lacking to create a genuine Western Alliance in either political or strategic terms. Prolonged indecision over the Army's priorities also did nothing to improve the already strained relations between the Services, one result being that Army–Air Force co-operation was, to put it mildly, still in a rudimentary state in 1940.

In spite of the great recent outpouring of books on British policy and military strategy in the 1930s there is no consensus among historians on some of the major issues, especially where the emotive term 'appeasement' is involved. Nor is further intense scrutiny of the official records likely to resolve many of the points at issue since so much depends on each particular author's vantage point. This volume has been written in the conviction that military policy, its relationships with diplomacy and its effect on the Army's preparedness for war, have been insufficiently taken into account in most studies of the Munich era.

Those who write about comparatively recent history are under considerable pressure to provide 'lessons' that are of continuing relevance in the nuclear age, but I offer no apology for examining the inter-war period on its own terms and for its own intrinsic interest. Nevertheless it has been impossible to avoid the depressing thought that many of the intractable problems confronting the makers of British defence policy in the 1930s are still with us today. Our economic problems, though in some respects very different from those of the 1930s, seem equally baffling; unemployment figures are distressingly high and Army recruiting figures low; while Parliament, the Press, and the public seem, if possible, even less concerned about our military weaknesses than before Munich. Nor, it is safe to predict, will future historians of British defence policy in the 1970s be able to draw upon such lively and radical debates *within* the Services—as reflected in the professional journals—as occurred in the 1930s. Admittedly there is now no overt military threat as obvious as that of Hitler's Germany, and it is tempting to assume fatalistically that a war between the super powers would automatically lead to a nuclear holocaust. In one respect British defence policy towards Europe since 1945 has differed sharply from that of the 1930s: successive Governments have unequivocally accepted a continental military commitment which, in principle at any rate, has become more rather than less important with the passing years. Whether, however, the majority of her political representatives and the electorate as a whole have fully accepted that Britain is strategically inseparable from Western Europe is another matter. One can only hope that, in contrast to the 1930s, deterrence will continue to work and that military weaknesses caused by a combination of complacency, indifference, and deliberate neglect will not again be exposed to the test of battle.

NOTES

Notes to Introduction

[1] Correlli Barnett, *The Collapse of British Power*, (1972), p. 305.

[2] N. H. Gibbs, 'British Strategic Doctrine 1918–1939', in Michael Howard (ed.), *The Theory and Practice of War* (1965), p. 194.

[3] H. Essame, *The Battle for Europe 1918* (1972). J. Terraine, *Impacts of War 1914 and 1918* (1970), and *To Win a War: 1918, the Year of Victory* (1978).

[4] J. E. Edmonds, *Military Operations: France and Belgium 1918*, vol. v (1947), pp. 570–600.

[5] Brian Bond *The Victorian Army and the Staff College, 1854–1914* (1972), pp. 299–329, 338–40. I am indebted to John Terraine for information concerning the number of p.s.c.s in the Army List in 1914 and the number of staff officers in France in 1918.

[6] *Statistics of the Military Effort of the British Empire, 1914–1920* (1922), pp. 561, 624, 639, 739–40.

[7] J. H. Boraston (ed.), *Sir Douglas Haig's Despatches* (1919, new ed. 1979), pp. xviii–xix, 299. Essame, pp. 145, 188.

[8] Essame, pp. 23–4, 145, 181, 194. *Haig's Despatches*, pp. 333, 335, 339.

[9] Edmonds, pp. 599–600. Essame, pp. 145, 181.

[10] Essame, pp. 23–5, 194. *Haig's Despatches*, pp. 304–8, 334–40.

[11] *Haig's Despatches*, p. 299.

[12] Brian Bond, *Chief of Staff: the Diaries of Lt. General Sir Henry Pownall*, vol. i (1972), *Liddell Hart: a Study of His Military Thought* (1977), *France and Belgium 1939–1940* (1975).

[13] Notably N. H. Gibbs, *Grand Strategy* vol. i (1976), and Michael Howard, *The Continental Commitment* (1972).

[14] For example S. W. Roskill, *Naval Policy Between the Wars*, 2 vols. (1968 and 1976), and H. Montgomery Hyde, *British Air Policy Between the Wars 1918–1939* (1976).

Notes to Chapter 1

[1] Michael Howard, *The Continental Commitment* (1972), pp. 72–5. Max Beloff, *Imperial Sunset*, vol. i (1969), p. 344.

[2] Keith Jeffery, 'The Military Defence of the British Empire, 1918–1922' (Ph.D. thesis, University of Cambridge, 1978), chapter 1. A. J. P. Taylor, *English History 1914–1945* (1965), p. 191.

[3] Beloff, p. 282.

[4] Ibid. 309–15. Nationalist sentiment was strongly opposed to the use of Indian native troops for imperial purposes, see for example Cab 4/7, CID252-B: 'Indian troops in these garrisons [i.e. in Mesopotamia, Aden, Palestine, and the Black Sea] are really mercenaries, and it must always be borne in mind that our policy in most of these countries does not commend itself to Indian public opinion, so far as it has been expressed.' For a discussion of British military policy regarding India see chapter 4.

[5] Beloff, pp. 345–7. A. P. Thornton, *The Imperial Idea and Its Enemies* (1959).

[6] Beloff, pp. 340, 350. Professor Howard, pp. 74–5, refers to the sentiments of mourning after 1918 evoked by the repeated intoning of that most melancholy of all hymns 'Oh God Our Help In Ages Past', but in the author's experience this hymn is usually sung to a cheerful and bracing tune. 'Abide With Me' sounds more likely, particularly as it is habitually sung on public occasions, including the FA Cup Final.

[7] Howard, pp. 64–5.

[8] Cited ibid. 66.

[9] Ibid. 70–7. For an excellent detailed discussion of British military policy towards the Middle East and South Russia between 1918 and 1922 see Jeffery, chapters 6–8.

[10] Beloff, p. 274.

[11] Ibid. 327–8. Martin Gilbert, *Winston S. Churchill*, vol. iv *1917–1922*, (1975), p. 234. Robin Higham, *Armed Forces in Peacetime: Britain 1918–1939* (1962), pp. 28–33. WO33/1004, Memorandum by the CIGS, 6 June 1920. Jeffery, pp. 204–5.

[12] Beloff, pp. 283, 297–301. Major-General Sir C. E. Callwell, *Field-Marshal Sir Henry Wilson* vol. ii (1927), pp. 244, 254–5, 261. On air substitution for troops in Iraq see Winston S. Churchill, *The Aftermath* (1941), pp. 461–6. E. Monroe, *Britain's Moment in the Middle East* (1965), chapter 3.

[13] Higham, pp. 59–63. Sir Charles W. Gwynn, *Imperial Policing* (1936), chapter vi. Cab 24/94, CP282.

[14] Callwell, pp. 183–7, 198 ff. Higham, pp. 26–8. General Sir Alexander Godley, *Life of an Irish Soldier* (1939), chapter xxi. In 1923,

after the evacuation of Constantinople, there were 71 infantry battalions at home (including eight on the Rhine) and 11 cavalry regiments (including one on the Rhine)—an approximate total of 63,000 troops. This compared unfavourably with 83 infantry battalions and 14 cavalry regiments (79,000 troops) at home in 1914, see WO32/5943.

[15] Beloff, p. 314–18. Jeffery, chapter 4.

[16] Charles Townshend, *The British Campaign in Ireland 1919–1921* (1975), p. 204. Higham, pp. 50–4, aptly entitles this subsection 'Military Nightmare'. Callwell, p. 236–321. General Sir Nevil Macready, *Annals of an Active Life* (n.d., but *c.* 1924), ii. 425–565.

[17] Townshend, pp. 122, 159, 190, 206.

[18] Montgomery, *Memoirs* (paperback edition, 1961), pp. 39–40.

[19] On the question of the Irish naval bases see Gibbs, *Grand Strategy*, vol. i, Appendix I.

[20] Higham, pp. 5–6. Churchill, *The Aftermath*, chapter 3.

[21] Higham, pp. 12–16. Churchill, *The Aftermath*, pp. 61–3.

[22] Churchill, *The Aftermath*, chapter 3. Martin Gilbert, pp. 181–96. Higham, p. 14. Keith Jeffery, 'Sir Henry Wilson and the Defence of the British Empire, 1918–1922', in *Journal of Imperial and Commonwealth History*, vol. v, No. 3 (May 1977) 270–93

[23] Beloff, pp. 278, 348. Higham, p. 68. For an excellent discussion of Britain's decline as a great power after and in part as a result of the First World War see Paul M. Kennedy *The Rise and Fall of British Naval Mastery* (1976), chapters 9 and 10.

[24] WO Paper A 2277 of 1919, Committee on the Organization of the After War Army.

[25] Gibbs, *Grand Strategy*, i. 3–6. Stephen Roskill, *Naval Policy Between the Wars* i 214–15. F. A. Johnson, *Defence by Committee* (1960), pp. 198–200.

[26] Cp. the diametrically opposed views of Peter Silverman and Ken Booth in *RUSI Journal*, March and September 1971, respectively.

[27] Stephen Roskill, *Hankey: Man of Secrets*, vol. ii (1972), p. 112, and 'The Ten Year Rule—the Historical Facts' in *RUSI Journal* (Mar. 1972).

[28] Gibbs, ii 4–6.

[29] Cab 23/15, 15 Aug. 1919.

[30] WO32/9314, M. Hankey's memorandum to Mr E. E. B. Speed, 14 Dec. 1923. In this memorandum Hankey also falsely asserted that the conclusion ('no great war for ten years') was never given Cabinet authority.

[31] *Interim Report of Committee on National Expenditure*, Cmd. 1581 (1922), Report on the Army Estimates, pp. 53–86. It is interesting that the interim report noted that research and experimentation carries in

their train 'much indirect increase of expenditure, also the substitution of new material for old, and of alterations in the engines of war. [They] inevitably also create a tendency in the minds of technical advisers to prescribe an accelerated rate of obsolescence in war material.' Cab 24/132, Memorandum by the General Staff, 20 Jan. 1922.

32 Higham, p. 86. Cab 4/7, CID276, General Staff Note on Disarmament, 5 Oct. 1921.

33 Keith Jeffery's doctoral dissertation referred to above constitutes the most scholarly assessment of Wilson's term as CIGS.

34 Wilson diary, 30 Nov. 1919 (partly reproduced by Callwell, p. 216) and 31 Dec. 1919 (ibid. 219). Quotations from Wilson's diary, other than those published by Callwell, are drawn from Jeffery's article cited in note 22 above.

35 See for example the diary entries for 13 Mar., 15 July (Callwell, p. 253), and 5 Aug. 1920.

36 Ibid., diary 2 Apr. 1921 (Callwell, p. 283).

37 Ibid., diary 5 July 1921 (Callwell, p. 298). After Wilson's confrontation with Lloyd George he addressed the Imperial Conference and told the Dominions' Premiers: '[The] Navy had a two-power standard and a one-power standard. We soldiers had no standard. A voluntary army answered no military war problem. War could not be considered in the abstract, an enemy must be named and plans prepared.'

38 By coincidence the inter-war period ended in a similar situation with the then CIGS, Lord Gort, refusing to deal with the Secretary of State for War, Hore-Belisha, in person.

39 WO33/1004, Britain's Military Liabilities, Memorandum by the CIGS, 6 June 1920.

40 Ibid., Military Liabilities of the Empire, 27 July 1920. Also to be found in Cab 4/7 CID255.

41 Gibbs, p. 52.

42 Ibid. See also Cab 24/159, CP200(23), Future Size of our Regular Army, Note by Secretary of State for War covering a memorandum by the General Staff.

43 In the CID in 1922 the Board of Trade representative pointed out that even the War Office's modest Expeditionary Force of 65,000 troops and 14,000 horses could not be equipped and provided with sea transport in less than three months. The Board of Trade insisted that it was organizing shipping for a long sea voyage, for example to India, not the conveyance of troops across the Channel. Early in 1923 the Government ruled that provision should not be made to meet a national war so that certain savings could be made in equipment and transport. The War Office, for example, could dispense with hospital

ships. See Cab 2/3, CID 155th, 156th, and 169th meetings.

[44] Cab 24/159, CP200(23). See also WO32/5943, Strength of the Military Forces in Relation to Military Commitments, Note by the CIGS, 20 Mar. 1923.

[45] Cavan Papers 1/2, Cavan to Robertson, 30 Sept. 1924.

[46] Higham, p. 326, provides a table of Service estimates between the wars.

[47] Cab 4/7, CID255 and 257, Survey of the Military Liabilities of the Empire, 27 July and Sept. 1920.

Notes to Chapter 2

[1] Michael Howard, 'The Liddell Hart Memoirs', in *RUSI Journal* (Feb. 1966), 58–61.

[2] J. Connell, *Wavell: Soldier and Scholar* (1964), pp. 149–50, 174, henceforth referred to as 'Connell'.

[3] J. F. C. Fuller, *The Army in My Time* (1935), pp. 174–5.

[4] Cab 53/1, COS 30th meeting, Annual Review of Defence Policy, 27 May 1926.

[5] Sir Giffard Martel, *An Outspoken Soldier* (1949), pp. 30–2. R. J. Collins, *Lord Wavell: A Military Biography* (1947), henceforth referred to as 'Collins'. Sir Philip Neame, VC, *Playing With Strife: the Autobiography of a Soldier* (1947), pp. 79–80, 110–11. Liddell Hart Papers 7/1921/32, Gort to Liddell Hart, 3 May 1921.

[6] J. F. C. Fuller, *Memoirs of an Unconventional Soldier* (1936), p. 411.

[7] Hampden Gordon, *The War Office* (1935), p. 330.

[8] Sir Alexander Godley, *Life of an Irish Soldier*, p. 274. Sir Frederick Morgan, *Peace and War: A Soldier's Life* (1961), p. 88. Lord Ismay, *Memoirs* (1960), p. 68. Burnett-Stuart, Unpublished Memoirs, p. 23. These memoirs are quoted by kind permission of Burnett-Stuart's daughter, the late Mrs Elizabeth Arthur.

[9] Interview with Sir Ian Jacob, 29 June 1971. Martel, pp. 328–9. Fuller, *Memoirs of an Unconventional Soldier*, pp. 381–6.

[10] Cited by Brian Bond, 'Richard Burdon Haldane at the War Office, 1905–1912', in *Army Quarterly* (Apr. 1963), 33.

[11] Major Harold Raymond Winton, 'General Sir John Burnett-Stuart and British Military Reform, 1927–1938' (unpublished Ph.D. thesis, Stanford University, California, 1977), pp. 242–3. Duff Cooper, *Old Men Forget* (1955), pp. 194–5.

[12] Higham, *Armed Forces in Peacetime*, pp. 45, 258, 260–1. Winton, p. 107. B. E. Bradshaw-Ellis, 'Seven Lean Years: the Organization and Administration of the Imperial General Staff, 1926–1933' (unpublished MA thesis, University of New Brunswick, 1973), p. 126.

[13] Gordon, pp. 7–10, 261. Bradshaw-Ellis, pp. 126–8. In 1936 the Master-General of the Ordnance was superseded by the Director-General of Munitions Production, and in 1937 Hore-Belisha added the Director-General of the Territorial Army to the Army Council.

[14] Fuller, *Memoirs,* pp. 365–6, 371–3. Martel, pp. 330–1. Winton, p. 53.

[15] Godley, p. 274. Ironside to Liddell Hart, 30 Nov. 1930. Macleod to Liddell Hart, 5 and 19 July 1936. Morgan, pp. 124–5.

[16] Col. The Hon. M. A. Wingfield, 'The Supply and Training of Officers for the Army', *RUSI Journal* (Aug. 1924), 433–44. E. S. Turner, *Gallant Gentlemen* (1956), p. 294.

[17] Montgomery, *Memoirs,* p.40.

[18] Collins, p. 109.

[19] Ibid., pp. 105, 111, 137, 148. Brigadier-General A. B. Beauman, *Then a Soldier* (1960), pp. 61, 76, 91. Neame, pp. 81–2.

[20] Collins, p. 125, Connell pp. 152–3. Sir Douglas Brownrigg, *Unexpected* (n.d. but *c.* 1941), p. 98. Ironside to Liddell Hart, 9 Nov. and 17 Dec. 1929, 17 May 1933.

[21] Sir Philip Chetwode to Liddell Hart 1 May 1937. Liddell Hart Papers 11/1933/23, Talk with General Pope-Hennessey, 14 Oct.

[22] Captain J. R. Kennedy, *This, Our Army* (1935), pp. 80–7.

[23] Morgan, p. 111. Major-General H. L. Birks Interview, Imperial War Museum Accession No. 00870/09.

[24] Kennedy, pp. 92–5. Kennedy hinted that Ironside, who was 53 in 1933, had been sent to India as QMG to get him out of the way as a critic of the establishment. In an analysis of the Army List of October 1936, Liddell Hart concluded that of the 27 generals or lieutenant-generals 11 were definitely 'duds' while 12 more showed signs of deteriorating. Of the 27 at least 16 were conservatives and only three definitely progressive (Burnett-Stuart, Ironside, and Kirke). Six would be over 65 at the end of their present appointment and 12 over 63. Of the 70 major-generals, Liddell Hart rated only eight as first class with another 19 as good second grade. Out of some 300 colonels only 11 seemed first class and a further 35 good second class. All these officers were listed by name with ratings and comments alongside. Contemporary comments and subsequent performances suggest that Liddell Hart's analysis was remarkably accurate. See Liddell Hart Papers 11/1931/45 and 46.

[25] Godley, pp. 264, 308. Ironside to Liddell Hart, 17 Dec. 1929 and 30 June 1934. Martel, pp. 31–2, 48. Beauman, pp. 85–6.

[26] Fuller retired at the age of 56 in 1934. On 2 January 1933 Ironside wrote to Liddell Hart predicting that Fuller would not be employed again: 'It is a great pity. I am not saying that he has not been stupid, but he was not handled properly just because his critical

spirit was considered disloyalty.' In eight years of close co-operation Ironside had not found Fuller disloyal. The Liddell Hart Papers contain numerous references to able officers whom he and others considered to have been badly treated by the War Office. Not even Liddell Hart was able to save some of the officers he had listed as highly promising, such as Tollemache and Karslake, from the Hore-Belisha 'axe' in 1937. On the extraordinary history of the establishment's prejudice against Tollemache see Liddell Hart's *Memoirs*, ii. 64–5, and 11/1938/8, Talk with Brigadier E. D. H. Tollemache, 11 Jan. 1938.

[27] Macleod to Liddell Hart, 19 Apr. 1937. Ironside to Liddell Hart, 2 Jan. 1933 and 30 June 1934.

[28] Liddell Hart Papers 11/1933/21, Talk with Martel, 2 Sept. Fuller to Liddell Hart, 7 Nov. 1936. Burnett-Stuart to Liddell Hart, 10 Nov. 1936, and Unpublished Memoirs, pp. 106–7. Interview with Brigadier John Stephenson, 14 Sept. 1976.

[29] Liddell Hart, *The Defence of Britain* (1939), pp. 350–8.

[30] Ibid. 359–61, 364. Although promotion to major was now guaranteed, under the new regulations a captain's pay might actually be reduced for several years. See also Turner, p. 298.

[31] Liddell Hart, *The Defence of Britain*, pp. 365–7.

[32] *RUSI Journal* (Feb. 1966) 61. On anti-Semitism in the British Army see R. J. Minney, *The Private Papers of Hore-Belisha* (1960), p. 18. It is only fair to record that several officers who served in this period have assured the author that they were unaware of any anti-Semitism in the Army.

[33] Beauman, p. 66. Liddell Hart emphatically endorsed these remarks in his copy. Ironside to Liddell Hart, 8 Nov. 1931.

[34] J. R. Colville, *Man of Valour: Field Marshal Lord Gort V.C.* (1972), pp. 62, 68–9. When Gort was appointed Commandant of the Staff College a brother officer remarked: 'He will have all the beds made of concrete and hosed down with cold water nightly,' ibid. 68.

[35] Brian Montgomery, *A Field-Marshal in the Family* (1973), pp. 198–238. Alun Chalfont, *Montgomery of Alamein* (1976), pp. 71–99.

[36] This is the theme of Brigadier C. N. Barclay's *On Their Shoulders: British Generalship in the Lean Years 1939–1942* (1964).

[37] *RUSI Journal* (May 1925), 207–9.

[38] M. A. Garnier, 'Social Class and Military Socialization: A Study of R.M.A. Sandhurst' (Ph.D. thesis, University of California, 1969), pp. 199–200, 223. Garnier's thesis contains numerous examples of regimental customs and lore, e.g. p. 122, the tradition of guards officers eating breakfast with their hats on. See also John Keegan, 'Regimental Ideology', in G. Best and A. Wheatcroft (eds.), *War, Economy and the Military Mind* (1976), pp. 3–18.

[39] Michael Howard, 'Soldiers in Politics', *Encounter* (Sept. 1962), 77–81.

[40] Kennedy, pp. 115–19. Compare Keegan's notion of the regiments' 'pecking order' in his 'Regimental Ideology', p. 6, with Simon Raven's celebrated contribution, 'Perish by the Sword', in Hugh Thomas (ed.), *The Establishment* (1959). According to Raven the degree of censorship passed on private morals is always a good indication of a regiment's social status: 'in "Etonian" regiments moral comment is seldom heard, the further down the scale we go, the more grindingly insistent it becomes'.

[41] WO32/2820. WO163/38, Report of Committee on Regimental Officers, May 1932. Lindsay to Knox, 29 Oct. 1932, Lindsay Papers. See also Winton, pp. 110, 289–90.

[42] Interview with Brigadier John Stephenson, 14 Sept. 1976.

[43] Keegan, p.16. See also John Baynes's excellent study of the 2nd Scottish Rifles (Cameronians) before and during the First World War, *Morale: a Study of Men and Courage* (1967). For a brilliant account of regimental soldiering in India in the 1930s see John Masters, *Bugles and a Tiger* (1956).

[44] Correlli Barnett, *The Desert Generals* (paperback edition, 1962), pp. 105–10. In Barnett's opinion, 'Within the Army's own structure this nineteenth or even eighteenth century mentality was reflected by the veneration for the regiment, which had long ceased to be a functional unit on the battlefield.'

[45] Turner, p. 295. Burnett-Stuart to Liddell Hart, 20 Sept. 1932. Ironside to Liddell Hart, 1 Mar. 1933.

[46] Fuller, *The Army In My Time,* p. 188. Burnett-Stuart to Liddell Hart, 9 Dec. 1931. See also Collins, *Wavell,* p. 155.

[47] By Lt.-Col. V. Prescott-Westcar (1937). For an amusing account of sport and horses in the inter-war Army by a well-known cavalry officer see Geoffrey Brooke, *Good Company* (1954). Two additional titles redolent with a similar atmosphere are General Sir Beauvoir De Lisle, *Reminiscences of Sport and War* (1939) and General Sir James Willcocks *The Romance of Soldiering and Sport* (1925).

[48] The lecture was by Sir Percy Hambro on 'The Horse and the Machine in War', *RUSI Journal* (Feb. 1927).

[49] Interviews with Brigadier Stephenson and Major-General J. Lunt. Correlli Barnett argues that even after mechanization in the late 1930s the cavalry spirit remained all-pervasive. In the North African desert 'The holy odour of the horse clung to British armour', *The Desert Generals,* p. 110.

[50] M. C. A. Henniker, *Memoirs of a Junior Officer* (1951), pp. 48, 86–7. For a ranker's vivid account of life in the Army between the wars see Spike Mays, *Fall Out The Officers* (1969). General Lunt recalls

a cockney lad who was eager to work with horses being attracted by a recruiting poster advertizing the West Riding regiment.

[51] Godley, pp. 290–1, 302–3.

[52] Neame, pp. 84–7. See Martel, *An Outspoken Soldier,* pp. 4–8, 37–48. Martel first won the Army Welter Weight Championship in 1912 but he continued to box regularly until he lost an eye in an explosion in 1944. He also played rugby. For the exploits of another outstanding all-round athlete, Charles Gairdner, see Philip Mason, *A Shaft of Sunlight* (1978), p. 117.

[53] Henniker, pp. 92–3. Morgan, pp. 67–8, 93.

[54] Martel, p. 5. The Liddell Hart Papers contain several references to officers being seriously injured in riding accidents. Major-General C. P. Heywood, tipped by Liddell Hart as a future CIGS, died from a heart attack while out hunting in October 1936. See Liddell Hart, *Memoirs,* ii. 32n. Sir John Dill also suffered a riding accident which militated against his chances of succeeding Deverell as CIGS. See Minney, p. 68.

[55] Wingfield, in *RUSI Journal* (Aug. 1924).

[56] Chetwode to Liddell Hart, 1 May 1937. An abbreviated version of Chetwode's Quetta address is located in the Chetwode file, Liddell Hart Papers. Many officers privately endorsed Liddell Hart's criticisms of the Army. Brigadier C. D. Baker-Carr, for example, wrote from Cyprus on 4 March 1936: 'What a queer nation we are! We shall start the war of 193? as if we are fighting on 12 November 1918. I expect you are as unpopular in high circles as I was in 1915–16. You try to make the Military Mind *think,* a most unpardonable offence.'

[57] Romer to Liddell Hart, 2 Feb. 1933. Ironside to Liddell Hart, 17 Dec. 1929. Connell, pp. 160–3.

[58] Stephenson interview. Ironside to Liddell Hart, Mar. 1932.

[59] For an amusing example of a non-meeting of British and French military minds see A. Beaufre, *1940: the Fall of France* (1967), pp. 52–3.

[60] Liddell Hart Papers 11/1939/63, Talk with Major-General C. N. F. Broad, 11 July.

[61] Ibid. 11/1936/107, Talk with General Karslake, 20 Nov., and 11/1937/74, Deverell, 14 Sept. Author's interviews with General Sir Ronald Adam, 17 Feb. 1978, and with Major-General Birks, 14 Mar. 1978. Liddell Hart, *Memoirs,* i. 79.

Notes to Chapter 3

[1] Howard, *The Continental Commitment,* pp. 81–5. Johnson, *Defence by Committee,* pp. 192–200. Howard Graham Welch, 'The Origins and Development of the Chiefs of Staff Sub-Committee of the Committee

of Imperial Defence: 1923–1939' (unpublished Ph.D. thesis, University of London, 1973, henceforth cited as Welch), chapter 1 *passim*.

[2] WO32/3489. Cab 53/14, COS141, Imperial Defence Policy, 1928, pp. 4–9.

[3] Major B. C. Dening, *The Future Of The British Army* (1928), pp. 58–60. The Cardwell System is more fully discussed in the next chapter.

[4] Welch, p. 71.

[5] Ibid. 72.

[6] Cavan Papers 1/2, Churchill College, Cambridge. On his accepting the appointment of CIGS Lord Byng advised Cavan, 'All you have to do is to attend the War Office daily, sit in a comfortable chair and ring a bell on your desk. Sit very tight for a year saying and writing as little as possible and by that time you will know the job.'

[7] Cab 63/48, Hankey to Sir Edward Grigg, 23 Mar. 1934, quoted by Welch, p. 73.

[8] Cab 2/4, CID 187th meeting, 28 July 1924, Note for the Office file by Hankey, 20 Nov. 1924. The chairman at that meeting, Lord Curzon, agreed with Chamberlain but suggested that Germany, although disarmed at present, should not be overlooked for the future.

[9] Cab 53/1, COS 6th meeting, 8 Jan. 1924. The latter part of Cavan's remark may sound reactionary but it proved very apt as regards the COS's relationships with Churchill during the Second World War.

[10] Gibbs, i. 35–8. WO79/69, Cavan Papers, Typed note for Secretary of State of War, 28 Apr. 1925. Foch also told Cavan that he could not be satisfied that Britain would be able to reinforce the Rhine Army immediately unless a force was specially maintained for that purpose.

[11] Cab 4/11, CID516, French Security, Memorandum by the General Staff, 29 Sept. 1924. Gibbs, i. 39.

[12] Cab 4/12, CID597, French Security (also in Cab 24/172, CP116(25)). See also John C. Cairns, 'Perplexities of a "Nation of Shopkeepers" in search of a suitable France, 1919–1940', in *American Historical Review*, 79, No. 3 (June 1974), 710–43.

[13] Cab 4/12, CID571, British, French and Belgian Security, Note by Hankey, 23 Jan. 1925.

[14] WO32/5799, The Present and Future Military Situation in Germany, 29 Jan. 1925 (also in Cab 4/12, CID562). Gibbs, i. 40–1.

[15] Cab 2/4, CID 195th, 196th, and 201st meetings.

[16] Gibbs, i. 42–4.

[17] Howard, p. 95.

[18] Ibid. 94–95. Gibbs, i. 52–4. Cab 4/15 CID701, A Review of Imperial Defence, 22 July 1926.

[19] CID701, p. 6. Gibbs, i. 54.

[20] Cab 53/1, COS 30th meeting. WO32/3460, Expeditionary Force Committee, Note by CIGS, 8 July 1926.

[21] Cab 24/180, CP303(26). Cab 2/5, CID 229th meeting, 14 July 1927, quoted by Welch, p. 99.

[22] Cab 2/5, CID 236th meeting, 5 July 1928. Cab 53/2, COS 73rd meeting, 6 July 1928.

[23] Cab 53/12, COS45 and 48, Afghanistan. Cab 53/13, COS95, Measures to put pressure on Russia. Cab 53/16, COS164(JP), Possible subsidiary operations against Russia. Howard, p. 90.

[24] See the following chapter for a full discussion of British strategic thinking on the security of the North West Frontier and Afghanistan in the late 1920s.

[25] Cab 4/17, CID847, The Present Distribution and Strength of the British Army in relation to its duties, Memorandum by the CIGS, Nov. 1927. Cab 4/17, CID900, Annual Review of Imperial Defence Policy, 1928. WO32/3489, Commitments and Liabilities, Memorandum of Secretary of State for War, June 1929. Also Welch, pp. 99–100.

[26] Howard, p. 92. Brigadier R. H. Dewing, *The Army* (1938), pp. 63–71.

[27] Cab 53/17, COS191, Annual Review of Imperial Defence Policy, 1929 (see also Cab 4/18, CP948). WO32/3489, p. 16.

[28] Monroe, *Britain's Moment in the Middle East*, pp. 80–2.

[29] Ibid. 80. Cab 53/14, COS141, Memorandum by CIGS, pp. 6–7.

[30] Sir John Slessor, *The Central Blue* (1956), pp. 51–61. As an Army expert on the Middle East wrote frankly in 1923, 'The friction and jealousy between the War Office and the Air Ministry . . . is now acute, the War Office wishing to abolish the Air Ministry as they regard all Air Forces as an ancillary to ground forces.' Colonel R. Meinertzhagen, *Middle East Diary* (1959), p. 131. Ismay, for one, was suspicious of the value of air control: 'Another . . . claim was that . . . bombing utterly demoralized the dervishes. I can only say that I attacked Jid Ali almost immediately after two aeroplanes had aimed all their bombs at it, and that I found no trace of demoralisation among the garrison. On the contrary, they were cheerful, utterly defiant, and grossly slanderous about my parentage!' Lord Ismay, *Memoirs* (1960), p. 35.

[31] Cab 53/2, COS 43rd meeting, 25 Jan. 1927. Cab 23/55, Cabinet 52nd meeting conclusion (9a), 26 Oct. 1927, both quoted by Welch, pp. 85–7.

[32] The Air Staff paper was entitled 'The Fuller Employment of Air Power in Imperial Defence', Slessor, pp. 70–4. Bradshaw-Ellis, p. 156. This Air Staff paper was by no means the only controversial

memorandum presented by Trenchard. For the CIGS's reaction to an equally controversial one on strategic bombing see Cab 53/16, The War Object of an Air Force, Note by the CIGS, 16 May 1928.

[33] Meinertzhagen, pp. 129–36. Monroe, chapter 3. In chapter 4 Miss Monroe stresses that oil was not a major consideration in Britain's policy regarding the Middle East for the greater part of the inter-war period. In 1938, for example, Middle East oil production amounted to less than one twentieth of the world's output and in 1948 it was still only one-eighth.

[34] Monroe, pp. 78–81. Dewing, pp. 73–6. Slessor, pp. 52–3, denies that the Air Staff ever believed that the system of air control was suitable for Palestine.

[35] Sir Charles Gwynn, *Imperial Policing,* (1936), chapter ix. Dewing, pp. 73–4.

[36] Monroe, pp. 81, 85 ff. Dewing, pp. 74–5. Howard, p. 93, refers to the Palestine garrison's 'endless and hopeless policing tasks to which the Second World War provided an almost welcome, though, alas temporary relief'.

[37] Gwynn, pp. 201–2.

[38] Ibid., chapter viii *passim*. Colville *Man of Valour,* pp. 60–2. Gort, Duncan's GSO1, risked his life in an attempt to rescue nuns and children from a convent at Chapei, but shortly afterwards found Japanese social customs more of an ordeal.

[39] Cab 53/14, COS141. In another note entitled 'Singapore: Scale of Attack' (Cab 53/14, COS122), the CIGS doubted if the Japanese would risk an attack on Singapore when they could more easily go for Hong Kong. In the latter event British naval forces already in the Far East would play the major role by trying to intercept them. It was also the Navy's responsibility to reduce the time for the relief force from Britain to arrive. In Milne's view 32 days was too long.

[40] WO32/3488, Strength, Distribution and Organization of the British Army in relation to its Duties, 1931. Bradshaw-Ellis, pp. 22–9.

[41] Cab 4/17, CID847, 900.

[42] Cab 2/5, CID 231st meeting, 19 Dec. 1927. Cab 4/17, CID861, Memorandum by Secretary of State for War, 12 Mar. 1928. In a Memorandum for the Secretary of State for War (WO32/3489) signed by all the members of the Army Council it was stressed that even with the slow rate of mobilization envisaged, it was doubtful if the Expeditionary Force could be completed in time. There was a shortage, for example, of 40,000 men as well as insufficient vehicles and equipment.

[43] Cab 4/20, CID1009, Annual Review of Imperial Defence Policy, 1930, pp. 1–3.

[44] Cab 4/12, CID562, The Present and Future Military Situation in Germany, 29 Jan. 1925.

[45] Cab 2/5, CID 239th meeting, 13 Dec. 1928. Cab 4/18, CID926, Military Situation in Germany, memorandum by Secretary of State for War covering a memorandum by CIGS. See Welch, pp. 101–2.

[46] Cab 4/18, CID945, Cab 4/19, CID979, Cab 2/5, CID 248th meeting, 29 May 1930, cited by Welch, p. 102.

[47] Cab 53/2, COS 66th meeting, 1 Mar. 1928. WO32/3488, Hankey to Creedy, 5 Feb. 1931. Welch, p. 100.

[48] Gibbs, i. 63–4.

[49] Ibid. 78–80. Cab 4/21, CID1082.

[50] Cab 4/21, CID1087, Note by Treasury on COS Annual Review, 1932, 11 Mar. 1932.

[51] Gibbs, i. 80.

[52] For example, Johnson, p. 198, Roskill *Hankey: Man of Secrets*, ii. 107. See also K. Booth, 'The Ten Year Rule—an Unfinished Debate', *RUSI Journal* (Sept. 1971), a reply to P. Silverman's 'The Ten Year Rule', *RUSI Journal* (Mar. 1971).

[53] Gibbs, i. 62–4.

Notes to Chapter 4

[1] Responsibility for command and administration of the Indian Defence forces under the Government of India may be summarized as follows: (*a*) Secretary of State's Advisory Council contained two military members—the Military Secretary (an officer of the Indian Army) and one retired Indian Army officer of high rank; (*b*) The Governor-General's Executive Council constituted the supreme executive authority in all military matters under the Secretary of State for India's direction. The Commander-in-Chief in India was a member; (*c*) Army Headquarters. The C.-in-C. assisted by a CGS, AG, QMG, and other senior officers was responsible for administering the Army; (*d*) The Army Department was one of the departments of the Government of India to which the C.-in-C. and General Staff were responsible. It was headed by a civilian Secretary who represented the Department in the Legislative Assembly. Military matters were, however, far less subject to legislative discussion and control than in Britain.

[2] As late as 1939 the COS noted that the normal six-year tour in India was the greatest deterrent to recruiting and recommended four years instead, Cab 53/47, COS874.

[3] See Brian Bond, 'The Effect of the Cardwell Reforms', in *RUSI Journal* (Nov. 1960), 229–36, and 'Cardwell's Army Reforms', in *Army Quarterly* (Apr. 1962), 108–17. On Arnold-Forster's military measures

see J. K. Dunlop, *The Development of the British Army, 1899–1914* (1938), and W. S. Hamer, *The British Army: Civil–Military Relations 1885–1905* (1970).

[4] Cab 16/47, ND-14, Future Size of Our Regular Army, memorandum by the Secretary of State for War, 17 Apr. 1923. WO33/1488, Report of the Committee on the Cardwell System, 1937.

[5] Dening, *The Future of the British Army*, pp. 60–1.

[6] See, for example, the following *RUSI Journal* articles and lectures: Capt. G. R. Appleton, 'The Cardwell System', (Aug. 1927), 591–9; B. C. Dening, 'The Obstacles in the Way of Mechanization of the Army' (Nov. 1927), 784–8; Capt. J. K. Edwards's Second Military Prize Essay, (Aug. 1928), 458–73; and Col. G. N. Macready's lecture, 'The Trend of Organisation in the Army' (Feb. 1935), 1–20.

[7] I am heavily indebted throughout this chapter to J. O. Rawson's unpublished D.Phil. thesis (Oxford University, 1976), 'The Role of India in Imperial Defence beyond Indian frontiers and home waters, 1919–1939'. Professor Gibbs provides a concise summary of Dr Rawson's main arguments in *Grand Strategy*, i, Appendix II. I am also grateful to Mark Jacobsen for allowing me to read the draft chapters of his Ph.D. thesis on the modernization of the Indian Army 1925–1939 (University of California, Irvine, 1979).

[8] Rawson, pp. 92–124. Between 1918 and 1923 Britain depended largely on Indian forces to hold her possessions and mandates in the Middle East. As late as April 1921, for example, there were still 32 Indian infantry battalions, five cavalry regiments, five pack batteries, and 10 sapper and miner companies in Mesopotamia and Persia.

[9] Cab 16/38, CID Sub-Committee on Indian Military Requirements. Report paras. 81–9. The ratio of British to Indian troops in 1922 was 1:6 in the Covering Force, 2:2.5 in the Field Army, and 1.24:1 in the Internal Security Force.

[10] Rawson, pp. 152–7.

[11] Liddell Hart Papers, Ironside to Liddell Hart, 13 Dec. 1926, 26 Jan., 29 May, and 27 Sept. 1929, 17 Jan. 1931. In fairness to the cavalry, however, it must be noted that the arm still had an important role to play in India, both in frontier warfare and internal security.

[12] Ibid., Karslake to Liddell Hart, 7 Feb. 1929. Author's interview with Major-General H. L. Birks, 14 Mar. 1978.

[13] Martel to Liddell Hart, 17 May 1929, 15 Jan., and 7 Apr. 1930, 19 Oct. 1932, and 20 June 1933. Major-General C. P. Heywood echoed Martel's phrase, 'It seems to me that India is now setting the pace', in rebutting a newspaper article by General Sir Hubert Gough, Heywood to Liddell Hart, 19 Dec. 1933. Liddell Hart Papers.

[14] Cab 16/83, CID Defence of India, First Report of Sub-Committee, 19 Dec. 1927. See also Gibbs, i. 826–7.

[15] Cab 16/83, Report, DI 3rd and 4th meetings, DI5, DI8, DI16, and DI23. For a concise statement on the significance of the Brikenhead Committee's findings see Howard, *The Continental Commitment*, pp. 90–2.

[16] Gibbs, i. 827–30. For the Pink Plan see WO33/1266. The Soviet–Afghanistan saga continues. On 27 April 1978 President Mohammed Daoud was assassinated in Kabul in a pro-Soviet *coup d'état*. On 7th August 1978 a *Daily Telegraph* editorial stated that 'strategic Afghanistan has now been firmly absorbed into the ever-spreading Soviet bloc'.

[17] In 1938 there were still only 8 RAF squadrons in India and all were needed for frontier defence. The Indian Army successfully resisted a major air substitution of its troops on the North West Frontier until the end of the Second World War.

[18] Cab 16/85, DI 16th meeting and DI42. Rawson, pp. 68–85.

[19] Rawson, pp. 63, 281–90.

[20] Minney, *The Private Papers of Hore-Belisha*, pp. 53–4, 66, 69.

[21] Liddell Hart, *The Defence of Britain*, pp. 262–3. *Memoirs*, ii. 5, 7.

[22] WO33/1488. In addition to Sir Victor Warrender, the members were Major-Generals M. G. H. Barker and R. H. Haining, Lieutenant-General G. W. Howard, and Mr F. C. Bovenschen (Deputy Under-Secretary of State at the War Office). There was not a progressive or radically minded member among them.

[23] The remedies considered included short tours in the Mediterranean by nominally 'home' battalions, organization of the home battalions into very large groups, general enlistment in the infantry as distinct from enlistment in a particular regiment, reduction of establishment, reduction in the terms of service, and the creation of distinct long- and short-service armies.

[24] Liddell Hart, *Memoirs*, ii. 8–11, 240. Hobart to Liddell Hart, 21 Aug. and 25 Nov. 1937.

[25] Pownall Diary, 2 and 28 Feb. 1938. In the latter Pownall under-estimated the astute War Minister when he wrote: 'He is particularly likely to go off them [the rails] in regard to India. Despite what he has been told he cannot get it into his head that Indian military affairs are not his pidgeon. He is as likely as not to put his foot right into it about India—if he does he'll take it right in the neck for the constitutional position of Indian defence matters is very jealously guarded by those who are responsible.'

[26] Liddell Hart, *The Defence of Britain*, pp. 305–6, and *Memoirs*, ii. 91, 94, 97. (Two infantry battalions, making a total of 45, were stationed in Burma which was separated from India for defence purposes only in 1937.)

[27] WO33/1502, The Organisation of the Army for its Role in War

(summary in Gibbs, i. 830–2).

28 Liddell Hart Papers 11/1938/83, Talk with Rowlands, 4 July, and Rowlands to Liddell Hart, 2 Aug. 1938. *Memoirs,* ii. 183–5.

29 Pownall Diary, 25 Apr. and 2 May 1938. Slessor, *The Central Blue,* pp. 195–9.

30 The Pownall Sub-Committee's report is Appendix 2 in Cab 53/39, COS737 (summary in Gibbs, i. 832–3.)

31 J. Connell, *Auchinleck* (1959), pp. 68–9. Auchinleck's Committee showed that the progressive element in the Indian Army was prepared to put its own house in order and accept a reduction of units. It played a vital role in paving the way for the Chatfield Committee which otherwise would have been fiercely opposed by the Commander-in-Chief in India, General Cassels.

32 Cab 53/9, COS 241st meeting, 21 June 1938. Cab 53/39 COS737, 2 July 1938.

33 Cab 27/653, Defence of India Committee.

34 Rawson, pp. 310–22.

35 See Lord Chatfield, *It Might Happen Again* (1947), pp. 144–59, and Connell, *Auchinleck,* pp. 70–1.

36 Gibbs, i. 833–4. Rawson, pp. 322–31.

37 Cab 53/47 COS874, 12 May 1939.

38 Rawson, pp. 334–5.

39 Ibid. 341–52.

Notes to Chapter 5

1 For example Fuller's *Memoirs of an Unconventional Soldier* and *The Army In My Time;* Liddell Hart's *Memoirs.* For an uncritical pro-mechanization account see J. Wheldon, *Machine Age Armies* (1968).

2 Dr Harold Winton's doctoral thesis provides an admirably detached view. I am heavily indebted to this work, particularly in this and the next chapter. Dr Winton's decision to build his thesis around the career of Burnett-Stuart—a progressive conservative—bears an interesting similarity to the study by his supervisor, Peter Paret, of the Prussian General Yorck, a soldier of similiar outlook though perhaps lacking the Scotsman's sense of humour.

3 G. Le Q. Martel, *In The Wake Of The Tank* (2nd edn., 1935), henceforth cited as 'Martel', pp. 70–9.

4 Winton, pp. 20–4.

5 Ibid. 20–4, 52. General Egerton's remarks followed a lecture by Major-General Sir Percy Hambro on 'The Horse and the Machine in War', *RUSI Journal* (Feb. 1927), 85–100. Liddell Hart, *Memoirs,* i. 94.

6 Winton, pp. 47–53.

[7] Liddell Hart, *Memoirs,* i. 79–80, 89. Major-General H. L. Birks supports the view that the tank men's greasy overalls tended to provoke an attitude of snobbish disdain in some officers of the older arms. Conversation with the author, 14 Mar. 1978.

[8] R. Lewin, *Man of Armour: a Study of Lieut.-General Vyvyan Pope* (1976), p. 52.

[9] Martel, pp. 91–9.

[10] Ibid. 100–5. Winton, pp. 45–6.

[11] Winton, pp. 40–1. A similar view of Parliamentary attitudes to mechanization in the 1920s was formed by G. P. Armstrong, 'The Controversy over Tanks in the British Army, 1919–1933' (unpublished Ph.D. thesis, University of London, 1975).

[12] M. M. Postan *British War Production* (1952), pp. 2, 6. Cavan Papers 1/2, Cavan to Robertson, 30 Sept. 1924, and Cavan's unpublished memoirs, 'Recollections Hazy But Happy'. See also Winton, pp. 44–5.

[13] A. J. Trythall, *'Boney' Fuller: The Intellectual General* (1977), p. 75 ff.

[14] Ibid. 82–5.

[15] Ibid. 92–3. Bond, *Liddell Hart,* pp. 27–30. Winton, pp. 36–8.

[16] Trythall, pp. 98–100, 106, 111. For examples of Montgomery-Massingberd's intemperate criticisms of Fuller see his letters to Liddell Hart in Liddell Hart Papers, 24 Apr. and 3 May 1926 and 7 Jan. 1927.

[17] Liddell Hart Papers, Karslake to Liddell Hart, 12 Oct. 1925. Winton, pp. 57–8.

[18] Liddell Hart *The Tanks* (1959), i. 234. Winton, pp. 103–4.

[19] Trythall, pp. 118–20. Liddell Hart, *Memoirs,* i. 111. B. E. Bradshaw-Ellis's MA thesis makes a spirited defence of Milne's achievements as CIGS but is based on a limited range of sources. Graham Nicol's biography *'Uncle George'* (1976) has little to say on this period of Milne's career.

[20] Liddell Hart, *Memoirs,* i. 110 and *The Tanks,* i. 242.

[21] Trythall, pp. 134–42. Liddell Hart, *Memoirs,* i. 112–15. Burnett-Stuart's reply, 18th February 1927, to Fuller's letter complaining about the conditions of his appointment to Tidworth is printed in full by Winton, pp. 114–15. Contrary to Liddell Hart's impression at the time, Burnett-Stuart showed considerable tolerance towards Fuller even if he did not intercede on his behalf with the CIGS.

[22] Liddell Hart, *Memoirs,* i. 116–17. Martel, pp. 147–9. The force comprised a tank battalion, an armoured car company, a field brigade (RA), a pack battery (RA), a field company (RE), a signal unit, and an infantry battalion equipped with machine guns.

[23] Liddell Hart, *Memoirs,* i. 115–17. Martel to Liddell Hart, 11 Oct. 1927. Winton, pp. 118, 139.

[24] Liddell Hart, *Memoirs,* i. 127–8. *The Tanks,* i. 250, 253–4. Martel, pp. 159–65. K. Macksey, *Armoured Crusader: Major-General Sir Percy Hobart* (1967), pp. 93–4. Winton, pp. 120–5.

[25] Liddell Hart, *Memoirs,* i. 128–30 and Papers 11/1927/7, typed copy of Milne's Tidworth Address and 11/1927/12 for Knox's reaction. Winton, pp. 123–4, is right in suggesting that Milne was sounder on matters of national strategy than on tactics.

[26] Liddell Hart Papers, Karslake to Liddell Hart, 4 Oct. 1927. Winton, pp. 127–8, 187. Martel, p. 187 ff. Lewin, *Man of Armour,* pp. 71–2.

[27] Liddell Hart Papers 11/1927/15, Broad to Liddell Hart, 26 Sept. 1927, and 11/1928/2, Talk with Colonel C. N. F. Broad, 2 Jan. 1928.

[28] Ibid. 11/1928/2 and 13. *Memoirs,* i. 132–3. WO32/2842, Final Report of the Cavalry Committee (1927), and see Bradshaw-Ellis, pp. 56–7. Winton, pp. 56–7, 130–2.

[29] *The Tanks* i. 258–9. Winton, pp. 197–8. A doctoral dissertation on Army–RAF relations 1918–39 is currently being prepared by D. J. P. Waldie, Department of War Studies, King's College, London. See chapter 11 for a fuller discussion of this subject.

[30] Liddell Hart, *Memoirs,* i. 131. Winton, pp. 128–30.

[31] Liddell Hart Papers 11/1928/3, Talk with Martel, 28 Jan.

[32] Liddell Hart, *Memoirs,* i. 134–5. Martel, pp. 150–4, 168. Winton, pp. 149–53.

[33] Liddell Hart, *Memoirs,* i. 135–6 and Papers 11/1928/19. Burnett-Stuart, Unpublished Memoirs, pp. 43–4. Winton, pp. 164–7 including the extract from Montgomery-Massingberd's memoirs.

[34] Martel, p. 169. Liddell Hart Papers, Martel to Liddell Hart, 12 Mar. 1931, and 11/1928/19, Talk with Colonel Pile, 28 Nov.

[35] Winton, pp. 168–70.

[36] Liddell Hart, *Memoirs,* i. 174–5 and Liddell Hart Papers 11/1929/21, Talk with Lord Thomson, 30 Nov.

[37] Liddell Hart Papers 11/1929/2, Talk with Pile, 23 Jan., and 11/1929/4, Talk with Lindsay, 28 Jan.

[38] *The Tanks,* i. 261–4. Bradshaw-Ellis, p. 60.

[39] Winton, pp. 188–9.

[40] Liddell Hart Papers 11/1929/20, Talk with Tim Pile, 7 Nov.

[41] Ibid. 11/1930/8, Talk with Pile, 15 Oct.

[42] Winton, pp. 189–91.

[43] Liddell Hart, *Memoirs,* i. 160–2 and Liddell Hart Papers, Broad to Liddell Hart, 23 Nov. 1928. Martel, p. 227, confusingly refers to the 'Mauve Manual' which he describes 'as a mildly futuristic book'. See also Winton, pp. 192–8.

[44] *RUSI Journal* (Nov. 1929), 744–58.

[45] Liddell Hart, *Memoirs,* i. 161. Martel, *An Outspoken Soldier* pp. 65–6. Though published later the author stresses that he voiced these criticisms at the time.

[46] *The Tanks* i. 276–9. Winton, p. 226.

[47] *Committee on National Expenditure* (Cmd. 3920, 1931). WO32/2786, The May Committee Report. See Bradshaw-Ellis, pp. 128–32.

[48] Liddell Hart Papers, Pile to Liddell Hart, 16 Sept. 1931, and 11/1931/15, Talk with Pile, 24 Sept.

[49] Liddell Hart Papers 11/1931/5, Talk with Pile, 24 Sept. Winton, pp. 244–8, takes a similarly critical view of most of these senior officers.

[50] Liddell Hart, *Memoirs,* i. 177–80. Martel, pp. 239–40. Macksey, *Armoured Crusader,* pp. 103–4.

[51] Liddell Hart, *Memoirs,* i. 181. Macksey, pp. 99–100. Martel, *Our Armoured Forces* (1945), p. 42.

[52] Liddell Hart Papers 11/1933/40. Winton, pp. 250–5.

[53] Bradshaw-Ellis, pp. 60–1. Milne not surprisingly emerges very well from a study based largely on War Office Papers.

[54] Liddell Hart, *Memoirs* i. 227–8 and Liddell Hart Papers 11/1929/18, Talk with Sir Sam Hoare, 31 Oct. 11/1929/20, Talk with Pile, 7 Nov. 11/1932/46, Talk with Fuller and [Major A. H.] Killick, 23 Nov. Martel to Liddell Hart, Jan. 1932.

Notes to Chapter 6

[1] For example Liddell Hart in various works, Dr R. J. O'Neill, and Kenneth Macksey; see Brian Bond, *Liddell Hart,* chapter 8.

[2] Kennedy, *This, Our Army,* pp. 218–21. Winton, pp. 277–8.

[3] Liddell Hart Papers, Liddell Hart to Hankey, 2 Dec. 1932. (All references to private correspondence are from the Liddell Hart Papers unless otherwise stated.)

[4] 11/1936/28, Talk with Duff Cooper, 18 Jan. 1936. See also *The Tanks,* i. 301–2.

[5] 11/1935/114, Talk with General Sir Charles Bonham-Carter, 12 Dec. 1935. Hobart to Liddell Hart, 24 July 1934 and 18 Nov. 1936. 11/1936/107, Talk with General Karslake, 20 Nov. 1936. 11/1934/48, Talk with Martel, 9 Sept. 1934.

[6] Lindsay Papers, Hobart to Lindsay, 16 Dec. 1933, and 16 Apr. 1934. *The Tanks,* i. 321–3. Liddell Hart, *Memoirs,* i. 235–6.

[7] Liddell Hart, *Memoirs,* i. 238, *The Tanks,* i. 305–7.

[8] Ibid. pp. 245–8 and pp. 317–18.

[9] Interview with Colonel Offord, 8 Nov. 1972, in Winton, pp. 348–52, and cf. *The Tanks,* i. 311–12.

[10] *The Tanks,* i. 328–31, and *Memoirs,* i. 249–52. In his criticism of Lindsay, Major-General H. L. Birks, who was in good position to comment, felt that he had spent too much time at his headquarters at Hungerford and had not got out and about enough, interview with General Birks, 14 Mar. 1978. On the other hand, Lord Bridgeman thought that as Lindsay was only given his staff two days before the exercise he should have refused to take part, Bridgeman Interview, Imperial War Museum.

[11] *The Tanks,* i. 332–3. Winton, pp. 353–61. Lord Bridgeman remains convinced that Burnett-Stuart deliberately wrecked the exercise, Bridgeman Interview, Imperial War Museum. Kennedy, pp. 222–34, provides a vivid description of the exercise but clearly at the time of writing had no notion of the artificial difficulties put in Lindsay's way.

[12] Winton, pp. 254–8. Bridgeman Interview, Imperial War Museum. *The Tanks,* i. 333–4. If a later reflection by Pile is to be believed Lindsay was also handicapped by the attitude of Colonel William Platt, commanding 7th Infantry Brigade. In a talk with Liddell Hart on 7 May 1938 Pile asserted that Platt was 'the nigger in the woodpile at the Mobile Division exercise which wrecked George Lindsay's career', 11/1938/52.

[13] Hobart to Lindsay, 7 Oct. 1934, Lindsay Papers. Hobart's correspondence with Lindsay immediately after the exercise does not suggest that there was a deep personal rift between them.

[14] *The Tanks,* i. 335–7. Winton, pp. 361–2. Martel, *An Outspoken Soldier,* p. 67. 11/1934/52, Notes on RUSI Lecture by Colonel Macready, 14 Nov. 1934.

[15] Hobart to Liddell Hart, 27 Apr. and 14 Aug. 1935. Burnett-Stuart to Liddell Hart (?) 1934 (p. 13 in typed copy of their correspondence). Liddell Hart, *Memoirs,* i. 264–5.

[16] *Memoirs,* i. 267–9. Hobart to Liddell Hart, 14 Aug. 1935. Macksey, *Armoured Crusader,* p. 126. Winton, pp. 362–3.

[17] *Memoirs,* i. 265–6, 275. Winton fails to reconcile the anti-continental views of his subject, Burnett-Stuart, with his own perception that a continental commitment was the strongest card in the hand of those who favoured mechanization in general and armoured formations in particular, cf. Winton, pp. 374–6, 382–3, and 439–41.

[18] Martel, *In the Wake of the Tank* (1935 edn.), pp. 280, 308–10.

[19] Pile to Liddell Hart, 27 Sept. and 25 Oct. 1935.

[20] Hobart to Liddell Hart, 21 Sept. and 18 Nov. 1936. See also 11/1936/126, 1st Tank Brigade 1936. In 1936 the Army possessed only 375 tanks (209 light and 166 medium) of which 304 were officially classed as obsolete and nearly all the remainder out of date. Even the newest models, 69 light tanks Marks V and VI, were armed only with

machine guns, see Postan, *British War Production*, p. 7.

21 Winton, pp. 382–3. On the fate of the Colonel of the Scots Greys see 11/1937/82, Talk with Major-General C. C. Armitage, 1 Nov. 1937, and *Memoirs*, ii. 48.

22 Pile to Liddell Hart, 25 Oct. 1935 and 1 Jan. 1936. Major-General H. L. Birks, Transcript of Interview, Imperial War Museum.

23 Winton, pp. 379–81. 11/1936/118, Talk with Deverell, 6 Dec. 1936. Kennedy, pp. 155–6.

24 *The Tanks*, i. 400–1. 11/1938/58, Lunch with Hobart, 24 May 1938.

25 Winton, p. 408. Between 1927 and 1936 the sums available annually for tank development varied between £22,500 and £93,750. Lack of money led to the trial of many new components in obsolete vehicles. Between 1936 and 1939 the War Office requirement for tanks (not all expended) rose from £12 million to £36 million, see M. M. Postan, D. Hay, and J. D. Scott, *Design and Development of Weapons* (1964), pp. 304–8.

26 E. W. Sheppard, *Tanks in the Next War* (1938), pp. 80–7. Liddell Hart, *Memoirs*, i. 385–8. Bond, *Liddell Hart*, pp. 108–9.

27 PREM 1/242, Hore-Belisha to Neville Chamberlain, 31 Jan. 1938. On the steps taken by the War Office to evade strict Treasury control see Postan, *British War Production*, pp. 43–7.

28 *Memoirs*, i. 388–9. *The Tanks*, i. 372. 11/1937/85, Talk with Duff Cooper, 4 Nov. 1937. 11/1936/98, Talk with Major-General J. Kennedy, 11 Nov. 1936, and 11/1936/107, Talk with General Karslake, 20 Nov. 1936.

29 *Memoirs*, i. 389. Martel (11/1934/48) informed Liddell Hart that Elles, Brough, and Studd were all 'good fellows' but knew nothing about mechanics. Crawford, the fourth in seniority, was the only qualified engineer in the branch.

30 *Memoirs*, i. 390–3. Martel, *Our Armoured Forces*, pp. 46–8, and *Outspoken Soldier*, pp. 129–31. Sheppard, pp 80–7.

31 For a detailed account of this complex question see Postan, Hay, and Scott, pp. 309–21.

32 For Pownall's hostile attitude towards Pile see Bond (ed.), *Chief of Staff*, i. 131, 148, 150–1. See also Winton, pp. 405–7.

33 Winton, p. 424. *Memoirs*, ii. 20–3. 11/1937/70 lists eligible officers with mechanized experience. In addition to those mentioned in the text Lt.-Generals Elles and Karslake were well-qualified but too senior to be considered for command of the Mobile Division.

34 R. Macleod and D. Kelly (eds.), *Ironside Diaries, 1937–1940* (1962) pp. 33–4.

35 Pile to Liddell Hart, 21 and 30 Oct. 1937. *Memoirs*, ii. 33–7, 40–4, 48–9.

[36] *Memoirs*, ii. 156. Winton, pp. 406–7.

[37] Burnett-Stuart, Unpublished Memoirs, pp. 112–16, 123. Broad to Liddell Hart, 22 Sept. 1937. For the organization of the Mobile Division see Martel, *Our Armoured Forces*, pp. 48, 378–81.

[38] Hobart to Liddell Hart, 25 Nov. 1937. In May 1938 (11/1938/58) Hobart told Liddell Hart that Wavell's ideas on mobility were badly out of date. Under his general direction the Mobile Division was testing methods which the Tank Brigade had tried and rejected.

[39] Hobart to Liddell Hart, 10 July and 26 Sept. 1938. Macksey, *Armoured Crusader*, pp. 153–7.

[40] Pile to Liddell Hart, 17 Aug. 1933, and 16 Apr. 1935. Lindsay to Liddell Hart, 14 Oct. 1930. Winton, pp. 297–301, 308–17.

[41] Lewin, *Man of Armour*, pp. 82–8. The author of this work agrees that 'the 1st (Light) Battalion RTC' on line 6 p. 86 should be deleted for the sentence to make sense.

[42] Macksey, pp. 153–73, *The Tanks*, i. 402–4, *Memoirs*, ii. 193–4. In his interview with the author, General Birks said he believed Lady Finlayson contributed to Hobart's removal from Egypt by refusing to receive Mrs Hobart on social occasions.

[43] Lewin, p. 90. Hobart to Liddell Hart, 5 Dec. 1936.

[44] For Gort's quarrel with Broad see Liddell Hart, *Memoirs*, ii. 35. 11/1937/96, Dinner with Gort, 22 Nov. 1937. 11/1939/52, Talk with Pile, 7 May 1938. For Broad's tactlessness at Quetta see 11/1937/66, Talk with Karslake, 16 Aug. 1937, and 11/1937/82 for the opinions of Armitage and Hutton. See also Winton, p. 461.

[45] 11/HB1937/58, Lunch with Hore-Belisha, 19 Oct. 1937.

[46] Winton, p. 461. *The Tanks*, ii. 11–13, 317–18. My impression that Liddell Hart thought Martel had made a poor impression at Arras is derived from Liddell Hart's marginal note in his copy of L. F. Ellis, *The War in France and Flanders 1939–1940* (1953), and from a conversation arising from the note.

[47] Winton, pp. 443–5. 11/1938/69, Talk with Martel, 21 June 1938, and 11/1938/122, 28 Nov. See also Sheppard, pp. 121–5. As the official historians of *Design and Development of Weapons* point out, British tank models in 1939–40 were in most respects as good as or superior to existing German models but there were fewer of them and they were less reliable. Not a single British tank type in production in 1939 was still being produced in 1945, see Postan, Hay, and Scott, pp. 247–8, 316–17.

[48] Winton, pp. 445–8.

[49] On 1 September 1939 Germany possessed 3,195 tanks (excluding Czech models): 1,445 Panzer Is, 1,226 Panzer IIs, 98 Panzer IIIs, 211 Panzer IVs, and 215 command tanks, see R. M. Ogorkiewicz, *Armour* (1960), p. 212. See also Jim Kemeny, 'Tank Doctrines from the First

to the Second World War', in *Australian Journal of Defence Studies*, vol. I, No. 2 (Oct. 1977), 133–48.

50 Martel, *Our Armoured Forces*, pp. 57–8. Winton, p. 458.

51 See Dr Winton's admirable concluding survey, pp. 466–81.

52 See John Gooch's forthcoming article, 'Mr Haldane's Army: Military Organization and Foreign Policy in England, 1906–7', in *Bulletin of the Institute of Historical Research.*

53 Winton, p. 441. As remarked earlier, Dr Winton does not consistently apply this perception when criticizing Montgomery-Massingberd and praising Burnett-Stuart. The official historians of *Design and Development of Weapons* agree that the chief obstacle to tank development was continuing uncertainty over the Army's role, see Postan, Hay, and Scott, pp. 306, 309–11.

54 Hobart's seven-page typed memorandum 'A.F.V.'s and the Field Force' is dated 11 October 1937 but was sent to Liddell Hart with his letter of 21 October. Macksey, pp. 139–46, quotes lengthy extracts from this document. Liddell Hart's copy contains his marginal queries and note of appraisal.

55 11/1937/83, Talk with Pile, 2 Nov. 1937.

Notes to Chapter 7

1 For example in Gibbs, Howard, Welch, and Johnson. See also K. Middlemas and J. Barnes, *Baldwin: a Biography* (1969), and P. Dennis, *Decision by Default* (1972).

2 Duff Cooper's remarks are quoted by Gibbs, i. 82. In this and subsequent discussions of financial policy I am indebted to G. C. Peden's doctoral dissertation, 'The Influence of the Treasury on British Rearmament, 1932–1939' (Oxford University, 1976) published as *British Rearmament and the Treasury 1932–1939* (1979). All page references are to the book. Since the first draft of this study was completed I have benefited greatly from Robert Paul Shay Jr.'s excellent *British Rearmament in the Thirties: Politics and Profits* (Princeton, 1977). Shay takes a broader view of rearmament in its political, financial, and business context than Peden and is more critical of the inhibiting effects of the Treasury's financial orthodoxy.

3 Gibbs, i. 82–5.

4 Cab 53/4, COS 111th meeting, 20 June 1933.

5 Cab 53/23, COS310, Imperial Defence Policy Annual Review 1933, 12 Oct. 1933.

6 Dennis, pp. 34–5. Colonel Pownall, as secretary of the DRC, kept a diary which vividly illustrates the problems of presenting a unanimous report.

[7] Howard, p. 105. On 15 February 1934 Pownall noted that Hankey considered Warren Fisher rather mad: 'Apparently he has some mysterious nerve disorder and his judgement is affected thereby. The papers he occasionally puts in are astonishing, long tirades far removed from the point and irrelevant to the Committee's terms of reference.'

[8] Chatfield was among the few senior serving officers in the inter-war period to publish personal memoirs—*The Navy and Defence* (1942) and *It Might Happen Again* (1947). For Pownall's views of Montgomery-Massingberd see his Diary for 11 Apr. 1933 and 23 Jan. 1934. The first volume of Liddell Hart's *Memoirs* create a decidedly unfavourable impression of Montgomery-Massingberd but should be viewed as the case for the prosecution.

[9] On Ellington see Pownall Diary, 23 Jan., 15, and 28 Feb. 1934, Gibbs, i. 97–8, and Montgomery Hyde, *British Air Policy Between the Wars*, pp. 297–8.

[10] Howard, p. 100. Roskill, *Hankey: Man of Secrets*, iii. 94, states that Hankey feared a new continental commitment but this is scarcely supported by his determination to ensure that the DRC squarely faced the problem. As a naval enthusiast who nevertheless appreciated the limitations of sea power and the need for an expeditionary force, Hankey was following in the footsteps of Sir Julian Corbett. It is also of course pertinent that he had begun his professional career as a Royal Marine.

[11] Pownall Diary, 14 Nov. 1933, and 28 Feb. 1934, Howard, pp. 105–6.

[12] Cab 16/109, DRC Report, p. 9.

[13] Ibid. 21–2 and DRC 10th meeting, 16 Feb. 1934 (pp. 236–7).

[14] Pownall Diary, 11 Jan. 1934.

[15] Ibid. 18 Dec. 1933 and Cab 16/110, 41st Conclusions DC(M), 3 May 1934.

[16] Cab 16/109, DRC 7th meeting, 25 Jan. 1934 (p. 178). Cab 21/434, Hankey to Vansittart, 8 Mar., and ibid., Vansittart to Dill, 12 Mar. 1934, cited by Dennis, p. 39.

[17] Gibbs, i. 99–100. Gibbs, i. 103n, gives the list of members of the DC(M).

[18] Pownall Diary, 3 and 9 May 1934.

[19] For the COS's replies to the DC(M)'s questionnaire see Cab 53/23, COS335, and Cab 16/111, DC(M)32 109. Question 3 suggested that a British financial contribution to the construction costs of the Belgian frontier fortifications would be more effective than an expeditionary force. Question 5 asked why, if German air forces operating from the Low Countries could make Britain untenable, Britain could not, assuming superior air forces, make the Low Countries

untenable for them? For a good summary of this discussion see Dennis, pp. 40–2.

[20] Cab 53/23, COS335 and 336. Dennis, pp. 43–4, Howard, pp. 107–8. Ironically, Hankey boasted to the Prime Minister that the machinery of the CID had worked very smoothly. 'The C.O.S. reeled off Report after Report for the Ministerial Committee without a discordant note', Cab 21/434, Hankey to the Prime Minister, 3 Aug. 1934.

[21] Cab 53/4, COS 125th meeting, 4 May 1934. At their previous meeting the COS calculated (with a map) the similar problems Britain and Germany would face in trying to bomb each other from their home countries. Taking the radius of action of the new night bomber at 335 miles and the day bomber at 288 miles they reckoned that if Britain avoided neutral territory her planes could not even reach the Ruhr, whereas operating from the Low Countries they could penetrate just beyond Berlin. Germany would be similarly handicapped against Britain if operating from her homeland and respecting neutral territory. Even this ominous analysis did not point out, however, that London was relatively more important and more vulnerable than Berlin.

[22] Gibbs, i. 105, 114–15.

[23] Pownall Diary, 13 Mar. 1934. Liddell Hart Papers 11/1934/1, 26 Oct., and 11/1934/43, Talk with Sir Christopher Bullock, 5 July 1934. Bullock was of course mistaken in reporting that Hailsham had gained an additional sum for the Expeditionary Force.

[24] Cab 16/110 contains the proceedings of DC(M)32. The most important meetings for the discussions of the role of the Army were 3 May (41st Conclusions), 10 and 15 May (44th and 45th Conclusions), 25 and 26 June (50th and 51st Conclusions), 2 July (52nd Conclusions). For a concise summary see Gibbs, i. 114–17.

[25] Cab 16/110, 17 July (54th Conclusions), Pownall Diary, 17 July 1934.

[26] Pownall's Diary note for 24 July 1934 reveals that the protracted discussion of the Army's role and share of the deficiency budget ended in anticlimax: 'Today the last meeting (?) of the Ministerial Committee. The Army proposals for spending £20 million polished off in the briskest way. They had forgotten about it till Hailsham reminded them and no one had read his paper. A strange way of going about things. Indeed before the word "approved" was used Hailsham had to go out for a discussion in the Lords.'

[27] Cab 24/250, CP205(34), Summary of conclusions, pp. 9–10.

[28] Cab 2/6, CID 266th meeting, 22 Nov. 1934.

[29] Gibbs, i. 107, 111–14. Pownall, who was present, noted the political implications of Baldwin's remark, Diary 30 July 1934.

[30] Liddell Hart Papers 11/1934/48–50.

[31] Duff Cooper is quoted by Dennis, p. 45. Cab 53/24, COS350, Defence Plans Memorandum by CIGS, 4 Oct. 1934.

[32] Welch, pp. 167–70.

[33] Cab 53/4, COS 130th meeting, Air Threat from Germany, June 27 1934. Cab 53/5, COS 132nd meeting, 24 July 1934. Cab 53/5, COS 153rd meeting, Defence Plans for the event of war against Germany, 29 Oct. 1935.

[34] Cab 53/5, COS 133rd meeting, Defence Plans, 9 Oct. 1934. Welch, p. 168.

[35] Welch, pp. 157–9, 163–4, 180, 206. The timidity of the Chiefs of Staff in failing to press for the large amounts of money their Services really needed has been noted earlier, see Howard, pp. 105–6.

[36] Pownall Diary, 18 June 1934.

[37] Gibbs, i. 126–7.

Notes to Chapter 8

[1] Gibbs, i. 178–80. Pownall Diary, 15 July 1935. Shay, p. 54 ff.

[2] Cab 53/24 COS372, Annual Review, 29 Apr. 1935, paras. 35–6.

[3] Bond, *Liddell Hart,* chapters 3 and 4.

[4] See Winton's doctoral thesis, 'General Sir John Burnett-Stuart and British Military Reform, 1927–1938'.

[5] This supports Duff Cooper's belief that Chamberlain had imbibed the 'pernicious doctrine' of limited liability from 'a distinguished General, whom he had met fishing' *Old Men Forget,* p. 194.

[6] Liddell Hart Papers 11/1935/90, Talk with General Sir John Burnett-Stuart, 26 Aug. 1935.

[7] Burnett-Stuart, Unpublished Memoirs, pp. 120–2. These memoirs were not seen by Dr Winton.

[8] Dennis, pp, 55–6. Dr Dennis cites some evidence in support of his thesis that the continental commitment entailed conscription, but in peacetime at any rate the War Office and the General Staff regarded five Regular and 12 TA divisions as the maximum force that could be put into the field.

[9] Liddell Hart Papers 11/1935/120, Martel, 26 Dec. 1935.

[10] Pownall Diary, 27 Jan. 1936.

[11] L. R. Pratt, *East of Malta, West of Suez: Britain's Mediterranean Crisis 1936–1939* (1975), pp. 22–5. Gibbs, i. 215, stresses that ministers needed little persuading by the COS that war with Italy should be avoided.

[12] R. Quartararo, 'Imperial Defence in the Mediterranean on the eve of the Ethiopian Crisis (July–October 1935)', *Historical Journal,*

20, I (1977), 185–220. See also Pownall's pessimistic assessment of the situation in his Diary, 16 Sept. 1935.

[13] Cab 53/5, COS 149th, 150th, 158th meetings on 6 and 13 Sept., and 5 Dec. 1935. See also Cab 53/25, COS394, and Cab 53/26, COS411. In this paragraph I have followed generally Welch, pp. 218–24.

[14] Welch, pp. 225–7. Gibbs, i. 215–16. Pownall Diary, 9, 16, and 23 Sept., 3 and 9 Oct., 4, 7, 25 Nov. 1935.

[15] For example Gibbs, Pratt, and Quartararo.

[16] Quartararo remarks that the Italian confrontation of 1935–6 can be regarded as the 'dress rehearsal' for the coming of the real war in 1940–2.

[17] Gibbs, i. 254.

[18] Cab 16/112, DRC Third Report, 21 Nov. 1935. Gibbs, i. 257–8, 261–3.

[19] Pownall's Diary entry begins on Monday 13 January 1936 but the week's events were probably all written up at the following weekend.

[20] Ibid. Pownall found Weir's ideas on the relative roles of the Army and RAF 'fairly absurd'. He also thought Weir's remarks about the inability of industry to carry out the production programme excessively pessimistic, perhaps because of his innate Scottish caution. 'I should have thought that if firms are told clearly what is wanted they will themselves do more than is anticipated if only for the financial gains that will accrue.' The Air Ministry, however, did have some difficulty with firms unwilling to invest in new plant and machinery. For the Ministerial discussions (DPR) of the DRC Report see Cab 16/123.

[21] Weir marked and retained copies of Liddell Hart's three articles on 'The Army Today' in *The Times*, Nov. 1935, see Weir Papers 17/10 139–41. In turn a senior RAF officer briefed Liddell Hart on Weir's reasons as to why the Government should give the RAF priority over the other two Services, Liddell Hart Papers 11/1936/30, Talk with R. H. Peck, 24 Jan. 1936. At this period Liddell Hart persuasively put the 'limited liability' case to Lord Halifax, see Liddell Hart Papers 11/1936/29, Talk with Lord Halifax, 22 Jan. 1936 (Brooks' Club). Cf. Peden, p. 123, who makes a good case for Trenchard's prior influence on Chamberlain in 1934.

[22] W. J. Reader, *Architect of Air Power* (1968), pp. 230–1. Middlemas and Barnes, *Baldwin*, p. 903.

[23] Cab 16/123, 2nd, 4th, and 7th meetings and memorandum No. 6. Duff Cooper also put his case for a continental commitment of the Field Force at a dinner party at Buck's Club on 14 February 1936 where his guests were Churchill, Fuller, Trenchard, and Liddell

Hart. See Liddell Hart Papers 11/1936/40.

[24] Cab 21/422(A), DPR(DR).

[25] Cab 16/123, 4th meeting. Reader, pp. 234–5. Shay, pp. 87–9, notes that Baldwin had lost political prestige over the Hoare–Laval fiasco and was in poor health. In his final months of office he failed to provide decisive leadership, especially in rearmament.

[26] Cab 4/24, CID1211-B, 27 Jan. 1936. Gibbs, i. 228–34. Middlemas and Barnes, p. 924n.

[27] Gibbs, i. 242–9. Middlemas and Barnes, p. 924.

[28] Cab 53/5, COS166, Memorandum on the International Situation, 12 Mar. 1936. See also Cab 53/27, COS441 (JP), Condition of our Forces to meet a possible war with Germany, 16 Mar. 1936. Three weeks after mobilization the first contingent of the Field Force (2 divisions) would still be without any tank units and would be 'largely on a horsed basis'. There would be no anti-tank weapons or infantry mortars and only sufficient artillery ammunition for four months.

[29] Pownall Diary, 8 and 9 Mar. 1936, probably written up the following weekend, 14–15 March. Note the hostile tone of his references to the French.

[30] Liddell Hart Papers 11/1936/45, Note on the Re-occupation of the Rhineland, 7 Mar. 1936.

[31] Middlemas and Barnes, p. 925.

[32] Pownall Diary, 30 Mar., 7 and 15 Apr. 1936. Cab 53/27, COS452, 454 (JP), and 455 (JP). The last paper cited contains a list of the War Office questions which could be put to the French and Belgians. After a CID discussion of the forthcoming Staff conversations on 3 April 1936 (Cab 2/6, 276th meeting), Hankey added the following gloss: 'The Committee recognized that the French and Belgians might be disagreeably surprised at the information we had to convey; nevertheless it was thought desirable that the exact position should be described, although undue emphasis need not be laid on our deficiencies.'

[33] Dill to Montgomery-Massingberd, 20 Apr. 1936 (copy in Dill Papers). Liddell Hart Papers 11/1936/64, Talk with Paget and Adam, 15 May 1936. Dennis, pp. 68–9.

[34] Cab 53/28, COS472. Eden's letter to the Prime Minister, 6 June 1936, was referred to the COS for their opinion. In ibid. COS478, Eden informed Inskip that the French were now inquiring about the British taking over Belgium's coastal defences. See also Cab 23/84 30(36) 1. For Eden's later account see his *Facing the Dictators* (1962), pp. 370–4, 389–90.

[35] Gibbs, i. 253–4.

[36] WO33/1370, War Office and Air Ministry Exercise, 1935. Burnett-Stuart, Unpublished Memoirs, pp. 130–7. Liddell Hart Papers 3/106, Liddell Hart to Barrington-Ward, 18 Sept. 1936.

[37] Cab 53/27, COS460 (JP), 29 Apr. 1936. If the recent Mediterranean commitments could be cancelled the Field Force might be improved by one Air Defence Brigade, one light tank battalion, 12th Lancers (armoured cars), and certain ancillary troops. The scale of transport vehicles and other stores could also be increased.

[38] The RAF aspect of the plans was equally sketchy. It was suggested that initially British light bombers would attack Germany from continental bases while heavy bombers would operate from England. If the Field Force was in reserve it would be allocated only two air co-operation squadrons. Ibid. 24.

[39] Cab 53/6, COS 174th meeting, The Situation in Europe, 13 May 1936.

[40] See Kieft, *Belgium's Return to Neutrality* (1972).

[41] Ibid. 56. Dr Kieft argues persuasively that Belgian foreign policy in 1936 was largely determined by the domestic rivalry between Flemings and Walloons but later shifts his ground to suggest that Britain's failure to provide a counterweight to Germany was of great significance. He is, however, right to insist (p. 164) that 'Britain wanted Western European co-operation without being willing or able to pay the price for it.'

[42] Ibid. 107–15. Cab 53/6, COS 187th meeting, 20th Oct. 1936. In a rambling discussion the COS inclined to the view that Belgian neutrality, which had just been proclaimed, was an advantage to Britain. Deverell remarked that according to the Military Attaché in Paris Gamelin had said the whole of the French General Staff's plans were based on the assumption that in event of war with Germany they would lend immediate and maximum military support to Belgium. Now France would have to continue her fortifications to the sea.

[43] Kieft, pp. 73–7. Under her new policy of strict neutrality Belgium broke off all official military contacts with Britain and France and prepared to defend herself against the latter as well as Germany. Unofficially, however, King Leopold encouraged continuing contacts with both France and Britain, see *Les Relations militaires franco-belges Mars 1936–10 Mai 1940* (Paris, 1968). For the COS opposition to staff talks see Cab 53/6, COS 178th meeting, 16 June 1936.

[44] Kieft, pp. 136–44. Cab 53/6, COS 189th meeting, The Position of Belgium in a Five Power Conference, 9 Dec. 1936. See also Cab 53/29, COS528.

[45] Chatfield frequently complained in the COS Committee about the lack of Foreign Office guidance on long-range policy, and on one occasion (20 October 1936) he queried 'if we had no agreement at all with France would Germany ever want to go to war with us?' Chatfield's memorandum to Hoare on 'The Situation as regards Belgium', 11 Dec. 1936 (Chatfield Papers), is cited by Welch, p. 243n.

See also Roskill *Hankey*, iii. 227.

[46] Duff Cooper, *Old Men Forget,* chapter 12. Middlemas and Barnes, pp. 941–2, 949. Pownall Diary, 25 May, 8 and 15 June 1936.

[47] Cab 53/28, COS497 (491 JP). Pownall also favoured cutting the ties with France and coming to an arrangement with Germany, Diary, 25 May 1936.

[48] Cab 55/8, COS 155th meeting (JP), 26 Oct. 1936, and Cab 53/29, COS513 (JP).

[49] Cab 21/509. In June 1936 Pownall submitted to Hankey an 11-page memorandum on 'The Role of the Army in a Major Continental War' which ably marshalled the arguments in favour of preparedness for such a role. Hankey minuted that 'This is first rate and most opportune' and that Dill considered it 'magnificent'. Haining and Inskip also saw it. Hankey used Pownall's memorandum as the basis for his own of 18 January 1937. On Vansittart's views see Dennis, pp. 86–8, 94.

[50] Liddell Hart Papers 11/1936/99, Talk with Field-Marshal Sir Cyril Deverell, 12 Nov. 1936. See also Dennis, pp. 82–3.

[51] Cab 53/29, COS537, 21 Dec. 1936. Appendices A–D comprise the combative memoranda exchanged by Duff Cooper and Neville Chamberlain. While Duff Cooper stressed the deplorable unreadiness of even the first two divisions of the Regular Field Force, whose cavalry, field artillery, and transport was still dependent largely on horses, the Chancellor emphasized 'the political temper of people in this country' which was 'strongly opposed to Continental adventures' and 'suspicious of any preparations made in peacetime with a view to large-scale military operations on the Continent'.

[52] Cab 23/86 75(36)3, The Role of the British Army, 16 Dec. 1936. Shay, pp. 136–7.

[53] Cab 21/509, Hankey to Inskip (typed copy), 17 Dec. 1936.

[54] Cab 53/6, COS 192nd and 193rd meetings.

[55] Cab 53/30, COS550.

[56] Cab 24/267, CP46(37), The Role of the Army, memorandum by Inskip, 2 Feb. 1937. Shay, pp. 138–9. See also Gibbs, i. 454–5.

[57] Cab 23/88 37(4), 5 May 1937. Gibbs, i. 456–8. Dennis, pp. 95–9.

[58] Welch admirably brings out the COS's persisting internal disagreements which were seldom even hinted at in their reports. For the suggestion of growing opposition to the continental land commitment within the Air Ministry I am indebted to Uri Bialer's unpublished doctoral thesis (University of London, 1974), 'Some aspects of the Fear of Bombardment from the Air and the Making of British Defence and Foreign Policy 1932–1939', see especially pp. 250–71. See also his 'The British Chiefs of Staff and the Limited Liability Formula of

1938, a Note', in *Military Affairs*, xlii, No. 2 (Apr. 1978) 98–9.

59 Welch, p. 265, and see also pp. 253–4.

60 Gibbs, i. 454n.

61 Ibid. 458–60.

62 Liddell Hart Papers 11/1937/49, Note, 3 June 1937. *Old Men Forget*, pp. 194–5. Shay, p. 158, suggests that Chamberlain decided to keep Duff Cooper in the Cabinet as a lesser evil than adding him to the Conservative back-bench critics of the rearmament programme.

63 Cab 24/273, CP316(37), Interim Report on Defence Expenditure in Future Years, 15 Dec. 1937, cited by Shay, p. 166.

64 Ibid. 166–8.

Notes to Chapter 9

1 Minney *The Private Papers of Hore-Belish*, p. 18. Dennis, pp. 100–1.

2 *The Ironside Diaries*, p. 24. For Deverell's later account of his relationship with Hore-Belisha see Deverell Papers, Deverell to Brigadier H. Sandilands, 8 Aug. 1945, and 26 Jan. 1947.

3 Liddell Hart, *Memoirs*, ii. In addition to documents now available in the PRO, several published accounts throw new light on the Hore-Belisha ministry; for example, Brian Bond (ed.), *Chief of Staff*, I (Pownall), and Colville, *Man of Valour* (Gort).

4 See Bond, *Liddell Hart*, chapters 3 and 4.

5 Liddell Hart Papers 11/1937/113.

6 Liddell Hart, *Memoirs*, ii. 3–8, 146.

7 Minney, p. 35, Dennis, pp. 102–3, Gibbs, i. 465. Shay, p. 164.

8 *Ironside Diaries*, p. 26.

9 Dr Peden's *British Rearmament and the Treasury 1932–1939* is largely presented from the Treasury viewpoint and tends to defend its policies and actions. By contrast, Shay's *British Rearmament in the Thirties* is concerned with the wider issue of the Government's handling of rearmament and is more critical of the Treasury's doctrine and influence, see particularly pp. 95–7, 103–6, 125–32, 148–53, 159–63, 207, 247–9, 263, 276–7, 286–95.

10 Keith Middlemas, *Diplomacy of Illusion: the British Government and Germany, 1937–1939* (1972), pp. 124–7.

11 Peden, pp. 118–21, 127–30, 137–8, 182. See also Shay, pp. 183–8.

12 Middlemas, pp. 81–2.

13 Ibid. 121–3. Pownall Diary, 18 Feb. 1938.

14 Liddell Hart, *Memoirs*, i. 386. Minney, p. 54.

15 Liddell Hart, *Memoirs*, ii. 13–28.

[16] Ibid. 37. Minney, pp. 59–60, 69. Cab 21/554, Ismay to Hankey, 6 Jan. 1938, and Ismay's note on talks with General Lelong, 28 Jan. 1938. Cab 21/575, Deverell's report on the French and German manœuvres, 15 Oct. 1937.

[17] Cab 21/509, Entries between 29 Oct. and 2 Nov. 1937.

[18] Liddell Hart Papers 11/1937/94, Talk with Deverell, 18 Nov. 1937. Beaufre, *1940: the Fall of France*, pp. 52–3.

[19] *Ironside Diaries*, pp. 38–9. Pownall Diary, 1 Jan. 1938.

[20] Middlemas, p. 125. In January 1938 Hore-Belisha wrote to Chamberlain that, because of the Army's new priorities, no medium tanks were required, and there was no provision even to design a heavy tank for use in a European war. Dennis, p. 130, also notes that Liddell Hart overlooked the necessity of strong artillery to protect the Field Force.

[21] Bond, *Liddell Hart*, chapter 4.

[22] Roskill, *Hankey*, iii. (1974), pp. 285, 290–1. See also Middlemas, p. 68.

[23] Peden, pp. 138–9. Shay, pp. 138–9, points out that by this time Hankey and Inskip were in close collaboration.

[24] Gibbs, i. 467–73. Dennis, pp. 109–12. Middlemas, 123–5. Howard, *The Continental Commitment*, p. 117.

[25] Howard, *The Continental Commitment*, p. 117.

[26] Pownall Diary, 1 and 3 Jan. 1938.

[27] *Ironside Diaries*, pp. 42–3, 46–8. Dennis, p. 118.

[28] Peden, pp. 135–45.

[29] See Barry D. Powers, *Strategy Without Slide-Rule* (1976).

[30] Cab 2/7, CID 313th meeting, 17 Mar. 1938.

[31] Gibbs, i. 460–4. *Ironside Diaries*, p. 47. The amount of space given to air defence matters in the second volume of the Liddell Hart *Memoirs* indicates the extent of War Office concern with the subject.

[32] *Ironside Diaries*, pp. 46–7, 57–60.

[33] Liddell Hart Papers 11/1938/58, Lunch with Hobart, 24 May 1938, and 11/1938/89, Outline of the Opposition to the Development of the AA Defence of Great Britain, 30 July 1938.

[34] Cab 53/8, COS 227th meeting Military Preparations in relation to Imperial Defence, 19 Jan. 1938.

[35] Cab 21/510, Ismay to Hankey, 1 Dec. 1937. Peden, p. 126.

[36] Cab 16/181, DP(P) minutes of meeting, 19 Apr. 1937. *Ironside Diaries*, p. 46.

[37] See especially Pratt, *East of Malta, West of Suez: Britain's Mediterranean Crisis, 1936–1939*.

[38] Ibid. 69, 93–7, 115–17, 123.

[39] Gibbs, i. 473, 483–6. *Ironside Diaries*, p. 45.

[40] Pratt, pp. 124–9. See also M. J. Cohen, 'British Strategy and the

Palestine Question 1936–39', in *Journal of Contemporary History*, 7 (July–Oct. 1972), 157–83.

41 Pratt, pp. 162–3. Pownall Diary, 4 July, 29 Aug., 26 Sept. 1938.

42 Pratt, p. 164.

43 Liddell Hart, *Memoirs*, ii. 89–99. Gibbs, i. 481. Pownall Diary, 21 Feb. 1938. Shay, pp. 189–93.

44 WO33/1502, The Organisation of the Army for its Role in War 10 Feb. 1938. Dennis, pp. 119–21.

45 Dennis, pp. 123–6, Minney, pp. 92–8.

46 Gibbs, i. 481. *Ironside Diaries*, pp. 53–5.

47 Middlemas, pp. 180–3, 193–5. Liddell Hart, *Memoirs*, ii. 143–5. Pownall Diary, 7 Mar., 30 May, 13 June 1938.

48 Middlemas, p. 63. Cab 16/181, p. 14. Cab 4/27, CID 1391-B, p. 2. Pownall Diary, 14, 21, and 25 Feb. 1938. *Ironside Diaries*, p. 51. Pratt, pp. 100–1.

49 Gibbs, i. 623–32. Cab 53/8, COS 228th meeting Staff Conversations with France and Belgium, 28 Jan. 1938. Cab 53/35, (JP) ibid, 21 Jan. 1938 (accepted as COS680 on 4 Feb.). Cab 53/37, COS706, ibid., Note by Secretary, 7 Apr. 1938.

50 Cab 2/7, CID 319th meeting, 11 Apr. 1938. Gibbs, i. 632–6. See also the running commentary on the approach to staff conversations in the Pownall Diary, April 1938.

51 Gibbs, i. 637–40. Minney, p. 120.

52 Gibbs, pp. 640–1. Dennis, pp. 132–3. Liddell Hart Papers 11/1938/64, Extract from Notes on a Talk with M. de Margerie. 3 June, and 11/1938/82, Note for Barrington-Ward, 4 July.

53 Cab 53/37, COS698, (Revise), Military Implications of German aggression against Czechoslovakia, 28 Mar. 1938. Gibbs, i. 642–6.

54 *Ironside Diaries*, pp. 28–30, 40–1, 62.

55 Pownall Diary, 21 Feb., 7 Mar. 1938.

56 *Ironside Diaries*, p. 29. Pownall Diary, 26 Sept. 1938. Cab 53/9, COS 245th meeting, 25 July 1938. Gamelin's ambivalent intentions about a French advance into Germany were communicated to the British on 26 September, but the CIGS and CAS were unable to tell him anything about their plans, see Cab 21/595. For the influence of the pessimistic French high command on its Government see Robert J. Young, 'French Policy and the Munich Crisis of 1938: a Reappraisal', in Canadian Historical Association's *Historical Papers* (1970), 186–206.

57 Cab 53/40, COS755, Draft Appreciation of the Situation in event of war with Germany in April 1939.

58 This paragraph generally follows Gibbs, i. 646–8, but for a different view see R. Skidelsky's review article, 'Going to War with Germany', in *Encounter* (July 1972). Skidelsky stresses that Chamberlain

wanted an agreement with Hitler without any major re-distribution of power in Germany's favour. Thus if Hitler sought revisionism in Central Europe he had to act quickly and brutally before Britain and France rearmed.

59 Cab 53/41, COS765, (Revise), Appreciation of the Situation in event of war against Germany, 14 Sept. 1938. Ibid. COS770, The Czech Crisis, 23 Sept. 1938. For the Joint Planning Committee's gloomy analysis on which the COS reports were founded see Cab 55/13, COS309 (JP), 13 Sept. 1938.

60 Gibbs, i. 646. Middlemas, p. 330. Howard, p. 125. Cab 21/544, Memorandum by Ismay, 20 Sept. 1938. Roy Douglas, *In the Year of Munich* (1977), p. 57. Ismay subsequently changed his mind completely and recorded that 'From the purely military point of view, it would have paid us to go to war in 1938', Lord Ismay, *Memoirs*, p. 92.

61 For Brigadier Stronge's account of his role during the Czech crisis see B. Bond and I. Roy (eds.), *War and Society Yearbook*, 1 (1976), pp. 162–77. Milan Hauner, 'Czechoslovakia as a Military Factor in British Considerations of 1938', *Journal of Strategic Studies*, i, No. 2 (Sept. 1978), 194–222. This study fills a serious gap by its careful analysis of the military balance between Czechoslovakia and Germany in 1938 and also of the problem of Czech military morale. For D. Vital, 'Czechoslovakia and the Powers September 1938', see Hans W. Gatzke (ed.), *European Diplomacy Between Two Wars 1919–1939* (Chicago, 1972) or *Journal of Contemporary History*, i (Oct. 1966). Pownall Diary, 27 Sept. 1938, confirms the importance of Mason-Macfarlane's flight to London on that day. See also A. Adamthwaite *France and the Coming of the Second World War* (1977), pp. 231–8, Middlemas, pp. 246–7, 387, and Douglas, p. 67.

62 Middlemas, p. 401. Cab 53/9 COS 250th meeting, 13 Sept. 1938. The chairman and CAS Newall advocated closer collaboration with France whose military plans were then unknown to the COS.

63 Liddell Hart Papers 11/1938/103, Appreciation of the War which now threatens. See also *Memoirs*, ii. 118, 141–6, 151–4.

64 Middlemas, pp. 283–4, 354. Douglas, pp. 76–7.

65 Peden, p. 145.

66 Williamson Murray, 'German Air Power and the Munich Crisis', in B. Bond and I. Roy (eds.), *War and Society Yearbook* 2 (1977), pp. 107–18. See also Adamthwaite, pp 233–44. But grandiose plans for long-range bombers were adumbrated in Germany in the 1930s, see R. J. Overy, 'From "Uralbomber" to "Amerikabomber": the Luftwaffe and Strategic Bombing', in *Journal of Strategic Studies*, i, No. 2 (Sept. 1978), 154–78.

67 Middlemas, pp 410–13. Skidelsky, in *Encounter* (July 1972), differs from Middlemas in believing that Chamberlain had not lost

the chance to strike a bargain with Hitler at Munich provided he was willing to give Hitler a free hand in central and south-eastern Europe. According to this view Chamberlain fell between the two stools of armed resistancce and genuine appeasement.

[68] Liddell Hart, *Memoirs*, ii. 168. On the sixth day of mobilization barely half Britain's anti-aircraft guns were in a position to engage an attacker.

[69] Ibid. 161–2, 166, 170, 193–4. Douglas, p. 73. Hauner's conclusion (see n. 61 above) is that 'In 1939 Britain and France were strategically in a much worse position than before 30th September 1938.'

[70] Pownall Diary, 13 Jan. 1938. Howard makes a similar point in *The Continental Commitment*, p. 120.

Notes to Chapter 10

[1] Middlemas, p. 421. Dennis, pp. 143–4, 149. *Ironside Diaries*, p. 70.

[2] Cab 24/279, CP234(38), Defence Preparations: forecast of supply position and basic of future policy.

[3] Adamthwaite, pp. 226–7, 278–81. For a contrary view that Daladier's attitude during the Munich crisis was greatly influenced by his belief in French military weakness see Young, 'French Policy and the Munich Crisis of 1938'.

[4] Adamthwaite, pp. 245–8. Dennis, p. 150. Middlemas, pp. 445–6, 451–4. See also Robert J. Young, 'The Aftermath of Munich: the Course of French Diplomacy, October 1938 to March 1939', in *French Historical Studies*, viii, No. 2 (Fall 1973), 305–22.

[5] Cab 21/510, Committee on Defence Programmes and Acceleration D (38)3, 1 Nov. Pownall Diary, 3 and 17 Oct., 7 Nov. On Hankey see Roskill, *Hankey*, iii. 393 and Douglas, p. 80. On Liddell Hart see his *Memoirs*, ii. 193–6.

[6] Dennis, p. 156. The letters were published on 8, 16, 19, 22, 28 November 1938. See also Adamthwaite, p. 251. Brigadier Martel expressed anxiety to Liddell Hart lest Burnett-Stuart's letter in *The Times* on 28 November should check the development of tanks. Liddell Hart Papers 11/1938/122.

[7] Cab 23/95, 56/38, Anglo-French Staff Conversations, 18 Nov. 1938. Pownall Diary, 21 Nov. 1938.

[8] Dennis, pp. 151–4. Adamthwaite, pp. 249–51. Middlemas, pp. 443–5.

[9] Pownall Diary, 14 and 28 Nov. 1938.

[10] Adamthwaite, pp. 249–51. Dennis, p. 156.

[11] Pownall Diary, 5 Dec. 1938.

[12] Cab 24/282, CP27(39), Preparedness of the Army in relation to its role. Gibbs, i. 503–4.

[13] Cab 2/8, CID 341st meeting, 15 Dec. 1938.

[14] Cab 53/10, COS 265th meeting, 21 Dec. 1938. Even making allowance for new commitments since the First World War and the increased importance of ADGB, the CIGS believed it would be possible to maintain at least the whole of the Territorial divisions when war potential had been fully developed, and if preparations were made in peacetime it should be easy to put four Territorial divisions into the field at four-monthly intervals, see Cab 51/510, Gort to Ismay, 21 Dec. 1938.

[15] Dennis, pp. 155–9. Cab 53/44, COS827(JP), Strategic Position in a European War (Enclosure to Annex 1), 25 Jan. 1939. See also Cab 21/510, Inskip to Ismay, 4 Jan. 1939.

[16] Pownall Diary, 2 and 23 Jan. 1939. Cab 21/511, Backhouse to Ismay, 9 and 16 Jan., Ismay to Backhouse, 12 Jan. Backhouse's sympathetic view of the continental commitment may in part have reflected his sharp reaction against his predecessor's obsession with preparing the fleet for war against Japan, see R. John Pritchard, 'The Far East as an Influence on the Chamberlain Government's Pre-War European Policies', in *Millenium,* 2, No. 3 (Winter 1973–4), 15.

[17] Cab 53/10, COS 268th meeting, 18 Jan. 1939.

[18] Cab 53/44, COS827, The State of Preparedness of the Army in Relation to its Role. Gibbs, i. 504–8.

[19] Cab 2/8, CID 345th meeting, Supply Organisation in War, 26 Jan. 1939. Minney, pp. 171–2.

[20] Cab 53/44, COS829, German aggression against Holland, 24 Jan. 1939. Cab 24/282, CP3(39), Possible German aggression against Holland, Report of FPC, 27 Jan. Cab 23/3, (39)1, Review of the International Situation, 1 Feb. See also Gibbs, i. 499–500, and Middlemas, pp. 427, 438–9.

[21] Cab 23/97, 5(39), Preparedness of the Army in relation to its role, 2 Feb. Gibbs, pp. 509–11.

[22] Cab 23/97, 8(39), idem, 22 Feb. Pownall Diary, 30 Jan. Gibbs, i. 512–13.

[23] Adamthwaite, p. 254. Dennis, pp. 170–1, 182. Shay, pp. 236–8.

[24] Cab 23/97, 8(39). Cab 55/15, COS375(JP), Enclosed extracts from draft minutes of Strategical Appreciation Sub-Committee, 13 Mar. 1939. For the minutes of this committee's six meetings between 1 March and 17 April 1939 see Cab 16/209. Gibbs, i. 423n, lists its members.

[25] Liddell Hart Papers 11/1939/6 and *Memoirs,* ii. 211. Bond, *Liddell Hart,* p. 104. Dennis, pp. 171–2.

26 Minney, pp. 173–9. Dennis, pp. 176–8. Pownall Diary, 12 Mar. 1939.

27 Dennis, pp. 178–82. Minney, pp. 181–2. Liddell Hart, *Memoirs*, ii. 223–4.

28 Adamthwaite, pp. 300–6. Middlemas, p. 400. S. Aster, *1939: The Making of the Second World War* (1973) pp. 92–4. In *March 1939: The British Guarantee to Poland* (1976) Simon Newman concludes that 'Appeasement' did not fail because it was never seriously tried. By this paradoxical statement he means that, although Chamberlain was not prepared to make a military stand over Czechoslovakia, he was not prepared either to give Hitler *carte blanche* to expand in eastern and south-eastern Europe but rather attempted to raise political and economic barriers to further German expansion. Dr Newman demonstrates that as a consequence of Prague Halifax and the Foreign Office were prepared to face the risk of war by guaranteeing Poland, but he does not show that Chamberlain experienced a comparable conversion. Dr Newman generally follows Robert Skidelsky's interpretation in his review article in *Encounter* (July 1972). This argues that Chamberlain, having assumed at Munich that Hitler's objectives were strictly limited, swung to the other extreme after Prague and believed him to be bent on world conquest.

29 Newman, pp. 120–1, shows that political rather than strategic considerations prepared the way for the guarantee to Poland. See also Adamthwaite, p. 305.

30 Minney, pp. 187–8. Dennis, pp. 197–200. Shay, pp. 275–7.

31 Ismay, *Memoirs*, p. 93. Slessor, *The Central Blue*, pp. 183–4. Pownall Diary, 3 Apr. 1939.

32 Newman, pp. 112, 136, 150–6, 186–97, 204, 219. See also Aster, p. 105. Middlemas, p. 457.

33 Cab 53/10, COS 285th and 286th meetings, 28 and 30 Mar. 1939. Cab 53/47, COS872, Military Implications of an Anglo-French guarantee of Poland and Roumania, Report, 3 Apr. 1939. See also Aster, pp. 96–9, 105–9, 127, and Dennis, pp. 201–5.

34 Newman, pp. 139–42. Pownall Diary, 3 Apr. Slessor, pp. 229–31.

35 Dennis, pp. 193–5, 215. Adamthwaite, 313–14.

36 Minney, pp. 195–9. Churchill, who greatly admired Hore-Belisha's struggle with Chamberlain over conscription, remarked: 'I saw something of him in this ordeal, and he was never sure that each day in office would not be his last.' Even Sir John Simon, who as Home Secretary had resigned on the issue in 1916, accepted the necessity for conscription in 1939 before the Prime Minister.

37 Dennis, pp. 212, 217. Minney, pp. 191–2.

38 Pownall Diary, 30 Apr. Minney, pp. 193, 206.

[39] Dennis, pp. 217, 222, 225. Newman, p. 221, comes close to suggesting that Britain was more responsible than Germany for the outbreak of the Second World War.

Notes to Chapter 11

[1] On the COS's attitude to staff talks see Cab 53/44, COS838, 6 Feb. 1939. For a detailed summary of the staff talks in 1939 see Gibbs, i. 653–84.

[2] Cab 53/47, COS877, Anglo-French Staff Conversations, Report on Stage 1, 11 Apr. 1939. See also Aster, pp. 143–4, and Gibbs, pp. 668–74.

[3] Cab 53/48, COS900(JP), 5 May 1939. Cab 53/49, COS914, Anglo-French Staff Conversations, Report on Stage 2, 11 May 1939. Aster, pp. 145–6.

[4] Cab 53/50, COS927. The British delegation comprised Brigadier E. Clayton, Captain H. B. Rawlings, and Group-Captain A. P. Davidson.

[5] Cab 53/51, COS939 (Revise), 18 July 1939. Cab 53/51, COS940(JP), 7 July 1939. Aster, pp. 147–9.

[6] Pratt, pp. 173–93. Gibbs, i. 668.

[7] Williamson Murray, 'The Role of Italy in British Strategy 1938–1939', *RUSI Journal* (Sept. 1979).

[8] Sir John Kennedy, *The Business of War* (1957), p. 9. The unpublished portions of Ironside's diary for the summer of 1939 contain numerous references to his belief that Britain must give priority to the Middle East and offensive operations against Italy. On Ironside's views see Pile's letter to Liddell Hart of 20 August in Liddell Hart Papers 11/1939/72. See also *idem,* 11/1939/37, for the naval view that in April 1939 British strategy aimed to knock out Italy in six weeks.

[9] Cab 2/8, CID 360th meeting, 12 June 1939. Cab 53/52, COS942(JP), 12 July 1939.

[10] *Ironside Diaries,* pp. 78–83. Kennedy, pp. 12–13. Aster, pp. 149–50, 212–13.

[11] Cab 53/48, COS887.

[12] *Ironside Diaries,* p. 78. Aster, pp. 150–1 and chapter 6, for British attitudes to an alliance with the Soviet Union. For ambivalent French views of the Soviet Union see Adamthwaite, pp. 272–4, 311–12. For a vivid first-hand account of the Anglo-French mission to Moscow see Beaufre, *1940: the Fall of France,* chapter 6.

[13] Adamthwaite, pp. 332–3. Pownall Diary, 5 June.

[14] Pownall Diary, 16 July. Kennedy, pp. 10–11. Gamelin struck Kennedy as 'a slick and clever talker, and rather a "political" soldier'.

He was 'an insignificant little man who shook hands flabbily, and without looking one in the face'. Worse still, he failed Gort's standard test by not knowing the name of the commander of the French guard of honour. Not a propitious beginning.

15 Gibbs, i. 679–80. Adamthwaite, p. 333.

16 Cab 53/11, COS 309th meeting, 19 July 1939. Kennedy, p. 11. On the continuing disagreement and friction among the COS about air matters in 1939 see Welch, pp. 325–31. In the summer of 1939 personal relations among the COS were as bad as during the Beatty–Trenchard era and the CAS was still the odd man out because both the senior Services felt they had a right to more air support and air forces under their own control. Dr Welch concludes that 'Continual consultation among the C.O.S. had not produced a better understanding among the Services; familiarity with each other's views had bred contempt rather than compromise.'

17 The following section (notes 18–30 inclusive) is based largely upon a draft chapter of Derek Waldie's forthcoming doctoral dissertation on 'Relations between the Army and the Royal Air Force, 1918–1939'. I am most grateful to Mr Waldie for permission to draw upon his research.

18 Air 9/30, 19 and 28 Apr. 1926.

19 *Flight Magazine*, vol. xix (10 Mar. 1927), 135. Major R. G. Cherry, 'The R.A.F. and Army Cooperation', in *Journal of the U.S.I. of India*, vol. lv (Oct. 1925), 32, both cited by Waldie. Sir Charles Broad recalled that, after he had persuaded some pilots to give a demonstration of ground straffing at a practice camp in the late 1920s, the War Office was admonished by the Air Ministry for encouraging young airmen to contravene official policy. Broad to Liddell Hart, 7 Jan. 1966, Liddell Hart Papers.

20 Cab 53/5, COS 134th meeting, 1 Nov. 1934. Air Vice Marshal Capel was interviewed by Waldie in April 1977.

21 Cab 53/8, COS 219th meeting, 19 Oct. 1937. Cab 53/33, COS624 (JIC), 6 Oct. 1937.

22 Air 2/2895, Joint Committee on Air Requirements for the Field Force, 30 June 1939.

23 WO32/3115, Notes on Certain Lessons of the Great War, p. 12. C. M. McAlery, 'The Air Arm in the Army Manoeuvres', *The Aeroplane*, vol. xlix (25 Sept. 1935), 377, cited by Waldie.

24 Waldie, pp. 64–6.

25 Meeting held on 11 December 1935, referred to in Cab 53/50, COS924, and Air 2/2895.

26 Copy of the Army Council's memorandum, 31 March 1939, attached to Cab 53/48, COS881. Cab 21/521, Gort to CID Secretary, circulated as COS881.

[27] Cab 21/521, 12 June 1939, circulated as COS924, Cab 53/50, 14 June 1939.

[28] Cab 53/11, COS 292nd meeting minute 8, 1 May 1939.

[29] Air 2/2895, note by Director of Plans, 29 June 1939.

[30] Air 2/2895, Joint WO/Air Ministry Committee, 30 June 1939.

[31] L. F. Ellis, *The War in France and Flanders 1939–1940* (1953), p. 7. Lord Ismay, *Memoirs*, p. 104.

[32] Pownall Diary, 23 Apr. 1939.

[33] L. Carr to P. C. S. Hobart, 2 June 1939, Hobart Correspondence with Liddell Hart (folder 1) in Liddell Hart Papers.

[34] *Ironside Diaries*, pp. 51–88 J. R. M. Butler, *Grand Strategy*, vol. ii (1957), pp. 27–9. Gibbs, i. 516n, 524–6. See also Postan, *British War Production*, p. 73, for the great increase in War Office requirements of certain items between December 1938 and April 1940, for example tanks and carriers from 5,025 to 18,743; motor vehicles and motor cycles from 25,545 to 376,299; shells (excluding anti-aircraft) from 14.8 million to 64.4 million.

[35] Montgomery, *Memoirs*, pp. 49–50.

[36] Minney, pp. 39–47, 95–7, 179–80, 206–9. Liddell Hart, *The Defence of Britain*, pp. 329–33, 384–410.

[37] Colville, *Man of Valour*, p. 134.

[38] Liddell Hart, *Memoirs*, ii. 238–9. *Ironside Diaries*, pp. 76, 79. Kennedy, *The Business of War*, p. 18.

[39] Liddell Hart, *Memoirs*, ii. 261. Minney, pp. 229–30. *Ironside Diaries*, pp. 93–4. Pownall Diary, 3 Sept. 1939.

[40] Colville, pp. 137–8, 145.

[41] Major-General L. A. Hawes, 'The Story of the "W" Plan: the move of our forces to France in 1939', in *Army Quarterly* (July 1971), 445–56. According to Hawes the first Anglo-French staff conversations held in France in 1939 were completely onesided. 'There were no interpreters present and General Gamelin spoke so quickly that I am quite sure half of what he said was not understood by the British . . . General Gamelin would talk at great length very rapidly for some minutes about the various proposals and General Gort would reply at once: "D'accord".'

[42] Ellis, pp. 9–10.

[43] Ibid. 15–17.

APPENDIX I

Biographical notes

Adam, Ronald Forbes, 2nd Bt. (General Sir Ronald), b. 1885. Educated Eton and Woolwich. First World War (France and Italy). GSO1 Staff College, Camberley, 1932–5. GSO1 War Office, 1935–6. DDMO, 1936. Commandant Staff College, 1937. DCIGS, 1938–9. AG, 1941–6. General, 1942.

Alexander, Harold Rupert Leofric George, 'Alex' (Field-Marshal Viscount Alexander), b. 1891. Educated Harrow and Sandhurst. First World War (France), wounded, dispatches five times, DSO, MC. IDC, 1930. GSO1 Northern Command, 1932–4. Commander Nowshera Brigade, 1934–8, including Mohmand operations 1935. Commander 1st Division and I Corps, 1938–40. C.-in-C. Middle East, 1942–3, and Allied Armies in Italy, 1943–4. Supreme Allied Commander Mediterranean Theatre, 1944–5. Field-Marshal, 1944.

Armitage, Charles Clement (General Sir Clement), b. 1881. South African War and First World War. Commander School of Artillery, 1927–9. Commander 7th Infantry Bde., 1929–32. Commandant Staff College, Camberley, 1934–6. Commander 1st Division, 1936–8. MGO India, 1938–42.

Auchinleck, Claude John Eyre, 'The Auk' (Field-Marshal Sir Claude), b. 1884. Educated Wellington. First World War (Egypt 1914–15, Mesopotamia, 1916–19). IDC, 1927. Instructor Staff College, Quetta, 1930–3. Commander Peshawar Bde., 1933–6, including Mohmand operations. DCGS India, 1936–8. C.-in-C. India, 1941 and 1943–7. C.-in-C. Middle East, 1941–2.

Backhouse, Roger Roland Charles (Admiral of the Fleet Sir Roger), b. 1878. First World War. Commander 3rd Battle Squadron Atlantic Fleet, 1926–7. Third Sea Lord, 1928–32. Commander 1st Battle Squadron Mediterranean Fleet, 1932–4. C.-in-C. Home Fleet, 1935–8. First Sea Lord and CNS, 1938–9. Admiral, 1934, and Admiral of the Fleet, 1939.

Bartholomew, William Henry, 'Barty' (General Sir William), b. 1877. Educated Newton College, Devon, and Woolwich. Entered RA, 1897. First World War. Commanded 6th Infantry Bde., 1923–6. DRO, 1927–8. Commandant IDC, 1929–31. DMO and I, 1931–4. CGS India, 1934–37. GOC.-in-C. Northern Command, 1937–40.

Beauman, Archibald Bentley (Brig.-Gen.), b. 1889. Educated Malvern and Sandhurst. Joined South Staffs. Regt., 1908. First World War (France and Italy) commanded 69th Infantry Bde., in Italy 1918–19 as one of the youngest brigadiers in the Army. GSO2 Baluchistan District, 1921–5. Chief Instructor, Woolwich, 1926–7. Chief Instructor Small Arms School, Netheravon, 1932–4. Commander 15th Infantry Bde., 1934–8. Retired 1938 but recalled to command a division ('Beauforce') in France in June 1940.

Beaumont-Nesbitt, Frederick George (Major-General), b. 1893. Educated Eton and Sandhurst. Joined Grenadier Guards, 1912. First World War. Military Attaché, Paris, 1936–8. DDMI, 1938–9. DMI, 1939–40. Maj.-Gen. General Staff, 1941–5.

Birch, James Frederick Noel, 'Curly' (General Sir Noel), b. 1865. Educated Marlborough and Woolwich. Entered RA, 1885. South African War. First World War: Commander 7th Bde. RHA, Brig.-Gen. General Staff Cavalry Corps, GOC RA. 7st Division, I Corps, and 1st Army, Artillery Adviser to C.-in-C. France 1916–19 (dispatches eleven times, promoted Lt.-Gen., KCMG). Director-General of the TA, 1921–3. MGO and Member of Army Council, 1923–7. The experimental 'Birch gun' was named after him. Retired 1927.

Birks, Horace Leslie (Maj.-Gen.), b. 1897. Educated University College School. First World War (France 1915–17), joined Tank Corps. Instructor RTC Schools, 1919–24. General Staff appointments Western Command and War Office, 1930–7. Instructor Staff College, Quetta, 1937–9. Served with armour in Second World War, commanding 10th Armoured Division in 1943.

Blakiston-Houston, John (Maj.-Gen.), b. 1881. Educated Cheltenham. South African and First World Wars. Commanded 2nd Cavalry Bde., 1927–31. Commandant Equitation School, Weedon, and Inspector of Cavalry, 1934–8. Retired in 1938 but recalled to command 59th Division, 1939.

Bols, Louis Jean (Lt.-Gen. Sir Louis), b. 1867. Joined Devon Regt., 1887. Bde. commander in France 1915, Brig.-Gen. and Maj.-Gen. on Staff in France 1915–17, Divisional Commander France 1917, CGS Eastern Expeditionary Force, 1917–19. Divisional Commander Southern Command, 1920–4. Governor and C.-in-

C. Bermuda, 1927–30.

Bonham-Carter, Charles (General Sir Charles), b. 1876. Educated Clifton and Sandhurst. South African and First World Wars. DSD, 1927–31. Commander 4th Division 1931–3. Director-General of TA, 1933–6. General, 1937.

Braithwaite, Walter Pipon (General Sir Walter), b. 1865. Educated Bedford and Sandhurst. Joined Somerset Light Infantry, 1886. Commandant Staff College, Quetta, 1911–14. DSD, 1914–15. CGS Mediterranean Expeditionary Force (Gallipoli), 1915, Commander 62nd Division, 1915–18 and IX Corps, 1918–19. GOC.-in-C. Western Command India, 1920–3. Scottish Command, 1923–6. Eastern Command, 1926–7. AG, 1927–31. Retired 1931.

Bridges, Edward (Sir Edward) b. 1892, only son of the Poet Laureate Robert Bridges. Educated Eton and Oxford. First World War: Capt. and Adjutant 4th Bn. Oxford and Bucks Light Infantry. Fellow of All Souls College, Oxford, 1920–7. Entered Treasury, 1919. Assistant Secretary, 1934, and Principal Assistant Secretary, 1937. KCB, 1939. Secretary of the Cabinet, 1938–46.

Broad, Charles Noel Frank (Lt.-Gen. Sir Charles), b. 1882. Educated Wellington and Cambridge. Entered RA, 1905. First World War. Tank Corps, 1916. Commandant Tank Gunnery School, 1924–7. DSD, 1927. Author of official manual *Mechanised and Armoured Formations* ('The Purple Primer') 1929. Commanded armoured brigade in 1931 exercises. Brigadier on General Staff Aldershot Command, 1931–4. Bde. Commander India, 1935–7. Maj.-Gen. i/c administration Aldershot Command, 1937–9. GOC.-in-C. Aldershot Command, 1939–40. GOC.-in-C. Eastern Army India, 1940–2. Retired 1942.

Brooke, Alan Francis, 'Brookie' (Field-Marshal Viscount Alanbrooke), b. 1883. Educated Woolwich and joined RFA in 1902. First World War: GSO2 (RA) Canadian Corps 1917, GSO1 (RA) 1st Army, 1918–19. Instructor Staff College, Camberley, 1923–7. IDC, 1927. Commander 8th Infantry Bde., 1934–5. DMT, 1936–7. Commander of Mobile Division, 1937–8. Commander AA Corps, 1938–9, and GOC.-in-C. AA Command, 1939. Commander II Corps in France, 1939–40. CIGS, 1941–6.

Brough, Alan (Maj.-Gen.), b. 1876. Educated Cheltenham. First World War and South Russia (1919–20). Assistant Director Engineering, War Office, 1927–31. Director of Mechanization, 1932–6. Retired 1936.

Brownrigg, W. D. S. (Lt.-Gen. Sir Douglas), b. 1886. Educated Mulgrave Castle and Sandhurst. Joined Sherwood Foresters 1905. First World War (Gallipoli 1915, Mesopotamia 1915–18).

GSO1, War Office, 1923–7. On Quartermaster's staff, Shanghai. Defence Force, 1927. North China and China Command, 1928–31. Commander 159th Infantry Bde., 1931–3, and 11th Infantry Bde., 1933–4. Commander 51st (Highland) TA Division, 1935–8. Military Secretary to Secretary of State for War, 1938–9. Director-General of the TA, 1939. AG BEF in France, 1939–40.

Campbell, David Graham Muschet (General Sir David), b. 1869. Educated Clifton. Joined 9th Lancers 1889. A noted equestrian who won many famous races including the Grand National (in 1896). South African War. First World War, commanded successively 9th Lancers, a Cavalry Bde., and 21st Division (1916–19). GOC Baluchistan District, 1920–4. Military Secretary to Secretary of State for War 1926–7. C.-in-C. Aldershot Command, 1927–31. Governor and C.-in-C. Malta, 1931–6. Died 1936.

Campbell, Walter (Lt.-Gen. Sir Walter), b. 1864. Educated Wellington, Cambridge, and Sandhurst. Joined Gordon Highlanders 1887. Served in several Indian frontier wars, South Africa, and the First World War. Maj.-Gen. i/c Administration Aldershot Command, 1919–21. QMG, 1923–7. Retired 1927.

Capel, Arthur John (Air Vice Marshal), b. 1894. Educated Marlborough, Oxford, and Sandhurst. France, 1914–18, RFC and RAF. Commandant Army School of Co-operation, Old Sarum, 1936–8. IDC, 1939. Served in France, Britain, and the Middle East, 1939–45.

Carr, Laurence (Lt.-Gen.), b. 1886. Educated Uppingham and Sandhurst. First World War. GSO1, War Office, 1931–4; Directing Staff IDC, 1934–6. Commander 2nd Infantry Bde., 1936–8. DSD, 1938–9. Asst. CIGS, 1939–40. Commander I Corps, 1940–1. GOC.-in-C. Eastern Command, 1941–2.

Cassels, Robert Archibald (General Sir Robert), b. 1876. First World War. Commanded Peshawar District, 1923–8. AG in India, 1928–30. GOC.-in-C. Northern Command India, 1930–4. C.-in-C. of Army in India, 1935–41.

Cavan, Frederick Rudolph Lambert, 'Fatty' (Field-Marshal the Earl of Cavan), b. 1865. South African War and First World War: commanded Bde. of Guards Division, commanded XIV Corps and in charge of operations of 10th Italian Army on Piave front in 1918. C.-in-C. Aldershot, 1920–2. CIGS, 1922–6. Field-Marshal, 1932.

Charles, James Ronald Edmonston (Lt.-Gen. Sir Ronald), b. 1875. Educated Winchester and Woolwich. South Africa. Mohmand Field Force, 1908. First World War: commanded 25th Division, 1918–19. Commanded Waziristan Field Force, 1923. Commandant Woolwich, 1924–6. DMO and I, 1926–31. MGO, 1931–4. Retired 1934.

Chatfield, Alfred Ernle Montacute (Admiral of the Fleet Lord Chatfield), b. 1873. Entered Royal Navy 1886. In First World War saw action at Heligoland (1914), Dogger Bank (1915), and Jutland (1916). Third Sea Lord, 1925–8. C.-in-C. Atlantic Fleet, 1929–30. C.-in-C. Mediterranean, 1930–2. First Sea Lord and CNS, 1933–8. Minister for the Co-ordination of Defence, 1939–40.

Chetwode, Philip Walhouse (Field-Marshal Sir Philip), b. 1869. Educated Eton. Entered Army 1889. Burma campaign (1892–3), South Africa, and First World War. Commanded 5th Cavalry Bde. 1914–15, 2nd Cavalry Division 1915–16, Desert Corps Egypt 1916–17, XX Army Corps, 1917–18, in Palestine and Syria. Military Secretary, War Office, 1919–1920. DCIGS, 1920–2. AG, 1922–3. C.-in-C. Aldershot Command, 1923–7. CGS India, 1928–30. C.-in-C. of the Army in India, 1930–5. Field-Marshal, 1933.

Collins, Robert John, 'Jack' (Maj-Gen.) b. 1880. Educated Marlborough. South Africa. First World War: commanded 73rd Infantry Bde., 1918–19. Instructor Staff College, 1919–23. DMT in India, 1924–6. Commanded 9th Infantry Bde., 1926–7, and 7th Infantry Bde. (including the Experimental Mechanised Force), 1927–8. GOC 3rd (Meerut) Indian Division, 1934–8. Retired 1938.

Davidson, Alexander Elliot (Maj.-Gen.), b. 1880. Educated Blackheath and Woolwich. Entered RE, 1899. South African and First World Wars. Chairman Technical Committee, Mechanical Warfare Board, 1927–31. Asst. Director of Works, War Office, 1931–5.

Deverell, Cyril John 'Butcher' (Field-Marshal Sir Cyril), b. 1874. Educated Bedford School. Joined West Yorks Regt. 1895. Bde. Major and General Staff India, 1908–14. Bde. Major BEF 1914–15, Commander 20th Infantry Bde. 1915–16, 3rd Division 1916–19. Promoted Maj.-Gen. for distinguished service in the field, 1919. Commanded United Provinces District India, 1921–5. QMG in India, 1927–30. CGS India, 1930–1. GOC.-in-C. Western Command, 1931–3. GOC.-in-C. Eastern Command, 1933–6. Field-Marshal, 1936. CIGS, 1936–7.

Dill, John Greer (Field-Marshal Sir John), b. 1881. Educated Cheltenham and Sandhurst. Entered Army 1901. South Africa. First World War: Brig.-Gen. (and the outstanding officer) in the Operations Section of Haig's Headquarters in 1918. Commanded 2nd Infantry Bde., 1923–6. Instructor at IDC, 1926–8. Brigadier on General Staff India, 1929–30. Commandant Staff College,

Camberley, 1931–4. DMO and I, 1934–6. Commander British Forces in Palestine, 1936–7. GOC.-in-C. Aldershot Command, 1937–9. Commander I Corps BEF in France, 1939–40. CIGS, 1940–1. Head of British Military Mission in Washington from 1941 until his death in November 1944.

Dowding, Hugh Caswell Tremenheere, 'Stuffy' (Air Chief Marshal Lord Dowding), b. 1882. Educated Winchester and Woolwich. Joined RA in 1900 and transferred to RFC in First World War. Director of Training, Air Ministry, 1926–9. Air Member for Research and Development, Air Council, 1930–6. Air Officer in Chief Fighter Command, 1936–40. Retired 1942.

Duncan, John (Maj.-Gen. Sir John), b. 1872. NW Frontier India, 1897–8. South Africa. First World War: Gallipoli 1915, commanded 78th Infantry Bde. 1916–17, and 22nd Division in Macedonia 1917–19. Maj.-Gen. General Staff Army of the Black Sea, 1919. Commanded Shanghai Defence Force, 1927–8. GOC 1st Division Aldershot, 1928. Retired 1928.

Elles, Hugh Jamieson (General Sir Hugh), b. 1880. Educated Clifton and Woolwich. Joined RE 1899. South Africa. First World War: commanded Tank Corps in France, 1917–19. Commandant Tank Centre, 1920–3. Inspector RTC, 1923. Bde. Commander Southern Command, 1923–6. DMT, 1930–3. Commander 42nd (East Lancs.) Division, 1933–4. MGO, 1934–8. Retired 1938.

Ellington, Edward Leonard (Marshal of the Royal Air Force Sir Edward), b. 1877. Educated Clifton and Woolwich. Joined RA but learnt to fly in 1912 and served on staff of RFC during the First World War. Member of Air Council, 1918–22. Commanded RAF in Middle East 1922–3, in India 1923–6, and in Iraq 1926–8. AOC.-in-C. ADGB, 1929–31. On Air Council, 1931–3. CAS, 1933–7.

Evans, Roger (Maj.-Gen.), b. 1886. Joined Royal Inniskilling Dragoon Guards. First World War: Mesopotamia, 1917–18. IDC, 1934. Brigadier on General Staff India, 1935–7. DDMI, 1938. Commander 1st Armoured Division, 1938–40. Retired 1944.

Fraser, William Hon. (Brigadier), b. 1890. Educated Charterhouse and Sandhurst. Served with Gordon Highlanders in Egypt and India. First World War. Military Attaché Brussels and The Hague, 1931–5, and Paris, 1938–9.

Fuller, John Frederick Charles, 'Boney' (Maj.-Gen.), b. 1878. Educated Malvern and Sandhurst. Joined Oxfordshire Light Infantry. South Africa. First World War: GSO2 37th Division and 3rd Army 1916, GSO2 HQ Heavy Branch Machine Gun Corps, and GSO1 Tank Corps 1917. Staff Duties Directorate War Office, 1918–22. Chief Instructor Staff College, Camberley, 1922–6.

Military Assistant to CIGS, 1926–7. Declined command of Experimental Mechanized Force. GSO1 2nd Division, 1927–9. Bde. Commander BAOR, July–Oct. 1929, and 13 Infantry Bde., 1929–30. Maj.-Gen. on half-pay, 1930–4. Retired 1934.

Gathorne-Hardy, John Francis (General Hon. Sir Francis), b. 1874. Educated Eton and Sandhurst. Joined Grenadier Guards 1894. South Africa. First World War: GSO1 7th Division 1915–16, Brig.-Gen. General Staff XIV Corps 1916–18, Maj.-Gen. General Staff British Forces in Italy and Italian 10th Army, 1918–19. DMT, 1922–5. Commander Deccan District, 1926–8. GOC.-in-C. Northern Command, 1931–3, and Aldershot Command, 1933–7. Worsted by Deverell in 1935 manœuvres and lost chance of becoming CIGS. Retired 1937.

Gillman, Webb 'Gillie' (General Sir Webb), b. 1870. Educated Dulwich College and Woolwich. Entered RFA 1889. South Africa. First World War: promoted Maj.-Gen. Commandant Woolwich, 1920–4. Inspector of Artillery, 1924–7. MGO and Member of Army Council, 1927–31. Died 1933.

Godley, Alexander John, 'Lord God' (General Sir Alexander), b. 1867. Educated Haileybury and Sandhurst. Joined Royal Dublin Fusiliers 1886. South African War: staff officer with Generals Baden-Powell and Plumer. Commanded a division and corps at Dardanelles and in Egypt, 1914–16. Commanded XXII Corps in France and Germany, 1916–19. Military Secretary, War Office, 1920–2. C.-in-C. Gibraltar, 1928–33. Retired 1933.

Gordon-Finlayson, Robert, 'Copper' (General Sir Robert), b. 1881. Entered Army 1900. First World War and North Russia (1919). Commanded Rawalpindi District, 1931–4, and 3rd Division, 1934–6. Commander British Troops in Egypt, 1938–9. Adjutant-General, 1939.

Gort, John Standish Surtees Prendergast Vereker, 'Fat Boy' (Field-Marshal Lord Gort), b. 1886. Educated Harrow and Sandhurst. Entered Grenadier Guards 1905. First World War: dispatches nine times, MC, DSO (2 bars), VC, and commanded 1st and 4th Bns. Grenadier Guards. GSO1 Shanghai Defence Force, Aug. 1927. GSO1 4th Division, 1927–30. Commander 4th Guards Bde., 1930–2. DMT India, 1932–6. Maj.-Gen. and Commandant Staff College, Camberley, 1936–7. Lt.-Gen. and General, 1937. Military Secretary to Secretary of State for War, Sept.–Dec. 1937. CIGS, 1937–9. C.-in-C. BEF in France, 1939–40. Governor of Malta, 1942–4.

Haining, Robert Hadden 'Bob' (Lt.-Gen. Sir Robert), b. 1882. Educated Uppingham and Woolwich. Entered RA 1901. First World War: dispatches six times, DSO. Barrister-at-Law, 1919. IDC,

1927. GSO1 4th Division, 1930–1. MOI, War Office, 1931–3. DDMO and I, 1933–4. Commandant IDC, 1935–6. DMO and I, 1936–7. GOC British Forces in Palestine and Trans-Jordan, 1938–9.

Harington, Charles 'Tim' (General Sir Charles), b. 1872. Educated Cheltenham and Sandhurst. Staff officer in South African and First World Wars: Chief of Staff Second Army. Commander Army of the Black Sea and Allied Forces of Occupation in Turkey, 1920–3. Northern Command, 1923–7. Western Command India, 1927–31. GOC.-in-C. Aldershot Command, 1931–3. Governor and C.-in-C. Gibraltar, 1933–8.

Hawes, Leonard Arthur (Maj.-Gen.), b. 1892. Educated Bedford and Woolwich. Joined Royal Garrison Artillery 1911. First World War: dispatches seven times, wounded, DSO, MC. Instructor Staff College, Quetta, 1934–7. As GSO1 (Plans), War Office, from June 1938 made arrangements for dispatch of BEF to France in 1939.

Heywood, Cecil Percival, 'Guffin' (Maj.-Gen.), b. 1880. Educated Eton and Sandhurst. South African and First World Wars: dispatches seven times, DSO, CMG, commanded 3rd Guards Bde. 1918 (wounded). DMT India, 1930–2. DSD, 1934–6. Died 1936.

Hobart, Percy Cleghorn Stanley 'Hobo' (Maj.-Gen. Sir Percy), b. 1885. Educated Clifton and Woolwich. Joined RE 1904. First World War: France 1915, Mesopotamia 1916–18 (wounded and POW), Palestine 1918. Joined RTC 1923. Inspector RTC, 1933–6. Commander 1st Tank Bde., 1934–7. DDSD, 1937. DMT, 1937–8. Raised 7th Armoured Division in Egypt, 1938–9. Retired 1940. Corporal in Home Guard. Recalled in 1941 and raised 11th and 79th Armoured Divisions, commanding latter in NW European campaign, 1944–5.

Hopkins, Richard Valentine Nind (Rt. Hon. Sir Richard), b. 1880. Educated King Edward's Birmingham and Cambridge. Controller of Finance and Supply Services Treasury, 1927–32. Second Secretary Treasury, 1932–42. Permanent Secretary to Treasury 1942–5.

Hotblack, Frederick Elliot, 'Boots' (Maj.-Gen.), b. 1887. Joined Tank Corps in First World War. Instructor Staff College, Camberley, 1932–5. Military Attaché, Berlin, 1935–7. General Staff, War Office, 1937–9. General Staff BEF, 1939. Selected to command force at Trondheim in April 1940 but suffered a stroke or accident in London blackout. Retired 1941.

Howard, Geoffrey Weston (Lt.-Gen. Sir Geoffrey), b. 1876. Entered Army 1897. South African and First World Wars: dispatches seven times, CMG. Commander 9th Infantry Bde., 1927–31. Maj.-Gen i/c administration Eastern Command, 1931–4. Commander 5th Division, 1934–7. Retired 1938.

Howard-Vyse, Richard Granville Hilton, 'Wombat' (Maj.-Gen. Sir Richard), b. 1883. Entered Army 1902. First World War: Bde. Major 5th Cavalry Bde. and Chief Staff Officer 5th Cavalry Division. Chief Staff Officer Desert Mounted Corps and Commander 10th Cavalry Bde. in Palestine, 1917–18. Commander Royal Horse Guards, 1922–6. Inspector of Cavalry, 1930–4. Retired 1935. Head of Military Mission with French High Command, 1939–40.

Hutton, Thomas (Lt.-Gen. Sir Thomas), b. 1890. Educated Rossall and Woolwich. Joined RA in 1909. First World War: dispatches four times, wounded three times, MC and bar. Military Assistant to CIGS, 1927–30. GSO1 Military Operations, War Office, 1933–6. GSO1 1st Division, 1936–8. DCGS Army HQ India, 1940–1. CGS, 1941. GOC Burma, 1942.

Ironside, William Edmund, 'Tiny' (Field-Marshal Lord Ironside), b. 1880. Educated Tonbridge School and Woolwich. Joined RA 1899. South African and First World Wars: commanded 99th Infantry Bde., 1918. C.-in-C. British Forces in Russia, 1918–19, and North Persia, 1920–1. Commandant Staff College, Camberley, 1922–6. Commander 2nd Division, 1926–8. Commander Meerut District India, 1928–31. QMG in India, 1933–6. GOC.-in-C. Eastern Command, 1936–8. Governor and C.-in-C. Gibraltar, 1938–9. Inspector-General of Overseas Forces, 1939. CIGS, Sept. 1939–May 1940. C.-in-C. Home Forces, 1940. Field-Marshal, 1940.

Ismay, Hastings Lionel, 'Pug' (General Lord Ismay), b. 1887. Educated Charterhouse and Sandhurst. Entered Army 1905. Served in India and Middle East, 1908–25. Asst. Sec. CID, 1926–30. Military Secretary to Viceroy of India, 1930–3. GSO1, War Office, 1933–6. Deputy Sec. CID, 1936–8, and Secretary CID, 1938–40. Chief of Staff to Minister of Defence, 1940–6.

Jacob, Claud William (Field-Marshal Sir Claud), b. 1863. Educated Sherborne and Sandhurst. Entered Indian Army 1882. First World War: commanded Dehra Dun Bde. 1915, Meerut and 21st Divisions 1915, II Corps 1916–19. CGS India, 1925. Secretary Military Dept. of India Office, 1926–30. Field-Marshal, 1926.

Joubert de la Ferté, Philip Bennet (Air Chief Marshal Sir Philip). Educated Harrow and Woolwich. Joined RFA 1907, seconded to RFC, 1913. First World War: France 1914–15, Egypt 1916–17, Italy 1917–18. RAF Instructor at IDC, 1927–9. Commandant

RAF Staff College, 1930–4. AOC Fighting Area, 1934–6. AOC.-in-C. Coastal Command, 1936–7. AOC RAF India, 1937–9. C.-in-C. Coastal Command, 1941–3.

Karslake, Henry (Lt.-Gen. Sir Henry), b. 1879. Educated Harrow and Woolwich. Joined RGA 1898. South Africa and First World Wars: transferred to Tank Corps, Brigadier-General Tank Corps, 1918. GSO1 HQ Peshawar, 1920–3. GSO1 War Office, 1923–5. Colonel on General Staff Southern Command, 1925–8. Brigadier and Maj.-Gen. in Staff appts. India, 1928–33. Commander Baluchistan District, 1933–5, and in charge at Quetta during the earthquake. Lt.-General, 1936. Retired 1938.

Kennedy, John C. (Maj.-Gen. Sir John) b. 1878. Educated Haileybury. Joined Argyll and Sutherland Highlanders 1898. First World War (France and Belgium): commanded 26th (Highland) Bde., 1917–18. Commander 19th Indian bde. 1926–32, 44th (TA) Division 1932–4, and 1st Division 1934–6, including operations against the Mobile Force in 1934 exercise. Maj.-Gen., 1931. Retired due to ill health, 1936.

Kennedy, John Noble (Maj.-Gen. Sir John), b. 1893. Educated Stranraer and Woolwich. Entered Royal Navy 1911 and transferred to RA 1915. First World War: RN 1914–15, France, Flanders, and Egypt 1915–18, South Russia 1919–20. DDMO, 1938. Director of Plans, 1939. Commander (RA) 52nd Division in France, 1940. DMO, 1940–3. Asst. CIGS, 1943–5.

Kirke, Walter Mervyn St George (General Sir Walter), b. 1877. Educated Haileybury and Woolwich. Entered RA 1896. Waziristan (1901–2) and South Chin Hills (1905–6) operations. First World War. Colonel on Staff Aldershot, 1922–4. DCGS. in India, 1926–9. Commander 5th Division, 1929–31. Chairman of WO Committee on Lessons of the Great War, 1932. GOC.-in-C. Western Command, 1933–6. Director-General TA, 1936–9. Inspector-General and C.-in-C. Home Forces, 1939–40.

Knox, Harry Hugh Sidney (General Sir Harry), b. 1873. Educated St Columba's College, Dublin. Joined 5th Royal Irish Rifles 1890. Served in NW Frontier campaigns in 1890s and in Uganda 1900–1. First World War: GSO1 15th (Scottish) Division 1915–17, Brig.-Gen. General Staff XV Corps 1917–19, temporary commander 29th Division Aug. 1918. Commander 3rd Infantry Bde., 1923–6. DMT, 1926–30. Commander 3rd Division, 1930–2. Adjutant-General, 1935–7. Retired 1938.

Laird, Kenneth Macgregor (Brigadier), b. 1880. Educated Charterhouse and Sandhurst. South African and First World Wars (France, Macedonia, Serbia, Bulgaria, and Turkey). Joined Tank Corps 1921. Commanded RTC Centre, 1927–8. Inspector RTC,

1929–33, and commanded 1st Tank Bde. during 1932 training season. Bde. Commander India, 1933–5. Retired 1935.

Leigh-Mallory, Trafford (Air Chief Marshal Sir Trafford). Educated Haileybury and Cambridge (LL.B). First World War. Commandant School of Army Co-operation, 1927–30. Instructor at Staff College, Camberley, 1930–1. DDSD, Air Ministry, 1931–4. Senior Air Staff Officer Iraq, 1936–7. AOC No. 12 Fighter Group, 1937–40. Killed in air crash *en route* to South East Asia Command, 1944.

Liddell, Clive Gerard (Lt.-Gen. Sir Clive), b. 1883. Educated Uppingham and Sandhurst. Entered Army 1902. First World War: AAG, War Office, 1917–18. Instructor Staff College, Camberley, 1920–2. GSO1, War Office, 1928–31. Commander 8th Infantry Bde., 1931–4. Commander 4th Division, 1935–7. AG, 1937–9.

Lindsay, George Mackintosh (Maj.-Gen.), b. 1880. Educated Radley. Joined Rifle Brigade 1900. South African and First World Wars: Army Machine Gun Officer 1st Army, 1918. Commander No. 1 Armoured Car Group Iraq, 1921–3. Transferred to RTC as Lt.-Col. and Chief Instructor Tank Corps, Central Schools, 1923. Inspector RTC, 1925–9, and Member of Mechanical Warfare Board, 1926–9. Brigadier, General Staff Egypt, 1929–32. Commander 7th Infantry Bde., 1932–4, and commanded Mobile Force in 1934 manœuvres. Commander Assam District India, 1935–9. Retired 1939.

Macready, Cecil Frederick Nevil (General Rt. Hon. Sir Nevil), b. 1862. Educated Marlborough and Cheltenham. Joined Gordon Highlanders 1881. Egypt (1882), South Africa, and First World War. AG BEF, 1914–16, AG, War Office, 1916–18. Commissioner of Metropolitan Police, 1918–20. GOC.-in-C. Forces in Ireland, 1920–2. Retired 1923.

Macready, Gordon Nevil (Lt.-Gen. Sir Gordon), b. 1891. Only son of Rt. Hon. Sir Nevil Macready (above). Educated Cheltenham and Woolwich. First World War. Asst. Sec. CID, 1926–32. IDC, 1933. GSO1, War Office, 1934–6. DDSD, 1936–8. Asst. CIGS, 1940–2. Chief of British Army Staff at Washington, 1942.

Martel, Giffard Le Quesne (Lt.-Gen. Sir Giffard), b. 1889. Educated Wellington and Woolwich. Joined RE. First World War: GSO2 Machine Gun Corps and Tank Corps, 1917–18. Deputy Assistant Director Fortifications and Works, 1923–26. Designed and constructed one man 'tankette' in 1925. Instructor at Staff College, Quetta, 1930–4. IDC, 1935. Asst. Director of Mechanization, War Office, 1936–8, and Deputy Director, 1938–9. Commander 50th (TA) Division including counter-attack at Arras, 21 May

1940. Commander Royal Armoured Corps, 1940. Head of Military Mission at Moscow, 1943. Col. Commandant RE, 1944. Retired 1945.

Mason-MacFarlane, Frank Noel (Lt.-Gen. Sir Frank), b. 1889. Educated Rugby and Woolwich. First World War (France and Mesopotamia). Military Attaché at Budapest, Vienna, and Berne, 1931–4, and at Berlin and Copenhagen, 1937–9. DMI with BEF in France, 1939–40. Head of British Military Mission at Moscow, 1941–2.

Milne, George Francis, 'Uncle George' (Field-Marshal Lord Milne), b. Aberdeen 1866. Entered RA 1885. Sudan campaign (1898), South Africa, and First World War: rapidly promoted to Maj.-Gen., General Staff Second Army, commander 27th Division, and (January 1916) Commander XVI Corps Salonika, and Commander British Salonika Force and Army of the Black Sea, 1916–20. Lt. of the Tower of London, 1920–3. GOC.-in-C. Eastern Command, 1923–6. CIGS, 1926–33. Field-Marshal, 1928. Governor and Constable of the Tower of London, 1933–8. Died 1948.

Montgomery, Bernard Law, 'Monty' (Field-Marshal Viscount Montgomery) b. 1887. Educated St Paul's and Sandhurst. Joined Royal Warwickshire Regt. 1908. First World War: DSO and Bt. Major. GSO1 Staff College, Quetta, 1934–7. Commander 9th Infantry Bde., 1937–8, and 8th Division, 1938–9. Commander 3rd Division in France, 1939–40. Commander 8th Army 1942–3, 21st Army Group 1944–5, BAOR 1945–6. CIGS, 1946–8. Field-Marshal, 1944.

Montgomery-Massingberd, Archibald Armar, 'Archie' (Field-Marshal Sir Archibald), b. Fivemiletown Co Tyrone 1871, second son of Rt. Hon. Hugh de F. Montgomery PC. Added Massingberd in 1926 when his wife inherited the Massingberd estates. Educated Charterhouse and Woolwich. Joined RA 1891. South Africa. First World War: GSO1, 4th Division on the Marne in 1914 when Sir Henry Rawlinson took command, accompanied him as his chief of staff with IV Corps and Fourth Army, 1916–18. Rose from Major to Maj.-Gen. in two and a half years. DCGS (also to Rawlinson) in India, 1920–2. Commander 1st Division, 1923–6. Lt.-Gen., 1926. GOC.-in-C. Southern Command, 1926–31. AG, 1931–3. CIGS, 1933–6.

Morgan, Frederick Edgworth, 'Freddie' (Lt.-Gen. Sir Frederick), b. 1894. Educated Clifton and Woolwich. Joined RA 1913. First World War: Capt. 1916. Served in India in late 1920s and early 1930s. GSO2, War Office, 1936–8. GSO1 3rd Division, 1938–9. Colonel, 1938. Chief of Staff to Supreme Allied Commander

(COSSAC), 1943–4.

Neame, Philip (Lt.-Gen. Sir Philip), b. 1888. Educated Cheltenham and Woolwich. Joined RE 1908. First World War: VC in 1914, Brigade Major infantry bde. and on general staff of a division, corps, and army. Directing Staff Camberley, 1919–23. Served with RE units in India for most of inter-war period. Commandant Woolwich, 1938–9. DCGS of BEF in France, 1939–40. Commander British Forces in Cyrenaica against Rommel's first attack Mar.–Apr. 1941. POW, 1941–3 (escaped). Retired 1947.

Newall, Cyril Louis Norton (Air Chief Marshal Sir Cyril), b. 1880. Educated Bedford School and Sandhurst. Joined Royal Warwickshire Regt. 1905, transferring to Indian Army 1909 and to RAF 1919. First World War: Bt. Major. Director of Operations and Intelligence and DCAS, 1926–31. AOC RAF Middle East, 1931–4. Member of Air Council for Supply and Organisation, 1935–7. CAS, 1937–40.

Paget, Bernard Charles Tolver (General Sir Bernard), b. 1888, third son of the Bishop of Oxford. Educated Shrewsbury and Sandhurst. First World War: DSO, MC, Bt. Major. Colonel, 1929. GSO1 Staff College, Quetta, 1932–4. GSO1 (Military Intelligence) War Office, 1934–6. Commander Quetta Bde., 1936–7. Maj.-Gen., 1937. Commandant Staff College, Camberley, 1938–9. Commanded force at Trondheim in April 1940. C.-in-C. Home Forces, 1941–3. C.-in-C. Middle East Forces, 1944–6.

Peck, Sydney Capel (Maj.-Gen.), b. 1871. Educated The Perse School and Cambridge. (MA). First World War: DSO. Bt. Lt.-Col. Director of Artillery, 1924. Director of Mechanization, 1927–32. Retired 1933.

Pile, Frederick Alfred, 'Tim' (General Sir Frederick), b. 1884, elder son of Sir T. D. Pile 1st baron whom he succeeded in 1931. Joined RA 1904. First World War: DSO, MC. Commanded 3rd Tank Bn. RTC in Experimental Mechanized Force, 1927–8. Asst. Director of Mechanization, 1928–32. Commander Canal Bde. Egypt, 1932–6. Commander 1st AA Division (TA), 1937–9. GOC.-in-C. AA Command, 1939–45.

Pope, Vyvyan Vavasour (Lt.-Gen.), b. 1891. Educated Lancing. Joined North Staffs. Regt. 1912. First World War: wounded three times, DSO, MC. Bt. Major. Joined RTC 1923. Bde. Major RTC Centre, 1926–7. GSO2 War Office, 1931–3. IDC, 1934. Organized Mobile Force in Egypt during Abyssinian crisis, 1936. GSO1 Directorate of Military Training, 1936–7. Brigadier General Staff Southern Command, 1938–9. Chief Staff Officer II Corps in France, 1939–40. Promoted Lt.-Gen. on appointment to command an armoured corps in 8th Army in Sept 1941 but killed in an air crash 5 Oct 1941.

Pownall, Henry Royds (Lt.-Gen. Sir Henry), b. 1887. Educated Rugby and Woolwich. Served in RFA and RHA in England and India, 1906–14. First World War: DSO, MC, Bde. Major RA 17th Division, 1917–19. Asst. Sec. and Deputy Sec. CID, 1933–6. DMO and I, 1938–9. CGS BEF in France, 1939–40. VCIGS, 1941. C.-in-C. Far East, 1941–2. Lt.-Gen., 1942. Chief of Staff to Supreme Allied Commander SE Asia, 1943–4.

Radcliffe, Percy Pollexfen de Blaquiere (General Sir Percy), b. 1874. Educated Winchester and Woolwich. Entered RA 1893. South African and First World Wars: dispatches six times, DSO, KCMG, Bt. Col. DMO, War Office, 1918–22. Commander 48th Division (TA), 1923–6, and 4th Division, 1926–7. GOC.-in-C. Scottish Command, 1930–3, and Southern Command, 1933.

Rawlinson, Henry Seymour, 'Rawly' (General Lord Rawlinson), b. 1864, elder son of Maj.-Gen. Sir Henry Rawlinson Bt. whom he succeeded in 1895. Educated Eton and Sandhurst. Joined Rifle Brigade 1884 and exchanged into Coldstream Guards 1892. Sudan (1898) and South Africa. Commandant Staff College, 1903–6. Commander 3rd Division, 1910–14. First World War: commanded 4th Division Sept.–Oct. 1914, IV Corps Oct. 1914–Dec. 1915, and Fourth Army Dec. 1915–Mar. 1919. GOC.-in-C. Aldershot, 1919–20. C.-in-C. India, Nov. 1920–5. Died after an operation 28 March 1925.

Ready, Felix Fordati (General Sir Felix), b. 1872. Entered Army 1891. Sudan, South Africa, and First World War. GOC Northern Ireland District, 1926–8. GOC 1st Division Aldershot, 1929–30. Lt.-Gen., 1930. QMG, 1931–5. Retired 1935.

Romer, Cecil Francis, 'Romeo' (General Sir Cecil), b. 1869. Joined Royal Dublin Fusiliers 1890. South African and First World Wars: CB, CMG, and promoted Maj.-Gen. GOC 1st Division, 1926–7. GOC.-in-C. Southern Command, 1931–3. AG, 1933–5. Retired 1935.

Rowlands, Archibald (Sir), b. 1892. Educated Penarth, Univ. College of Wales, and Oxford. First World War (Mesopotamia). Private Secretary to Secretary of the War Office (Sir Herbert Creedy), 1920–2. Principal Private Sec. to successive Secretaries of State for War (Lord Hailsham, Lord Halifax, Duff Cooper). IDC, 1936. Financial Adviser to Government of India, 1937–9. KCB, 1941.

Sergison-Brooke, Bertram Norman (Lt.-Gen. Sir Bertram), b. 1880. Entered Army 1899. South African and First World Wars: DSO, CMG, Bt. Lt.-Col. Commanded 1st Guards Bde. Aldershot, 1928–31. Brig.-Gen. General Staff Eastern Command India,

1931–4. GOC London District, 1934–8 and 1939–42.

Skeen, Andrew (General Sir Andrew), b. 1873. NW Frontier operations (1897–8), China (1900), East Africa (1902–4), First World War, 3rd Afghan War (1919), and Waziristan (1919–20). Commander Peshawar District, 1922–3. GOC.-in-C. Southern Command India, 1923–4. CGS Indian Army, 1924–8. General, 1929.

Slessor, John Cotesworth (Marshal of the Royal Air Force Sir John), b. 1897. Educated Haileybury. Served in RFC 1915–18 in France, Egypt, and Sudan (MC). Air Staff, 1928–30. Instructor Staff College, Camberley, 1931–4. With RAF in India, 1935–7, and took part in Waziristan operations. Director of Plans, Air Ministry, 1937–41. KCB, 1943. AOC.-in-C. Coastal Command, 1943–4. C. in C. RAF in Mediterranean and Middle East, 1944–5.

Slim, William Joseph (Field-Marshal Viscount Slim), b. 1891. Educated King Edward's Birmingham and Sandhurst. Joined Royal Warwickshire Regt. First World War: Gallipoli (wounded), France, Mesopotamia (wounded and MC). Joined Indian Army. Instructor Staff College, Camberley, 1934–6. In Second World War commanded I Burma Corps, XV Indian Corps, 14th Army, and Allied Forces South East Asia.

Stronge, Humphrey Cecil Travell (Brigadier), b. 1891. Educated The Oratory and Sandhurst. Joined the Buffs 1910. First World War: Cameroons, German East Africa, and France (DSO, MC). GSO2, War Office, 1928–30, and GSO1, War Office, 1934–6. Military Attaché, Belgrade and Prague, 1936–9.

Studd, Malden Augustus (Brigadier), b. 1887. Joined RA 1907. First World War. Joined Tank Corps. Asst. Director of Mechanization, War Office, 1932–6. Brigadier i/c Administration Malaya, 1937–40.

Thomson, Christopher Birdwood (Brig.-Gen. Lord Thomson), b. in India 1875, son of a major.-gen. Educated Cheltenham and Woolwich. Joined RE 1894. South African War (Bt. Major). Staff College, Camberley, 1909–10. First World War: Belgium, Military Attaché Bucharest, Palestine (1917), Brig.-Gen., 1918. Joined Labour Party 1919. Secretary of State for Air 1924, 1929–30. Created baron 1924. Died in airship R 101 disaster in 1930.

Thorne, Augustus Francis Andrew Nicol, 'Bulgy' (General Sir Andrew), b. 1885. Educated Eton and Sandhurst. Joined Grenadier Guards 1904. First World War: dispatches seven times, DSO and two bars. Commanded 184th Infantry Bde., Oct. 1918–Mar. 1919. Military Assistant to CIGS, 1925–6. Military Attaché Berlin, 1932–5. Commander 1st Guards Bde., 1935–8.

GOC London District, 1938–9. Commander 48th Division in France 1939–40, and XII Corps 1940–1. GOC.-in-C. Scottish Command, 1941–5.

Trenchard, Hugh Montague, 'Boom' (Marshal of the Royal Air Force Viscount Trenchard), b. 1873. Entered Army 1893. South African War (dangerously wounded). First World War: GOC RFC in France, 1915–17. Maj.-Gen. 1916. CAS, 1918–29. Marshal of the RAF, 1927. Commissioner Metropolitan Police, 1931–5.

Vesey, Ivo Lucius Beresford (General Sir Ivo), b. 1876. First World War: CMG, DSO. DRO, 1919–23. Director of Organisation and Staff Duties, Air Ministry, 1923–9. Commander 48th (TA) Division, 1930–1. DSD, 1931–4. GOC.-in-C. Western Command India, 1935–6 and Southern Command India, 1936–7. CGS India, 1937–9. Retired 1939.

Wardrop, Alexander Ernest (General Sir Alexander), b. 1872. Joined RA 1892. First World War (France): Brig.-Gen. (RA) 1915–18, and Maj.-Gen. (RA) 1918–19. Commander Troops in Palestine, 1921–2. District Commander India, 1923–7. GOC North China, 1927–9. QMG India, 1930–3. GOC.-in-C. Northern Command (York), 1933–7.

Wavell, Archibald Percival (Field-Marshal Earl Wavell), b. 1883. Educated Winchester and Sandhurst. Joined Black Watch 1901. South African and First World Wars: France, 1914–16 (wounded and MC). Military Attaché with Russian Army in Caucasus 1916–17, and Egyptian Expeditionary Force 1917–20. Brig.-Gen. General Staff XX Corps, 1918–19. Commander 6th Infantry Bde. 1930–4 and 2nd Division Aldershot 1935–7. Commander Troops in Palestine and Trans-Jordan, 1937–8. GOC.-in-C. Southern Command, 1938–9. GOC.-in-C. Middle East, 1939–41. C.-in-C. India, 1941–3. Viceroy, 1943–6.

Weir, William Douglas (Viscount Weir), b. 1877. Controller of Aeronautical Supplies and Member of Air Board, 1917–18. Director-General of Aircraft Production, 1918. Secretary of State for Air and President of Air Council, Apr.–Dec. 1918. Barony and PC, 1918. Member of Advisory Panel to Principal Supply Officers' Committee, 1933–5. Adviser to Air Ministry on Aircraft Production, May 1935–May 1938 (resigned when Lord Swinton was dismissed as Secretary of State), and Member of Defence Policy and Requirements Sub-Committee, 1936–7. Viscount, 1938. Director-General of Explosives, Ministry of Supply, 1939–42. Chairman of Tank Board, 1942.

Whigham, Robert Dundas (General Sir Robert), b. 1865. Educated Fettes and Sandhurst. Joined Royal Warwickshire Regt. 1885.

Sudan (1898), South African War, and First World War: DCIGS, 1916–18. Commanded 62nd Division in France in 1918. AG, 1923–7. GOC.-in-C. Eastern Command, 1927–31. Retired 1931.

Wilson, Henry Hughes, (Field-Marshal Sir Henry), b. 1864. Educated Marlborough. Joined Royal Irish Regt. and transferred to Rifle Brigade 1884. Burma campaigns (1885–9), South Africa (DSO, Bt. Lt.-Col.). Commandant Staff College, Camberley, 1906–10. DMO and I, 1910–14. First World War: Sub-Chief of General Staff BEF 1914, Chief Liaison Officer with French Armies 1915, Commander IV Corps 1916, Chief Liaison Officer with Pétain and Nivelle 1917, Military Representative on Supreme War Council Nov. 1917–Feb. 1918, CIGS Feb. 1918–Feb. 1922, MP for North Down 1922. Assassinated 22 June 1922.

Wilson, Henry Maitland, 'Jumbo' (Field-Marshal Lord Wilson), b. 1881. Educated Eton. South African and First World Wars (DSO). GSO1 Staff College, Camberley, 1930–3. Commander 6th Infantry Bde., 1934–5. Commander 2nd Division, 1937–9. GOC.-in-C. Egypt, 1939, and Cyrenaica, 1941. C.-in-C. Persia–Iraq Command, 1942–3. C.-in-C. Middle East, 1943. Supreme Allied Commander Mediterranean Theatre, 1944. Field-Marshal 1944. Head of Joint Staff Mission in Washington, 1945–7.

APPENDIX II

Military Departments and Directorates of the War Office

Chief of the Imperial General Staff	Adjutant-General	Quartermaster-General	Master-General of the Ordnance
Director of Staff Duties	Director of Recruiting and Organization	Director of Movements and Quartering	Director of Artillery (I)
Director of Military Operations and Intelligence	Director of Personnel Services	Director of Supplies and Transport	Director of Artillery (II)[1]
Director of Military Training	Director of General of Army Medical Services	Director of Remounts	Director of Fortification and Works[2]
		Director General of Army Veterinary Services	
		Director of Equipment and Army Ordnance Stores[3]	

1 Renamed Director of Mechanization in October 1927.
2 Transferred to control of QMG in October 1927. Renamed Director of Works.
3 Transferred to control of MGO in October 1927. Renamed Director of Ordnance Services.

APPENDIX III

Members of the Army Council, 1918–1939

Secretary of State for War	Date Appointed
Winston Churchill	10 Jan. 1919
Sir Laming Worthington-Evans	13 Feb. 1921
The Earl of Derby	24 Oct. 1922
Stephen Walsh	22 Jan. 1924
Sir Laming Worthington-Evans	7 Nov. 1924
Thomas Shaw	8 June 1929
The Marquess of Crewe	26 Aug. 1931
Viscount Hailsham	9 Nov. 1931
Viscount Halifax	7 June 1935
A. Duff Cooper	27 Nov. 1935
Leslie Hore-Belisha	28 May 1937
Parliamentary Under-Secretary	
Viscount Peel	14 Jan. 1919
Sir R. A. Sanders	2 Apr. 1921
Hon. W. E. Guinness	31 Oct. 1922
C. R. Attlee	23 Jan. 1924
The Earl of Onslow	12 Nov. 1924
The Duke of Sutherland	4 Dec. 1928
The Earl de la Warr	10 June 1929
Lord Marley	13 June 1930
Earl Stanhope	11 Nov. 1931
Lord Strathcona and Mount Royal	3 Feb. 1934
The Earl of Munster	31 Jan. 1939
Financial Secretary	
H. W. Forster	19 June 1915
Sir A. Williamson	23 Dec. 1919
Hon. G. F. Stanley	2 Apr. 1921
R. S. Gwynne	16 Mar. 1923
J. J. Lawson	23 Jan. 1924
H. D. King	12 Nov. 1924
A. Duff Cooper	14 Jan. 1928
E. Shinwell	10 June 1929
W. S. Sanders	6 June 1930
A. Duff Cooper	1 Sept. 1931
Douglas Hacking	2 July 1934
Sir Victor Warrender	29 Nov. 1935

Permanent Under-Secretary

Sir Reginald Brade	15 Jan. 1914
Sir Herbert Creedy	15 Jan. 1920

Chief of the Imperial General Staff

Field-Marshal Sir Henry Wilson	19 Feb. 1918
General The Earl of Cavan	19 Feb. 1922
General Sir George Milne	19 Feb. 1926
General Sir Archibald Montgomery-Massingberd	19 Feb. 1933
Field-Marshal Sir Cyril Deverell	7 Apr. 1936
General The Viscount Gort	6 Dec. 1937

Adjutant-General to the Forces

Lt.-Gen. Sir G. M. W. Macdonogh	11 Sept. 1918
Lt.-Gen. Sir Robert Whigham	1 Mar. 1923
General Sir Walter Braithwaite	1 Mar. 1927
General Sir Archibald Montgomery-Massingberd	1 Mar. 1931
General Sir Cecil Romer	19 Feb. 1933
Lt.-Gen. Sir Harry Knox	1 Mar. 1935
Lt.-Gen. Sir Clive Liddell	13 Dec. 1937

Master-General of the Ordnance[1]

Lt.-Gen. Sir William Furse	4 Dec. 1916
Lt.-Gen. Sir John Du Cane	1 Jan. 1920
Lt.-Gen. Sir Noel Birch	1 Oct. 1923
Lt.-Gen. Sir Webb Gillman	1 Oct. 1927
Maj.-Gen. Sir Ronald Charles	1 Mar. 1931
Lt.-Gen. Sir Hugh Elles	5 May 1934

Quartermaster-General

Lt.-Gen. Sir Travers Clarke	16 Mar. 1919
Lt.-Gen. Sir Walter Campbell	16 Mar. 1923
Lt.-Gen. Sir Hastings Anderson	16 Mar. 1927
Lt.-Gen. Sir Felix Ready	2 Feb. 1931
Lt.-Gen. Sir Reginald May	2 Feb. 1935
Lt.-Gen. Sir Walter Venning	1 Feb. 1939

Director-General of Munitions Production[2]

Vice-Admiral Harold A. Brown	14 Sept. 1936

Director-General of the Territorial Army[3]

Lt.-Gen. Sir Walter Kirke	1 Apr. 1936

[1] The MGO ceased to be a member of the Army Council after 1937.

[2] Established as a member of the Army Council by Order in Council of 26 September 1936.

[3] Established as a member of the Army Council by Order in Council of 22 October 1937.

SELECT BIBLIOGRAPHY

Public Record Office

Cabinet

The following classes of Cabinet Papers proved most valuable for this study:

Cab 2	Committee of Imperial Defence, minutes of meetings.
Cab 4	CID Miscellaneous Memoranda ('B' Papers).
Cab 16	CID Sub-Committees, including the Defence Requirements Committee.
Cab 21	Registered files.
Cab 23	Minutes of Cabinet meetings, officially known as Conclusions.
Cab 24	Cabinet Papers (CP).
Cab 27	Cabinet Committees, including the Disarmament Conference Ministerial Committee DC(M), 1932–5.
Cab 29	Conference Reports and Notes, including Anglo-French Staff Conversations.
Cab 53	Meetings and Memoranda of the Chiefs of Staff (COS) from 1923 and also of the Deputy Chiefs of Staff (DCOS) from 1932.
Cab 55	Meetings and Memoranda of the Joint Planning Sub-Committee (from 1927).
Cab 63	Hankey Papers.

War Office Papers

WO32 and WO33	Miscellaneous documents.
WO79	Cavan Papers.
WO106	Directorate of Military Operations and Intelligence documents.
WO163	Minutes and Précis of the Army Council.

Air Ministry documents

Air/2 Miscellaneous documents.

Other archives

Centre for Military Archives King's College, London

Liddell Hart Papers. And General Sir William Bartholomew, Field-Marshal Sir Cyril Deverell, Field-Marshal Sir John Dill, Major-General George Lindsay, Field-Marshal Sir Archibald Montgomery-Massingberd.

Churchill College, Cambridge

Field-Marshal The Earl of Cavan and Viscount Weir. Also consulted Sir Thomas Inskip (Viscount Caldecote).

Imperial War Museum

Recorded interviews with Lord Bridgeman, Major-General H. L. Birks and Field-Marshal Lord Carver. The Museum also contains the Papers of Field-Marshal Sir Henry Wilson, including his diaries (microfilm) and correspondence.

Private Papers

Burnett-Stuart, General Sir John. Unpublished Memoirs made available by his daughter, the late Mrs Elizabeth Arthur.

Macleod, Colonel Roderick. Documents relating mainly to the military career of Field-Marshal Lord Ironside.

Pownall, Lieut.-General Sir Henry. Diaries on loan from J. W. Pownall-Gray Esq.

Ph.D. theses

Armstrong, G. P., 'The Controversy over Tanks in the British Army, 1919–1933', University of London, 1975.

Bialer, Uri, 'Some Aspects of the Fear of Bombardment from the Air and the Making of British Defence and Foreign Policy, 1932–1939', University of London, 1974.

Bradshaw-Ellis, B. E., 'Seven Lean Years: the Organisation and Administration of the Imperial General Staff, 1926–1933' (Master's thesis), University of New Brunswick, 1976.

Garnier, Maurice, A., 'Social Class and Military Socialization: a Study of R. M. A. Sandhurst', University of California, 1969.

Jacobsen, Mark, 'The Modernization of the Indian Army, 1925–1939', University of California, Irvine, 1979.

Jeffery, Keith, 'The Military Defence of the British Empire, 1918–1922', University of Cambridge, 1978.

Murray, Williamson, 'The Change in the European Balance of Power, 1938–1939', University of Yale, 1975.

Peden, G. C., 'The Influence of the Treasury on British Rearmament, 1932–39', University of Oxford, 1976.

Rawson, J. O., 'The Role of India in Imperial Defence beyond Indian Frontiers and Home Waters, 1919–1939', University of Oxford, 1976.

Waldie, D. J. P., 'Relations between the British Army and the Royal Air Force, 1918–1939', King's College, London (in progress).

Welch, H. G., 'The Origins and Development of the Chiefs of Staff Sub-Committee of the Committee of Imperial Defence, 1923–1939', University of London, 1973.

Winton, H. R., 'General Sir John Burnett-Stuart and British Military Reform, 1927–1938', University of Stanford, 1977.

SECONDARY SOURCES

Adamthwaite, Anthony, *France and the Coming of the Second World War, 1936–1939,* Cass, 1977.
Aster, Sidney, *1939: the Making of the Second World War,* Deutsch, 1973.
Barnett, Correlli, *The Desert Generals*, Kimber 1960. Pan Books, 1962.
—— *The Collapse of British Power,* Eyre Methuen, 1972.
Beaufre, André, *1940: the Fall of France*, Cassell, 1967.
Beauman, A. B., *Then a Soldier,* P. R. Macmillan, 1960.
Beloff, Max, *Imperial Sunset: Britain's Liberal Empire, 1897–1921,* Methuen, 1969.
Best, Geoffrey and Wheatcroft, Andrew (eds.), *War, Economy and the Military Mind,* Croom Helm, 1976.
Bidwell, Shelford, *Gunners At War,* Arms and Armour Press, 1970.
Bond, Brian, *France and Belgium 1939–1940,* Davis-Poynter, 1975.
—— Liddell Hart: a Study of His Military Thought, Cassell, 1977.
—— (ed.), *Chief of Staff: the Diaries of Lt. Gen. Sir Henry Pownall, Vol. I 1933–1940,* Leo Cooper, 1972.
—— and Roy, Ian (eds.), *War and Society Yearbook,* two vols., Croom Helm, 1976–7.
Brownrigg, Sir Douglas, *Unexpected,* Hutchinson, n.d., but *c.* 1941.
Callwell, Major-General Sir C. E. (ed.), *Field Marshal Sir Henry Wilson,* 2 vols., *Vol. II,* Cassell, 1927.
Chatfield, Admiral of the Fleet Lord, *The Navy and Defence,* Heinemann, 1942.
—— *It Might Happen Again,* Heinemann, 1947.
Cole, D. H., *Imperial Military Geography,* 8th edn., Sifton Praed, 1936.
Collins, R. J., *Lord Wavell: a Military Biography, 1883–1941,* Hodder and Stoughton, 1947.
Colville, J. R., *Man of Valour: Field Marshal Lord Gort V.C.,* Collins, 1972.
Connell, John, *Auchinleck,* Cassell, 1959.
—— *Wavell: Soldier and Scholar,* Collins, 1964.
Cooper, Alfred Duff, *Old Men Forget,* Hart-Davis, 1954, Readers Union 1955 edn.

Dening, B. C., *The Future of the British Army*, Witherby, 1928.
Dennis, Peter, *Decision by Default: Peacetime Conscription and British Defence, 1919–1939*, Routledge and Kegan Paul, 1972.
Dewing, R. H., *The Army*, Hodge, 1938.
Douglas, Roy, *In the Year of Munich*, Macmillan, 1977.
Eden, Anthony (Earl of Avon), *Facing the Dictators*, Cassell, 1962.
Ellis, L. F., *The War in France and Flanders 1939–1940*, HMSO, 1953.
Essame, Hubert, *The Battle for Europe, 1918*, Batsford, 1972.
Feiling, Keith, *The Life of Neville Chamberlain*, Macmillan, 1946.
Fuller, J. F. C., *The Army in My Time*, Rich and Cowan, 1935.
—— *Memoirs of an Unconventional Soldier*, Nicolson and Watson, 1936.
Gatzke, Hans W, (ed.), *European Diplomacy Between Two Wars, 1919–1939*, Chicago, Quadrangle Books, 1972.
Gibbs, N. H., *Grand Strategy Vol. I*, HMSO, 1976.
Gilbert, Martin, *Winston, S. Churchill Vol. IV 1916–1922*, Heinemann 1975.
Godley, Sir Alexander, *Life of an Irish Soldier*, Murray, 1939.
Gordon, Hampden, *The War Office*, Putnam, 1935.
Gwynn, Sir Charles W., *Imperial Policing*, Macmillan, 1936.
Henniker, M. C. A., *Memoirs of a Junior Officer*, Blackwood, 1951.
Higham, Robin, *Armed Forces in Peacetime: Britain 1918–1939*, Foulis, 1962.
—— *The Military Intellectuals in Britain, 1918–1939*, New Brunswick, N.J.,: Rutgers University Press, 1966.
Howard, Michael, *The Continental Commitment*, Temple Smith, 1972.
—— (ed.), *The Theory and Practice of War*, Cassell, 1965.
Hyde, H. Montgomery, *British Air Policy Between the Wars, 1918–1939*, Heinemann, 1976.
Ismay, Lord, *Memoirs*, Heinemann, 1960.
Johnson, F. A., *Defence by Committee: the British Committee of Imperial Defence, 1885–1959*, Oxford University Press, 1960.
Kennedy, Sir John, *The Business of War*, Hutchinson, 1957.
Kennedy, J. R., *This, Our Army*, Hutchinson, 1935.
Kennedy, Paul M., *The Rise and Fall of British Naval Mastery*, Allen Lane, 1976.
Kieft, D. O., *Belgium's Return to Neutrality*, Oxford, Clarendon Press, 1972.
Lewin, Ronald, *Man of Armour: a Study of Lieut.-General Vyvyan Pope*, Leo Cooper, 1976.
Liddell Hart, B. H., *The Defence of Britain*, Faber, 1939.
—— *The Tanks*, 2 vols., Cassell, 1959.
—— *Memoirs*, 2 vols., Cassell, 1965.
Macksey, Kenneth, *Armoured Crusader: Major-General Sir Percy Hobart*, Hutchinson, 1967.

Macleod, Roderick and Kelly, Denis (eds.), *The Ironside Diaries, 1937–1940,* Constable, 1962.
Macready, Sir Gordon, *In the Wake of the Great,* Clowes, 1965.
Macready, Sir Nevil, *Annals of an Active Life*, 2 vols., *Vol. II*, Hutchinson, 1924.
Martel, Sir Giffard, *In the Wake of the Tank,* Sifton Praed, 2nd edn., 1935.
—— *Our Armoured Forces,* Faber, 1945.
—— *An Outspoken Soldier,* Sifton Praed, 1949.
Mason, Philip, *A Matter of Honour: an Account of the Indian Army, its Officers and Men,* Cape, 1974.
Masters, John, *Bugles and a Tiger,* Joseph, 1956.
Meinertzhagen, Richard, *Middle East Diary, 1917–1956,* The Cresset Press, 1959.
Middlemas, Keith, *Diplomacy of Illusion: the British Government and Germany, 1937–1939,* Weidenfeld and Nicolson, 1972.
—— and Barnes, John, *Baldwin: a Biography,* Weidenfeld and Nicolson, 1969.
Minney, R. J., *The Private Papers of Hore-Belisha,* Collins, 1960.
Monroe, Elizabeth, *Britain's Moment in the Middle East,* Methuen, 1965.
Montgomery, Field-Marshal Viscount, *Memoirs,* Collins, 1958, Fontana Paperback, 1961 edn.
Morgan, Sir Frederick, *Peace and War: a Soldier's Life,* Hodder and Stoughton, 1961.
Neame, Sir Philip, *Playing With Strife,* Harrap, 1947.
Newman, Simon, *March 1939: the British Guarantee to Poland*, Oxford, Clarendon Press, 1976.
Nicol, Graham, *Uncle George: Field-Marshal Lord Milne of Salonika and Rubislaw,* Reedminster Publications, 1976.
Ogorkiewicz, Richard M., *Armour,* Stevens, 1960.
Peden, G. C., *The Treasury and British Rearmament, 1932–1939,* Scottish Academic Press, 1979.
Postan, M. M., *British War Production,* HMSO, 1952.
—— ,Hay, D., and Scott, J. D., *Design and Development of Weapons,* HMSO, 1964.
Powers, Barry D., *Strategy Without Slide-Rule,* Croom Helm, 1976.
Pratt, L. R., *East of Malta, West of Suez: Britain's Mediterranean Crisis 1936–1939,* Cambridge University Press, 1975.
Preston, Adrian (ed.), *General Staffs and Diplomacy before the Second World War,* Croom Helm, 1978.
Reader, W. J., *Architect of Air Power: the Life of the First Viscount Weir,* Collins, 1968.
Rock, William R., *British Appeasement in the 1930's* Arnold, 1977.

Roskill, S. W., *Naval Policy between the Wars*, 2 vols., Collins, 1968 and 1976.
—— *Hankey: Man of Secrets*, vols. 2 and 3, Collins, 1972 and 1974.
Shay, Robert Paul Jr., *British Rearmament in the Thirties: Politics and Profits*, Princeton University Press, 1977.
Sheppard, E. W., *Tanks in the Next War*, Bles, 1938.
Sixsmith, E. K. G., *British Generalship in the Twentieth Century*, Arms and Armour Press, 1970.
Slessor, Sir John, *The Central Blue*, Cassell, 1956.
Terraine, John, *Impacts of War 1914 and 1918*, Hutchinson, 1970.
Thomas, Hugh (ed.), *The Establishment*, Blond, 1959. Ace Books, 1962.
Townshend, Charles, *The British Campaign in Ireland, 1919–1921*, Oxford University Press, 1975.
Trythall, A. J., *'Boney' Fuller: the Intellectual General*, Cassell, 1977.
Turner, E. S., *Gallant Gentlemen: a Portrait of the British Officer, 1600–1956*, Joseph, 1956.
Watt, D. C., *Personalities and Policies*, Longmans, 1965.
—— *Too Serious a Business: European Armed Forces and the Approach to the Second World War*, Temple Smith, 1975.
Young, Robert J., *In Command of France: French Foreign Policy and Military Planning, 1933–1940*, Cambridge, Mass. and London, Harvard University Press, 1978.

INDEX